The Militant Song Movement
in Latin America

The Militant Song Movement in Latin America

Chile, Uruguay, and Argentina

Edited by Pablo Vila

LEXINGTON BOOKS
Lanham • Boulder • New York • Toronto • Plymouth, UK

Fragments of the cantata Montoneros, by Huerque Mapu et al.; "Juana Azurduy," by Félix Luna and Ariel Ramírez; "Canción por el fusil y la flor," by Bernardo Palombo and Damián Sánchez; "El sueño de Celedonio Olmos," by Ernesto Sábato and Eduardo Falú; "El Poeta," "Camino del indio," "El arriero va," "El payador perseguido," "Preguntitas sobre Dios [Las preguntitas]," by Atahualpa Yupanqui; "No sé porque piensas tú," by Horacio Guarany and Nicolás Guillen; "Si se calla el cantor," by Eraclio Rodríguez; "Coplera del prisionero," by Eraclio Rodríguez and Armando Tejada Gómez; "Zamba de los humildes," "Coplera del viento," by Oscar Matus and Armando Tejada Gómez; "Canción para un niño en la calle," by Ángel Ritrovato and Armando Tejada Gomez; "El cóndor vuelve," by Eduardo Aragón and Armando Tejada Gómez; "Triunfo agrario," "Canción con todos," by César Isella and Armando Tejada Gómez; "Sueño carpero," by Francisco Romero and Armando Tejada Gómez; "Cuando tenga la tierra," by Ariel Petrocelli and Daniel Toro; "Para el pueblo lo que es del pueblo," by Piero and José Tcherkaski; "María Pueblo," by Roberto Paglia and María Gómez; "La calle de la cárcel," by María Parrondo and "Si un hijo quieren de mí," by Angel Ritrovato and Leonardo Castillo reprinted with permission of SADAIC (Sociedad Argentina de Autores y Compositores de Música).

The songs "La flor de la verbena," by Luis Araneda; "Cueca de la solidaridad" and "Cueca de la libertad," by Eduardo Carrasco reprinted with permissions of the authors.

Published by Lexington Books
A wholly owned subsidiary of Rowman & Littlefield
4501 Forbes Boulevard, Suite 200, Lanham, Maryland 20706
www.rowman.com

10 Thornbury Road, Plymouth PL6 7PP, United Kingdom

Copyright © 2014 by Lexington Books

British Library Cataloguing in Publication Information Available

Library of Congress Cataloging-in-Publication Data

The militant song movement in Latin America : Chile, Uruguay, and Argentina / edited by Pablo Vila.
pages cm
Includes bibliographical references and index.
ISBN 978-0-7391-8324-3 (cloth : alk. paper) -- ISBN 978-0-7391-8325-0 (electronic)
1. Political ballads and songs--Latin America--History and criticism. 2. Popular music--Latin America--History and criticism. I. Vila, Pablo, 1952- editor.
ML3575.M45 2014
782.42'1599098--dc23
2014000342

∞™ The paper used in this publication meets the minimum requirements of American National Standard for Information Sciences Permanence of Paper for Printed Library Materials, ANSI/NISO Z39.48-1992.

Printed in the United States of America

To Jan Fairley, a true pioneer studying the Latin American New Song, who desperately wanted to finish her chapter for this collection, but her untimely death cut her effort short. We have lost not only an outstanding academician, but, above all, a great friend.

Contents

Acknowledgments

Numerous people helped to make this book possible. I have already mentioned in the dedication the special role Jan Fairley played in the development of this collection. For years we were planning the volume together and, even though she tried until the last minute to finish her chapter, her untimely death didn't allow her to do so. Special thanks go to all the contributors for their hard work. Other people who gave me very good advice on the journey were Ramón Pelinski, Alberto Nadra, and Jairo Moreno. Ed Avery-Natale was very helpful with the index and Peggy Westwell with the translations. Mercedes Nachón Ramírez did a wonderful job transcribing the interviews with the Argentine members of the movement, to whom I also extend my gratitude (Horacio Guarany, Gloriana Tejada Gómez; César Isella, Marián and Chango Farías Gómez, Rodolfo Poggini, Carlos Pino, Víctor Heredia, Oscar Rovito). For all of them, many, many thanks. Carlos Molinero deserves a special place in the acknowledgment section for sharing with me his vast knowledge on the topic, well beyond his role as a coauthor of two chapters. Finally, I must acknowledge my children, Juanchi, Paloma, and Malena, and my wife, Julia Chindemi Vila, for all their support.

Introduction

Pablo Vila

Latin America in the 1950s, 1960s, and 1970s underwent a profound and often violent process of social change. From the Cuban Revolution to the massive guerrilla movements in Argentina, Uruguay, Peru, Colombia, and most of Central America, to the democratic socialist experiment of Salvador Allende in Chile, to the increased popularity of socialist oriented parties in Uruguay, or "socialist-leaning" movements, such as the Juventud Peronista in Argentina, the idea of a really possible social change was in the air. Although this topic has been explored from a political and social point of view, there is an aspect that has remained fairly unexplored. The cultural, and especially musical dimension of this movement, so vital in order to comprehend the extent of its emotional appeal, has not been fully documented. Literally, people put constantly their lives at risk opposing authoritarian regimes and participating in rallies to support their political parties, all the while singing militant songs that gave them the courage to do so. "There is no revolution without songs" proclaimed the huge banner installed behind the stage where newly elected President Salvador Allende (surrounded by the most important members of "Nueva Canción Chilena"—Chilean New Song) first celebrated his electoral victory in 1970.

Political actors are not purely rational players that make decisions from a mere cost-benefit point of view. What's more, they often risk their lives following ideologies they barely comprehend. Without an understanding of the emotional component of political involvement it is impossible to fully understand a movement for social change such as the one operating in Latin America at that time. Without an account of how music was pervasively used in the construction of these emotional components, the political and social explanation of what occurred in Latin America during that period will be always inexcusably partial. This book is an initial attempt to overcome this

1

deficit. In this collection of essays, we examine the history of the militant song movement[1] in Chile, Uruguay, and Argentina at the peak of its popularity (from the mid-1960s to the different—but suspiciously coincident—coup d'états in the mid-1970s), considering their different political stances and musical deportments, as well as their development after the coup d'états when they became quite important for the legions of exiles from Chile, Uruguay, and Argentina who escaped the repression in their countries of origin. In the different chapters of the book the contribution of the most important musicians of the movement (Violeta Parra, Víctor Jara, Patricio Manns, Quilapayún, Inti-Illimani, etc., in Chile; Daniel Viglietti, Alfredo Zitarrosa, Los Olimareños, etc., in Uruguay; Atahualpa Yupanqui, Horacio Guarany, Mercedes Sosa, Marián Farías Gómez, Armando Tejada Gómez, César Isella, Víctor Heredia, Los Trovadores, etc., in Argentina) are highlighted; and some of the most important conceptual extended oeuvres of the period (called "cantatas") are analyzed (such as *La Cantata Popular Santa María de Iquique* in the Chilean case and *Montoneros* in the Argentine case). The different chapters of the book deal with the complex relationship that the aesthetic of the movement established between the political content of the lyrics and the musical and performative aspects of the most popular songs of the period. Because the "militant" many of the songs of the period refer to was actually "a male militant," issues of gender are also part of the analysis of some chapters.

WHY MILITANT AND NOT "PROTEST" SONG?

While many of the collaborators of this collection use "protest song" in their chapters, if on the one hand I wanted to respect their own approaches to the issue of how to address this peculiar musical movement, I still named the book "The Militant Song Movement in Latin America," using "militant" instead of "protest" to qualify the noun "song." I did so because, following Molinero (2011), I want to depart from the traditional appellation by which this type of music is understood: "protest music" or "protest song." This was (and still is) the way this music is usually named. If the 1967 Congress in Cuba that congregated the most important Latin American members of the movement was called the first *"Encuentro de la Canción Protesta"* [First Encounter of Protest Song], while writing this introduction (November 2013), in Lucca, Italy, the *Protest Music in the Twentieth Century Congress* is being organized by the Centro Studi Opera Omnia Luigi Boccherini.

As Molinero reminds us (2011: 53), the name "protest song" originated in the United States in the early 1930s, and was linked to both the political left and protest against segregationist/racist policies. Eventually the term was extended further in the 1960s encompassing the protest against the war in

Vietnam, and gender discrimination. It is quite obvious that its use in Latin America follows this origin, if we take into account that the name of the referred above Cuban congress of 1967 is not called *Encuentro de la Canción DE Protesta* (the grammatically correct way to say it in Spanish), but *Encuentro de la Canción Protesta* (a literal translation from English). The Festival was followed by the creation of a cultural association for the dissemination of the protest song in the rest of the world, which lasted for at least five years, and contributed to the spread of the term in the rest of Latin America. If the name was somehow appropriate in the United States, referring to "protest" in the sense of "demonstrate" with banners (but in this case through music), my claim is that this had little to do with the theme and features of the militant song movement in Latin America.

The point I want to make here is that the Latin American militant song movement did not generally protest *against* a given situation (although in some cases it did so); instead, it *denounced* (in the double sense of making public and alerting about) a situation. This did not entail taking on the voice of an "oppositional group" (Kaliman 2004) and even less advocating for a specific measure regarding the situation being portrayed, such as putting an end to war or adopting anti-discrimination laws (Molinero 2011: 53). This became quite clear for the practitioners of the movement themselves, and became inscribed in the different national names that the movement actually acquired in Chile, Uruguay, and Argentina, none of them having the name "protest" on it: *"Nueva Canción Chilena"* (Chilean New Song), *"Canto Popular"* ([Uruguayan] Popular Song), and *"Movimiento del Nuevo Cancionero"* (New Song Movement) respectively. The only exception to this trend is the creation of the *"Centro de la Canción Protesta"* in Montevideo in the late 1960s as a multi-disciplinary meeting place for poets, musicians, composers, educators. However, the center had a short life: first it changed its name to *"Centro de la Canción Popular Uruguaya"* (Popular Uruguayan Song Center) replacing "protest" by "popular" in order to try to avoid censorship and being shut down, something that was completely unsuccessful, because, a few years later, it was forcibly closed by the government. [2]

Beyond the official names the different national movements ended up using, there were several other labels that were utilized to describe the militant songs of the time, such as *"canción de denuncia"* (denunciation song), *"canción contestataria"* ("song of contestation"), names that I could have used to name the book. However, I have several reservations regarding those names. The most important is that, even though many of the works composed during the 1960s and 1970s in Chile, Uruguay, and Argentina can easily be identified with these labels (*"La Cantata Popular Santa Maria de Iquique,"* by Quilapayún, in the case of Chile; *"A desalambrar"* ("Tear Down the Wire Fences") by Viglietti, in the case of Uruguay; *"No te cases con minero"* ("Don't Marry a Miner") by Guarany, in the case of Argentina, for instance), there were many others that, instead of "contesting" or "denouncing" a particular social situation, offered a message of hope for the social subordinates, auguring the arrival of better times in a near future that was conceived as "scientifically secured" (according to the Marxist lore of the time). At the same time, when, for instance, in the case of Chile those "better times" actually arrived and a democratic socialist experiment was under way, the Chilean New Song (without stopping their denunciations), started a complete new set of songs asking for concrete political actions: like encouraging people to vote for the Popular Union's candidates in the parliamentary elections of 1973, to support the Allende's government when under attack by the opposition, so on and so forth.[3] Therefore I do not consider "denunciation song" or "song of contestation" encompassing enough to name the entire production of the movement.

Another common name at the time was "canción testimonial" (testimonial song). This label was quite alluring for me to use for naming the book for several reasons. As Molinero points out (2011: 54), "[I]ts mere meaning sounds as poetry, and to 'give testimony' from one person to another . . . or, by extension, from one generation to the next one." However I concur with Molinero that this label leaves out the more radicalized part of the militant song movement, those singers and songwriters who more than offering only a testimony (in the sense of portraying and transmitting) of a particularly negative social situation, sought to convince, mobilize, sensitize toward the advancement of radical social change.

Those are the main reasons why I have chosen "militant song" instead. Because "militant" prefigures, without determining or narrowing it, a committed political position. A political position that is not necessarily a traditional leftist one, allowing, in this way, to incorporate the musical production of the different branches of Peronism in Argentina in the militant movement, which would have been left aside if only pro-socialist songs were allowed into the corpus. At the same time this militant position is broader than a mere "protest" as it focuses on broad political propositions as well. As Molinero points out (2011: 56),

> The term "militant" is not explicitly partisan, although it implies that the goal of the song was to be part of a comprehensive strategy, external to the song itself. Part of a movement. . . . The idea of being part of a process that integrates to a whole that transcends it and to which it contributes (even with different brands of militancy), is what we consider the distinctive characteristic of this subgenre.[4]

VARIANCES

While the militant song movements in each country are quite similar to each other in terms of time-span, song thematic, relationship with institutional politics, and the like, they also have some noticeable differences that are worth mentioning. In this introduction I will concentrate, for obvious reasons of space, on only two of them: the gender dimension and the perdurability of their song production.

THE "HOMBRE NUEVO" (NEW MAN) OF THE SONGS WAS CLEARLY MALE, BUT WHO SANG FOR HIM?

As it is clear when we analyze the songs, most of the production of the time is, in terms of thematic, "male oriented": the "hombre nuevo" was clearly a man (Carrillo Rodríguez's chapter delves in-depth on this issue). However, depending on the country we are talking about, there is a very important difference in terms of how gender plays at the level of composition, and above all, interpretation. In the Chilean case, not by chance Violeta Parra is considered the "mother" of the militant song in the sub-continent (while Atahualpa Yupanqui, from Argentina, would be the "father"). However, most critics concur that beyond Violeta and her daughter Isabel Parra, most of the composers and interpreters of the genre were male, and this is quite intriguing, considering the importance of female interpreters before and after the militant song movement. The fact that Violeta died in 1967, before the Chilean New Song movement was in full throttle, adds another dimension to understand the supremacy of male composer and interpreters when the move-ment was at its peak, in the late 1960s and early 1970s. In other words, Violeta Parra is considered a "precursor" (who happened to be a female) of a movement mostly composed of males (Jara, Quilapayún, Inti-Illimani, Illapu, Patricio Manns, etc.): a "mother" who had only one female child, and many male children.

The Uruguayan case is still more extreme: even though a very important composer is active in the militant song movement, Idea Vilariño, before the coup d'état we cannot find any major female interpreter that can be linked to the movement, and after the coup, only Cristina Fernández became impor-tant, usually in terms of the duo she formed with her husband, Washington Carrasco. We can add to this markedly masculine characteristic of the Uru-guayan case the public persona many of the singer/songwriters of the time adopted, who emphasized a very traditional male image and posture.

We find a whole different scenario in the case of Argentina. Even though the presence of female composers is often forgotten,[5] the opposite is true when we consider interpreters. Without any doubt the public image of the

Movimiento del Nuevo Cancionero has a female (and mestizo, by the way) face: Mercedes Sosa. And Mercedes Sosa became, over time, the public image of the entire Argentine militant song movement as an interpreter. At the same time, while not as popular as Horacio Guarany, César Isella, or Los Trovadores, for instance, Marián Farías Gómez was a very important actor of the movement. She not only literally replaced Mercedes Sosa in many instances when Mercedes had other commitments and could not participate in shows linked to the leftist Nuevo Cancionero (the shows mounted by Tejada Gómez in 1967; the tour to Eastern Europe of the mid-1960s; and the like); but also she was highly involved in the activities of the peronist José Podestá group that eventually lead to the "Cancionero de la liberación," which, by the way, had another very important female participant: Marilina Ross. As we can see, a complete different scenario compared to what was going on with the Chilean and Uruguayan branches of the militant song movement.

SONGS FORGOTTEN VERSUS REMEMBERED SONGS

Forty years have passed since the militant song movement was at its peak, and many of the songs that were popular at its time have disappeared from the popular memory, while a few others survived the passage of time. At the same time, many of the non-militant songs that were part of the habitual repertoire of the singers and composers of the movement in the 1960s and 1970s are still remembered and, some of them, have definitively entered the "canon" of the national folklore of their countries of origin. Interestingly enough there are marked differences in the way that this process has proceeded in Chile, Uruguay, and Argentina. In the case of Chile, most of the songs people remember from the militant movement's artists are the politically committed ones, such as "*El pueblo unido jamás será vencido*" ("The People United Will Never Be Defeated"), "*El Aparecido*" ("The Apparition"), "*La muralla*" ("The Wall"), "*Vamos mujer*" ("Let's Go Woman"), "*Plegaria a un labrador*" ("Prayer to a Peasant"), "*Te recuerdo Amanda*" ("I Remember Amanda"), "*La carta*" ("The Letter"), and so on. One exception is the production of Violeta Parra (beyond "The Letter"), where "*Volver a los 17*" ("To Be 17 Again"), and, above all, "*Gracias a la vida*" ("Thanks to Life")—which even though it does not have any explicit political content many people still consider it a kind of "anthem" of the New Song in Latin America (among them, our beloved Jan Fairley), are still very popular.

In the case of Uruguay, the situation is more mixed. On the one hand most people remember today the songs of the militant movement interpreters that are not politically oriented, but, at the same time, they also somehow remember the others, but the listening experience itself "de-politicizes" them, in the sense of using those songs to remember a time when dreams of social change were the order of the day, but without paying much attention to the specific political messages those songs carried out at the time of their composition. In this regard, from Zitarrosa's repertoire the militant songs that are still popular are, "*Adagio en mi país*" ("Adagio in My Country"), "*Diez décimas de saludo al pueblo argentino*" ("Ten Stanzas Greeting the Argentine People") and "*Doña Soledad*." But many of his non-militant songs are quite popular nowadays as well, such as "*El violín de Becho*" ("Becho's Violin"), "*Recordándote*" ("Remembering You") "*Zamba por vos*" ("Zamba for You") and "*Pál que se va*" ("For the One Who Is Leaving"). From Los Olimareños' repertoire, the militant songs that are still remembered are "*Milonga de pelo largo*" ("Long Hair's Milonga"), "*Cielo del 69*" ("Sky 69"), and "*El Orejano*," but many of their non-militant songs are quite popular as well, like "*A don José*" ("To Don Jose [Artigas]").

And Argentina is a completely different story, because what most people remember of the repertoire of Yupanqui, Guarany, Mercedes Sosa, Tejada Gómez, Isella, Los Trovadores, and the like are the non-militant songs, not the politically oriented ones. In that regard, the songs that currently people listen to most on the radio, on television, at festivals and the like are Yupanqui's "*Piedra y camino*" ("Stone and Road"), "*La pobrecita*" ("The Poor One"), "*Chacarera de las piedras*" ("Stones' Chacarera"), and so on, but not "*Las preguntitas*" ("The Little Questions"), for instance. Víctor Heredia's most well-known song is "*El viejo Matías*" ("Old Man Matias") not any of his more militant ones. In the case of Horacio Guarany, without any doubt his more famous songs are the non-militant ones: "*Volver en vino*" ("Coming Back in Wine"), "*Piel morena*" ("Tanned Skin"), "*Puerto de Santa Cruz*" ("Santa Cruz Port"), and "*Pescador y Guitarrero*" ("Fisherman and Guitar Player"); however, one of his most famous militant songs is still popular: "*Si se calla el cantor*" ("If the Singer Becomes Silent"). Something similar occurs with the production of Tejada Gómez and Isella, because if on the one hand the most popular songs today are the non-militant ones ("*Zamba del laurel*" ["Laurel's Zamba"] and "*Canción de las simples cosas*" ["Song of Simple Things"] for instance), on the other hand, "*Canción con todos*" ("Song with Everybody"), one of the most important militant songs of the 1960s/1970s, has been definitively incorporated into the folk song canon of the country and, actually, the entire continent.[6]

That it is in Chile where the militant songs are remembered the most is not by chance, because those songs are emotionally linked to what was (albeit for a very brief period of time) a successful process of democratic social change interrupted by a violent coup d'état. While Peronism also governed Argentina for a similar brief period of time (1973–1976) during the same decade, only the few months when Cámpora was president (in one version of the story), or the year Cámpora and Perón were in the presidency (in another version of the story) can count as deserving the qualification of "progressive" governments that, somehow, fulfilled the desires for social change promoted by the militant song movement in Argentina. Additionally, the massacre that followed the peronist government of the 1970s, to which the guerrilla groups that continued their armed struggle under the democratic government of Cámpora and Perón contributed to a certain degree,[7] disavows any naïve remembrance of the "heroic" revolutionary times of the early 1970s in Argentina nowadays, their militant songs included. In the case of Uruguay, there was nothing close to the brief access to power experienced by the left in Chile and Argentina. Therefore, remembering the militant songs more than the other type of music production of the members of the militant song movement makes much more sense in the case of Chile, than in the case of Argentina and Uruguay.

NAVIGATING THE BOOK

In chapter 1, "New Song in Chile: Half a Century of Musical Activism," Nancy Morris explains how the Chilean New Song formed in the 1960s in response to a number of factors that were shared throughout Latin America, including the exchange of political and musical ideas in the region; the denunciation of foreign domination, particularly by the United States; and the concomitant political militancy and search for identity expression. *Nueva Canción Chilena* emerged during the time that Salvador Allende was achieving prominence as a Chilean political leader, and New Song musicians actively supported his 1970 election campaign and subsequent presidency. When Allende was overthrown in a military coup d'état in 1973, well-known New Song musician Víctor Jara was killed, and most of the other prominent New Song musicians became exiles.

The military dictatorship of Augusto Pinochet crushed New Song music. In an atmosphere of repression and fear, young musicians revived New Song in a different form inside Chile. Using metaphorical lyrics to evade the regime's censorship, dictatorship-era New Song provided an outlet of expression for veiled opposition sentiments and a voice of resistance that varied in tone and explicitness depending on the level of authoritarian repression, which itself varied with changing conditions during the Pinochet regime. Outside of Chile, exiled New Song musicians toured the world, exposing audiences on all continents to their music, and encouraging opposition to the dictatorship. Many of the exiles moved back to Chile with the country's return to democracy in 1990, and they continue with their music and social activism, along with their younger colleagues.

As a message carrier intentionally attuned to political conditions, Chilean New Song has had an influence beyond the musical realm throughout its existence. As a genre of popular culture, New Song has been both a reflector and a reflection of the society that generated it. This chapter traces the history of Chilean New Song delineating the social and political circumstances that generated it, that distinguish it and that are inseparable from it. Focusing on the conditions and events that constituted the setting for New Song, the chapter explores the interweaving of politics and this form of cultural expression across a span of some fifty eventful years in Chile.

In chapter 2 "'Remembrance Is Not Enough . . .' ('No basta solo el recuerdo . . .'): The Cantata Popular Santa María de Iquique 40 Years after Its Release," Eileen Karmy Bolton analyzes the trajectory of the *"Cantata Popular Santa María de Iquique,"* which was composed by Luis Advis in 1969 and recorded by Quilapayún in 1970. Without any doubt the Cantata is one of the most relevant works of Chilean music, establishing an important landmark in the development of the Chilean New Song movement, extending the format of the song and setting up the basis of a compositional poetic. Also, the Cantata went far beyond the frontiers of what was defined as erudite and popular music, and expanded its influence to the rest of Latin America in the format of "cantata popular."

In the chapter Karmy Bolton shows how Quilapayún, an iconic group in the Chilean New Song movement, through their popularity and political support, brought an important staging and musical trend that was characteristic of this movement, in both Chile and Latin America. In addition, Quilapayún's influence gave to the Cantata a very particular meaning. In spite of the years that have gone by, the sociocultural, political, and economic changes that the country has suffered, the *"Cantata Popular de Santa María de Iquique"* has succeeded being in vogue with its message for more than forty years, being itself, at the same time, a historical source that can tell about the 1907 massacre of workers that originated the oeuvre, as well as the socio-politic happenings of the 1970s, when the Cantata was originally performed.

Additionally, through its various versions, it can tell about the recent Chilean history, establishing connections with other musical traditions. This Cantata is kept updated by means of the social resignification that each of its versions has been able to give to it. In this chapter, Karmy Bolton reviews some versions of the Cantata in order to study its resignifications from a hermeneutic standpoint. Methodologically, the author uses an intertextual analysis, based on the Cantata's history since it was released. The versions chosen for the analysis have a different approach from traditional formats of the "Cantata"—resignifying it and proposing a new meaning and new ways to approach the concepts proposed by the Chilean New Song during the time this work was originally released. But also and especially through these versions, we can understand the social significations that the Cantata acquires over time, and the deep meanings that this work takes in each of its versions.

The main objective of chapter 3, "The Chilean New Song's *cueca larga,"* by Laura Jordán González, is to examine the place held by the complex musical-poetical-choreographic form known as the *cueca,* within the Chilean New Song (CNS) foundational project of building a "soundtrack" for revolutionary Latin America during the 1960s, 1970s, and 1980s. As such, the examination Jordán González undertakes seeks first to respond to a broader question regarding the sound qualities of the Chilean New Song by using the particular instance of the *cueca* as a case study. Secondly, Jordán González intends to propose an understanding of the relation between the selection/ exclusion/predilection of certain musical traditions within the repertoire of the Chilean New Song, as well as the political discourse of the musicians involved.

The first section is devoted to defining what the author understands to be the Chilean New Song, discussing both its political and sound dimensions, and by defining the term *cueca,* underlining some formal characteristics at stake in this study. Even though there appears to be a consensus that the CNS undertook a political project side by side with leftist political parties, promoting and accompanying social changes, Jordán González stresses the fact that the political dimension of the CNS exceeds the militant activity undertaken by some musicians. In reality, the very artistic project, in its material and sound qualities, was erected on the aspiration of *creating* an actual *Latin-American* sound, a genuine expression of the continent to which these musicians belonged. This attempt was combined with a curiosity for learning and adopting music from neighboring countries.

By examining the place held by the *cueca* in the CNS, largely considered the "Chilean national dance," in the second section the author attempts to advance some understanding of how Chilean traditions were inserted in the project. First, Jordán González gives an overview of the *cueca*'s place in the general repertoire of this genre and examine some of the most well-known *cuecas* within it, such as *"Los pueblos Americanos"* ("The American Peoples"), *"Cueca de la CUT"* ("CUT'S cueca"), and *"Cueca de Joaquín Murieta."* Second, she analyzes four specific pieces of *cueca*: *"Me gusta Valparaíso"* ("I Like Valparaíso") and "Juanito Orrego" by Aparcoa; *"Cueca de la libertad"* ("Cueca of Liberty") and *"Cueca de la solidaridad"* ("Solidarity's cueca") by Quilapayún. The analyses emphasize various aspects of form and vocal performance, observing their relation to traditional and innovative practices. The third and final section ponders the results of her analyses and puts forth some meanings associated with the *cueca,* especially related to exile, to reveal the negotiations of *chileanity* within the Latin-Americanist discourse.

Chapter 4 moves us from Chile to Uruguay. In "Modern Foundations of Uruguayan Popular Music," Abril Trigo explains to us that Uruguayan popular music is a relatively recent cultural phenomenon that was established in three phases. The 1960s (characterized by the revolutionary optimism inspired by the Cuban Revolution, the irreversible socio-political crisis of the no longer viable "Switzerland of America," and the emergence of the youth as a new cultural and political actor), witnessed the simultaneous development of a socially committed "protest song" doubly inspired in local rural folk and the overwhelming Argentine folkloric wave, and a largely derivative though locally adapted and widely eclectic, rock-and-roll. After the military coup of 1973, which imposed brutal political repression, cultural and artistic bans, and harsh media censorship, many musicians went into exile, while some were imprisoned and others went underground. By the mid-1970s a new generation of artists and musicians, inspired by their elders of the "committed" or "protest song" movement, had filled their shoes by developing a formidable space of cultural resistance that would be known as "*canto popular*," or "popular song." By the end of the 1970s, "canto popular" became increasingly experimental and gradually shifted from rural folk forms to urban folk genres, prominently the carnival rhythms of *murga* and *candombe*, variously fused with different shapes of rock and pop. The return in 1985 to liberal democracy, however restricted, opened the gates to a plethora of cultural manifestations while making palpable the consolidation of an original musical landscape. The process that had started in the early 1960s had finally come to produce a distinctively Uruguayan musical identity.

The chapter analyzes the cultural and ideological legacy of the first foundational moment, when an outstanding generation of singers, musicians, and poets, part of a larger countercultural movement that set the stage for the ulterior development of a left national front (the currently governing Frente Amplio), coalesced under an extraordinary set of circumstances, and set the foundations of contemporary Uruguayan popular music. Trigo focuses on the popular music of primarily rural folk inspiration produced by Alfredo Zitarrosa, Daniel Viglietti, and the duo Los Olimareños, integrated by Braulio López and José Luis Guerra, who are indisputably the emblematic artists of this period.

Chapter 5, "Popular Music and the Avant-garde in Uruguay: The Second Canto Popular Generation in the 1970s," by Camila Juárez, analyzes the second generation of Popular Song in Uruguay, which develops between 1977 and 1985. Juárez points out that in its artistic production different compositional traditions coexist, with a multiplicity of genres ranging from rock and folk to vanguard international music. This generation of Popular Song can be thought of as a social movement, due to its political vision of the cultural reality of the country, acting as a bloc of opposition to the dictatorship officially established in 1973. In this chapter Juárez analyzes the historical and political conditions that made possible the emergence of a compositional strategy linked to vanguard international music and applied to the urban popular song. To understand the development of vanguard musical thinking among the young musicians of the 1970s, the author focuses on the institutional update process that takes place in the Uruguayan music field since the 1960s. A figure of importance in this process is Coriún Aharonián who co-founded a number of institutions among which the Latin American Courses for Contemporary Music (1971–1989) occupies center stage. Many of the composers of the second generation of the Popular Song movement attend to these musical training courses that promote new ways of approaching the song from a program that is political as well.

Chapter 6 "The Rhythm of Values: Poets and Musicians in Ekphrasis and the Case of Uruguay, 1960–1985," by María L. Figueredo, explains how the links between music, poetry, and socio-political movements forged in Latin America during the second half of the twentieth century (especially those that became evident in the New Song movements in several countries in the 1960s, 1970s, and 1980s), bridge diverse genres and styles and problematize the former strict categorization of artistic forms. The effects of the resignification of the poetic text, when rearticulated within a popular musical structure, became a key characteristic of these interdisciplinary, and often times intercultural, identitarian expressions. As a poetic text became embedded in popular music, it integrates a new reality of language in song that calls into question notions of identity within specific new socio-political circumstances. Figueredo takes the Uruguayan case to exemplify how the interaction of poetry and music in the 1960s, 1970s, and 1980s renews, reinvents and questions the concepts of identity in which texts of poets such as Wáshington Benavides, Mario Benedetti, Líber Falco, Julio Herrera y Reissig, Circe Maia, Idea Vilariño, and others, are set to music by artists such as Washington Carrasco and Cristina Fernández, Eduardo Darnauchans, Los Olimareños, Daniel Viglietti, and Alfredo Zitarrosa, among others. The first part of the chapter presents her findings on the way in which collaborations between poets and musicians served as a mode of affirmative resistance in times of heightened socio-political tensions. In the second section, the reception of a selected sample of songs, based on prepublished poems, serves to focus a theme relevant from each of the three decades of the phenomenon of *Canto Popular Uruguayo*. What is highlighted through the detailed analysis of three representative examples from the corpus is the role that the interaction between the recognizable rhythms, rooted in specific spatial forms of identity and articulations of language in popular music, become a new mode of reception for the poems; as well it reveals in what specific ways the new musical settings of the poems perform a resignification of the inherent content of the poems with political and aesthetic effects which, though these dissipate after the end of the dictatorship era in Uruguay (1985), they subsequently shift the perception of the nature of revolt in musico-poetic language.

Chapter 7 moves us from Uruguay to Argentina and also to the historical origin of the Militant Song Movement in Latin America: Atahualpa Yupanqui. In "Atahualpa Yupanqui: The Latin American Precursor of the Militant Song Movement," Carlos Molinero and Pablo Vila show us how, well before the militant song movement became a force for social change in Latin America in the 1960s, Atahualpa Yupanqui was writing and singing songs in the 1940s that, in hindsight, were laying the groundwork for it. The authors claim that the part Yupanqui played in pioneering the militant song, and the conceptual strictures he placed on it, had decisive consequences for the development of a movement that, eventually, would spread continent-wide. According to Molinero and Vila, as precursor, Yupanqui's primary contribution to the Latin American militant song movement is two-fold: he introduced important themes that would be developed over time, and he provided the sense of mission essential to any movement, musical or otherwise. Out of Yupanqui's vast repertoire, the authors have singled out for discussion in the chapter two themes that, in their view, were landmarks in the subsequent militant song movement: the vindication of actors previously made invisible by the power structure (indigenous population), and critical commentary on the socio-political conditions of his time.

In that regard, the first part of the chapter is dedicated to an analysis of Yupanqui's stances, political writings, and songs that specifically vindicate indigenous Argentines. Starting from his artistic name (his real name was Héctor Roberto Chavero), that is, an indigenous appellation that was a first for any folk musician in Latin America and required the passage of many decades to become fashionable; following his political writings for the official Communist Party newspaper; and, more importantly, analyzing some of his most well-known songs (like "*Camino del Indio*" ["Indian Trail"]), Molinero and Vila show the different ways in which Yupanqui, for the first time in Latin American popular music, gave the "Indians" a voice of their own. The second part of the chapter addresses Yupanqui's "invention" of the so-called "protest song" in Latin America (here rebaptized as "militant song") analyzing "*El Arriero va*," which, written in 1944, is universally considered the "first" militant song of the sub-continent. Following "*El Arriero va*" (["The Drover Goes"] which claims that "Sorrows and cattle, they go down the same path/ The sorrows are ours/The cattle are someone else's"), and still a member of the Argentine Communist party, Yupanqui wrote a series of militant songs, such as "*Las Preguntitas*" ("The Little Questions"—which states that "Whether God looks out for men/maybe yes, maybe no/but there's no doubt he lunches/at the boss's table"), "*El pintor*" ("The Painter"—which claims that the painter was a bad one "since he only painted my poncho/and forgot about my hunger") and "*El poeta*" ("The Poet"—which posits that "You're like a poor blind man/who doesn't know where he's going/Go look at the miners. . . . And sing to those who fight/for a crust of bread") criticizing different aspects of Argentine's social formation that became a sort of "blue-print" for the subsequent production of militant songs all over Latin America.

The chapter also analyses Atahualpa's most explicit, integrative message relating to the militant song, which is found in his first and best-known long work, *"El Payador Perseguido"* ("The Persecuted Payador" [Troubadour]). In it his two thematic innovations—Indianism and social criticism—are on full display. Molinero and Vila end the chapter showing how, in the latter part of his career, Yupanqui tried to detach his image from that of the "protest singer." He did so, on the one hand, vindicating his entire musical production, not only his militant songs, which, according to him, were only a minimal part of his vast production. On the other hand, criticizing the poetic and musical limitations of the genre known as "protest song." In doing so he also took the opportunity to harshly criticize the "protest singers" popular at that time.

Chapter 8, "A Brief History of the Militant Song Movement in Argentina" by Carlos Molinero and Pablo Vila, chronicles the development of the militant song movement in Argentina from the mid-1950s to the mid-1970s. The authors show in the chapter how folk music was transformed by the militant artists from a mere "representation" of the past in the present to a "political weapon" to bring the future now (a future that, according to the lore of the time, was "scientifically" predicted as "socialist"). In the process, a kind of "militant Decalogue" was, step by step, being developed. The Decalogue included *Indigenismo* (vindicating indigenous people), *Americanism* (the search for the union of all Latin American people), *historical reinterpretation* of the Argentine past, *hope* (or even certainty) for a better future, *social change, fighting pacifism, popular leadership*, the immortality of the freedom fighter (a kind of *unreligious religiosity*), and the primordial *role of the song* in the revolutionary transformation. And the tenth: *specific political propose*, in the last part of the decade.

The first part of the chapter deals with the career of Horacio Guarany. Molinero and Vila claim that Guarany, more than any other member of the leftist branch of the militant song movement in Argentina, represents the classic role of "official singer of the party." Not only because he was always present in Communist Party (CP) congresses, celebrations, and the like (usually explicitly admitting his liaison with the CP), but also because his lyric production was very closely related to what the CP was advocating at different points in time; and still, even more importantly, because his performances were sometimes more reminiscent of a political leader than those of a popular singer. From there the chapter moves to the most recognizable actor of the militant song movement in Argentina, the Nuevo Cancionero movement. From its very inception in the early 1960s, the MNC proclaimed itself the critical vanguard for ascertaining the quality and meaning of folk songs in Argentina, only accepting as valid those that proposed social change.

Their members explicitly wanted to change folk music so that it accompanies the life and struggles of the people, thus placing the accent on the future more than on the past. Molinero and Via analyze the most important songs written by the pillars of the movement (such as Tejada Gómez, Isella, and the like), and popularized by singers like Los Trovadores, El Quinteto Tiempo, Daniel Toro, Mercedes Sosa, and Marián Farías Gómez, the two latter being analyzed in depth due to their centrality in the popularization of the Nuevo Cancionero's songs (Marián being also a "hinge" between the MNC and Peronism).

The last part of the article is dedicated to the analysis of the most important peronist group associated with the militant song movement in Argentina: The José Podestá Group that was behind the *Cancionero de la Liberación* (The Liberation Songbook). Molinero and Vila account for the politico-musical activities of Oscar Rovito, Piero, Marilina Ross, Chango Farías Gómez, and Leonor Benedetto (among others), who were the authors and interpreters of what can be called "songs for the political moment," or "circumstantial songs." Interestingly enough, the members of the José Podestá Group were not apologetic at all for the "directly political" message of their songs, which could be discredited as *"panfletaria"* (a political pamphlet, instead of an artistic song) by many people (then and now). On the contrary, they saw themselves as composing those songs out of the urgency of the real struggle for power they were undergoing in the late 1960s and early 1970s around the *"Luche y vuelve"* ("Fight, and He Returns") campaign peronism was engaged in to secure the return of Perón to Argentina and, eventually, power.

Chapter 9, "The Revolutionary Patria and Its New (Wo)Men: Gendered Tropes of Political Agency and Popular Identity in Argentine Folk Music of the Long 1960s" by Illa Carrillo Rodríguez, closes the book showing how the socially and politically committed music movements that flourished throughout the Americas from the 1950s to the 1970s critically engaged with the continent's national folksong traditions, putting them to work in the articulation of a "popular-revolutionary" voice and identity. Interestingly enough, even though this version of identity was fraught with highly gendered representations of political agency, the question of how these music movements (and the left-wing culture that encompassed them) contended with issues of gender remains largely unexamined. With this chapter, Carrillo Rodríguez tries to fill the gap, and posits that such gendered modes of enacting "popular" and "revolutionary" subjectivities are crucial sites of political signification in which key elements of the 1960s' and early 1970s' utopian imagination crystallized.

The first part of the chapter parses different folk music currents that wrestled with the issue of representing the "authentic *pueblo*" and, thereby, with the difficulties of enacting a politically committed aesthetic praxis. Her analysis moves back and forth from a discussion of the figurations of popular-revolutionary subjectivities in Argentina's *Nuevo Cancionero* Movement and a contemporaneous Latin American New Song repertoire, to a consideration of how these subjectivities were represented in a "militant" musical narrative (the cantata *Montoneros*) that stemmed from the official cultural program of an armed political organization.

In the second part of the chapter, Carrillo Rodríguez charts the gender paradigms that recur in this politically committed repertoire. There, she enlarges her scope of analysis by examining the tropes of femininity and masculinity through which other, less overtly politicized sectors of Argentina's folksong milieu articulated musical narratives of nationhood that evoked the figure of the guerrilla. The focus of this part of the chapter is on the ways in which these narratives, which reference the nineteenth century's struggles for independence and subsequent civil wars, bear the traces of deeply rooted assumptions about gender and nationhood.

In the final part of the chapter, Carrillo Rodríguez reflects on how the gender paradigms conveyed by 1960s and 1970s folk-music production made possible, but also disavowed, certain forms of political agency. In what ways, she asks, did such paradigms partake in the configuration of the period's dominant model of *militancia* (militantism)? To what extent did this model of revolutionary agency and its musical representations unsettle normative political, aesthetic, and gender regimes? Carrillo Rodríguez's discussion of the tense dialogue that this musical repertoire entertained with political praxis and historical discourse seeks precisely to interrogate the ways in which the period's cultural production not only reflected, but fundamentally partook of, the configuration of polysemous, often contradictory models of revolutionary action.

NOTES

1. When we refer to a "militant song movement" in this book we don't want to give the reader the impression that what occurred in the 1960s and 1970s was a well-organized and coordinated social movement. In that regard, our use of the "movement" concept does not refer to a homogeneous group of people, music genre, or cultural formation, but rather to a constellation of very diverse repertoires, performance personae, musical aesthetics, and cultural practices that shared, in one way or another, an intense connection to the socio-political at a time of major social mobilizations and attempts at transforming existing power structures. In other words, it is important for the reader to know that there was no single organic and organized movement as such and, on the other hand, that "militant" does not refer to a historical category, in the way that the Chilean New Song and *Canto Popular Uruguayo* do, but to a common quality that, upon close inspection, you can discern in this assemblage of heterogeneous cultural practices. I want to thank Illa Carrillo Rodríguez for helping me to fully articulate this point.

2. Interestingly enough, even though Daniel Viglietti made a compilation of militant songs in 1969 under the name of "Protest Songs," at the same time in a later stage of his career he used the term "propositional song" as a better alternative to "protest songs." I want to thank Camila Juárez from making me aware of this information.

3. I want to thank Eileen Karmy Bolton for bringing this information to my attention.

4. As Illa Carrillo Rodríguez correctly points out (personal communication), in proposing the term "militant" it is important "to discuss the different valences of the term in English and Spanish. For even though both the Spanish *militante* and the English 'militant' share the Latin root *mīlitāns* (soldier), their current uses and connotations are quite different in each language. In contemporary parlance, my sense is that the English 'militant' has largely lost its earlier, nineteenth-century meaning of 'having a combative attitude in support of a cause' (*Oxford English Dictionary*) and now seems to be more strictly associated with warfare and the military. In Spanish, instead, *militancia* has preserved the former sense and is used to encompass the modes of political commitment that in English would be called 'activism.'"

5. There are several songs that were crucial for the development of the movement that were composed by female composers: *"Romance de María Pueblo"* by Pocha Barros; *"Zamba del Zafrero"* by Alma García; *"Zamba del chaguanco"* by Hilda Herrera; and so on.

6. Of course, I am advancing these claims in the first part of the 2010s, being completely aware that the reception of each of these repertoires is constantly fluctuating.

7. As Illa Carrillo Rodríguez correctly points out (personal communication), "While it is true that political organizations like the ERP undertook armed actions during the democratically-elected Peronist government, it is worth noting here that the idea that these organizations 'contributed' to the period's massacres is still highly contentious. Though still debated, a less contentious claim is that these organizations contributed to the intensification of militarism and armed violence."

Chapter One

New Song in Chile

Half a Century of Musical Activism

Nancy Morris

Latin American New Song is generally known as a fusion of politically conscious lyrics with traditional musical styles. Chilean New Song coalesced in the late 1950s and 1960s from a number of factors that were shared throughout the region, including the cross-Latin American exchange of political and musical ideas, political militancy, and the concomitant search for identity expression. Due to the specific socio-political events in Chile, Chilean New Song became the best-known manifestation of the genre outside Latin America.

Nueva Canción Chilena—Chilean New Song—emerged as Salvador Allende was gaining prominence in Chilean politics, and New Song musicians actively supported his 1970 election campaign and subsequent presidency. When Allende was overthrown in a military coup d'etat in 1973, well-known New Song musician Víctor Jara was killed, and most of the other prominent participants became exiles. The military dictatorship of Augusto Pinochet censored New Song music. In an atmosphere of repression and fear, young musicians revived New Song in altered form inside Chile. Outside of Chile, exiled musicians toured the world, exposing audiences on all continents to their music, and promoting opposition to the dictatorship. Many of the exiles moved back to Chile with the country's return to democracy in 1990, and they continue with their music and social activism, along with their younger counterparts.

There are numerous facets of New Song that invite analysis, and many ways to approach the topic. This chapter traces the history of Chilean New Song delineating the socio-political context that generated it, that distinguishes it and that is inseparable from it. It explores the interweaving of political events, societal institutions, and this form of cultural expression across a span of some fifty turbulent years in Chile. Like any social phenomenon, New Song can be delimited in multiple ways with varying degrees of breadth. The focus here is comparatively narrow, centering on the core people and events associated with this musical genre. The chapter is based on primary and secondary written and recorded material; interviews with participants; and field observation during visits to Chile in 1983, 1984, 2010, 2011, and 2012. All translations from Spanish originals are my own.

ANTECEDENTS

In the mid-twentieth century, what was commonly identified as folk music in Chile consisted of bucolic songs venerating the Chilean countryside based on a narrow set of traditional rural forms, particularly the *tonada,* a gentle, Spanish-derived style featuring vocal harmonies, delicate guitar arrangements, and decorous performances. This sentimental music, which Chilean musicologist Juan Pablo González has termed "folkloristic" for its distance from the traditional folk styles that it is based on (1989: 268), was popularized by a number of singing groups. The best known were *Los Cuatro Huasos* (The Four *Huasos*) and *Los Huasos Quincheros* (The Rodeo *Huasos*), names that evoked the rural hacienda: "*huaso*" designates a ranch hand, or simply a person from the country, and is commonly translated as "cowboy" or "horseman." These ensembles purveyed "an idealistic and romantic view of country life, life that takes place in the farms owned by the bourgeoisie" (González 1989: 268). This musical reflection of Chile's hierarchical social structure belied changing conditions. Voter reform in the 1950s greatly expanded electoral participation (Chilcote & Edelstein 1974: 521), opening the way for "the onset of mass politics in Chile" (Sigmund 1977: 23).

Electoral inclusion, political party mobilization and labor union activity contributed to and reflected increasing political consciousness in Chile and across Latin America. This, in turn, was expressed in popular music. In the early 1960s, Chilean musicians, influenced by similar developments in Argentina, looked beyond the limited *huaso* style toward renovating traditional music. They sought a wider range of folk forms and a more straightforward delivery than the highly stylized *huasos*. Their desire to reduce the distance between the folk origins and urban adaptations of traditional music reflected their political sympathies, and created "a new soundtrack" for Chile that came to be termed "neofolklore" (González, Ohlsen & Rolle 2009: 337–338, 356). As they explored rural Chilean styles, neofolklore musicians also began providing "new content for the old forms" by writing songs that expressed their social concerns (Fairley 1984: 111). This new content represented a real change in folk-based songs. In the words of Chilean radio announcer Ricardo

García, neofolklore compositions showed that Chilean popular music could go beyond "the *tonada* that spoke of the difference between the landowner and the laborer with a decided bias toward the former" (Osorio 1996: 102).

García, a charismatic host of popular radio programs, discovered a different approach to music when he met the irrepressible self-trained folklorist Violeta Parra. Parra's passion for Chilean culture led to her unsponsored travels to unearth its diversity. With pencil, tape recorder, and a persuasive manner, she documented traditional musical styles that had received scant attention outside their communities (Parra 1985). Rejecting the music of the "those postcard *huasos* from the golf club" (Štambuk & Bravo 2011: 82), she collected songs from rural peasants, from the deserts and high plains of Northern Chile, from the archipielagos in the South, and, long before militant indigenous consciousness took hold across the continent, from Easter Island and from Chile's Mapuche people (Štambuck & Bravo 2011: 179).

As she gained recognition for the breadth and depth of her music collecting in the early 1950s, Parra appeared on García's radio program. The music she presented, García said, "signified for me the entrance into an absolutely fascinating world, where words and songs had a completely different feeling" (Osorio 1996: 51). Parra endeavored to document and preserve songs and styles that were nearly extinct, and she also expressed her own feelings through poetry and songwriting. In 1962 she wrote "*La Carta*," ("The Letter"), a composition that some have identified as the "birth of Chilean New Song" because it melded folkloric music with socially conscious lyrics (Barraza 1972: 37; González, Ohlsen & Rolle 2009: 389). The song described her brother's arrest in connection with the repression of a nationwide workers' strike:

> They sent me a letter in the early mail
> In this letter they tell me they took my brother off to jail
> And heartlessly they shackled him and dragged him through the streets, yes.
> (cited in Martínez Reverte 1976: 78)

While describing an event that affected her personally, with "The Letter" Parra also captured the social agitation unleashed in the 1950s, as the political mobilization of the working class altered the tenor of Chilean society (Constable & Valenzuela 1991: 22). This politicization was felt in universities as well: a vigorous student movement was calling for a greater voice in higher education.

In 1965, a trio of university students formed a new ensemble whose goals as a group joined musical and political realms: "We did not want to make concessions to commercialism," founding member Eduardo Carrasco explains, "we wanted to . . . make expressive music without adornment or exaggeration . . . search for our roots . . . and . . . make revolutionary music."

Rejecting "Anglo-Saxon penetration in our music," they looked instead toward Latin American styles as a foundation for expressing their identity, which entailed ideals of Latin American unity. For a name, they broke with the conventions of neofolkore groups and from the indigenous Mapuche language selected *Quilapayún*, "three bearded ones," which at the time described them (Carrasco 2003a: 11–25). As Quilapayún developed their vocal and instrumental skills and added new members, they approached Víctor Jara for guidance. Jara, a musician and theater director known for his imaginative work, became their artistic director (Carrasco 2003a: 81–84).

Although Quilapayún was concerned about the stage management involved in creating a smooth presentation for multiple musicians and instruments, they lacked access to theaters, and sang mostly at university events and small coffeehouse-bars called *peñas*. Their music was seldom played on the radio, which was a vehicle for the "Anglo-Saxon penetration" that they objected to. Beyond the occasional folk song, Chilean music heard on the air was principally by local imitators of Anglo-American rock 'n roll, sometimes singing in English, often Anglicizing their names (González, Ohlsen & Rolle 2009: 605–651; Taffet 1997: 94). Media owners and programmers were happy to feature popular culture that did not challenge the status quo. Ricardo García observed that because "the bourgeoisie, the masters of banking and industry . . . controlled everything," Violeta Parra's folk songs might be played on the radio but listeners were unlikely to hear a political song like "The Letter" (Osorio 1996: 103).

In 1965 Parra's oldest children, Isabel and Ángel, opened a space for the music that was emerging out of neofolklore by founding the *Peña de los Parra* (The Parras' *peña*) in Santiago. Inspired by the *Peña de los Parra*, a group of architecture students led by Osvaldo Rodríguez and Payo Grondona founded a *peña* in Valparaíso, Chile's major port city, and similar gathering spaces began to appear throughout the country (Bravo Chiappe & González Farfán 2009: 35). A contemporary observer noted that "this Chilean version of café-concert met immediate acceptance" particularly among a certain social sector: "At first the public was almost exclusively students, artists and intellectuals" (Barraza 1972: 39).

The *peñas* were the hub of activity for musicians who wanted to create music that, unlike the songs that they were hearing on the radio, would express their identity as Latin Americans. This "growing Latin Americanist sentiment" was in evidence as the *peñas* welcomed "all the folklore of the continent" (Valladares M. & Vilches P. 2009: 17). In the same spirit, Violeta Parra established *La Carpa de la Reina*, a performance space and multifaceted cultural center on the outskirts of Santiago. Many of the musicians who became the core of Chilean New Song circulated among the *peñas* and *La Carpa de la Reina*.

Violeta Parra did not live to see the immeasurable impact that she would have on New Song. By unearthing and honoring marginalized Chilean musical forms, by setting her political sentiments to folk rhythms, and by using traditional styles to undergird her own compositions of astonishing creativity, she opened the way for exploration and renewal. The New Song group Inti-Illimani explained, "Violeta introduced folkloric investigation, re-creation, elaboration, and abstraction which expanded the creative possibilities of all the other artists" (Orellana 1978: 124). Commenting on her painstaking work recovering and assembling rural songs and using these influences in her own compositions, Osvaldo Rodríguez said "in her most notable songs . . . rhythms flower which were not only forgotten, but practically no longer existed. . . . Violeta Parra is the fundamental core of Chilean New Song" (Orellana 1978: 130). Víctor Jara stated, "The presence of Violeta Parra is like a star that will never go out . . . Violeta . . . showed us the path; we do no more than follow it" (*Caimán Barbudo* 1972: 3).

Parra died in 1967, a year of significant events in Chilean music and politics. Chilean society was astir: Christian Democratic President Eduardo Frei, elected in 1964, advocated political participation and reforms favorable to the working class but was unable to both mollify the business sector and keep up with demands of miners and unionizing peasants (Sigmund 1977: 43–75; Chilcote 1974: 533, 541). In addition to work stoppages, demonstrations, and student strikes, the ongoing social turmoil was exacerbated by bank robberies and urban violence from the newly formed Movement of Revolutionary Left (MIR), which advocated armed struggle (Sigmund 1977: 61–67). This contrasted with the position of the Chilean Communist Party, which favored electoral progress toward social equality. The Party's deep roots in the Chilean working class and its support of cultural work drew the allegiance of activists and artists, among them many New Song musicians (Chaparro, Seves & Spener 2013: 25; Hite 2000: 32).

Musicians and activists were attentive to the international context, as were their counterparts around the world in the contentious 1960s. Political scientist Katherine Hite (2000: 17), analyzing Chilean leaders, notes that "the influence of the ideologically charged 1960s era on the identities of young people coming of political age cannot be overemphasized." The 1959 Cuban Revolution provided inspiration, and U.S. actions—the embargo of Cuba, the blatant influence in Latin American business and politics, and the escalating Vietnam War—generated resentment and animosity. Representing unwelcome domination, United States popular culture was ever-present, not only on top-40 radio, but also in Disney comic books and Hollywood films. The prevalence of media products imported from the unpopular North fed the drive to seek out Latin American roots.

Reflecting this interest in Latin America, a group of students formed the Inti-Illimani ensemble in 1967 (Salinas 2010; Coulon 2009: 40). While

Quilapayún had taken their name from the language of the Mapuche of Southern Chile, Inti-Illimani looked to the North. Their passion for Andean music was signaled in the combination of the word for "sun" in the Andean Aymara language with the name of a prominent Bolivian mountain (Inti-Illimani Histórico 2013).

In this period, urbanized styles drawing from highland music of Bolivia, Peru, Argentina, and Chile had been gaining audiences. The mingling of musicians from various Andean traditions in the clubs of Buenos Aires and across the ocean in nocturnal Paris played a pivotal role in this crosscutting interchange (Rios 2008). Travels to Argentina and Bolivia early in Inti-Illimani's existence increased their exposure to this mixture of influences (Cifuentes Seves 2000, Section 5), and to the resultant set of instruments that came to dominate "the Andean musical niche in much of the world" (Rios 2012: 5). Along with other nascent groups, they adopted the panpipes, or *zampoña*; the bamboo flute called the *quena*; the *charango*, a small ten-stringed instrument traditionally made from an armadillo shell; and the large *bombo* drum.

Also in 1967, Neofolklore musician Patricio Manns, accompanied by the group "Andean Voices," recorded "*Sueño Americano*" ("American Dream"), a long-form work that foreshadowed the artistic maturity that New Song would achieve. The album's twelve songs are set to Latin American musical forms from several countries. The lyrics, in the poetic language characteristic of this important artist, trace developments in Latin American history while denouncing exploitation and U.S. domination, and celebrating liberation.

The International Encounter of Protest Song, held in Cuba in 1967, served as catalyst to the establishment of New Song as a defined genre. Participants from sixteen countries, including Peggy Seeger from the United States, and Isabel and Ángel Parra and Rolando Alarcón from Chile, gathered to sing and discuss their music (Silber 1967: 29). The encounter heightened the trans-Latin American sentiments that were already evident in the Chileans' musical choices, and created closer ties with other musicians who attended, among them Oscar Matus of Argentina, and Daniel Viglietti and Alfredo Zitarrosa of Uruguay (Valladares M. & Vilches P. 2009: 106–7; Music-bazaar 2013).

The following year, Quilapayún sought to record their increasingly radical repertoire. They had previously released two folkloric records on the Odeon label, but their new material was outside Odeon's scope. With financial support from the Chilean Young Communist organization, they collaborated with Víctor Jara on *For Vietnam* (Carrasco 2003a: 128). The title song exhibits both international consciousness and anti-Americanism, warning "Yankee . . . you will fall" to "the heroic people of Vietnam" (Quilapayún 2012a).

The album was filled with overtly political songs: a Cuban folk song with updated pro-Castro lyrics; a Violeta Parra song denouncing political hypocrisy; a "Funeral Song for Che Guevara," who had died in Bolivia shortly before in the pursuit of Latin American revolution that made him a hero; a text by Chilean poet Pablo Neruda, set to the traditional *cueca* rhythm, about legendary Latin American resistance fighter Joaquín Murieta. Violeta Parra's compositions, Neruda's poetry, and the *cueca* form would be consistent features of Chilean New Song.

Although *For Vietnam* received no airplay, sales through trade unions, community organizations, and student groups made it an immediate success, leading the Young Communists to formalize the record label *Discoteca de Canto Popular* or DICAP ("Popular Song Records") as a way "to continue to distribute revolutionary music" (Carrasco 2003a: 129). DICAP released more than sixty records between 1968 and 1973 (MúsicaPopular.cl 2012). Many musicians also gained exposure through *Chile Ríe y Canta* ("Chile Laughs and Sings"), a live radio program that dispatched caravans of musicians to all corners of the country, and also operated a *peña* in Santiago (González, Ohlsen & Rolle 2009: 320).

This growing musical current had performance spaces and a recording company, but the lack of mainstream outlets carried through to music festivals. Such festivals—concerts or concert series with many performers, often structured as competitions—had multiplied throughout Chile from the 1950s. In 1960 a festival had been founded to showcase Chilean musicians and entice tourists to the seaside town of Viña del Mar. Radio personality Ricardo García played a central role in the Viña del Mar festival, promoting it vigorously on the air and in magazine commentaries, and serving as on-stage host of the show (González, Ohlsen & Rolle 2009: 241–246). The festival rapidly became successful but, as was the case with radio, the political music that was heard in *peñas*, at events, and on DICAP records was present only meagerly.

In 1969, with the Viña del Mar festival well established, García set out to put together a new festival that would provide visibility for alternative music. Pondering the idea, he mused, "I think there are new ways to say things. . . . I think that it's possible to speak of a new Chilean song" (Valladares M. & Vilches P. 2009: 125). This comment reflected a labeling trend in Latin America for socially conscious traditionally rooted musical styles. In the spirit of Argentina's *nuevo cancionero* (New Songbook), the event was dubbed "the First Festival of *Nueva Canción Chilena*" or Chilean New Song. In García's words it was "the only way to gather Chilean composers and demonstrate a new expression, open the way for them, a door, through a festival attended by workers and students, those who would best understand what this New Song is about" (Osorio 1996: 103).

The Festival was co-sponsored by the Catholic University of Chile, which had new liberal leadership as a result of university reform won by the students. University Rector Fernando Velasco Castillo emphasized the search for authenticity represented by this music in his opening remarks: "Perhaps popular song is the art that best defines a community. But lately in our country we are exposed to a reality that is not ours. . . . Our purpose here today is to search for an expression that describes our reality. . . . Let our fundamental concern be that our own art be deeply rooted in the Chilean spirit" (Velasco Castillo 1969). Following Chilean festival norms, the First Festival of Chilean New Song was organized as a competition among twelve invited participants. The judges divided the first prize between Richard Rojas and Víctor Jara. Jara, accompanied by Quilapayún, played his winning song advocating rural and urban working class unity *"Plegaria a un Labrador"* ("Prayer to a Peasant") to a packed Chile Stadium (Barraza 1972: 45).

The next year, García followed up with the Second Festival of Chilean New Song. Reflecting "the difference between this festival and similar contests organized by the recording industry" (Barraza 1972: 45), this time the event was not framed as a competition. The contrasting works presented at the Festival demonstrated the breadth of creation that had come to be encompassed within the rubric New Song. Included in the roster was *"Il Bosco,"* titled for a popular café in central Santiago which, as the lyrics relate, served as all-night headquarters for young people who could not find privacy for romance. This wry three-minute commentary on urban life was composed and performed by Payo Grondona, accompanying himself on banjo.

From a vastly different location on the musical spectrum came the *"Cantata Santa María de Iquique,"* a thirty-five-minute work written by conservatory-trained composer Luis Advis and performed by Quilapayún, using principally Andean instruments. The work recounts the 1907 massacre of striking miners and their family members in the Chilean city of Iquique, when military forces opened fire on a crowd of thousands gathered at the Santa María school. The reported number of deaths was around three hundred (Dibam n.d.); historians' estimates are higher; and in popular legend, including the Cantata, the figure is 2,000 to 3,000 (Stern 2006b: 290).

As described by Chilean composer Juan Orrego Salas (1985: 11), the *"Cantata Santa María de Iquique"* employs "songs, spoken or sung recitatives, instrumental and choral interludes, that is, all the components of the Baroque *cantata* assimilated to vernacular traditions . . . and presented in accessible language." The Cantata exemplified the deepening musical exploration and desire to bridge classical and popular music that Quilapayún member Eduardo Carrasco (1995) terms a characteristic of Chilean New Song. Advis was one of the key figures in this "new type of creation, which combined the distant academic world with Latin American popular culture" (González, Ohlsen & Rolle 2009: 303). In 1972, the Cantata was characterized as "the most important work of New Song" (Barraza 1972: 85), an evaluation that has held up in the ensuing decades. In 1984, Osvaldo Rodríguez noted that the Cantata "not only marked an era, but created a school" of long-form works that incorporate classical and popular elements (p. 135); in 2012, Jorge Coulon of Inti-Illimani described the impact of the Cantata as "a revolution within the revolution" of New Song (Arenas 2012: 42).

The Second Festival of Chilean New Song, with its culminating performance of the "*Cantata Santa María de Iquique*," was held during the final weeks of the fractious 1970 Chilean presidential election campaign. Nationwide strikes and continued violence by the MIR punctuated the ongoing social ferment. In the three-way contest, Socialist Party Senator Salvador Allende was the candidate of the Popular Unity coalition, an alliance dominated by the Socialist, Communist and Radical parties. The Popular Unity platform called for the restructuring of government and the economy, including universal health care and education and enhanced social benefits for workers and peasants (Unidad Popular 1969).

A historical account of military excess against workers, the *"Cantata Santa María de Iquique"* also had contemporary resonance. The work closes with an exhortation against complacency:

> All of you who have listened to this story please understand
> Don't just remain there seated thinking it's safely past . . .
> Perhaps tomorrow or the next day . . . it could all take place again. . . .
> We must battle to attain the rights due to everyone . . .
> We must join together as brothers, so no one can push us down . . .
> The day will arrive of justice and freedom for all at last.
> (Quilapayún 2012b)

With its call to action, this song echoed Allende's campaign song *"Venceremos"* ("We Will Triumph"), a collaboration among Inti-Illimani, Víctor Jara, Claudio Iturra, and composer Sergio Ortega—like Advis, a classically trained musician (Coulon 2009: 47–49). Unlike the Cantata, and in keeping with its mobilizing purpose, musically *"Venceremos"* was a simple march with basic instrumentation: flute, guitar, *charango*, and *bombo*.

> We will triumph, we will triumph. . . .
> Break the links, a thousand chains will be gone
> We will triumph, we will triumph
> We'll defeat misery and move on.
> (cited in Mellac 1974: 20)

New Song musicians participated in campaign activities, singing *"Venceremos"* at many functions, and writing other songs in support of Allende. For example, Isabel Parra composed a song describing a woman who was optimistic about a future Popular Unity government, explaining, "It was a song that nobody asked me to write and you'd realize later that it was sung all over Chile . . . that's how the songs were born, because we were involved in what was happening" (González Bermejo 1975: 49).

Allende won the election with a narrow plurality, the first Marxist ever to become head of state by popular vote. Carrasco describes the feeling among Allende supporters: "We were happy, everything seemed to be going in the direction of unstoppable progress, of justice, of democracy, everything seemed to indicate that Chile was a special country where all the dreams of our continent would be realized" (2003a: 165). A Chilean journalist encapsulates the reaction of Allende opponents, who "sunk into despair and drew their blinds in fear that the 'Marxist hordes' would attack" (González 2012: 43).

The distance between the dreams of a more egalitarian society that inspired Allende's followers and the fears that rattled his opponents created an acutely strained social climate. Allende took office amid continuing political strife and efforts to sabotage his election from within and without Chile (Valenzuela 1978: 49). In support of the Popular Unity government's programs, New Song musicians performed at official functions and at gatherings in shanty towns, parks, factories, universities, and trade union halls. Constant performing honed their musical abilities, and some who had started as amateurs began studying music with Sergio Ortega (Carrasco 2003b).

The commitment many artists felt to Popular Unity ideals elicited a body of work produced to support the government in a time of social upheaval. Among the long-form musical creations, the one most directly aligned with the government was an album setting the proposed policies of Popular Unity to music. A collaboration of Sergio Ortega, Luis Advis, and Inti-Illimani, with texts by Julio Rojas, *"Canto al Programa"* ("Song of the Program") contains such titles as "Waltz of Education for All" and "Song of Agrarian Reform." But reforms aimed at greater incorporation of peasants and workers into national life inevitably stoked the fears of powerful social sectors. The opposition was aided by the United States government, which, seeing Allende as a Marxist threat, cut aid to Chile and secretly supplied millions of dollars to efforts to bring down the Popular Unity government (Qureshi 2009; United States Department of State 1975).

As social conflict escalated, Nueva Canción participants produced a series of "pamphlet" songs that responded to conditions and events of the moment (Carrasco 2003a: 169–173). Such a song was Víctor Jara's *"Ni Chicha ni Limoná"* ("Neither One Thing nor the Other"), which mocked people who were unwilling to take a stand in favor of Popular Unity in a polarized time when inaction was seen as tantamount to supporting the opposition.

Folkloric musical exploration also continued. In 1971, "influenced by Chilean New Song and the ancestral Andean culture," a group of students in Northern Chile formed Illapu, an ensemble dedicated to investigating and playing Andean music (Illapu 2012). Their studies and their lifelong familiarity with the region led them to employ a greater range of indigenous forms and instruments than had previously been heard in Chilean New Song. Their inventive and energetic style elicited an invitation to perform in the February 1973 Viña del Mar festival (Padilla 1985; Illapu 2012).

By mid-1973 everyday life was chaotic. Inflation and strikes against Popular Unity policies in such key sectors as trucking, mining, public transportation and agriculture had brought about manufacturing delays, food shortages, and near-paralysis of routine transactions of every sort throughout the country. The "peaceful transition to Socialism" that Allende espoused had became an unpeaceful series of ideological and physical confrontations, an escalating cycle of demonstrations and counter-demonstrations as government supporters and opponents feverishly worked toward their contrary goals (Valenzuela 1978: 77–78; Sigmund 1997: 169). In August 1973, in this fraught atmosphere, Sergio Ortega and Quilapayún wrote the song "The People United Will Never Be Defeated" for the Popular Unity government (Carrasco 2003a: 219).

> And now the people
> Rising up in struggle
> With the voice of a giant
> Shouting out "Onward!"
> The people united will never be defeated! (Quilapayún 2013a)

SEPTEMBER 11, 1973

On September 11, 1973, a military coup d'etat brought an end to the Popular Unity government and its ambitions. That morning, announcing its "irrevocable decision to fight to the end to defeat the Marxist government" (Molina n.d.: 233), the military junta that engineered the coup, headed by General Augusto Pinochet, declared a State of Siege and moved into cities and regions throughout the country. The military took over the mass media, seized control of banks, closed the country's borders, suspended air traffic, and set a curfew. As tanks rolled through neighborhoods and bombers roared overhead, military edicts were read out on the radio: the populace was to remain calm, not to leave workplaces or homes, and to cooperate with authorities. Edict number 1 warned that any "act of sabotage" would be severely punished. Edict number 2 ordered evacuation of the government complex, a colonial palace in central Santiago called La Moneda, where President Allende was ensconced with members of his inner circle. "Effective immediately," stated Edict number 8, "the presence of groups of people in the streets is absolutely prohibited" (Molina n.d.: 234). Soldiers rounded up thousands of citizens and held them in stadiums. Edict number 10 named ninety-five Popular Unity government officials who were instructed to report to authorities. Accustomed to the rule of law, many did so, and found themselves sent to forced-labor concentration camps (Bitar 2009).

The most prominent New Song ensembles, Quilapayún and Inti-Illimani, were on tour in Europe when the coup took place. Although the atmosphere in Chile had been tense when they left and fears of a military takeover were widespread, they were stunned to hear news reports of house-to-house searches, mass arrests, and the bombing of La Moneda. In his memoir, Eduardo Carrasco of Quilapayún describes learning of the coup: "At that instant everything changed for us. . . . Information circulated . . . about killings in factories, deaths in shantytowns, torture, cadavers floating in rivers, massive searches, assaults, concentration camps. . . . In Santiago some of our houses had been ransacked; they were looking for us along with many other Chileans who had leftist connections" (2003a: 239, 244). Allende was dead. Pinochet had declared that Chile was "in a state of internal war" (Muñoz 2008: 46). The military was monitoring travel in and out of the country. It had closed most media outlets and controlled those that continued to function. The *Peña de los Parra* and the DICAP record company were among the many sites that had been raided (Perez Luna 1975; Jara 1984: 257). It was clear that New Song musicians could not safely return to Chile.

They were soon joined outside the country by most of their colleagues. To evade arrest and get out of Chile under conditions of border lockdown many Chileans took refuge in the embassies of sympathetic countries until safe conduct passes could be arranged (Wright & Oñate Zúñiga 2007: 33–34). Among those New Song musicians who left via embassy were Patricio Manns, Sergio Ortega, Isabel Parra, and Osvaldo Rodríguez (Lubetkin n.d.: 27; Dorfman 1998: 201).

Some were not so lucky. Ángel Parra was arrested, taken to the National Stadium with thousands of others, and then sent to a concentration camp (Perez Luna 1975). A clandestinely recorded cassette of a prison concert, smuggled out and made into a record in Mexico, testifies to his imprisonment (Parra 1977). He was released after four months, but forbidden to sing or to leave the country. About a year later, he snuck out of Chile (García 2006b; Perez Luna 1975).

To many people, the name of Víctor Jara has come to represent Chilean New Song. Jara was killed, as were hundreds of others, in the first days of the military takeover. Jara's widow, Joan (1984), sought out witnesses so she could reconstruct the events of his last days, which are corroborated in published testimonials of the coup (Villegas 1974: 59–66). Jara was arrested at his workplace at the Technical University when tanks besieged the campus.

Along with the University Rector and some six hundred other students and faculty, he was taken to Chile Stadium, where thousands were being held. A soldier recognized Jara, separated him from the group, and beat him. Later, Jara joined a group of friends in the stadium bleachers; they helped him tend his wounds. Conditions in the stadium revealed the attitude of the military toward those they perceived as enemies. The scant food supplied was insufficient, bright lights stayed on day and night, talking was prohibited (Villegas 1974: 22–23). After three days, soldiers again singled Jara out for removal from the crowd of prisoners. Taken to the stadium dressing rooms, he was beaten and taunted to sing. Witnesses say he responded with the first part of Allende's campaign song "*Venceremos*" before being dragged off. In the stands, he had been writing on a scrap of paper, which he handed to the person next to him when he was taken away "who in turn hid it in his sock . . . His friends had tried each one of them to learn the poem by heart as it was written, so as to carry it out of the Stadium with them. They never saw Victor again."

> There are five thousand of us here
> In this small part of the city. . . .
> I wonder how many we are in all
> In the cities and in the whole country?
> Here alone
> Are ten thousand hands which plant seeds
> And make factories run...
> How hard it is to sing
> When I must sing of horror.
> Horror which I am living
> Horror which I am dying . . . (Jara 1984: 246–51)

A week after the coup d'etat, summoned by a worker who took great personal risk to contact her, Joan Jara identified her husband's body, riddled with bullet wounds, wrists broken, in the Santiago morgue. She hastily arranged a burial before it became just another unidentified corpse among hundreds (Carmona 2013; Jara 1984: 241–243).

Víctor Jara was a creative artist whose work marked Chilean New Song in profound ways before he took on martyr status (Chaparro, Seves & Spener 2013). He was not only an important composer and solo performer, but he also sang with both Quilapayún and Inti-Illimani, and aided them with their stage management, molding professional ensembles out of unwieldy groups (Carrasco 2003a: 83–84; Coulon 2009: 40–41). His artistic talent put at the service of his political convictions, his collaborative spirit, and his bravery in the face of death have made Jara a touchstone for politically committed artists. As a Spanish music analyst stated in 1977, "Jara is a myth" (Aguirre González 1977: 25). His mythical status endures. Musicians all over the world pay homage to him, singing his songs or writing about him in theirs; Arlo Guthrie, the Clash, and U2 are among the English-language artists who have done so. Jara is the subject of numerous documentary films and written profiles. His name and story often appear in general works on the Popular Unity government and its overthrow.

The 1973 coup d'etat marked a signal divide in Chilean history and, accordingly, in New Song. With the principal New Song musicians outside of the country, and censorship and repression reigning inside, the path of New Song forked into New Song in exile and, eventually, a revived and altered New Song in Chile.

NEW SONG INSIDE CHILE

During the first year of military rule, a formal State of Siege and an informal state of fear prevailed, as the military endeavored to wipe out Marxism in Chile. Individuals were silenced by might and violence. Meticulous subsequent documentation has determined that about 3,000 people were killed or "disappeared" by the dictatorship and more than 150,000 detained, many of them tortured (Stern 2006a: 158–160). Discussion was silenced by edicts and surveillance. There would be no electoral politics: the military closed down Congress, outlawed Marxist parties and declared all others "in recess," destroyed voter lists, and harassed those party leaders who were not in exile or in prison (Sigmund 1977: 253; Valenzuela 1978: 109). There was to be no expression of leftist political ideas: books were burned in huge bonfires; the publisher associated with the Popular Unity government was shut down, its inventory incinerated and its publications outlawed; the poetry of Pablo Neruda—Nobel Literature Prize winner, Allende's Ambassador to France, and Communist Party member—was banned (Dorat Guerra & Weibel Barahona 2012: 183). The exuberant murals supporting the Allende government were whitewashed (Errázuriz & Leiva Quijada 2012). Military officers were put in charge of all universities; they dismissed thousands of professors and students (Constable & Valenzuela 1991: 249).

The silence that resulted from this wholesale intimidation and destruction came to be called the "cultural blackout" (*Araucaria de Chile* 1978): "Bookstalls closed, nightlife vanished, and radio stations replaced Andean protest ballads with Mexican *mariachis* and American pop songs" (Constable & Valenzuela 1991: 147). As a carrier of ideas and an ally of the Popular Unity government, New Song was included in the purge far beyond its removal from radio playlists. When the DICAP office and the *Peña de los Parra* were ransacked, master recordings were destroyed (Jara 1984: 257; Perez Luna 1975). A September 28, 1973, memo from the Odeon record company indicates that the military was concerned about the commercial recording industry as well: "Complying with the self-censorship of the Phonographic Industry that the Governing Junta has stipulated," Odeon informed its retail outlets that it would no longer manufacture certain titles—a list of twenty-eight records was provided—and insisted that "since the dispositions of the Junta are that these and other similar records be withdrawn from sale *immediately*," distributors return any existing inventory to the company without delay. The list included early records of Quilapayún, Inti-Illimani, Víctor Jara, and Violeta Parra, as well as an album by U.S. singer Joan Baez (Odeon 1973, emphasis in original).

Unlike neighboring countries, Chile had a long history of democratic rule, and the violence and intensity of the coup d'etat were shocking. Many believed that the military would hold power briefly and then cede to civilian government. This naiveté about the intentions of the new regime coupled with the concrete order of record industry "self-censorship" perhaps explains why an Odeon executive requested a meeting with officials some two months after the coup. Héctor Pavez, a musician who was present, described the meeting to a friend:

> We were not familiar with fascism, and we needed to know. The reality was much worse than we had thought. . . . They gave it to us straight: That they were going to be very tough, that they would examine our attitudes, our songs, with a magnifying glass, forget the flute, the *quena*, the *charango* because they were instruments identified with the socially conscious song; . . . that the *"Cantata Santa María"* was a historic crime of high treason . . . that Quilapayún were responsible for the divisions among Chilean youth. . . . Well, at that point we knew that there was nothing to be done, absolutely nothing, unless we became collaborators with the Junta (Largo Farías 1977: 39).

At around the same time, executives of EMI, Phillips, and RCA, the leading international record labels operating in Chile, were summoned to a meeting at which they were told to put Andean music "in the freezer" because its association with the Allende government threatened the "new institutionality" (García 2006b).

The news that it was dangerous to play Andean music circulated through what was left of the folk and New Song community. This startling turn of events was reflected in the decision of the Viña del Mar music festival organizers within months of the coup to suspend the festival competition in the folk music category (González 2013: 266).

The separation of Andean instruments from Nueva Canción songs and from popular music in general provided a way around the proscription. In late 1973, musician Jaime Soto León, a conservatory-trained student of Sergio Ortega who had been involved with New Song, formed a group he called Andean Baroque. In an interview he explained, "it occurred to me to make Baroque music with Andean instruments"—the Andean *quena* flute replacing the seventeenth-century recorder, for example, and the *charango* substituting for the mandolin. "Quilapayún were outside the country, and Inti-Illimani were outside the country, and Illapu didn't dare play and . . . I said if we play Bach, Handel, Vivaldi they can't suppress us, they're going to leave us be even if we're playing Andean instruments."

With performing spaces scarce to nonexistent, Andean Baroque began giving recitals in churches, which offered an added layer of protection. Although their music derived from the centuries-old classical canon, there was a shared sense that the instruments conveyed a political message (Acevedo 1995: 158). This notion was confirmed in interview comments from a Chilean cultural critic who was a teenager at the time. Seeing a flyer announcing an Andean Baroque recital at a church, and not knowing anything about this new group, he and a friend welcomed the opportunity to attend a live musical performance. When they heard the Andean instruments, "it made us nervous, because for me just hearing those sounds was like being in something prohibited, something bad. This was in, like, 1974." The same year an attempt to put together a *peña* foundered when the first performance was denounced to authorities by neighbors who heard singing at a "Communist meeting" (Bravo Chiappe & González Farfán 2009: 58).

By 1975, repression had become more selective, and traditional Andean music came out of the freezer. The group Illapu, whose music was deeply rooted in Andean forms, had remained in Northern Chile after the coup, continuing with their folkloric investigation far from the metropolitan center. After a period of silence, they began playing again (Padilla 1985; Cruz 1983: 17). Others followed, and the music became so popular that its resurgence was termed the "Andean Boom." Instrumentals and traditional nonpolitical songs were the order of the day. That order was literal: at a few short-lived efforts to open *peñas*, artists were instructed to avoid songs with political content (Bravo Chiappe & González Farfán 2009: 58–59). The first stable post-coup *peña* opened in 1975, founded by New Song musician Nano Acevedo (Acevedo 1995: 157–158; Bravo Chiappe & González Farfán 2009: 61). It was followed by others, and a performing circuit of *peñas*, churches and universities developed. In contrast to the pre-1973 bohemian norm, events were scheduled for early evening so that performers and audience could get home before the nightly curfew.

The music that emerged from these activities was sufficiently cohesive that it invited classification. Having named *Nueva Canción* with the 1969 Festival, Ricardo García also selected the term *Canto Nuevo* for its successor. He explained, "the need existed to label a movement. We sought a name that would meet two requirements: that it be easily remembered and that it suggest a tie with *Nueva Canción*" (Godoy 1981: 16). *Nueva Canción* and *Canto Nuevo* both translate into English as "New Song." These terms and variants of them are used indiscriminately throughout Latin America, except in Chile, where *Nueva Canción* denotes pre-1973 New Song, and *Canto Nuevo* refers to dictatorship-era music.

In 1976, a media window opened for *Canto Nuevo* in the form of a nightly radio show highlighting young Chilean musicians (Godoy 1981: 18), and a new record company. Ricardo García, who had been blacklisted from radio, founded Alerce Records "to rescue a series of scattered values. The leftovers of a movement—the *nueva canción*—tied to my own life." He chose to call the record label after the larch tree of his native Southern Chile: "hard wood, adaptable to all climates." The Alerce Records logo shows a fallen tree behind an upright one, "symbolizing the rebirth of popular song" (Godoy 1981: 15).

Reaching the potential audience was always a hurdle for *Canto Nuevo*. Unlike *Nueva Canción*, which had been integrally involved with the politics of its time and thus had a ready-made audience, *Canto Nuevo* was implicitly in opposition to a government that did not allow the voicing of opposition sentiments. Media were censored. Musical performers had to submit song lyrics to the authorities for approval. With social life drastically restricted, television had become the principal outlet for Chilean entertainment. Each television channel had a "chief of security" who monitored content and administered an unpublished blacklist of banned performers. "The lists and the rules behind them were variable," according to analysts of the era, "and the criteria unknown" (Contardo & García 2009: 20–21), but most *Canto Nuevo* musicians found themselves unwelcome on TV. Like churches, universities were somewhat protected spaces, despite being headed by appointed military officers. In 1977 students formed the "University Cultural Group," which held arts festivals and *peñas*.

Breaking out of small-scale performance spaces, Alerce Records held *La Gran Noche del Folklore* ("The Grand Night of Folklore"), a festival-like concert, in 1977. Large gatherings of any kind were still rare and the 7,000-seat theater sold out. The restrictions on interaction and the climate of fear that had prevailed since 1973 were illustrated by the comments of a musician who attended the event. "I saw people I hadn't seen since 1973, people I thought were in prison, or dead" (Morris 1986: 127–128). Included in the concert of mainly traditional folk songs, the group Aquelarre played a Patricio Manns composition about a nineteenth-century hero of the Chilean Independence Wars who "shone like the ray of freedom." The word "freedom," which comes in the middle of the song, brought the audience to cheers and lengthy applause, a moment captured on the Alerce recording of the concert (Discos Alerce 1978).

This incident illuminates the enormous difference between *Nueva Canción*, a vehicle for overt political statements, and *Canto Nuevo,* which was hindered from expressing political ideas. Applause at key moments was one communication code between performers and audience. Another was allegorical lyrics. After plumbing the possibilities of instrumentals and innocuous songs, musicians moved toward finding ways to say more, using "convoluted metaphors that tried to say something without saying anything," note Contardo and García, who interviewed more than one hundred participants in dictatorship-era Chilean popular culture. "Musicians . . . gathered in *peñas*, churches and universities to criticize the regime without mentioning it" (2009: 105–106).

Gone were tributes to Che Guevara and Chilean Communist party founder Luis Emilio Recabarren. Instead, there were songs about love and daily life, often with an undercurrent of sadness or rebellion (Díaz Inostrosa n.d.: 178–181). There were cautiously selected songs by Violeta Parra. In addition, there were songs about the shattered dreams of youth, about waiting for dawn to break, about a garden that would flourish at some undefined future time. The *Canto Nuevo* group Santiago del Nuevo Extremo sang of the springtime sun dying. An Eduardo Peralta song invited back a happy puppeteer who had gone away:

> Let us find a way to walk a brighter road
> Although to do so we must go against the tide (*La Bicicleta* 1982: 18).

The popular Schwenke-Nilo duo specialized in poetic allusions that were vague enough to get past censors but specific enough to carry meanings for those who sought them:

> You have to make yourself anew day after day
> We have to invent hope for ourselves . . .
> Re-paint this landscape,
> Find new contact lenses
> Get a new spelling book . . . (Pincheira Albrecht 2010: 39)

In the album notes to an Alerce Records *"Canto Nuevo"* compilation, Ricardo García wrote, "[W]e live in a different era, where words acquire new meanings, where the unsayable flowers in almost secret signals. Poetry is like that. Music is like that" (Discos Alerce 1977). Although to the initiated this statement may seem brazen, there is nothing specific for the censor to object to, illustrating García's savvy approach to a dangerous undertaking.

García was able to keep Alerce going in part because of his celebrity: a nationally-known radio announcer until the day of the coup, he had been beloved by the Chilean public for decades. The other part was because of his strategic decisions. His widow explained in an interview that he employed a right-wing accountant and made sure that the company's books were "impeccable" so as to not provide a pretext for unwanted attention. He also marketed Alerce records as examplars of Chilean culture, placing a conceptual barrier to shutdown by the ostentatiously patriotic military. Alerce record covers carried a graphic of the Chilean flag with the legend "authentic Chilean folklore."

Although Alerce stayed in business, García tangled constantly with officialdom. Permission to hold a *Canto Nuevo* Festival in 1978 was denied due to "negative reports from pertinent authorities" (Carabineros de Chile 1978). In 1979, permission to hold the Second Grand Night of Folklore was first granted and then revoked two days before the concert, when most of the tickets had been sold. In 1981 García was jailed for importing 800 cassettes of Cuban singer Silvio Rodríguez and of Víctor Jara's early folk music for distribution by Alerce. García was released after a week, and six months later an appeals court dropped the charges of subversion (*Hoy* 1981; *El Mercurio* 1981).

In addition to the vigilance of censors and other authorities, another impediment to *Canto Nuevo*'s development was the lack of financial possibilities for artists. By 1980, many of the original participants were finishing college and abandoning music for more secure livelihoods (Diaz Inostroza n.d.: 159). The difficulty of earning a living as musicians became a decision point for the members of Illapu. Finding that their success during the Andean Boom period was not sustainable, they left Chile for Europe in 1980. When they tried to return the following year, invited to appear on a Chilean television program, they were barred from entering the country on grounds that they were "Marxist activists who participate in an overseas campaign to hurt Chile's prestige" (*International Herald Tribune* 1981: 5). Despite the attrition, *Canto Nuevo* carried on. In 1981 the Viña del Mar festival's folklore competition was reinstated and a number of *Canto Nuevo* musicians participated (González 2013: 268).

Beginning in 1983, the Pinochet regime faced open protest. A series of demonstrations against the effects of the failing neoliberal economic model and in favor of democracy mobilized many Chileans. Though these protests were ruthlessly put down, repression and censorship eased as the regime grappled with internal disagreements and external opposition. As an expression, however masked, of dissent, *Canto Nuevo* thrived through the mid-1980s.

Like *Nueva Canción*, *Canto Nuevo* had begun with Andean sounds, and, like *Nueva Canción*, over time it became more varied and complex. Responding to multiple influences and searching for new ways to express themselves, artists entered the realms of electronic and classical music, jazz, and rock. At the same time, a growing assortment of pop, rock, and punk groups gained prominence. These groups were not associated with *Canto Nuevo*, although some had defiant names: *Los Prisioneros, Los Pinochet Boys, Emociones Clandestinas, La Ley, Los Ilegales* (The Prisoners, The Pinochet Boys, Clandestine Emotions, The Law, The Illegals). Purveyors of marginal, alternative music, some expressed rebellion, in the main without the reflectiveness of Canto Nuevo (Escárate 1995: 155; García 2006a; Party 2009: 680). Writing about Chilean society, historians Paul Drake and Iván Jaksić (1991: 10–11) consider the role of culture in the "revival of freedom and openness" in the late 1980s, noting "[e]ven the strident tones of the popular rock group Los Prisioneros rallied youth to the ideals of liberty." As these genres and groups attracted increasing numbers of fans, and as the restrictions on expression eased, "Canto Nuevo and its cryptic poetry fell into natural obsolescence" (Escárate 1995: 158).

NEW SONG IN EXILE

Outside Chile, the musical imperative was different. With the coup d'etat, *Nueva Canción* musicians, who had been touring as "cultural ambassadors" of the Popular Unity government (Carrasco 2003a: 240), suddenly became voices of opposition to the dictatorship. Inti-Illimani were in Rome on September 11, 1973. Their performance scheduled for that night became "a heartfelt homage to Allende" (Parot 2007). The highlight of Quilapayún's tour was to have been a show at the renowned Paris Olympia theater on September 15, four days after the coup. "In a sorrowful atmosphere and trying to carry on after the tragedy," says a group member, "amid deep breaths and tears, we whimpered more than sang the *Cantata Santa María*" (Carrasco 2003a: 244).

Most of the *Nueva Canción* artists who were in Chile did not remain, becoming part of the estimated 200,000 Chileans who left the country to escape the dicatorship (Wright & Oñate 1998: ix). Patricio Manns went first to Cuba and then settled in France. Many ended up in Paris, among them Isabel and Ángel Parra, Sergio Ortega, and Héctor Pavez, who left Chile after the disheartening meeting of musicians and record company representatives with the military regime. Payo Grondona and Osvaldo Rodríguez found asylum in East Germany, and Rodríguez subsequently resided in several European cities.

At first the exiled musicians gave voice to the sentiments that had been silenced inside Chile, singing of their anger and grief after the coup, their nostalgia for Chile and its past, the travails of the present, and hopes for the future. Songs were written in homage to Víctor Jara. A portion of Allende's final statement to the Chilean people, broadcast just before the seat of government was bombed, was put to music and recorded by exiled musicians: "These are my last words, and I am certain that my sacrifice will not be in vain . . ." (Allende 1973).

Nueva Canción artists continued to tour and record overseas. Ángel Parra explained in 1975, "the role we play now in the exterior is to keep alive the presence of our former government, and stimulate people to keep supporting us . . . because there are still . . . thousands of political prisoners, because there are people in constant danger of death" (Perez Luna 1975). Establishing themselves in Paris and Rome respectively, Quilapayún and Inti-Illimani performed around the world at Chile solidarity events. Both groups toured the United States multiple times, playing at colleges, community centers, theaters, and such prestigious venues as the Kennedy Center and Carnegie Hall.

What was at first self-preservation became forced exile. Within months of the coup, the dictatorship decreed that those who had left in irregular circumstances would have to petition to re-enter the country. *Nueva Canción* musicians were consistently denied permission to return. This situation prevailed for eight years, as exiles gradually realized that the military regime was going to stay in power, and shifted from living with their suitcases packed toward integrating into their new communities (Wright & Oñate 1998).

In 1982, the junta began publishing lists of exiles allowed to enter the country. Payo Grondona returned in 1983, the only New Song participant to do so (Godoy 1984). In 1984, the regime inverted the process, releasing lists of individuals who were barred from Chile. The first list of 4942 names included all of the well-known New Song musicians (*El Mercurio Internacional* 1984). Osvaldo Rodríguez wrote to a friend about his family's efforts to effect his return. "You ask if I won't do something to try to return? I reply: haven't you seen the lists? I'm right at the top. . . . My father visited lawyers, church officials, and judges. Nothing!" (Morris 2006: 158–159).

From exile, Patricio Manns wrote what many came to regard as the quintessential exile lament:

> When I think about my country
> A volcano in me bleeds
> When I think about my country
> I cease to exist
> When I think about my country
> Utter shipwreck
> When I think about my country (Manns 2004: 60)

A Quilapayún song about Isabel ("Chabela") Parra's unsuccessful efforts to return to Chile displayed a more sardonic tone:

> The stream enters into the river
> The river in the silent sea . . .
> The bird enters the nest . . .
> The robber is allowed entry,
> The smuggler of contraband
> But the folklorists—oh, no—
> No pardons granted to them!
> It's the last straw that they will not

allow Chabela entry. (Carrasco 2007: 92)

This song has a complex, modern sound, a far cry from traditional Andean music. It exemplifies the expansion of the exiles' music with their ongoing growth as artists, their exposure to varied musical currents and ideas as they traveled, and their felt imperative—in contrast to the reactive songs of the Allende period—to make durable art (Carrasco 2003a: 267).

NUEVA CANCIÓN AND CANTO NUEVO

During the seventeen years of the dictatorship, New Song musicians inside and outside of Chile continuously expanded their breadth and depth as artists. Quilapayún incorporated avant-garde arrangements and texts; Inti-Illimani explored Mediterranean sounds and enlarged their instrumental repertoire, while incorporating new members into the group. Exiled musicians used local folk forms to write compositions in appreciation of the welcome they received in their adopted countries. In Chile, *Canto Nuevo* musicians increasingly took their own paths, and looked outward to Cuban *nueva trova* and international pop ballad styles.

The currents of Chilean New Song interacted. Although *Nueva Canción* musicians could not enter the country, their recordings were clandestinely distributed in Chile. Features about exiled musicians appeared in the Chilean press, particularly the countercultural magazine *La Bicicleta,* which began publishing in 1978. When the dictatorship in neighboring Argentina gave way to democracy in 1983, exiled Chilean musicians organized performances in the border town of Mendoza, some two hundred miles from Santiago; thousands of Chileans crossed the Andes to attend (Inti-Illimani 2013; Quilapayún 2013b).

Canto Nuevo musicians also traveled. Eduardo Peralta visited Osvaldo Rodríguez and other exiled musicians during the ten months he spent in Europe. In an interview he noted that Eduardo Carrasco of Quilapayún introduced him to the music of French singer Georges Brassens, who became an important reference for Peralta. The popular *Canto Nuevo* group Santiago del Nuevo Extremo collaborated with Inti-Illimani, sharing the stage in Europe and recording a song together that came out in Chile on a Santiago del Nuevo Extremo release. In typically indirect language, "The Distant Half" alludes to a return "from that abyss" to "the embrace of a future re-encounter."

THE RETURN OF DEMOCRACY AND THE END OF EXILE

Democracy returned to Chile in 1990 through a formal process that the Pinochet regime mistakenly believed it could control. The military had promulgated a new constitution in 1980 that was ratified by the populace in a shoddy and dubious voting process (Arriagada 1988: 43–45; Garretón 1991: 217). The constitution included a provision for a yes/no "consultation on military rule" to be held in 1988. Opponents of the regime felt that this plebiscite, like the constitution's approval, would be rigged, and that should the "no" result prevail, it would somehow be prevented from taking force. After infighting and soul searching on whether to validate the process by participating in it, the opposition unified under the "Alliance of Parties for 'no,'" headed by predictatorship political leaders who had "operated in a semi-open and semi-clandestine sphere" during the years when political activity was proscribed (Garretón 1991: 218, 225–228). Seeking legitimacy and facing international pressure, the regime did not oppose transparent ballot boxes, public vote counting, and the placement of observers at every polling place, measures that would yield a process that was not amenable to fraud (Drake & Jaksić 1991: 12; Portales 1991: 266–267).

Less than two months before the plebiscite, the dictatorship announced the end of forced exile. Three weeks later, Inti-Illimani arrived in Chile, in the words of group member Jorge Coulon, "fifteen years and fifty-four days after we left on a three-month tour" (1995: 100). On October 5, 1988, 55 percent of Chilean voters said No to the dictatorship continuing in power, to 43 percent who voted for the Yes option (Drake & Jaksić 1991: 13).

The following year, in the first election since 1973, Christian Democrat Patricio Aylwin, representing the opposition alliance, won the presidency. The day after the formal inaugural ceremony in the Presidential palace, the new government held a celebration of the return to democracy at the National Stadium. Seventy thousand spectators attended a multifaceted show featuring singers, dancers, and acrobats, as well as relatives of those who had been "disappeared" by the dictatorship. The musical acts included *Nueva Canción* and *Canto Nuevo* groups in addition to younger singers who had spent almost their entire lives under military rule (Otano 2006: 131).

Over time, most of the exiled musicians went back to their country. Ricardo García commented in a newspaper column: "This fractured culture of ours begins to recover its pulse with each artist who returns" (Osorio 1996: 238). Returning musicians were met at the airport by mobs of fans. They gave emotional first concerts in Chile. Isabel Parra performed on a TV show, the set decorated to look like the *Peña de los Parra* (Osorio 1996: 237). Quilapayún opened their return concert with Violeta Parra's "The Letter," to a roar of applause. They sang new and old songs, including Víctor Jara's "*Te Recuerdo Amanda.*" For encores, they played the final song from the "*Cantata Santa María de Iquique*" and then, to fervent audience chanting, "The People United Will Never be Defeated" (Quilapayun 2003). In his inaugural concert after returning, Patricio Manns said "during practically all the years of exile, I was planning this night of return to my country with a friend of almost my entire life." He continued with a moving tribute to Ricardo García, "my friend, my brother," who had died shortly before (Manns 1995).

Reestablishing themselves in Chile was not always a smooth process for former exiles. Although the Aylwin government enacted policies to encourage their return, re-entry could be difficult. Some musicians struggled to integrate themselves into a very changed society. Osvaldo Rodríguez was well-received at first, but like many returnees found he was unable to make a living in Chile (Morris 2006: 163). Quilapayún and Inti-Illimani both suffered rancorous splits, resulting in each case in two groups composed of some original members and some new ones.

TWENTY-FIRST CENTURY NEW SONG

In twenty-first century Chile, New Song is present as a cultural referent and a contemporary form of social activism. The faces of Víctor Jara and Violeta Parra, along with Pablo Neruda and Salvador Allende, appear on murals, t-shirts, posters and tourist souvenirs. The Santiago airport shop carries an extensive selection of New Song CDs. Sidewalk musicians include New Song in their repertoires. The Chilean Museum of Memory and Human Rights, opened in 2010, houses New Song material in its physical and digital collections (Museo de la Memoria 2013). The Violeta Parra foundation, established by her children, is dedicated to preserving her legacy (Fundación Violeta Parra 2008). A movie about Violeta Parra was the most popular Chilean feature film of 2011 (Maza 2011).

Forty years after his death, Víctor Jara remains prominent. Chile Stadium, where he played in the First Festival of Chilean New Song in 1969 and where he was tortured and killed in 1973, has been renamed Víctor Jara Stadium and designated a National Monument so that it cannot be torn down (Coulon 2009: 90). As part of initiatives to gather evidence of abuses committed by the military, Jara's remains were exhumed in 2009; an autopsy found he had been struck by forty-four bullets. Thousands of people accompanied his casket to the Santiago cemetery for reburial (*La Nación* 2009; BBC 2009). Investigations prompted by Jara's family led to the identification of eight former soldiers involved in Jara's death. They were indicted by a Chilean court in 2012, two for Jara's murder and the other six as accomplices. One of those accused of homicide had left Chile in 1990; Chilean authorities sought his extradition from the United States (Bonnefoy 2012; Cooperativa 2012; Justicia Para Víctor 2013).

New Song is not solely a relic. "The People United Will Never Be Defeated" has become an anthem of resistance heard in many languages all over the world. In Chile, active musicians of all generations agitate for human rights with their music. Now grandparents, most of the surviving *Nueva Canción* musicians continue to tour the world and to support social justice causes inside and outside Chile. They have extensive websites, and communicate with fans, old and new, through Facebook and Twitter. The causes they advocate include the environment; the political, cultural, and territorial demands of Chile's Mapuche people; and the campaign of Chilean students for education reform. Collaborations among musicians of *Nueva Canción* and *Canto Nuevo* along with younger musicians across genres are increasingly common.

At the 2009 Viña del Mar music festival, an Isabel Parra composition won the folk music competition. Patricio Manns's song *"De Pascua Lama,"* an environmental message about the destructive effects of mining on Chile's glaciers, won the same prize in 2011. One of the principal acts invited to the 2011 Viña del Mar Festival was Calle 13, the internationally popular Puerto Rican group. Inti-Illimani and young Chilean singer Camila Moreno joined them on stage for the performance of Calle 13's signature song about Latin American unity (Calle 13 2011).

In 2012, some 50,000 people attended a stadium concert celebrating the one hundredth anniversary of the Chilean Communist Party. The musical acts traversed the history of New Song. The concert was headlined by revered Cuban New Song musician Silvio Rodríguez, who made spoken and sung references to Violeta Parra and Víctor Jara. *Nueva Canción* group Inti-Illimani, *Canto Nuevo* group Sol y Lluvia, and several young, up-and-coming musicians also performed. Bridging the generations was the Cantata Rock Collective, a group made up of musicians from a contemporary Chilean rock group along with the sons of members of both Quilapayún and Inti-Illimani, who are now themselves members of those ensembles. The Cantata Rock Collective created a rock version of the *"Cantata Santa María de Iquique,"* "without altering its essential character," in order to bring the work to a new audience (Colectivo Cantata Rock 2012).

CONCLUSION

In the 1960s, musicians and students reacting against a glut of imported commercial music that they felt was alien to their reality sought to assert and express their Chilean and Latin American identities. Their rejection of external domination and endemic social inequality was part of that reality and those identities. On a foundation of traditional Latin American folk music, they built compositions that depicted their values and views.

Throughout its trajectory, Chilean New Song came to describe, express, channel, and focus political ideals. Such was its success in doing so that the Popular Unity government sponsored it, the military that overthrew that government banned it, and the democracy that eventually supplanted the military dictatorship spotlighted it. Such was its power that the Popular Unity government used it as an instrument of communication, and artists and producers risked defying the military regime to use it as an instrument of resistance.

The corpus of New Song includes hastily written songs that provide snapshots of specific historical moments. New Song would be a valuable archival reference if those songs were its entirety. They are not: New Song includes short and long-form works of lasting artistic merit. The works created from the 1960s through the 1980s now exist as artifacts of times past. But New Song has a place in twenty-first-century Chile alongside other genres of popular music because while preserving and conveying social memory it has also adapted and reinvented itself. Many of the original participants continue to produce new music that reflects current conditions and their own evolution as artists.

As a message carrier that is intentionally attuned to political conditions, Chilean New Song has been part of events in the larger society beyond the musical realm. As a genre of popular culture, it has been both a reflector and a reflection of the society that generated it. Although many of its compositions stand alone as artistic achievements, New Song, like any cultural manifestation, cannot be fully understood without reference to its historical context. At the same time, the creations of New Song vividly convey the changing tenor of changing times; they are primary texts that enrich understanding of Chilean society and politics.

Both *Nueva Canción* and *Canto Nuevo* have outlived the historical conditions that engendered them. Across half a century of existence, the instrumental base, the musical styles, the nature and topics of lyrics, the performance venues, the makeup of the audience, and the reach of New Song have expanded far beyond what its originators could have imagined. Inside and outside of Chile, New Song continues to elicit popular, artistic and academic interest in its musical beauty, expressiveness, and inventiveness; its role in the quest for social justice; and the ways it interlocks with Chilean history.

NOTE

This research was supported by a Fulbright Scholar Program award, and a Temple University sabbatical leave and Grant-in-Aid.

Chapter Two

"Remembrance Is Not Enough . . ."
("No basta solo el recuerdo . . .")

The Cantata Popular Santa María de Iquique
Forty Years after Its Release

Eileen Karmy Bolton

During the boom of the *Nueva Canción Chilena* (Chilean New Song), a new work that represents a rupture within the local popular music scene, especially the one with folk roots and politically committed, is released. This work is the "*Cantata Popular[1] Santa María de Iquique*," composed by Luis Advis in 1969 and released by Quilapayún in 1970. Proposing a new musical style, this work expands the format of the song and crosses the borders between what is defined as art music and what is defined as popular music.

This work constitutes a particular breakthrough of the *Nueva Canción Chilena y Latinoamericana*, being the first folk cantata and thus inspiring the later creation of other works in this format not only in Chile but in Latin America, as well as giving a new nature to the musical development of the Chilean New Song, while making visible a historic event hidden in the official history of Chile.

The "*Cantata Popular Santa María de Iquique*" attains a particular relevance in many ways. On the one hand, it acquired an important historic value by making visible the Pampa workers' massacre on December 21, 1907, in response to a strike for better work conditions and wages in a time when Chile based much of its wealth on saltpeter production.

This massacre inspired a great amount of intellectual and artistic production, works that have contributed to the understanding of the social phenomenon that occurred in Iquique in 1907, but also transformed it since they "in one way or another, have *deconstructed* this event by narrating it in a present

45

perspective" (González 2007: 21). In this respect, the capacity of the *"Cantata Popular Santa María de Iquique"* to stay current for more than forty years, has contributed to transforming this very same work into a historical source that not only speaks of the massacre of 1907 but also about other events, for instance, the socio-historical moment in which this work was released.

On the other hand, this work acquires an aesthetic value that responds to its innovative mixture of musical styles, defined mainly as oppositions: art music, popular song, and folk creation. Advis, as a theater musician formed in the academy, composes a work with the structure of a baroque cantata but including important variants: instead of being about sacred or mythical matters it develops a subject of socio-political contingency that, besides vindicating an event from the past, calls for action and awareness to avoid such events occuring in the future. The other variant corresponds to stylistic—musical aspects with which he intended to merge "various melodic turnings, harmonic modulations and rhythmic cores of American or Hispano-American root" (Advis 1999: 5) with the ones of the classic cantata. A third innovative aspect was the instrumentation: "from the usual orchestra only the basses have been kept (violoncello and contrabass) as a support, adding two guitars, two *quenas*, a *charango* and a bass drum" (Advis 1999: 5). And last, "the classic Recitative song, has been substituted for a spoken Narrative that, nonetheless, contains rhythmic and metric elements, in order not to brake the utter sonorous" (Advis 1999: 5). As a result, Advis added to the name of this format the "popular" adjective giving his work the name of *"Cantata Popular Santa María de Iquique."*

It is important to underline the fact that this work was dedicated to Quilapayún, one of the first bands belonging to the Chilean New Song, and also one of the most popular ones in this movement. Quilapayún was known for their particular usage of male voices, along with the use of Andean traditional instruments and their staging, which integrated theater resources enhancing their expressive and interpretative level.[2] These elements, along with the mix of musical and instrumental styles, maximize the epic character of the *"Cantata Popular Santa María de Iquique,"* turning it into an emotional work with a high reach.

Even though other works with similar characteristics (long-form and thematic unity) existed prior to this one in other countries of Latin America, it has been stated that the *"Cantata Popular Santa María de Iquique"* laid the foundations for the constitution of the popular cantata genre (González, Norambuena & Opasso 2008: 28–29). It consists of a musical work of thematic unity of national character that has been expanded to the rest of Latin America. This idea entails an identity and nationalistic value, which will not be explained here,[3] but it is worth mentioning that beyond a national and generic definition of the popular cantata format, the compilation of works with this format and the corroboration of the existence of a continuity in this kind of compositions, both national and international, are interesting. This continuity of the popular cantata as a genre attests to the importance of the work of Advis, fundamentally for inventing this style, having set the standard for a compositional pattern and inspiring the creation of other cantatas since then.

Thus, the *"Cantata Popular Santa María de Iquique"* is considered today one of the most popular works of Luis Advis, as one of the most prominent of Quilapayún's repertoire. Five years after the Centennial of the massacre in the Santa María's School in Iquique, and after the commemorations of the Bicentennial of the Independence of Chile, it is also considered one of the most important works in Chilean music history, both for its historical and aesthetic value and for its relevance in the rumination on Chile's national and Latin-American identities.

Given this relevance and the high popularity that this work has gained, its signification is transformed according to different moments in the recent history of the country, and at the same time it attests to the different socio-historic contexts in which this work has been remade. Therefore, this chapter reviews the different versions of the *"Cantata Popular Santa María de Iquique,"* in order to understand how they provide new meanings, keeping this work current, despite the passage of time and socio-political changes.

The approach to the significations of the Cantata is done through a hermeneutic perspective whose analytical development incorporates both, formal elements of the work and nonmusical features, which are related to it, covering it with meaning. The analytical strategy is intertextual, through which I have tried to elucidate the meanings behind the relations laying between the texts, taking in consideration how features and elements of one text play into another.

Understood from this perspective, the *"Cantata Popular Santa María de Iquique"* has a "vertiginous capacity of transformation" (Genette 1989: 481) that can be seen and heard through the different versions made, which are, also, the strategies that resignify and renew the Cantata through time.

THE CHILEAN NEW SONG AND THE
UNIDAD POPULAR (1970–1973)

The *"Cantata Popular Santa María de Iquique"* is released during the cultural movement of the Chilean New Song, months before the presidential elections of 1970, which Salvador Allende won, as a representative of the *Unidad Popular*, consecrating him as the first democratically elected Socialist president in Chile.

The socio-political context in which the Chilean New Song is forged was characterized by strong social and political confrontations "at a time when it is considered that all dreams are possible, that the brightest future is at hand, that men can master and program their destiny" (Parada 1988: 3). This had an influence on the musicians that aimed to "interpret the social aspirations of the folk, the people" (Carrasco 2009; see also Morris's chapter in this collection).

The Chilean New Song was consolidated in this context, being characterized by a powerful source of autochthonous creativity and a strong defense of cultural identity, as well as by its "urgency, denunciation and propaganda character" (Parada, 1988: 4). This yearning for cultural identity focused on "the retrieval of folklore, the autochthonous, the indigenous [. . .] of Latin-American music" (Carrasco 2009).

This commitment to social and class issues becomes one of the main characteristics that differentiates the Chilean New Song from other musical references. This very quality "would irrevocably lead to the use of vocal interpretations more appropriate to the meaning of the texts, that contrasted sharply with the agogic usually used; aspect developed exemplarily by the assertive group Quilapayún" (Advis 1998: 25).

Therefore, what can be defined as Chilean New Song has a wide and mobile border, fundamentally because what has been created in this musical stream does not fit into the classical concept of what a song is, as the songs or musical pieces do openly, or even more the cantatas. Considering that the Chilean New Song used the free format of the popular songs (opposed to the traditional folklore rhythms and genres) and instruments that were non-representative of what is commonly understood as "Chilean," which were brought from other latitudes; as well as the fact that it included folklore rhythms and genres representative of other Latin-American countries, can we still characterize this movement as Chilean?

This movement attempted to establish a different relation with what was known at the moment as Chilean traditional music, making obvious the difficulties that the country has had assuming a plural and diverse identity, contributing to the awareness about the need of questioning the limits of the national consciousness.

If the Chilean New Song aims to answer problems related to the history of the country, what is new in this movement? As a possible answer, I propose that it widened the concept of tradition; it put forward a different vision of national music. It made a creative contribution toward a pluralistic perspective, open to the cultural diversity that is Chile, helping to recognize ourselves as Chileans in wider values than the ones offered by the tradition before as established patterns.

The main particularity of the Chilean New Song is that for the first time in the popular music domain in Chile, the creators raised questions about the development of an artistic expression, concerning the song, format, structure, harmony, subject, poetry, and instrumentation and interpretation issues.

"CANTATA POPULAR SANTA MARÍA DE IQUIQUE": ITS RELEASE AND IMPACT

In November 1969, Advis attended a concert of Quilapayún, where "the interpretational force and the musical color achieved with the northern instruments" (Carrasco 2003a: 151) caught his attention. He is convinced then that through this group his work could have a greater impact than if it were performed by a chamber orchestra (as he first conceived it), producing furthermore an interesting union between art music elements and folk music, which was already being studied in the musical academy, but without the expected impact their promoters were looking for.

Meanwhile, Quilapayún had approached musicians "that felt weary of the elitism of the conservatory and wanted to seek ways to the folk" (Carrasco 2003a: 153). This group started working with the composer Sergio Ortega, and during their search for widening the possibilities of the folk song, Advis suggested pulling together the *"Cantata Popular Santa María de Iquique."* Eduardo Carrasco remembers that "it was precisely what we were looking for; he, on his part, had done what we needed, without even having asking him. A little astonished by these happy coincidences, we started working with him" (2003a: 153).

On August 14 and 15, 1970, the Second Festival of the Chilean New Song took place, where this work was released, although it had been recorded a few weeks before. This time, the festival did not have a competitive character, but the idea was broadcasting the musical works of the participants. Among the songs that were presented was this composition of Advis, performed by Quilapayún.

It is interesting that this work was presented in the context of a *song* festival, widely surpassing this format. Carrasco agrees that there were some problems between the contestants, because some of them were opposed to the presentation of the Cantata in the festival. "Some feverishly tried to create a movement 'anticantata,' claiming that this festival was for songs and no others kinds of works like the one we wanted to present. Happily, in the end good sense was imposed, although we had to endure painful discussions in an assembly which I would rather forget" (2003a: 156).

The public, mainly composed of youth and students, praised the presentation with standing ovations, regardless of the difficulties encountered by Quilapayún and the narrator Marcelo Romo[4] while performing the work.[5] Advis was directing from the audience, but according to the recollections of the performers themselves, the stage lighting prevented them from seeing him. Nonetheless, "the presentation overall was more than acceptable" (Carrasco 2003a: 156) and "the public acceptance was spectacular. [. . .] People standing. It was Chile Stadium,[6] that is five thousand people. [. . .] It was packed, completely packed" (Parada 2010).

Days later, Quilapayún, this time with the actor Héctor Duvauchelle, performed the Cantata in the theater La Reforma,[7] at the University of Chile, which consecrated the work both in the musical academy and in the university circuit. "Héctor's voice coupled so perfectly to our sound, that I doubt that we have later surpassed the dramatic quality of this first performance" (Carrasco 2003a: 156, 157).

Ricardo Venegas, who was not yet part of the group but was present in the audience, remembers the emotion of the moment: "I recall seeing Luis Advis walking around the theater, I think that he directed a little, he was . . . very pleased, it was his first experience with this kind of music" (2010). About this second release, done in an area closer to Advis's world than Quilapayún's, Rodolfo Parada remembers that "it was a more or less selected public, friends, I don't know, people, politicians, musicians, intellectuals that naturally appreciated the work" (2010).

Days later, the album was available for sale,[8] something that contributed greatly to widespread listening of the work, since these two concerts were rather circumscribed to a specific type of public: the intellectual left wing of Santiago. About this, Alfonso Padilla, who knew the Cantata by listening to the album, remembers, "I was impressed, and that's when I started to hear things, for example, someone told me that, I don't know if I read it or I was told [. . .] that Ángel Parra would have said 'ok what do we do now.' This explains the following: the *Cantata Santa María* set the standards very high" (2011).

This work was also transmitted by Televisión Nacional on its program *Raíces del canto*, which was granted the third place in the best television program of 1970 by *Telecran*: "What counts in this case is not only the musical value of the work, but also the stage proposal and the communication ability of the group, which were decisive in making this transmission one of the breakthroughs of the year and a sign of success for the newly born state channel" (Telecran 69 in González, Ohlsen & Rolle 2009: 304).

Since then, and until the present, Quilapayún has kept on performing the "*Cantata Popular Santa María de Iquique*," included in its most successful repertoire. They have toured the world with this work, accompanied by different actors and presenting the narration in different languages.

Since its release, the Cantata has had an important impact, which cannot be measured based on sales or number of concerts made by Quilapayún, mainly due to the lack of reliable records. Because of the Coup of 1973 and the following dictatorship, many of the discography copies were eliminated and others hidden in clandestineness. But, also, under the theoretical perspective of this research, the impact of this work is not necessarily related to the *original* version or to the remakes and concerts made by Quilapayún, but to the appropriation that the listeners have made of it along its over forty years of existence.

This appropriation has been through the albums of the Cantata, considering mainly its general listening (by means of sold, loaned, and hand copied albums), the live presentations of this work (of Quilapayún and other groups that have pulled together this work), and also—and especially—the remakes that have been done of this work, which give to it new significations.

That is to say, the significant reception that the public has given to the Cantata not only has been forwarded to the listening of the album or the Quilapayún's concerts, but also to the remakes of the album and especially to the versions made of this work.[9] Quilapayún has performed the Cantata in different places in the world accompanied by different actors, orchestras, and choruses. In some of these performances the narrations have been in the languages of the countries where it was being performed, but in every case "people stay there, listening, and applauding, and it is not only Chileans any longer, they can be Finnish, Germans, Argentines, Spaniards, French, and they love it. So this is a message, I would say that it is related to Chile, but it is a universal message" (Venegas 2010).

The impact of the Cantata is also related to its ability to make visible an historical event that was hidden in the official history of Chile, and therefore, was unknown to most people. In this way, this work established an important relationship with historiography, since it has been considered both a historical source to reconstruct the facts of 1907 and a music that has made visible and popularized these events that "history does not want to remember" in the recent history of the country.

Even though this topic was already included in previous records, like *Canto a la Pampa (Song to the Pampa) (Por Vietnam [For Vietnam]* 1968), the narrative of events, linked until then to Pezoa's poem, is replaced in the *"Cantata Popular Santa María de Iquique"* by an interpretation of the story that seeks to contribute to an awareness of the possibilities of building a new future.

Thereby, the historical value of the Cantata suggests a new meaning: besides being able to revive an event that had been forgotten, it manifests a call to awareness about social injustices and to remain united to prevent such events from occurring again.

In the late 1960s, Quilapayún was a fundamental part of the Chilean New Song, one of the most representative groups of this movement and of the presidential campaign of Salvador Allende, presidential candidate of the Unidad Popular. This relationship between Quilapayún and the Unidad Popular is an important aspect to understand the *"Cantata Popular Santa María de Iquique"* from an intertextual analytic perspective, since its significance has transcended the massacre of 1907 and has settled in the socio-political context of 1970, but also in the contexts in which this work has been remade and re-signified after 1970.

About this topic, Ricardo Venegas wonders, "How many generations have listened to the Cantata Santa María? At least three generations, or maybe more. And so, the people who listen to it now, the youth that attend our concerts, and when we performed the Cantata in 2007, 2008, around then, or later, boys that might be twenty years old, nineteen, that did not experience the Chilean New Song, did not experience the Coup, nor the dictatorship, etc., but, nonetheless, are there and they take the Cantata Santa María and make it theirs" (2010).

Accordingly, as a result of this process of appropriation of the Cantata that has been done by several generations, it has been able to stay current for more than forty years, despite the socio-political changes that occurred in Chile, and the changes within the group that gave life to this work through its performance.[10] The Cantata has meanings, it brings memories, it evokes emotions in those who listen to it, and it also provokes feelings in its performers, a sense of belonging of the work, its music, its content and its history, identifying with it. Thus, it is signified over and over again, constantly, being able to account for each and every period in which this work has been remade: in the early 1970s, during the exile of Quilapayún and the Chilean New Song (1970s and 1980s), upon their return to Chile during the 1990s, and in the first decade of 2000.

"THE SINGING WON'T BE ENOUGH" ("*EL CANTO NO BASTARÁ*"): SIGNIFICATIONS 1907–1970

Quilapayún became the greatest diffuser of the Cantata; their huge popularity reached in Chile, and also abroad, meant the popularity of the Cantata and vice versa:

"The release of the Cantata occurred in an ambience of great political commotion, because of the conclusion of the electoral campaign of 1970. [. . .] There's optimism and trust in the supporters of the Unidad Popular coalition and the Cantata endorses it for, in spite of narrating a tragedy as a lament, it does it as a denunciation and announcement of better times to come" (González, Ohlsen & Rolle 2009: 304–305).

On September 4, 1970, Allende is elected President of the Republic, representing the Unidad Popular, whose cultural program proclaimed the incorporation of the masses to intellectual and artistic activities, reaffirming the aspiration to a revolutionary and class consciousness "overcoming the bourgeois values, on the basis of people socially aware and showing solidarity" (Albornoz 2005: 148). The musical movement that had been developing, sheltering this political project was the Chilean New Song, and it represented the dreams of equality and overcoming poverty. But with Allende's triumph "the chimera had to become praxis [. . .] now the challenge was, rather than to propose denounce or criticize, building" (Albornoz 2005: 148–149).

The *"Cantata Popular Santa María de Iquique"* did not only denounce the event of the 1907 massacre, but also made a call to unity and to awareness to avoid events like the one narrated to reoccur.

Eduardo Carrasco states that the *"Cantata Popular Santa María de Iquique"* was successful in its period because it represented, on the one hand, a consummation of the work done by the Chilean New Song Movement, and on the other hand, a faithful expression of the political convictions present in the Chilean society in the early 1970s (2009). During those months, Chile experienced a unique situation in its history. It was an electoral year, in which one of the candidates for the presidency was Salvador Allende, thus there was a great social effervescence from which none could remain disconnected. A new period in the history of the country began when Allende won the elections representing the Unidad Popular.

In this context, the Cantata represented a call to unity, to take history and to appropriate it. The Cantata "was also considered a very faithful expression of the spirit laying in society at that moment, that is, a spirit of social claims of unity, hope in what was to come, as long as the people joined. All these ideas were more or less the ideas of the Unidad Popular and that is why it had a huge success" (Carrasco 2009).

No doubt the socio-political and cultural context in which the Cantata was released maximized its wide welcoming and contributed to its high social significance, because it had a double meaning: besides denouncing a historical event and to awareness so that something like this never happened again in Chile. As Ricardo Venegas, who attended the release, describes:

> The people were touched but were left with the feeling that [. . .] this was not just a work that denounced something, that happened, terrible, and the massacre and all that, but suddenly there is *"Canción Final"* ("Final Song") in the Cantata, for example, that says "ok, this happened, but what do we do now." So the people left the concerts, and until today I think they leave the concert with that same feeling, with that image, with that impulse, with that energy, of saying "ok, we have to unite, we have to unite so that this never happens again in Chile" (2010).

We can summarize the significance that the Cantata had in the period of its release in the following way. On the one hand, the work allows the listeners to put themselves both in the socio-historic context of 1907, when the massacre of the pampa strikers occurs, and in the moment when the work is released: 1970. The way this work leads the listeners to reminisce both historical moments is expressed both through the poetic text (what is narrated and the poetry used to achieve that) and the music (in terms of its harmony, rhythm, instruments, and performance). Different musical and poetic re-

sources are used to achieve this representations, some of which are intentional (as, for instance, the use of Andean instruments to refer to the place where
the massacre occurred early in the century); while other exceeded the intentions of the composer, thus they can only be heard a posteriori (as do the
verses "*quizás mañana o pasado / o bien en un tiempo más / la historia que
han escuchado / de nuevo sucederá*" [maybe tomorrow or the day after / or
maybe later on / the story you have heard / shall happen again]). That is to
say, only once the events of 1973 occurred can the listener interpret the signs
that the Cantata provided. On the other hand, this work communicates a
message of unity that has different meanings and that also is renewed in time.
It is heard as a song of hope for a better future, what was assumed, in the
period of its release, with a positive significance and the premonitory elements present in this work were only given meaning after the Coup of 1973.

DICTATORSHIP AND EXILE: THE CANTATA AS A SONG OF RESISTANCE AND LIBERATION

Due to the Coup of 1973, Allende's death and the silencing of the most
important voices of the Chilean New Song, the "*Cantata Popular Santa
María de Iquique*" enters a new phase: the proscription of its music, the exile
of its performers, and the clandestine work of its author. Nonetheless, this
failed to make this music totally disappear. Clandestinely, it kept on playing
and in exile, the musicians kept singing it. The Cantata, as an iconic work of
the Chilean New Song Movement, resisted in Chile despite the prohibitions.
    One of the strategies of survival of this work was through remakes and
staging performances by groups other than the original performers. One of
those was the one put together by a group of political prisoners in
Concepción, in 1975, directed by Alfonso Padilla, now a musicologist, then
one of the leaders of the *Juventudes Comunistas* (Communist Youth):

> We didn't have a cello or a contrabass, but we had a narrator, and we per-
> formed it entirely. It was amazing. I think that the great majority of the people
> had never heard it live or even the album, they had heard that there was a
> Cantata that talked about that killing, but they didn't know more than that. So it
> was amazing because there were 160 political prisoners and several jail guards
> that also heard it, and it was, well, simply very emotional, people from the
> audience ended up crying. It was really very, very, very emotional" (Padilla
> 2011).

The significance that the Cantata acquires in this context was very powerful,
since its message of unity and hope referring to the Pampa strike was trans-
ferred to the political prisoners at jail in Concepción that listened to this live

remake, expressing to them messages of resistance and collaboration that helped them to survive the situation they were in.

During the dictatorship in Chile, the Cantata was able to resignify its message, representing the resistance and the struggle against the Pinochet regime, paralleling the Pampa massacre of 1907 to the violence pursued by the Chilean State commanded by the military since 1973. The Cantata communicated a message of life and hope, resignifying it in a new context: it didn't narrate either the Pampa massacre or the strike any longer, instead, it was able to talk about the violence of the dictatorship and the truncated dream of the democratic way to socialism, and to overcome this through a song of unity and hope adapted to the new political situations.

The Cantata represented liberation, not only in Chile but also elsewhere. To listen to it, and even more to perform it, inside the jail meant an act of rebellion that released those who suffered it from the ordeal of the political prison. Besides, it was able to communicate a message of hope and unity that helped the political prisoners to hold on to the eagerness of a better tomorrow, of a collective triumph, and to be able to fight the uncertainty and the distress they lived in.

Outside Chile and Latin America, the situation was different. As other representatives of the Chilean New Song, Quilapayún was abroad when the Coup of 1973 occurred. Subsequently, they began their exile in Paris by chance, during this new period, they continued performing and enriching their repertoire, performing also the *"Cantata Popular Santa María de Iquique."*

They performed it successfully in every country they visited around the world. Despite the painful events occurring in Chile and the confusion caused by this sudden exile, the musicians of Quilapayún clearly knew that their concerts could help as acts of solidarity, and as a group they could testify to the Chilean people's drama, but at the same time to become messengers of the democratic will of Chile (Carrasco 2003a: 242). In the communication of this message, the Cantata became a useful tool, which represented these very values and was able to renew and resignify them in different contexts. It could be performed in diverse countries around the world, in different languages and its message would be understood by the audience.

In the twilight of the dictatorship, when the growing popular opposition gradually gained a significant extent of legality against the Pinochet regime, that which was previously forbidden became more available. The album of the *"Cantata Popular Santa María de Iquique"* was reissued, opening the way for the return of Quilapayún and the rest of the people in exile.

In 1989, Quilapayún performs in Chile after sixteen years of absence. This concert is edited in the album *Quilapayún ¡En Chile!* (*Quilapayún, in Chile!*), whose penultimate song is the *"Canción final"* of the Cantata, followed by *"El pueblo unido jamás será vencido"* ("The People United Will

Never Be Defeated"), emphasizing the epic character of these songs that, together at the end of the concert, represent the return of the group to the country.

In this context, the *"Canción final"* resignifies the *"Cantata Popular Santa María de Iquique,"* placing it as a song of triumph of what was lived and also a song of hope by the expectations on the results of the plebiscite of October the year before, where the option "No" triumphed over the continuation of the regime. This new significance of the Cantata transcends the values of unity and protest that it represented at the time of its release. Here, the song of hope is imbued with the still recent pain. The verses *Quizás mañana o pasado / o bien en un tiempo más / la historia que han escuchado / de nuevo sucederá* (maybe tomorrow or the day after / or maybe later / the story you have heard / shall happen again) quite specifically signify the pain of those who suffered the consequences of Pinochet dictatorship. Similarly, the libertarian message[11] transmitted by this song was felt and fully appropriated in this atmosphere of hope for the end of the dictatorship.

RESIGNIFICATIONS OF THE *"CANTATA POPULAR SANTA MARÍA DE IQUIQUE"*: THE VERSIONS

Following the metaphor suggested by Lejuene, where the duplicity of the object can be represented "by means of the image of the palimpsest, in which it can be seen, on a parchment, how a text overlaps another without covering it entirely but making it visible through transparency" (Genette 1989: 495) the resignifications of the Cantata work are translucent in each of its versions.

There are two types of versions that have been made of the Cantata, the first type are the versions that have recreated this work with the intent to imitate the 1970 version, with an eye toward maintaining the authenticity of the first sound and staging, keeping the musical, instrumental and sound format, with the intention of (effectively reached or not) *sounding and being seen like* Quilapayún. These versions correspond to most accounts of the Cantata known so far, which have been performed live and not recorded.

Quilapayún has edited four different versions of this work,[12] without taking into account the times[13] when they have performed it live around the world, with different actors, presenting the narration in different languages, accompanied by orchestras, choruses, and even changing the text on some occasions.[14]

A second type of versions corresponds to those that have wanted to detach themselves from the version of 1970, presenting *creative transcriptions* of this work that are not characterized by searching to *sound like or be seen as* Quilapayún. Instead, these versions propose a new sound and attempt to recreate the work, of which we find four so far: the one of the *Conjunto Instrumental y Coral de la Universidad Austral de Chile* (1972) (Instrumental Ensemble and Choir of the University Austral of Chile) and other three that surfaced in the early 2000s, which deviate from the version of 1970, both for their aesthetic and performing proposals and for their innovative "intensions" of not *sounding or being seen as* Quilapayún.

1. *Conjunto Instrumental y Coral de la Universidad Austral de Chile* (1972):

The first version of the Cantata Popular Santa María was recorded by the Conjunto Instrumental y Coral de la Universidad Austral de Chile in 1972 in Valdivia (IRT). Franklin Thon, after discovering this work wanted to make a choral version of it. He discussed the idea with Advis and Quilapayún, to get their support and authorization, without foretelling the repercussions this version would have once edited in a luxury LP and once performed in Santiago and Valdivia.

The fact that this version is the first one, and that it was made only two years after the album edition of the Cantata, echoes the great reception and significance this work had from the very moment of its release. Musicians and students from the south of the country felt honored to recreate this work, contributing to make visible the Pampa events of 1907, and especially to spread in a greater way the message that the Cantata communicates.

The particularity of this version is related to its performance by a mixed choir, where female voices are included alongside the male voices. This is quite significant since the Cantata represents a breakthrough in the Chilean New Song; it also falls in the imaginary of the *Hombre Nuevo* (New Man), which gives a context to this cultural movement.

This *Hombre Nuevo* was meant to lead the revolution, to be the voice of the dispossessed, representing the youth, the worker, hope, and a better future. In this context, and according to this imaginary, Chilean New Song was mainly heard in male voices that, in addition, sang to a male subject: the worker, the miner, the farmer, and the lower class inhabitant.

Thereby, the insertion of a unisex choir to perform a central work of the Chilean New Song meant not only that men could invite women to participate in the revolutionary struggle, but it also specifically demonstrated that this endeavor was being carried out together. Men and women in one song could make the revolution.

This version includes a *creative transcription*. In terms of Corrado, and following Genette, this is a *trans-stylization transcription* with orchestration (1989: 482), for it not only maintains the original instruments of the Cantata, but it also adds choral arrangements for four voices, both female and male, innovating in the male aesthetic of the work of Quilapayún.

Nonetheless, as a consequence of the coup and the subsequent dictator-ship, during which all this music was proscribed, the master and the copies of the album were lost in the clandestinity. Besides, Valdivia's marginal condi-tion, compared to the centrality of Santiago, maximized the fact that this version was barely known, both in the moment of its release and afterwards. Today, this version can be found on some websites, but unofficially. Actual-ly, many of the participants in this recording do not have access to this album (Andrade 2011).

2. *Felo* (2002):

The album *Felo-Carril*, by the singer and humorist Felo, came out in 2002. It summarizes a live performance of twenty-one musical pieces that makes an *ironic* version of part of the Latin-American repertoire, especially the songs linked to the Chilean New Song (referring to Patricio Manns and Luis Advis) and the *Nueva Trova Cubana* (Cuban New Trova) that includes songs of Pablo Milanés and Silvio Rodríguez. In this context he presents the *"Cantata Santa María de Iquique"* in a "summarized" version,[15] where in less than forty seconds he connects the beginning of the *"Pregón"* ("Proclamation") with the last part of the *"Canción Final,"* explaining when this peculiar rendition is finished:

> I always like, even through a brief summary, to remember this wonderful work
> of Luis Advis that makes us recall those terrible facts that happened precisely
> in the Santa María's School in Iquique, in 1907, under the government of . . . I
> don't know if it was Pinochet at the time . . . Eh . . . no, in 1907 Pedro Montt
> governed, that's it. Pedro Montt . . . Ugarte,[16] now I remember.

The significance that this version carries can be summarized in two main points: on the one hand, it establishes a direct link between the tragic events of the strike/massacre of 1907 and the violent dictatorship of Pinochet, rein-forcing the idea that by listening to it today, the Cantata can speak also of the military dictatorship that began in 1973, and not only of the events that occurred in Iquique at the beginning of the century.

On the other hand, it proposes an original and particular way of approach-ing a work like the Cantata, a very confrontational one, because it makes it possible to mock a work even though it has been *mythologized* as a work of art, and *made sacred* in a political, intellectual, and serious way, as is the case of this work and much of the protest repertoire of New Song.

This version also attests to the deeply rooted character of the *"Cantata Popular Santa María de Iquique,"* so that it is not necessary to perform it entirely for the audience to recognize it and understand the message it car-ries.

3.   *Cuarteto Strappa* (Strappa String Quartet) (2007):

The *Cuarteto de Cuerdas Strappa*,[17] put together an instrumental version (without the text or the narration) of the Cantata, arranged by the compositor Osiel Vega. This version premiered in July 2007 in the auditorium Glenn Gould in Toronto, as part of the celebrations of the centenary of the strike/ massacre organized by the *Grupo Cultural Chile-Canadá* (Cultural Group Chile-Canada), supported by the *Casa Salvador Allende* (Salvador Allende's House), where Bryce Moloney made the narrations in English. On this occasion, they released the album *Santa María de Iquique*, which was recorded between May and June of the same year in the Isidora Zegers auditorium of the Facultad de Artes de la Universidad de Chile (the Faculty of Arts of the University of Chile), the same place where Quilapayún released this work thirty-seven years before.

Some of the most significant characteristics of this version respond to the fact that it does not take into account the song and spoken text of the *"Cantata Popular Santa María de Iquique."* Therefore, this version is called only *"Santa María de Iquique,"* omitting the words Cantata and Popular. This change in the name clearly reveals the art aspects of the 1970 version, not only for its instrumentation (which is exclusively art music instruments), but also for its musical adaptation (which doesn't consider the poetic text of the songs and the narration present in the original work).

One of its performers states that "it is incredible that the music makes us feel that without the text, the music alone reincarnates very well the whole drama of the saltpeter worker" (Reyes[18] 2007). However, from the point of view of the social relevance of this work, in all its versions, it is not the "music alone" that reincarnates the worker drama of 1907, but this version expresses the meanings and the significations the Cantata has acquired overtime, especially considering the contexts it was released in, where the audience had a prior link to this work.

As the version of Felo, this version also attests to the deeply rooted character of the *"Cantata Popular Santa María de Iquique"* in the collective memory, as it can be performed without the texts and the message is understood all the same.

Something similar can be affirmed about the versions performed by Quilapayún in different countries in the world, in which despite including the poetic text and narrations, many times the language in which it was performed was not understood by the audience.

4.   *Colectivo Cantata Rock* (The Cantata Rock Collective) (2007):

The most recent and innovative version of Advis work is the *"Cantata Rock Santa María de Iquique,"* recreated in the context of the commemorations of the centenary of the strike/massacre of 1907. The *Colectivo Cantata Rock* (from now on Colectivo) was in charge of this version, with Patricio Pimienta as narrator and directed by Ismael Oddó.

This Colectivo is composed by the band Chancho en Piedra[19] and young members of the band Inti-Illimani Histórico[20] (Historical Inti-Illimani) and Quilapayún.[21] These groups represent different generations and musical styles: the last two are icons of the Chilean New Song, while the first one represents a new generation, characterized by the ludic sense present in their texts and staging, and characterized also by a sound that mixes rock and funk in Spanish.

They looked for sounds from different musical traditions of the New Song, but from the same periods, which are remarked through *allusions*, *quotes*, and *intertextual topics* present in this version of the Cantata. Many of these intertextual relations correspond to *quotes with referential intentions*, namely, the deliberate search for a particular sonority, aiming to lead the audience to these other musical traditions, different from the New Song, thus placing the Cantata in a dialogue with music styles that had not been related so far.

The search for these sounds refers to the music of Chancho en Piedra, which is closer to classic rock and funk than to Latin-American folk and New Song. Similarly, it represents the generation to which the musicians of the Colectivo belong, born in the late 1970s, having lived a childhood and adolescence surrounded by this music. But it especially responds to the inquietude of the Colectivo of putting in dialogue different musical traditions that at certain point in time were conceived as antagonistic, and from that position, problematizing the recombination of these different musical styles.

The crossing provoked by this mixture of sounds coming from Anglo-Saxon rock and a work with a central role in the New Song, creates a meeting between two kinds of audiences and makes this version function as a *crossover*, facilitating "the moving of a track listened to by a specific audience or music scene, to another" (López Cano 2011: 3). The Cantata finds its way to a new generation, with different musical traditions than New Song and Latin-American folk, seeking to reach a more diverse audience, which is neither necessarily politicized nor familiar with the events that occurred in Iquique in 1907. The bassist of the Colectivo Cantata Rock states,

> Many people, as I when I was a little boy, were unaware that this occurred. And also, many people think the following: "ah, what does it matter." When the subject of the abuse perpetrated by the military during Pinochet's regime is on the table, "ah but it happened so long ago," and it didn't happen that long ago. And many people prefer to think that way "ah, it's in the past already." [. . .] people without memory don't have culture, don't have roots, don't know where they are going, don't have a future (Ilabaca 2011).

Thus, this version reveals the importance of historical memory, of exposing the past and creating the ability to talk about it, even to an audience that is not politicized. The past that this new version of the Cantata refers to is not only the strike/massacre of 1907, nor the wind of hope that was felt at the time of the release of this work in 1970, but especially the remembrance of the Coup of 1973 and the subsequent dictatorship.

Like Felo's version, the Cantata Rock links together the violent events of 1907 with the ones that occurred during the Coup of 1973 and the military dictatorship. But this rock version also resignifies this work, giving it new meanings, referring to new historical events and extending its message by being framed in a historical moment different from the one when the Cantata was released.

In so doing, this version grants new significations to the Cantata, particularly because it situates it in a socio-political and cultural context that is radically differentiated from the time of its release, essentially because of the economic conditions of the country (under a neoliberal market model), technological and digital developments (which were crucial for the diffusion of this version), the political situation (under a third government of the *Concertación de Partidos por la Democracia* [Coalition of Parties for Democracy]) that, even though of a center-left political orientation, has continued important aspects that were established by the dictatorship.

The *"Cantata Santa María de Iquique"* doesn't end in its version of 1970; it stays alive and resignifies itself with each of its versions. Especially, this rock version grants new meanings and problematizes the work based on new significations.

Through the *hypertextuality* relation that it establishes with the original version of 1970, it makes a *direct transformation* into an electrified and rock version that respects the core, the narration, and the format, but suggests a different style. This way, this new version constitutes a *creative transcription* (Corrado 1992: 28), since it maintains the formal elements of the work, but varies the stylistic elements and the instruments with which it is performed. It also corresponds to an *instrumental transformation through substitution* that replaces the instruments of the 1970 version with others, changing the language in which this musical work is communicated.

In the use of voices we find an important *quote with referential intentions*, according to the conceptualization of Corrado. Ismael Oddó, son of Willy Oddó (historic member of Quilapayún) sings as a soloist the song *"Soy obrero"* ("I Am a Worker"), performed by his father in all the Quilapayún versions until his death.[22] In the later versions made by Quilapayún, this song was performed by Ismael Oddó, who joined this group replacing his father in their reunion in Chile in 2003. This situation illustrates the idea of a generational continuum of the Cantata from Quilapayún to this Colectivo.

We can also find intertextual relations in this version of the Cantata with conceptual works of classic rock,[23] through *quotes, allusions* and other kinds of references. It's worth mentioning that this version is inspired in this kind of works (Oddó 2010), but these intertextual relations also account for the profound significations given both by the sonorities, the texts and the themes of the works referred to, such as the tragic nature of the narrated stories, the landscapes, and the death that the heroes face in these works.

The use of rock fulfills functions that maximize the dramatic nature of the Cantata, as emphasizing its message of hope, intensifying also its *ironies*. In addition, it maximizes the interpretative aspects present in Advis's work, exacerbating its epic nature with an exceptional interpretative strength that seems to increase not only the heroism of the Pampa people in 1907, but also that of the *Hombre Nuevo* (New Man) who survived the dictatorship that began in 1973.

Additionally, this new version of the Cantata establishes *hypertextual relations* with other works from the Chilean New Song, such as "*El derecho de vivir en paz*" (1971) ("The Right to Live in Peace"). In this song, Víctor Jara invites the band Los Blops to record with him, embellishing it "with distorted electric guitars and organs with a psychedelic accent" (Ponce 2008: 127), conferring to it a new character, rich in significations. Considering the relation established by the New Song and the Chilean left wing with rock music, this invitation is not innocuous. The music styles with an Anglo origin, especially rock, were criticized by the most orthodox sectors of the Chilean left wing, for constituting spaces for relaxation and entertainment, not conducive to the revolution and the awareness of the masses. They were criticized for evading reality and representing *imperialist* culture.

On the one hand, some sectors of the institutional left wing disapproved of the lack of political and social substance of this music. But on the other hand, many of this kind of musicians joined the Unidad Popular, which put them in an intermediate position. There were "signs of a rapprochement to the Chilean New Song that nonetheless, did not always lead to happy results, facing an officialdom that tends to be suspicious of a sort of choleric youth with an electric guitar" (Ponce 2008: 136). Juan Pablo Orrego, member of Los Blops, remembers, "The UP had that virtue. Despite not belonging to a party or fitting the canons of political music, we were allowed to show our music to the workers anyhow. It was crazy because after the concerts there were forums and every time someone would say that they had been taught that these instruments were imperialist" (in Ponce 2008: 128).

Víctor Jara was one of the promoters of New Song that didn't believe in this rhetoric, and thanks to his way of thinking, his critical and open-minded stance, he sought to experiment and integrate elements from rock in his repertoire still representing the Chilean New Song. Regarding this, Orrego remembers,

Víctor was a very open-minded person, he listened to all styles of music, and he was open to everything. And hence, he was a very cultured person. Víctor had been in England, he was a friend of Donovan, a Scottish singer and songwriter that was very popular at the time, very important. That is, Víctor was a person that had been around the world, and therefore, respected all kinds of expressions (2010).

It is worth mentioning that the process that Chile was going through at the beginning of the 1970s was not something that happened separately from the rest of the world, where important changes were occurring in a cultural, social, political, and, especially, artistic matter: "everything was changing. So we [Los Blops] were rather in a more open, more broad tendency, we didn't really want to typecast ourselves in the Chilean New Song" (Gatti 2010).

During the 1960s and 1970s the rock movements (psychedelic, folk, and others) became stronger, both in the United States and Europe (especially in England) and, opposed to the North American policies implemented during the years of the Cold War, they developed a particular sound and poetic rhetoric. These trends came to Latin America, and to Chile, as a fashion, but also as important references and inspirations for the local bands. The other references can be synthesized in the words of Eduardo Gatti: "we were looking toward Víctor Jara or Violeta Parra, even though we liked Cream or Jimi Hendrix" (Ponce 2008: 141).

Víctor Jara, incorporating elements such as rock in his repertoire, sought to criticize the totalizing imaginary that identified every Anglo-Saxon element as imperialist, challenging the dichotomy between the music of foreign origin (such as rock) and Latin-American music, as if it were oppositions such as falsehood/authenticity, imperialism/revolution, or oppressors/oppressed.

Therefore, the nuance of the Colectivo Cantata Rock to relate the work of Advis with Jara's proposal, seeks to "say another thing in a similar way" (Genette 1989: 16). This Colectivo seeks to revalorize the proposal of Jara, crossing musical frontiers that were defined dogmatically. Along with this, they seek to question again the dichotomy stated by the traditional Chilean left wing of the 1970s, that related directly and uncritically North-American sounds (including rock) to *yankee imperialism*. As a response to this question, Felipe Ilabaca (from the Colectivo Cantata Rock) says,

I just want to say that the fact of making a rock version is already a political statement, a political stance from our point of view. Rock was created by the *gringos*, completely *yankee*. The economic capitals that made possible the abuse of the saltpeter-workers were not exactly North-American, but English, the fathers of the North-Americans. The version of Luis Advis with Quilapayún, they didn't have, due to a political stance, the instruments of the

Nueva Ola (New Wave),[24] they used *quenas*, *zampoñas* and acoustic guitars and *bombos* to protest from here. We could also stand aside that stance, but the Cold War won. And we are sons of rock, and we love it and without any fear, we love Elvis, we love Chuck Berry, we love Daft Punk, we love everything that is happening because the world has already taken that color. But to shift the work into that format, means to tell the *gringos*: "hey! With your own machinegun: tatatata" (Ilabaca 2011).

In other words, the Colectivo Cantata Rock appropriates a musical language, which was considered imperialist, to perform Advis's work, to resignify it and communicate its message to new audiences. In addition, the creative development in the process of putting together the Cantata sought to grant more expressiveness to the work, to maximize its dramatic character, and especially, to fill it with new meanings and representations.

This search for sounds from different musical traditions than the Chilean New Song, but of the same period, brings into dialogue the Cantata with other musical styles characteristic and representative of the Anglo-Saxon classic and psychedelic rock of the early 1970s. These sounds that the Colectivo Cantata Rock looks for, besides being significant for the musicians' generation, are relevant since they represent a musical tradition that left its mark in the Anglo-Saxon world (though not exclusively) for its innovative artistic proposal.

It is important to consider that when the Colectivo Cantata Rock communicates the message of Advis's work in a new sound proposal, they become responsible for a historical memory and for the permanent renewal of this work's call to unity, awareness and action, in each of its different versions. This way, the Cantata Rock aims to a new generation, communicating a message that, while inspired in a massacre that occurred in the early twentieth century, today, in the first decade of the twenty-first century, maintains its validity and the same concern of the past.

CONCLUSION

To go over the forty years of the "*Cantata Popular Santa María de Iquique*" from the listening point of view and the social representations that this work has had, meant taking a position on it. The repercussions of this work have not only been related to its musical properties or to Advis's compositional virtuosity, or to the impressive Quilapayún's staging of the work. We cannot deny the key role of these elements, especially in defining the Cantata as a breakthrough in the Chilean New Song movement, and as a central reference in Chilean music in general. Nonetheless, these elements by themselves have not made the Cantata what it is today.

The significations and social representations that this work carries are due to a combination of elements that have occurred during these forty years. We analyzed these elements taking into consideration the different versions that have been made of the Cantata in order to understand its social representations and resignifications during its forty-year lifespan.

Two parallel processes occur. First, the version recorded by Quilapayún in 1970 is attenuated as the only reference version of the work. Even though it remains a reference version (assumed as the original) to the later versions, the work does not transcend in time nor resignify exclusively through this version. Neither has it remained as the only reference version for the audience, since the new generations have known the Cantata through more recent versions than the one of 1970.

Secondly, this work is transformed and resignifies itself, that is, it no longer represents only what was related in 1970, and it no longer mentions exclusively the events of Iquique in 1907, adding new issues and sociopolitical events in which it has been involved due to its own history, representing them in its musical rhetoric.

The processes through which the Cantata has gone have been the product of the significations that the audiences have given to it and not one of its music in a pure sense. These very significations have been the ones that have placed the Cantata in the position it is today: a breakthrough and a central reference in our national music.

The most transcendental characteristic of the Cantata is its ability to remain current, despite the passage of time, to resignify and to account for the different issues and events in our history through different musical languages, but communicating the same central message that Luis Advis meant to transmit in 1970, maximizing it through new significations and references.

After the long journey that this work has undertaken, we can see that its central message is communicated through its different versions, both the one recorded by Quilapayún in 1970 and the most recent and innovative ones.

The main message of the Cantata is one of unity. Luis Advis stated that unity (in 1907) was necessary to confront the injustices against the foreign capital that owned the saltpeter business. When reinterpreting the meaning of this message in the different phases that the Cantata has been through (via its versions), we have seen that in the version of 1970 (Quilapayún, DICAP) the concept of unity answered both Advis's proposal (when the Cantata's references focused on the events in Iquique at the beginning of the century) and the need for unity of the Chilean left wing to triumph in the presidential elections, representing a song of hope of a better future (a socialist, free, and independent country).

However, after the Coup of 1973 and the following military dictatorship, the Cantata underwent a resignification, interpreting new desires and accounting for other representations. During the dictatorship it was a song of resistance and unity, of liberty and hope, both to resist imprisonment, torture, and exile. At the same time, this work referred directly to the Unidad Popular, remembering it with nostalgia and pain. But above all, the Cantata was resignified as a premonitory song in which, through a call for unity and preparedness, it anticipated the violent events of 1973.

Meanwhile, in exile, the Cantata also resignified itself, establishing a linkage between nostalgia for a return to the country and the remembrance of the times of the Unidad Popular. This linkage leads the Cantata to be more representative of the Chile of the military dictatorship than the one of the beginning of the century described in the work. This is especially emphasized when the Cantata is performed by those who are in exile and who represent the proscribed music in Chile.

At the beginning of the second millennium, as a consequence of the *"Reencuentro"* ("Reunion") (2004) of Quilapayún in Chile, and of the presence in parallel of another Quilapayún in France, a legal dispute began between the two bands for the use of the name. This fact is quite paradoxical, since this group had represented the values of solidarity, community, and freedom, not only symbolically but also concretely, organizing workshops, forming parallel groups with the same name and aesthetic proposal to cooperate in the political campaigns of the Unidad Popular. In this regard, we state that the greatest damage suffered by the most important groups of the Chilean New Song was not exile itself, but the return to a transformed country that had little in common with the one they had left in 1973.

Thus, currently the *"Canción Final"* does not represent the song of hope it used to represent either during the moment of the release of the Cantata, or during the military dictatorship. We can interpret this as the end of a epoch, of a country whose political, social, economic, and cultural basis were changed drastically and dramatically in a structural way.

In these same years we also find a humoristic proposal that breaks the imaginary of seriousness and consecration of the committed chant. Felo makes his own version of the Cantata, along with other iconic works of the Latin-American repertoire of what is called the protest song, suggesting the laugh, the simplicity, and, especially in the case of the Cantata, a brief and synthesized speech in his performatic proposal.

This version attests to two fundamental elements. On the one hand, the significations of the Cantata are so fixed in our society that Felo could, in less than forty seconds, communicate his message with the same efficacy (but not with the same result) as if he had performed the entire work. On the other hand, this version makes evident the link established between the events in 1907 and the ones in 1973, equating the violence of the State facing the people's demonstrations that demand a social change.

At the one hundred year anniversary of the strike/massacre that occurred in Iquique in 1907, a number of tributes took place along the country, and especially by means of artistic expressions and new versions of the *"Cantata Popular Santa María de Iquique,"* as a work of reference of these events. One of them is the instrumental version (without texts or narration) of the Cantata (a Cantata without chant), called merely *"Santa María de Iquique."* This version re-enhances the most classic aspects of Advis's work, but it mainly attests to the universality of the message communicated in this work, through its transmission without the use of a poetic text, making evident the link that it establishes with the version of reference (Quilapayún, 1970) that says in words what this new version can leave out and still be understood.

A second version present one hundred years after the Pampa massacre of 1907 is the Cantata Rock that not only resignifies the message communicated by the work, but also maximizes it and renews it. We particularly highlighted this version in this chapter, not only because it is the most recent and innovative, but mainly because it has a greater meaningful value. First, by the means of using rock instruments, it has achieved a very accurate version of the one of 1970, overstepping the borders usually conceived between rock, art music, and popular music of folk roots that this work refers to.

In addition, it renews the message communicated by the Cantata, not only through the instruments it is performed with, but also through the contexts it is performed in: concerts for a youth audience that belongs to a new generation, born in democracy and not necessarily utterly aware of the events of 1907 or the ones that occurred in 1973. In this way, this version makes easier the passing from one music scene to another (*crossover*), communicating the message of the Cantata to a public that wouldn't have known about it through the versions of Quilapayún or other tribute bands of the Chilean New Song.

Secondly, this version of the Cantata was performed in tribute concerts both to the massacre of the Escuela Domingo Santa María in 1907 and to Salvador Allende, making evident the dual representation of this work (1907/ 1970). But this version (or part of it) has also been performed in concerts for Human Rights and the vindication of remembrance, establishing a direct link between the human rights violations perpetrated during the military dictatorship that began in 1973, accounting for its ability to represent three important moments in the history of Chile.

Thirdly, this version pays tribute to classic and psychedelic rock conceptual works of the 1960s and 1970s, referring, on the one hand, to these works and with them to other historical references, but dramatic and tragic all the same.

Rock was a music style that Víctor Jara and other Chilean musicians of that period approached from the New Song, being the subject of harsh criticism from sectors of the Chilean left wing, arguing about the use of a language related to what was North American, seen as an image of *imperialism*. One of those who criticized this approach was Quilapayún, in the voice of some of its members, a group that today approves of the Colectivo Cantata

Rock making a rock version of Advis's Cantata. This way, we can see that the Cantata Rock not only resignifies the work, but also brings its own performers (considered as the "original" ones and therefore, "legitimate") to reconsider their original positions as well.

The Cantata Rock proposes a new way of listening to this work and to attend to its live concerts: its performers are no longer dressed in black, but in white; the sound is no longer the one of *quenas* but of electric guitars and psychedelic keyboards; the voices are no longer representative of the New Song (the ones of Quilapayún) but of the characteristic timbre of the funk-rock Chilean band, Chancho en Piedra.

In this version, as a result of the socio-political events that characterize the recent context, the work no longer represents the three historical events mentioned before, but also the present. The verses *unámonos como hermanos / que nadie nos vencerá* (let's unite as brothers / that no one will defeat us) do not represent the unity of the working class or the need to unite as Chileans facing the interests of foreign capital (1907 and 1970). Neither do they refer so directly to the military dictatorship, and the song of resistance and liberation that it represented during the years of the Pinochet regime.

When the Colectivo Cantata Rock performed "*Canción Final*" in December 2011 in the concert "*Música x Memoria*" ("Music for Remembrance") in tribute to Human Rights, the Cantata referred again to the beginning of the century and especially to the military dictatorship of 1973, but also to the present. A similar situation occurs when Quilapayún performs the Cantata in August 2011 (in front of the main building of the Universidad de Chile) when the students' demonstrations were becoming stronger, jeopardizing the country's image of stability.

These facts are very significant, for insofar as the country sleeps (as happened most of the years of the government of *Concertación de Partidos por la Democracia*) the Cantata referred mainly to the past, to the beginning of the century, to the Unidad Popular and the military dictatorship, being unable to attest to a present, let alone to a future through their musical rhetoric.

It seems that today, during a right wing government, when the country has awakened and has reencountered itself with demonstrations (as mass marches and "*caceroleos*"—pot banging), the Cantata regains, in all of its versions, the ability to communicate its message for unity and social change, and especially, of understanding that our journey through life is more than a trace. It can leave an echo that resonates to the future, as we can today hear the echo of the Pampa workers from that distant time.

INTERVIEWS

Carrasco, Eduardo. Interviewee by Eileen Karmy. Santiago. June 26, 2009.

Gatti, Eduardo. Interviewee by Eileen Karmy. Santiago. July 8, 2010.
Ilabaca, Felipe and Patricio Pimienta. Interviewee by Eileen Karmy. Santiago. January 13, 2010.
Oddó, Ismael. Interviewee by Eileen Karmy. Santiago. December 18, 2009.
Padilla, Alfonso. Interviewee by Eileen Karmy. Santiago. June 23, 2011.
Parada, Rodolfo. Interviewee by Eileen Karmy. Santiago. July 23, 2010.
Venegas, Ricardo. Interviewee by Eileen Karmy. Santiago. April 26, 2010.

NOTES

1. Having the meaning of "People's Cantata" or "Folk Cantata." The use of "popular" in Latin America is different from its use in the Anglo-Saxon world, where it means widespread or famous.

2. These theatrical resources were provided by Víctor Jara, who directed the group between 1967 and 1969.

3. Concept developed in more detail in Karmy 2012.

4. In the recording of the album of the Cantata the narrator had been Héctor Duvauchelle, who couldn't attend to this concert and was replaced by the actor Marcelo Romo.

5. Some of these difficulties were related to the fact that the actor replacing Duvauchelle had joined the group only a few days before the rehearsals, so he made a few mistakes during the performance.

6. Since 2004 it is called Estadio Víctor Jara, in commemoration of this musician, murdered in that stadium in 1973.

7. Current Isidora Zegers auditorium of the Facultad de Artes de la Universidad de Chile (Faculty of Arts of the University of Chile).

8. Recorded by Ángel Araos for DICAP in June 1970, with Héctor Duvauchelle as narrator. Edited in the LP under the name of *"Cantata Popular Santa María de Iquique,"* its cover was designed by Antonio and Vicente Larrea, and the members of Quilapayún at the moment of the staging, recording, and release of this work were Eduardo Carrasco, Carlos Quezada, Willy Oddó, Patricio Castillo, Hernán Gómez, and Rodolfo Parada. The violoncello was performed by Eduardo Sienkiewicz and the contrabass by Luis Bignon.

9. On the one hand, the album of 1970 has been reedited in different countries around the world. For instance, in Chile it was reedited in a compact disc in 1998 by Warner Music Chile. This work was recorded again in 1978 (in a new version) in France, in the studios Pathe Marconi-EMI. On the other hand, this work has been reperformed and reversioned on countless occasions.

10. Quilapayún has been through exile in Europe, its return to Chile and its sequent scission in two "factions" confronted to each other in international lawsuits for registration and use of trademark, of which one resides in France, co-directed by Rodolfo Parada and Patricio Wang, and the other in Chile, directed by Eduardo Carrasco. Remembering the beginnings of Quilapayún, especially when its political motivations led to the formation of a series of groups working in parallel under the same name, in order to propagate a political and artistic message through their music, it is highly shocking to witness the existence and length of this conflict with such low purposes, that shreds into pieces the *hombre nuevo*, that Quilapayún flaunted to represent.

11. Represented in verses such as *Unámonos como hermanos, que nadie nos vencerá, si quieren esclavizarnos, jamás lo podrán lograr* (Let's unite as brothers, that no one will defeat us, if they want to enslave us, they will never be able to).

12. In 1970 (DICAP), in 1978 (one version in Spanish and one in French, Pathe Marconi), and in the second part of the album *Reencuentro* (*Reunion*) in 2004 (Macondo).

13. According to the calculations of Ricardo Venegas, Quilapayún may have had performed the *"Cantata Popular Santa María de Iquique"* at least four hundred times along its history (Venegas 2010).

14. Such as when Julio Cortázar intervened into the poetic text, with an eye on "fixing" the rhymes, recorded live by Quilapayun in 1978 with Héctor Duvauchelle in the album *Cantata Santa María de Iquique*, edited by EMI.

15. As Genette's suggested meaning, this version would be a transformation through transposition with the use of reduction by amputation under a ludic regime (parody) (Genette 1989).

16. Ugarte is the second last name (mother's last name) of Augusto Pinochet.

17. Composed by Javier Reyes (first violin), Jane Guerra (second violin), Polyana Castro (viola), and Francisca Reyes (violoncello).

18. Javier Reyes, interviewed by Andrés Florit (2007).

19. Felipe and Pablo Ilabaca, Lalo Ibeas, and Toño Corbalán.

20. Camilo Salinas (keyboard) and Fernando Julio (contrabass), who recorded the album and comprised the Colectivo until 2012. Nowadays, the Colectivo with dispenses the contrabass and incorporates the percussionist Danilo Donoso (Latin-American percussions), also a young member of Inti-Illimani Histórico.

21. Ricardo Venegas and Ismael Oddó.

22. Deceased in 1991.

23. Such as, "Echoes" (1971) of Pink Floyd or "Jesus Christ Super Star" (1971) of Andrew Lloyd Webber.

24. Nueva Ola is a different concept than "new wave." It corresponds to a trendy music in the 1970s, danceable, with simple lyrics (non-political) also known as "free music" (música libre).

Chapter Three

The Chilean New Song's *cueca larga*

Laura Jordán González

The Chilean New Song—*Nueva Canción Chilena*—has been mainly under-stood as a cultural "movement" rather than as a musical genre in and of itself. Most academic research has addressed this movement's political dimension regarding its social agency during the government led by Salvador Allende, or its involvement in the resistance struggles during the subsequent dictator-ship, in Chile as well as in exile. In several instances, some works have explored the Chilean New Song's sound dimension, taking the risk of defin-ing it as a musical genre and not merely as a movement. Thus, as I will show in more detail throughout the following pages, certain musical traits have been considered to be characteristic of pieces composed or performed by CNS musicians, among which hybridization[1] (or the mixing of different styles, genres and instruments) is one of the most prominent. The coming together of musicians from both erudite and popular music traditions is one clear example. This hybridization also embraced the configuration of an eclectic instrumental ensemble and the construction of performance styles applicable to a wide variety of rhythms and forms.

The main aim of this chapter is to examine the place[2] held by the complex musical-poetical-choreographic form known as the *cueca*, within the Chilean New Song foundational project of building a "soundtrack" for revolutionary Latin America during the 1960s, 1970s, and 1980s. As such, the examination I undertake seeks, first, to respond to a broader question regarding the sound qualities of the Chilean New Song, using the particular case of the *cueca* as a case study. Secondly, I intend to propose an understanding of the relation between the selection/exclusion/predilection of certain musical traditions within the Chilean New Song repertoire and the political discourse held by its musicians.

This chapter has three main sections. The first section is devoted to defining what I understand of Chilean New Song, discussing both its political and sound dimensions, and by defining the term *cueca*, underlining some formal characteristics that have a stake in this study. The second section approaches the *cueca* within the Chilean New Song in two parts: first, I give an overview of the *cueca*'s place in the general repertoire of this genre; second I analyze four specific pieces of *cueca*, two by Aparcoa and two by Quilapayún. The analyses emphasize various aspects of form and vocal performance, observing their relation to traditional[3] and innovative practices. The third and final section ponders the results of my analyses and provides some meanings associated with the *cueca*, especially related to exile, to reveal the negotiations of *chileanness* within the Latin-Americanist discourse.

PRIMERA PATITA—FIRST ROUND: CHILEAN NEW SONG AND *CUECA*

The Sound Dimension of the Chilean New Song

Recently, Tamar Dubuc proposed that the Chilean New Song be considered a musical genre, taking into account its prevailing musical aspects, as observable in Victor Jara's work (2008). In reality, since the beginning of the movement, various authors have tried to identify typical sound features, such as the case of Rodrigo Torres's *Perfil de la creación musical en la Nueva Canción Chilena desde sus orígenes hasta 1973*, an essay (1980) that offers the first systematization of this genre.

In a definition of "canto popular," including both the *Canto Nuevo* that emerged in Chile during the dictatorship and the *Nueva Canción* developed before and after the coup d'état, Torres identifies a variety of musical traditions nourishing it: art, popular, and folk music. Stefano Gavagnin later expanded the same argument, suggesting that the CNS is characterized by the integration of materials, techniques, and procedures from those three fields. For instance, the heritage of classical tradition would be manifested, following Gavagnin, through performance excellence, original formal schemes, use of erudite models such as cantata and *gebrauchsmusik*, and an instrumental style similar to chamber music. All these elements appear fragmentarily across the diverse musicians and bands, nevertheless a common awareness of the sound material seems evident to the author (Gavagnin 1986: 303–308).

Other than the convergence of these three traditions, the second main characteristic is the seeking of a Latin-American sound, widening the Chilean musical universe of reference. Both characteristics are expressed through creating a heterodox orchestra of vernacular instruments, diversifying forms and rhythms that serve as a basis for composition, developing heteroclite arrangements, creating large and complex pieces, and performing vocal polyphony and multi-instrumentalism. This musical portrayal was combined with a motivation to denounce social injustice and to promote social changes especially in Latin America.

In this chapter, I will focus on discussing both arrangements as well as a diversification of forms and rhythms as expressions of an attempted Latin Americanism, which is noticeable in the following quotes by Horacio Salinas and Gustavo Becerra, respectively:

> We [Chileans] have many lacks. If we put our musical heritage side by side with the heritage of Colombia, Brazil, Venezuela or Cuba we will see that our music is less attractive, a bit more hermetic and that it has been more difficult to develop. Therefore, since the 1960s, we Chilean musicians have looked outside and based almost all our experience on the musical wealth of our continent. By contemplating other people's music with astonishment, we have finally felt Latin Americans. [. . .] We integrated, little by little, different instruments and built a kind of eclectic band, which speaks a lot about the Latin American being situated in the depths of the Chilean musical culture[4] (Miranda & Salinas 2002: 103–104).
>
> Chile is culturally and economically indistinguishable from Argentina, Bolivia and Peru. This is something we need to start understanding so then we can understand why in our popular music we hear quenas, pincullos, light drums, and why in our folk music we need to talk about Bolivian, Argentine and Peruvian folk [music][5] (Orellana 1978).

By the early 1970s a well-established CNS orchestra including *charango* and *quena* would be recognizable, following Boyle and Canepa, a format that was later disseminated in exile (1987: 236). Regarding its configuration as a sort of "New Latin American orchestra" (Torres 2003: 294), Gavagnin emphasizes a "linguistic" purpose related to the ambition of building a new style recognizable as Chilean[6] (1986: 309–310). Hence, as Torres implies, constructing these new ensembles entails a strategy of distinction from other bands interpreting folk music (1980: 39). In order to distinguish themselves from *conjuntos de huasos*[7] such as Los Huasos Quincheros, the new ensembles resisted playing at the so-called commercial circuit,[8] and to distinguish themselves from *conjuntos de proyección folclórica* (folk projection combos) such as Cuncumén and Millaray, they explored new repertoires. CNS bands, as a primary feature, perform repertoire and use traditional instruments from the Andes. Therefore, integrating Latin-American elements involved not only diversifying instruments, but also varying the repertoire considerably. Thus, Torres understands this process undertaken by musicians that consists of opening themselves in relation to a discourse about the natural evolution of popular traditions, suggesting that musicians conceived their innovations as a continuation of people's culture. In musical terms, the result was the creation of original timbre constellations.

Bearing in mind the words of Horacio Salinas, who articulated the purpose of recalling an imaginary village where all Latin Americans live (2002: 102), integrating musical genres and forms should be comprehended within the framework of political and cultural demands. From this perspective, it is worthwhile to interrogate the selection processes at work in order to see a potential canonization[9] of certain genres and forms absorbed and rearticulated within the *genre* of Chilean New Song.

An overview of the repertoire reveals an effort to cover traditions from multiple Latin American countries: vals, landó, festejo, huayno, cueca, tango, zamba, chacarera, joropo, corrido, bolero, balada, tonada, sirilla, pericona, resbalosa, costillar, milonga, vidala, samba, bailecito, marinera, triste, malambo, galopa, décimas, son, guajira, mazurca, polka, trote nortino, and so on. (Orellana 1978; Barraza 1972: 31; Rodríguez 1989: 69). Some genres such as pop (Rolle 2005), American protest song[10] and rock (Richards 2005) were also incorporated from other geographies, although in a stylistic rather than on a formal level. Yet while Chilean New Song embraced diversity, despite the songwriters' best intentions, certain expressions found a privileged niche while others were marginalized. Although this study does not offer a systematic approach to the presence of diverse genres and forms in the repertoire, analysis of some examples will provide context for the place of *cueca* in Chilean New Song.

Some years ago, Agustín Ruiz examined the *cubanidad* in Quilapayun's work, underlining the integration of Cuban rhythms and sounds in order to provide a festive aura, while simultaneously indicating solidarity with the Cuban revolution (Ruiz 2006). Other case studies have exposed the revival of *sirilla* within CNS (González 1997) and the employment of pop and light music as a tool for irony in music (Rodríguez 2008). So-called Andean genres have been overlaid with a higher political value, either by virtue of their "marginal" origin in relation to a hegemonic[11] national culture (Bodiford 2007: 50–61), or for the sake of their predictable allusion to indigenous population as the quintessential subject representing relegated social classes (Fairley 1989); yet for being veritable transnational genres, which enables to obliterate the distinction between national and Latin American belonging. After the coup, the political meaning of Andean genres was also enhanced by the commitment of certain bands mainly associated with Andean sound, namely Quilapayún and Inti-Illimani (Van der Lee 1997: 28–33).

Having said all this, I now return to my original question: how does the *cueca* fit into this panorama? Does the *cueca* play any specific role in it? How present is it? How does it sound? Many more questions could be asked about the *cueca*'s place within the CNS, given the enormous value of the *cueca* in the context of Chilean popular music.[12] However, given that this is a thoroughly unexplored topic, I will limit my inquiry to addressing some considerations about the articulation of the *cueca*'s Chilean character within the frame of the Chilean New Song's Latin-Americanist stamp.

The Political Dimension of the Sound Dimension

With singer-songwriters such as Rolando Alarcón, Patricio Manns, Víctor Jara, Isabel Parra, Ángel Parra, Gonzalo "Payo" Grondona, Osvaldo Rodríguez, Kiko Álvarez, Richard Rojas, Julio Numhauser, among others, [13] and bands like Inti-Illimani, Quilapayún, Tiempo Nuevo, Aparcoa, Amancay, Illapu, Huamari, and Conjunto Lonquimay, the Chilean New Song is usually portrayed as a cultural cornerstone of Salvador Allende's coalition— *Unidad Popular* (UP). This portrayal has resulted not only because many of these musicians participated in various election campaigns (Rolle 2005), or simply because they were militant members of leftist political parties, or even because of their adherence to the protest song genre, but rather because their songs integrated the political experience of listeners, who participated in the "thousand days' government" [14] led by Allende.

As I previously stated, this has been the most discussed dimension of the Chilean New Song, particularly stressing the horrendous death of Víctor Jara and the exile of several musicians. Thus, many of the songs' "content" has been analyzed, various musicians' biographies have been told, and some songs' political uses examined in relation to clandestine practices (Bravo, Chiappe & González 2009; Jordán 2009) and to exile (Bessière 1980; Fairley 1989; Jordán 2010).

Even though there appears to be a consensus that the CNS undertook a political project side by side with the left parties, promoting and accompanying social changes, I would like to stress the fact that the political dimension of the CNS exceeds the militant activity undertaken by some musicians inside political parties or government institutions as some of them officially became "cultural ambassadors." In reality, the very artistic project, in its material and sound qualities, was erected on the aspiration of *creating* an actual *Latin-American* sound, a genuine expression of the continent to which these musicians belonged.

Here we see a different and less-explored facet of the political dimension of CNS coming to light: the construction of a cultural project whereby Latin-Americanist and pro-socialist musicians sought to implement the revolutionary principles of popular struggles through their music. The result was nothing less than a soundtrack for social changes carried out by Latin American peoples. This attempt was combined with a curiosity for learning and adopting music from neighboring countries.

It is interesting to recall that many CNS's musicians had been trained in ensembles dedicated to studying and diffusing the national folk tradition. Víctor Jara, Rolando Alarcón, and Patricio Manns are clear examples of this trend. From the *conjuntos de proyección folclórica*, the CNS conserved the objective of learning multiple traditions, but this time its scope was not limited to the national territory. It is worth remembering that various Latin American international genres were profusely dispersed in Chile. For instance the bolero had an exceptionally strong presence (Cf. González et al. 2008: 509–563). It was this influx of traditions, which up until that time were considered foreign, that the CNS transformed into elements of a Chilean Latin-American music proposal: the Chilean New Song played Latin-American music. Gavagnin described this phenomenon in which a Latin Americanism "of content" becomes one "of structure" (Gavagnin 1986: 305). Bolye and Canepa also observed the strong relationship between the idea and its sound result: "[I]t would seem that Chilean New Song in the 1960s was based in a search for 'Chileanness' and subsequently for 'Latin-Americanness' with the consequent processes of decantation, selection and integration of musical poetic styles and, above all, folklore instruments" (Boyle & Canepa 1987: 236).

So how does this Latin Americanism sound in the context of the Chilean New Song? Or maybe a better question is this: In recognizing the challenge of such a broad inquiry, what sound elements helped to configure Latin Americanness in the CNS? More specifically, I wonder if the construction of Latin-Americannes operates, at some extent, by a process of differentiation from a configuration restricted to *chileanness*,[15] and how Chilean traditions were inserted in the melting pot. By examining the place held by the *cueca* in the CNS, largely considered the "Chilean national dance," I will attempt to advance some understanding of this issue.

The *cueca*

The *cueca* is much more than just a kind of music. It is a type of choreography, a poetic form, and several styles of vocal and instrumental performance.[16] When one takes into account the places where it is practiced, its values systems, its circuits of fans, and its specialized musicians, the *cueca* can surely be considered to be a musical genre on its own according to Franco Fabbri's definition (2006). At the same time, the *cueca* can also be considered a musical form, a more limited category that includes specific compositional elements as well as some performative aspects, which directly affect the actual form.

In view of defining the *cueca* as a form, I make use of Serge Lacasse's conceptualization of musical parameters, which he divides between abstract, performative and technologic. Abstract parameters include rhythm, melody and form, all aspects related to composition; performative parameters refer to particularities of both vocal and instrumental performances; whereas technologic parameters are related to recording practices and effects, considered as creative elements that are constitutive of songs (Lacasse 2005: 27–33). Although in theory the three kinds of musical parameters can be clearly distinguished, when analyzing the *cueca* certain performance elements overlap with formal ones, in such a way that its form can only be extracted by considering some specific ways of singing it. Conversely, not all the vocal characteristics impact directly on the form, such as polyphony, timbre, and vocal technique, which belong to the realm of *cueca* as genre and not merely as a musical form. In defining the form, two main performance elements participate: disposition and repetition of poetical lines throughout the musical performance. On its own, that is, before it is performed, the *cueca*'s abstract poetical form contains a very rigid and invariable structure. However, when the *cueca* is sung, its abstract form is transformed through the introduction of vocal interjections, lines disposition, and repetitions. The results are varied based on traditional norms of the genre.

Regarding *cueca*'s most consistent musical traits,[17] there is a consensus about the poetical form, which consists of three sections: *cuarteta*, *seguirilla*, and *remate*.[18] In their abstract form, so before being materialized in sound, a *cueca* appears as follows:

Table 3.1.   Poetical form of "Cueca de Balmaceda"

Cuarteta	(1)	Ganó el bando liberal
	(2)	Y el conservador ganó
	(3)	Viva viva Balmaceda
	(4)	Cuyo partido triunfó.
Seguirilla	(5)	Triunfó como se sabe
	(6)	Es evidente
	(7)	Castigar al pechoño
	(8)	Por insolente.
	(9)	Por insolente sí,
	(10)	Y a los banqueros
	(11)	Y a los explotadores
	(12)	Por usureros.
Remate	(13)	Seré mientras yo exista
	(14)	Balmacedista.

Largo Farías 1976: 11

When compared with the study of its history, origins, and cultural meanings, the *cueca*'s musical form is not an issue that has been extensively addressed by researchers. A considerable exception is Carlos Vega's study *Forma de la cueca chilena* (1947), which minutely shows the conversion of poetic lines into musical phrases. Other authors have also described the way in which the

Table 3.2. Repetition of lines in the cuarteta of "*Cueca de Balmaceda*"

A) 1 1 2 2 3 4 1	B) 1 1 2 3 4 1	C) 1 2 2 3 4 1
Ganó el bando liberal	Ganó el bando liberal	Ganó el bando liberal
Ganó el bando liberal	Ganó el bando liberal	Y el conservador cayó
Y el conservador cayó	Y el conservador cayó	Y el conservador cayó
Y el conservador cayó	Viva viva Balmaceda	Viva viva Balmaceda
Viva viva Balmaceda	Cuyo partido triunfó	Cuyo partido triunfó
Cuyo partido triunfó	Ganó el bando liberal	Ganó el bando liberal
Ganó el bando liberal		

D) 1 2 2 3 4 1 1	E) 1 1 2 2 3 4	F) 1 2 2 3 4 4
Ganó el bando liberal	Ganó el bando liberal	Ganó el bando liberal
Y el conservador cayó	Ganó el bando liberal	Y el conservador cayó
Y el conservador cayó	Y el conservador cayó	Y el conservador cayó
Viva viva Balmaceda	Y el conservador cayó	Viva viva Balmaceda
Cuyo partido triunfó	Viva viva Balmaceda	Cuyo partido triunfó
Ganó el bando liberal	Cuyo partido triunfó	Cuyo partido triunfó
Ganó el bando liberal		

Santander 1983: 145–146

poetic text is transformed when sung to the detriment of metrics, rhythm, harmony, and form.

Vega recognizes eight different forms of the *cueca*, created by means of diverse developments of the *cuarteta* and the *seguirilla* sections. These developments implicate subdividing the original phrases. The main result is the transformation of the *cuarteta* in *octava*, [19] meaning that four lines give way to eight lines per stanza. At the same time, the transformed lines are repeated, according to different patterns of repetition that determine the *cueca*'s extension. In this way, following Pablo Garrido (1976) and Margot Loyola and Osvaldo Cadiz (2010), different patterns of repetition produce three standard durations, containing 48, 56, and 58 measures respectively. Examples of repetitions are shown in table 3.2.

> Gano el ba
> Gano el bando liberal
> Y el conser
> Y el conservador cayó
> Viva vi

Viva viva Balmaceda
Cuyo par
Cuyo partido triunfó
Octava in "*Cueca de Balmaceda*"

The *seguirilla*, which splits in two parts, also suffers transformations when it is sung. In the first part, from line (5) to line (8), a pair of lines is usually repeated, whether (5) and (6) or (7) and (8), although sometimes none of them are. In the second part, from line (9) to line (12), the repetition of (11) and (12) is optional. Lines in the *remate* are not repeated. Additionally, besides the lyrics corresponding to the poetic form, both the *cuarteta* and the *seguirilla* sections may include some interjections (*ripios* or *muletillas*) that not only alter the poetic form but also add new words or utterances.

Mi vida Gano el ba
Gano el bando liberal
Mi vida Y el conser
Y el conservador cayó
Mi vida Viva vi
Viva viva Balmaceda
Mi vida Cuyo par
Cuyo partido triunfó
Cuarteta transformed into *octava* plus the interjection "*Mi vida.*"

Other musical elements, such as melodic profile, harmony, and arrangement will not be examined in this chapter.[20]

SEGUNDA PATITA — SECOND ROUND: THE CHILEAN NEW SONG'S *CUECAS*

Violeta Parra and Héctor Pavez: The Most Recalled and Other *cuecas*

As I already indicated, the *proyección folclórica* groups had a strong impact on some of the Chilean New Song musicians, particularly on their training. Two figures implicated in the research on folk traditions, whose influence on the CNS was critical, produced probably the two most important *cuecas* within the CNS's repertoire, namely Violeta Parra and Héctor Pavez.

Violeta Parra's role as an indispensable precursor for the development of the Chilean New Song has gained a consensus among scholars and musicians. This is evident through the spread of her songs that had become a central part of the genre's repertoire, as well as her political ideas about the relationship between Latin-American musics and peoples. Daniel Party summarizes the expression of her influence through the construction of a Pan-

American sound (Party 2010: 673). According to Rodrigo Torres, her heritage manifests by means as diverse as broadening popular song topics, creating awareness about the need of voicing social consciousness with veracity, musicalizing national poetry, expanding musical forms, instruments and arrangements, and so forth (1980: 18–20). Moreover, her son Ángel and her daughter Isabel, whose first musical experiences involved Violeta, had an outstanding participation in building the Chilean New Song movement and sound. Regarding the *cueca*, Violeta's brother Roberto Parra contributed numerous original pieces, the so-called *"cuecas choras,"*[21] many of which were recorded by Ángel Parra, as I will examine later.

Table 3.3. Lyrics of *"Los pueblos americanos"*

Los pueblos americanos	The American People
Se sienten acongojados	They feel distressed
Porque los gobernadores	Because the rulers
Los tienen tan separados	Have them so separated
Cuándo será ese cuando,	When will the time come
Señor fiscal	[Mister prosecutor]
Que la América sea	That America will stand
Sólo un pilar	As one pillar
Sólo un pilar, ay sí	One pillar, ay yes
Y una bandera:	With one flag
Que terminen los ruidos	That ends the commotion
En las fronteras	At the borders
Por un puñado 'e tierra	Because I do not want a war
No quiero guerra.	For a handful of earth.

Translated by James Ryan Bodiford 2007: 80

Thus, it is not by chance that the most emblematic Chilean New Song's *cueca* is one composed by Violeta Parra under the title *"Los pueblos americanos"* ("The American Peoples"). Between 1968 and 1974, Isabel Parra and Patricio Castillo, Ángel Parra, Víctor Jara, and Quilapayún made different recordings of it.[22] It seems remarkable that, being one of the few "famous" CNS's *cuecas*, it addresses Latin Americanism rather than national or local topics. Yet, acknowledging the *cueca*'s ancient function of accounting for historical facts, people's realities and social demands,[23] Violeta's lyrics in this song clearly express the understanding of a common historical situation shared by people throughout the continent.

Table 3.4.   Repetitions of lines in the cuarteta of "*Los pueblos americanos*"

Mi vida	(1)	Los pueblos americanos
Mi vida	(1)	Los pueblos americanos
Mi vida	(2)	Se sienten acongojados
Mi vida	(2)	Se sienten acongojados
Mi vida	(3)	Porque los gobernadores
Mi vida	(4)	Los tienen tan separados
Mi vida	(1)	Los pueblos americanos

In its description of the May 1 demonstration held in Chile in 1972, René Largo Farías accounts for the symbolic meaning of "*Los pueblos americanos*" when he states that "after a heart-rending ovation, this *cueca* emerged as a flame among flags"[24] (1977: 26). In turn, Osvaldo Rodríguez Musso

explains that both this *cueca* and Rolando Alarcon's song "*Si somos americanos*" ("If We Are Americans") unveil the fact that "what was at stake during that period in Chile was not a problem about the Chilean music but one about the Latin-American music as a common expression"[25] (1984).

Recalling the former description of the *cueca*'s form and its various ways of being developed through singing, a quick observation of the form of "*Los pueblos americanos*" as it appears in Isabel Parra's performance, reveals a form of fifty-six measures, sometimes called *cueca campesina*,[26] as both the first and the second lines are repeated by the singer (see table 3.4), although this is not necessarily true, for every *cueca* of the CNS, as I will show later.

> *Mi vida*, Los pueblos
> Americanos
> *Mi vida*, Los pueblos
> Americanos
> *Mi vida*, Se sienten
> Acongojados
> *Mi vida*, Se sienten
> Acongojados
> *Mi vida*, Porque los
> Gobernadores
> *Mi vida*, Los tienen
> Tan separados
> *Mi vida*, Los pueblos
> Americanos
> *Octava* created through repetitions and interjections

Two other prominent *cuecas* were present in the early stages of the CNS. The first one, *"Cueca de la CUT*," composed by Héctor Pavez and recorded by Inti-Illimani in their album *Viva Chile* (1973), illustrated social struggles that were taking place in Chile. It is worth noting that this is the only *cueca* included by Torres in his list of the most important songs of struggle, along with *"Venceremos"* ("We Will Win"), *"Las ollitas"* ("The Small Pots"), *"Ni chicha ni limoná"* ("Neither One Thing nor the Other"), etc. (1980: 39). The second one is *"Cueca de Joaquín Murieta,"* composed by Sergio Ortega using a poem by Pablo Neruda and performed by Quilapayún in *"X Vietnam"* (1968).[27] It exemplifies the fruitful collaboration between classical and popular musicians. Víctor Jara recorded another renowned version of *"Cueca de Joaquín Murieta"* in his album *Pongo en tus manos abiertas* (*I Put That in Your Open Hands*) (1969).

Without trying to exhaust all possibilities, an overview of the CNS's discography from mid-1960s to the end of the 1980s, reveals an incipient number of traditional *cuecas*, such as *"Ojitos verdes"* ("Little Green Eyes"), (Víctor Jara, *"Víctor Jara"* 1966), *"Cueca de Balmaceda"* (Quilapayún, *"Basta"* ["Stop—but also Enough Is Enough"] 1969), *"Lárgueme la manga"* and *"El músico errante"* ("The Wandering Musician") (Inti-Illimani, *"Inti-Illimani"* 1969). Furthermore, an increasing number of original *cuecas* were recorded, such as *"Ta llegando gente al baile"* ("People Are Arriving to the Dance") (Patricio Manns, *"El sueño americano"* ["The American Dream"] 1965), *"Un cuarto de Tocopilla"* and *"Mataron a mi morena,"* (Patricio Manns, *"Entre mar y cordillera"* ["Between the Sea and the Mountains"] 1966), *"Frente popular (cueca 1)"* ("Popular Front Cueca 1), *"Frente popular (cueca 2)"* and *"Última canción (sajuriana y cueca)"* ("Last Song") (Huamari, *"Oratorio de los trabajadores"* 1972), Julio Rojas and Sergio Ortega's *"Cueca de los carabineros y las FFAA"* ("Cueca of the Police and the Military") (Inti-Illimani, *"Canto al programa"* ["Song for the Program"] 1970), Víctor Jara's *"Cuequita boliviana"* ("Bolivian Little Cueca") (Quilapayún, *"Quilapayún"* 1966), Cirilo Vila's *"Cueca de la libertad"* ("Liberty's Cueca") (Quilapayún, *"Quilapayún 5"* 1972), *"Cueca de la solidaridad"* ("Solidarity's Cueca") (Quilapayún, *"Adelante"* ["Go Ahead"] 1975), *"Recitativo y cueca autobiográfica"* (Quilapayún, *"Patria"* ["Homeland"] 1976), *"Cuecas del pañuelo"* ("Handkerchief Cueca") (Isabel Parra, *"Isabel Parra de Chile"* 1976), *"Sanjuanito y cueca de Murieta"* and dawn *"Madrugada y cueca"* ("Dawn and Cueca") (Patricio Castillo, *"La primavera muerta"* ["The Dead Spring"] 1977), *"Cueca sin fronteras"* ("Cueca Without Borders") (Trabunche, *"Terre chilienne"* ["Chilean Land"] 1976) and *"Alerta pueblos del mundo"* ("People of the World Be Alert") (Héctor Pavez in *"Chansons de la résistance chilienne"* ["Songs of the Chilean Resistance"] 1975).[28]

More extended incursions into the *cueca* genre were carried out by Ángel Parra, who in addition to the inclusion of some *cuecas* in his first LPs, recorded two whole albums of *cuecas*: *Las cuecas de Ángel Parra y Fernando Alegría* (1967), containing his setting to music of Alegrías's lyrics, and *Las cuecas del tío Roberto* (1972), singing a series of *cuecas choras* with his uncle. Moreover, the band Aparcoa articulated the closest connection between the Chilean New Song and the realm of urban *cueca*. This band dedicated half of their album *Aparcoa* (1972) to singing *cuecas*. The same year, they also performed Hernán "Nano" Núñez's *cueca "Dicen que Viña del Mar"* ("They Say That Viña del Mar") at the Festival de la Canción de Viña del Mar, obtaining second place in that folk competition (González et al. 2009: 432).

In this section I have examined some of the most well-known *cuecas* within the repertoire of the Chilean New Song, such as *"Los pueblos americanos," "Cueca de la CUT"* and *"Cueca de Joaquín Murieta."* In addition, I have mentioned a number of *cuecas* that occupy a place far from negligible. Even though the *cueca* played an important role for the CNS musicians, it is important to note that the *cueca* was not a form consistently promoted by these artists, which refutes the idea that every CNS album contained at least one or two *cuecas* (González et al. 2009: 425).

Two Peculiar Cases: Aparcoa and Quilapayún

Considering the vast history of this musical genre and the variety of its musicians, I will focus this section on two bands that used different performance styles to record several *cuecas*: Aparcoa and Quilapayún. I will examine two main aspects of their *cuecas*: the development of the poetic lines through singing, and the vocal performance; the first relates directly to the definition of form, and the second links musical style to musical genre.

Lines and forms

Aparcoa's album *Chile* was released in 1975, including two *cuecas* from Valparaíso: *"Me gusta Valparaíso"* and *"Juanito Orrego."* In both *cuecas* the immediate repetition of the second line as well as the reiteration of the first line at the end of the *cuarteta* stands out. Table 3.5 exemplifies the repetitions in *"Me gusta Valparaíso,"* while the lyrics show the transformation of the *cuarteta* into *octava*, following Carlos Vegas's terminology.

Me gusta
Valparaíso
Y la flor
De la verbena *ay, morena*
Y la flor
De la verbena *ay, morena*
Me gustan
Más tus ojitos

Que mi ban
dera chilena *ay, morena*
Me gusta
Valparaíso *ay, morena*
Octavas, repetitions and interjections in "*Me gusta Valparaíso*"

After examining the forms of "*Me gusta Valparaíso*" and "*Juanito Orrego*," it is not difficult to see their bond with a traditional way of singing the *cueca*, which is understandable in light of Aparcoa's connection to figures related to the urban *cueca*, such as Hernán Nano Núñez and Fernando González Marabolí.

In turn, from a variety of *cuecas* sung by Quilapayún, I would like to analyze two original pieces recorded during the 1970s: "*Cueca de la libertad*" and "*Cueca de la solidaridad*." Neither of them corresponds, strictly speaking, to a traditional *cueca* form, considering the characteristics discussed above. The earliest one, "*Cueca de la libertad*," which was composed by Cirilo Vila and appeared in 1972 in *Quilapayún 5*, possesses an unusual form. First, while no interjection is added in the *cuarteta*, the words "La vida," which are usually introduced as an interjection, are here included as part of the actual poetic line. By doing so, the piece is "characterized" as *cueca*, relying on the listeners' prior knowledge. This characterization would manage to hide the actual absence of a conventional *cueca* form. Yet, there is a second element that aids in the process of veneering the piece with the appearance of the *cueca*, consisting in the inclusion of typical traits of the *remate* in the last two lines. Moreover, the disposition of three consecutive verses before the *remate* seems to emulate the traditional sections: *cuarteta* / first part of the *seguirilla* / second part of the *seguirilla* (table 3.6). The end of the second verse repeats the first line of the *cueca*, similarly emulating the manner in which the traditional *cuarteta* is developed (see lines in italics in table 3.6). Another way to analyze them also leads to the traditional sung form. In fact, the two first verses could be read as a *cuarteta* transformed into *octava*, including also the repetition of some lines (table 3.7). The main difference, in such a reading of it, would be the length of lines. The whole singing performance expands over forty measures, due to structural deviations of sections. "*Cueca de la libertad*" contains two "rounds" of *cueca* (*pies de cueca*).

"*Cueca de la solidaridad*," for its part, was created in exile and displays an autobiographic stamp. Regarding the lyrics, it presents the same characteristics stated above about "*Cueca de la libertad*," which is the inclusion of the words "La vida" within the poetic line and not as an interjection. This time, these words are reiterated in every line of the *cuarteta*. The length of the traditional sung *cuarteta* remains: six lines. However, only the first line is reiterated at the end of the verse, in such a way that instead of repeating two

Table 3.5.   **Repetition of lines and interjections in "*Me gusta Valparaíso*"**

(1) Me gusta Valparaíso	
(2) Y la flor de la	*ay,*
verbena	*morena*
(2) Y la flor de la	*ay,*
verbena	*morena*
(3) Me gustan más tus	
ojitos	*ay,*
(4) Que mi bandera	*morena*
chilena	*ay,*
(1) Me gusta Valparaíso	*morena*
(5) Cuando me fui pa'l	
puerto	
(6) Llegué cantando	
(7) Y ahora al	*ay,*
despedirme	*morena*
(8) Me voy llorando	
(5) Cuando me fui pa'l	*ay,*
puerto	*morena*
(6) Llegué cantando	
(9) Me voy llorando, sí	
(10) Porque en Barón	
(11) Dejaré los recuerdos	*ay,*
(12) De un gran amor	*morena*
(13) Tiene encanto y	*caramba*
hechizo	
(14) Valparaíso	

of the conventional four poetic lines this *cuarteta* is constructed with *five* different poetic lines. In turn, the *seguirilla* is developed following traditional patterns, that is: repeating lines (5) and (6) by the end of the first half.

Juan Orrego Salas describes "*Cueca de la solidaridad*" as a "faithful replica" of folk music, gifted with spontaneity, a typical trait of musicians when performing traditional *cueca* (1980: 6). However, after analyzing this

Table 3.6.   Lyrics of "*Cueca de la libertad*"

(1a)	*La vida, Tanto me gusta*
(2a)	*El paisaje de mi tierra*
(3a)	Que no quiero estar en ella
(4a)	Como si extranjero fuera
(3a)	Que no quiero estar en ella
(4a)	Como si extranjero fuera
(1b)	Y quiero mar y montaña
(2b)	Hablando mi propia lengua
(3b)	Y a nadie pedir permiso
(4b)	Pa' construir la patria nueva
(1a)	*La vida, Tanto me gusta*
(2a)	*El paisaje de mi tierra*
(1c)	Y con lo del libertad
(2c)	La vida, Nadie me engaña
(3c)	Que mientras haya miseria
(4c)	No hay libertad que valga
(3c)	Que mientras haya miseria
(4c)	No hay libertad que valga
(13)	Caramba, no hay libertad
(14)	Si falta la dignidad
	*****************************
(1d)	*La libertad ha llegado*
(2d)	*Conquista del pueblo ha sido*
(3d)	En el corazón chileno
(4d)	Su llama se ha encendido
(3d)	En el corazón chileno
(4d)	Su llama se ha encendido
(1e)	Y siempre aquí quedará
(2e)	La patria está decidida
(3e)	Con unidad y trabajo

(4e)	No habrá fuerza que lo impida
(1d*)	*La libertad va a llegar*
(2d)	*Conquista del pueblo ha sido*
(1f)	Esta sí que es libertad
(2f)	Con la patria rescatada
(3f)	Con la justicia en la frente
(4f)	Y nuestra tierra liberada
(3f)	Con la justicia en la frente
(4f)	Y nuestra tierra liberada
(13b)	El pueblo y su dignidad
(14b)	Conquista su libertad

cueca, what does the repetition and disposition of lines denote? What can the form reveal about meanings at stake? As I have shown, Quilapayún did not repeat the lines according to the tradition in *"Cueca de la libertad,"* while in *"Cueca de la solidaridad"* they added a fifth line to the *cuarteta*, all while keeping the conventional extension of verses. In spite of all these original elements, there is an area where Quilapayún does not innovate significantly: the total extension of the *cueca*. This fact should not be overlooked, because it implicitly entails the potentiality of their *cuecas* to be *danced*. From my point of view, this also has strong implications in exile, where these *cuecas* were mostly disseminated. In fact, it becomes more remarkable considering that the practice of dancing was a powerful expression of the *cuecas* played by CNS bands for some Chilean communities in exile, as it has been previously pointed out (Fairley 1989; Knudsen 2006; Jordán 2010). I will return later to this issue.

Vocals

By listening to both versions of *"Me gusta Valparaíso"* and *"Juanito Orrego"* recorded by Aparcoa, it seems evident that the singers perform according to traditional principles of urban *cueca*, specifically related to vocal roles and polyphony. Julio Alegría, leader of the band, described in 1978 the technique by which they were inspired.

> Urban *cueca* is a male singing practice. Instead of getting together to dance, they get together for a singing competition. Competing with melodies and lyrics. A group is formed with no less than four singers. Each one sings one of the four verses. The one who begins is considered the main vocalist of the first

Table 3.7. *Octava* **and repetitions in the** *cuarteta* **of "***Cueca de la libertad***"**

La vida, Tanto me gusta	La vida, Tanto me gusta
El paisaje de mi tierra	El paisaje de mi tierra
Que no quiero estar en ella	Que no quiero estar en ella
Como si extranjero fuera	Como si extranjero fuera
Y quiero mar y montaña	*Que no quiero estar en ella*
Hablando mi propia lengua	*Como si extranjero fuera*
Y a nadie pedir permiso	Y quiero mar y montaña
Pa' construir la patria nueva	Hablando mi propia lengua
	Y a nadie pedir permiso
	Pa' construir la patria nueva
	La vida, Tanto me gusta
	El paisaje de mi tierra

verse, while the rest of them sing lower parallel thirds in unison (Alegría 1981: 125).[29]

In fact, members of Aparcoa take the leading voice in turns. Likewise, they do backing vocals to accompany the principal melody; just the way Alegría described it, which is explained by Margot Loyola in similar terms:

> The way of singing urban *cueca* [*cueca brava*] produces an interesting alterna-tion of voices in parallel thirds; the leading voice and two backing vocals sing the cuarteta. At the beginning of the first half of the seguirilla, one of the singers that was singing-back-up takes the leading voice, while the singer who previously sang it starts singing backing vocals. During the second half of the seguirilla the third singer performs the leading voice and the other two singers sing backing vocals (Loyola & Cádiz 2010: 123).[30]

Me gus-ta____ Val-pa-ra - í-so   Y la flor___ de la ver-be - na ay ___mo-re-na____

Figure 3.1.

In addition, they introduce multiple interjections, such as "*calacalacá.*" Moreover, the high tessiture of the sung melody is outstanding, particularly if compared to the *cuecas* performed by Quilapayún. The high tessiture is widely appreciated in traditional urban *cueca* genre, which values vocals with a piercing and loud sound (Claro et al. 1994: 152–154).

The performance style of the CNS bands has been generally described in terms of an eminently collective way of singing, which is demonstrable both

Table 3.8.   Repetition of lines in *"Cueca de la solidaridad"*

(1)	La vida, Por Chile amado
(2)	La vida, Todos los pueblos
(3)	La vida, Se han hermanado
(4)	La vida, Todas las manos
(3*)	La vida, Se han estrechado
(1)	La vida, Por Chile amado
(5)	El clamor solidario
(6)	Del mundo entero
(7)	Se levanta en defensa
(8)	De los obreros
(5)	El clamor solidario
(6)	Del mundo entero
(9)	De los obreros, sí
(10)	Del compañero
(11)	No estás solo en tu lucha
(12)	Pueblo chileno
(13)	Más temprano que tarde
(14)	Caerá el cobarde

in Aparcoa and Quilapayún. The conventional figure of the soloist singer in popular music is counterbalanced through the alternation of roles and a solid polyphonic development. This is especially true in the case of Quilapayún, whose arrangements reveal the traces of classical composers that worked with the band. Furthermore, the complexity of their contrapuntal arrangements has been read as a mark of performance versatility (Santander 1983: 38), while the construction of a collective vocal sound has been interpreted as a tool for expressing the "unity" of the people (González et al. 2009: 417).

A global overview of the vocal performance in the two previously discussed *cuecas* by Quilapayún raises the prominence of two stylistic elements. Firstly, *"Cueca de la libertad"* demonstrates the search for a rough sound, achieved by using dissonances—what Karen Linn describes as "rich vocal harmonies" (1984: 61)—and selecting a low tessiture. As a result, the vocal delivery resembles spoken voice, which suggests effortlessness. The various melodies are displayed in a narrow ambitus (vocal range), playing several unisons that challenge a quick identification of the leading voice (see figure 3.2).[31] Secondly, in *"Cueca de la solidaridad,"* a variety of textures are interspersed throughout the piece. For instance, a section where many vocalists sing in unison is alternated with a duo section. The two vocalists sing different melodies that, later in the studio, are respectively placed in two extremes of the sound space (right-left), through a typical stereo location (Moylan 2007: 51). This effect underlines the clearness of both melodies. Additionally, it suggests the use of incipient technological parameters (in terms of Lacasse 2005), with which Quilapayún manipulates by using different "positions" of the main melody, in both foreground/background and right/left axis.

In this section dedicated to examine the vocal performance, I have underlined some particularities of Aparcoa's and Quilapayún's manner of singing *cueca*, using the example of four pieces from the 1970s. The innovations carried out by the latter band are considered to serve as an illustration of the will to creatively contribute to the development of popular music traditions, embodied by the Chilean New Song. On the other hand, Aparcoa represents an exceptional case within the CNS, explainable by their close relationship with musicians belonging to the urban *cueca* tradition.

La vi-da tan-to me   gus-ta   el pai-sa-je de mi   tie-rra   que

no pue-do es tar   en   e-lla co-mo   si ex-tran-je-ro   fue-ra   que

Figure 3.2.

REMATE—ROUNDING OFF: THE *CUECA* IN EXILE AND SOME CONCLUSIONS

The *cueca* was danced in exile. Many listeners of the CNS, frequently militants and sympathetic leftists, developed a new attitude toward dance after their forced exit from Chile. As Martín Bowen has stated in reference to the opinion vented by Osvaldo Rodríguez before the coup d'état, "dancing was unfairly rejected both as a way of understanding the world and as a medium for expressing ideas"[32] (Bowen 2006, paragraph 33). Thus, when explaining the fact that not every new song created by a Chilean musician had to be considered part of the Chilean New Song, Fernando Barraza exemplified this idea with *cumbia* made in Chile during the *Unidad Popular* period, which, in his view, should not be properly considered Chilean New Song (1972: 9). After the coup and in exile a shift occurs. In a previous research about listening practices in exile (Jordán 2010), I have shown how the dancing practice seems to occupy a new critical place. Such a turn was partially due to the contact between Chileans and other Latin-American immigrants but also to a process of renewing the very relationship of Chilean exiles with their country and its music. One of the paradoxical dimensions of this new political situation was the ever-increasing need of the exiles to find collective recreation activities and spaces of joy even as they labored intensely in solidarity with the resistance in Chile. Dancing took a place of importance in satisfying this need, although skepticism toward entertainment remained anchored on an old leftist ethos.

Hence, the dancing of the *cueca* requires a particular attention. Even if it is not the most prominent form within the Chilean New Song, René Largo Farías referred to the *cueca* as the sole living traditional dance, considering it the "sovereign" and "soul" of Chilean *fiestas* (1976: 16). In fact, the dictatorship's attempt to capture the various meanings connecting the *cueca* to *chileanness* by means of fomenting a nationalistic rhetoric was unsuccessful, leading instead toward a multiplication of "resistant" *cuecas* (Rojas 2009). At the same time, the *cueca* did not enjoy great visibility during Salvador Allende's government. Conversely, many militant songs had taken the shape of marches, such as "*El pueblo unido*" and "*Venceremos.*" In exile, even if these songs lost their currency (Clouzet 1975: 102), they continued to be sung. However their meanings changed, as I have formerly argued regarding the case of "*Venceremos*" (Jordán 2010: 97–98).

I have indicated that during the dictatorship the relationship of exiled leftists to the *cueca* changed. On the one hand, many musicians participating in the *Canto Nuevo* movement stayed away from the *cueca*, in view of the association between *cueca* and the rightwing authoritarian government (Manuel 1990: 71). On the other hand, multiple musicians, especially linked to the *proyección folclórica* groups, continued performing *cueca* in different political activities of resistance (Rojas 2009: 59–66). Particularly in exile, a very powerful turn toward the *cueca* took place. Chilean got together founding community-based organizations in different cities around the world. In this context, they used to listen to and play the most famous songs of the Chilean New Song repertoire. Although the so-called Andean music was trendier among exiles, they additionally explored other kinds of popular music considered more "traditional," like the *cueca*. In Norway, for instance, the *cueca* acquired a critical role on building collective identity, in a process where community members actively participated.

> Resistance groups fighting the dictatorship, both within Chile and in exile, were very aware of the powerful symbolic content of the cueca, and they too employed it politically in a variety of ways. Most Nueva Canción groups in exile included at least one cueca in their repertoire, though rarely as a dance

performance; but if it was danced, it was generally performed without the folk costumes. In an effort to redefine the dance as the popular culture of resistance, cuecas were composed and performed in ways that were intended to liberate the dance from its chauvinistic overtones. The lyrics of these cuecas dealt with political struggle, labour unions or political parties, instead of the traditional cueca themes of love, humour and country life. (Knudsen 2006: 134)

In this passage, Jan Sverre Knudsen shows how the Chilean community in Oslo tried to avoid the "reactionary" meaning of the *cueca*. Similarly, in Montreal I have observed at least two antagonistic views about the *cueca*: one in which it is regarded as a tradition connected with the upper classes, thus detached from the "people" and therefore contemptible; and another view that emphasizes its "Chilean" stamp, underlining in a rather positive perspective the connection to national belonging. In exile, the need for featuring the Chilean element within a Latin-American framework increased. That is why an internationalist socialist discourse—or what Bodiford has called Pan-Latin-Americanism Cosmopolite Socialist—is juxtaposed with a discourse centered on the nation. In the context of Chilean forced migration, using the nation as a reference point becomes an important mark of embodying difference in relation to other immigrants as well as building cohesion in an exiled community's cultural practices.

In this way, avid listeners hungry for "tradition" received the Chilean New Song's *cuecas*. Although from the beginning the CNS was considered a genre distinct from the folk tradition (Barraza 1972: 33), its musicians put forward their legitimacy to explore and create on the basis of traditional forms, claiming the dynamic quality of popular traditions (Medeiros 2006). As I have argued already, this is true in the case of the CNS's *cuecas* since certain traditional elements of them remained while others did not. I consider highly significant the fact that Quilapayún did not dare to significantly modify the *form* of their *cuecas* in exile,[33] which regarding their reception in the Chilean community-in-exile was particularly meaningful because the form was intimately connected to the possibility of dancing. Thus, considering exile a situation in which creative experimentation was deepened—as Juan Pablo González has stated regarding the case of Inti-Illimani (2007)—this result is noteworthy given that negotiations between the traditional and innovative elements had the outcome of making the *cueca* recognizable as a traditional dance-oriented form of music.

A brief explanation of the lyrics of the *cuecas* also provides an interesting insight. Both *cuecas* by Quilapayún analyzed here talk about the historic situation surrounding their respective creation. "*Cueca de la libertad*" addresses the political project of Salvador Allende and the *Unidad Popular*, whereas "*Cueca de la solidaridad*" accounts for the international movement of solidarity with the Chilean people resisting dictatorship. The latter could be connected to the following description by Quilapayún's director Eduardo Carrasco of the first stage of their work in exile, characterized by a complete devotion to the solidarity movement: "In the first stage, our creativity was disturbed by the activism in which we were involved due to political obligations that we could not elude. As it is well known, the solidarity movement with Chile was one of the most active and popular of our era, may be only comparable to the one triggered by the Vietnam War" (Carrasco 2003: 265).[34]

In his book about the Chilean New Song, Largo Farías presented "*Cueca de Balmaceda*" as one of the first precedents of politically committed song, a *cueca* dating from circa 1886 and recorded by Quilapayún in one of their first albums. The truth is that political commentary has been a consistent topic for traditional *cueca* lyrics. Indeed, Peter Manuel has read the inclusion of *cuecas* in Víctor Jara's repertoire as a sort of continuation of an ancient tradition of accounting for social issues through the *cueca* (Manuel 1990: 70). Rodrigo Torres also included the *cueca* in his list of popular music genres connected to songs of struggle, along with anthem, march, and *cumbia* (1980: 39).

In turn, the *cuecas* performed by Aparcoa, whose lyrics do not address social issues, correspond to a popular repertoire that is vindicated by means of including a faithful replica into the Chilean New Song repertoire. Aparcoa's versions turn out to be an authentic vanishing point of two different musical genres.

The aspiration of understanding the *cueca*'s place within the Chilean New Song requires contemplating its political dimension within the genre in at least two ways: the use of it as a vehicle by militant musicians in a movement of international solidarity, and the meanings of it in the context of an exiled community that was forced to reconfigure its collective identity of national belonging. The convergence of both leads to the emergence of a third one, which is the insertion of certain "Chilean" expressions into the Latin-American sound of the Chilean New Song. Here, I must clarify that I do not want to imply that the *cueca* is an eminently Chilean genre and form; instead, I wanted to suggest the importance of considering the *cueca*'s enormous burden of *chileanness* in order to understand its articulation in the framework of a Latin-Americanist project such as the CNS.

"It is very difficult to define nueva cancion as a musical style. It seems to slip continually into other stylistic manifestations depending on its national site of origination and the specificity of the performance context" (Tumas-Serna 1992: 48). This assertion provides a stimulus for my conclusions. Tumas-Serna finds it difficult to define the New Song as a style, style being roughly equivalent to Fabbri's definition of genre. However, in view of the national belonging of styles and genres, and the contextual specificity of the songs' lyrics, I have tried to demonstrate precisely how they provide complex meanings to the sounds in Chilean New Song, meanings that pass over any direct connection between genre and nation, genre and territory, genre and political affiliation.

It would be quite dangerous, I think, to admit the existence of a homogenous sound creation by the Chilean New Song, because conversely it seems urgent to examine in detail the internal composition of this Latin-Americanist project that propelled it to diversify instruments and repertoire, as I discussed above. Not every genre and form is treated equally, nor do they convey all the same meanings. The presence of some of them in the CNS is more prominent than others. Recalling the argument stressed by Javier Osorio in his warning about the subordination of popular traditions under the umbrella of folk traditional music (Osorio 2005: 6), a similar concern could appear regarding the CNS-Latin-Americanist project. A significant contribution to that discussion would be to stop considering their musicians as agents of an abstract hybridization and to start scrutinizing their concrete material outcome.

In this chapter I attempted to demonstrate how the inclusion of the *cueca* in the repertoire of the Chilean New Song was developed according to different procedures, such as the innovation in singing style and vocal arrangements in Quilapayún and the conservation of some traditional elements particularly related to form, which is unmistakable in Aparcoa and to some extent in Quilapayún. I have argued that by keeping the form recognizable these bands also allow listeners to practice the traditional dance, which was particularly meaningful in exile. Multiple aspects remain to be examined through future analyses, such as instrumental arrangements, harmony, and vocal technique. Any examination of them should take into account the fact that sound elements are ineluctably related to meanings and social usages that constitute music practices in any given society.

NOTES

I would like to thank Tim Gauger and Sam Bick for proofreading the manuscript. Unless otherwise indicated, translations are mine.

1. Throughout this chapter I use the term "hybridization" according to its meanings as they appear in some musicians' discourses as well as in certain researchers' allusions to the Chilean New Song movement or genre, both expressed contemporarily to the production of the music at stake. This clarification aims to dissociate this discussion from other very interesting and necessary discussions about the problematic use of this term in a market-oriented context and the risk of essentializing the idea of "hybridization" implying the existence of pre-hybrid cultures. For more on this, see Hutnyk 2000: 31–42.

2. I refer to "place" in order to stress the role of the *cueca*, alluding to the possibility of mapping its meanings and importance within the Chilean New Song. Conversely, I am not making reference to some prolific debates about music and place, space, city, and so on.

3. I use "traditional" to refer to the diversity of uses and practices belonging to the genre of *cueca*, which is considered part of the "*música folclórica*," taking into account both perspectives of musicians and researchers.

4. "Nosotros [los chilenos] tenemos muchas carencias. Si ponemos nuestro patrimonio musical al lado del de Colombia, Brasil, Venezuela o Cuba, notaremos que nuestra música es menos vistosa, un poquito más hermética y que tiene mucha dificultad en su desarrollo. De ahí que desde los años 1960 los músicos chilenos hayamos mirado y casi basado nuestra experiencia en la riqueza musical de nuestro continente. Nos hemos sentido latinoamericanos mirando desde aquí con mucho asombro la música de los demás pueblos. (. . .) [F]uimos incorporando instrumentos y armando una banda un poco ecléctica, que habla mucho del ser latinoamericano que la cultura musical chilena lleva muy dentro" (Miranda & Salinas 2002: 103–104).

5. "Chile es cultural, económicamente, una cosa indisoluble con la Argentina, con Bolivia y con el Perú. Esta es una cosa que hay que empezar por entender y entonces nosotros recién entenderemos por qué en nuestra música popular se oyen quenas, pincullos, tambores ligeros, por qué en nuestro folklore tenemos que hablar de folklore boliviano, argentino, peruano" (Orellana 1978).

6. Conversely to such an idea, this chapter is devoted to clearing up certain creative procedures with which a particular sound that is variously considered to be very "Chilean," "Latin American," or "leftist" was built.

7. The figure of the *huaso* in this context corresponds to the substitution of the peasant (*campesino*) archetype for a landlord (*patrón*) archetype. The *conjuntos de huasos* were the quintessential ensemble of the Música Típica genre. This genre exclusively included musical traditions from the central zone (Zona Central) of Chile and it is recognized as a promoter of conservative ideas. *Tonadas* and *cuecas* were at the core of their repertoire (Costa 2009: 16). Certain bands of the *Neofolklore* wave are considered to be their successors, such as Los Cuatro Cuartos, whose repertoire is also constituted of traditional music although performed in a much more stylized way (ibid: 21–22).

8. Even though some Chilean New Song artists signed contracts with big recording companies, a great portion of them distributed their repertoire through the label DICAP, run by the Communist Youth of Chile.

9. No discussion on this topic has been yet undertaken in depth. However, as early as in 1978, Osvaldo Rodríguez claimed that the *tonada* had been almost excluded from the Chilean New Song repertoire (cf. Orellana 1978).

10. Nicolás Román has recently addressed the particular process of hybridization undertaken by Víctor Jara, who would have built a new artistic figure by combining both the *cantor de oficio* folk tradition and the protest singers' tradition (2011).

11. Several studies have analyzed different projects of construction of national culture. Traditions from the central zone (Zona Central) of Chile have been consistently considered hegemonic, especially as they have been promoted by *conjuntos de huasos* and their successors. Large debates have been carried out on the subject of configuring identity on the basis of folk traditions (cf. Donoso 2009; Costa 2009).

12. Considered successor of the ancient *zamacueca*, the *cueca* has been called the "national dance" of Chile since the mid-nineteenth century. Many studies have examined the *cueca* and its important presence in popular culture (cf. Acevedo Hernández 1953; Garrido 1979). Recently, its values and meanings associated to the political sphere have been stressed by Araucaria Rojas (2009).

13. Those are the most well-known names. However sometimes lists also include Fernando Ugarte, Marta Contreras, Héctor Pavez, Nano Acevedo, Tito Fernández, Homero Caro (Torres 1980: 38). It is interesting to note the inclusion of Héctor Pavez on this list, given that he was not fully integrated into the movement, remaining closer to the *proyección folclórica* groups.

14. Other than participating in mass-oriented political acts, some musical creations merged with some government projects, such as "*Canto al Programa*" (Julio Rojas, Luis Advis, Sergio Ortega, and Inti-Illimani, 1970) and "*La merluza*" (Carlos Puebla and Quilapayún, 1970).

15. The expansion from a mainly Chilean to a Latin-American cultural framework allows us to think about how some processes of constructing "national" culture serve also to understand "Latin-American" culture, regarding the common allusion to an "imagined community," in terms of Anderson (1983), to which belonging is articulated. I thank Alejandro Vera for his insightful comments.

16. See for example Loyola and Cádiz 2010 and Garrido 1976.

17. Choreography has also a very rigid structure. Further information can be consulted in Loyola and Cádiz 2010: 150-154.

18. Also called estrambote, dístico, pareado, coda, or cola.

19. Carlos Vega identifies four main forms of the *octava*, where the *cuarteta*'s four lines come to be eight lines alternating [1] 4 and 5 syllables, [2] 7 and 5 syllables, [3] 4 and 8 syllables, and [4] seven and 8 syllables, plus their variations.

20. I will provide just a general description. The *cueca* is usually constituted of two musical stanzas: antecedent phrase and consequent phrase. Both melodies are invariably repeated throughout the *cueca*. In the first section (the *cuarteta*), each octosyllabic line fits with one of the two melodies, while in the second (*seguirilla*) and third (*remate*) sections, each line of five or seven syllables corresponds to half of either stanza. Harmony is usually tonal and harmonic development is either major or minor, depending on the region. An instrumental introduction is usually played with guitar, harp, piano, or accordion, as well as various membranophones and idiophones, such as pandero and tormento.

21. It is interesting that Fernando Barraza included the "cueca chora" as part of the Chilean New Song in his book published during the *Unidad Popular* government (1972: 31).

22. See the albums "*Vientos del pueblo*" ("Winds of People") (Isabel Parra, 1974), "*La Peña de los Parra vol. 1*" (Isabel and Ángel Parra, 1969), "*En México*" (Víctor Jara, 1996), "*X Vietnam*" (Quilapayún 1968).

23. Antonio Acevedo Hernández says, "aborda la crónica noticiosa, lo que puede llamarse político, la protesta, no solamente amorosa sino ciudadana, que clama contra los hechos que lesionan los intereses de la colectividad, abarcando todo género de injusticias" (1953: 162).

24. "[L]uego de la ovación estremecida, la cueca surgiendo como una llamarada entre las banderas"

25. "[L]o que se planteaba en aquellos años en Chile no era un problema acerca de la música chilena sino de la música latinoamericana como expresión común" (Rodríguez Musso 1984).

26. Several references, obtained from websites and oral sources, account for the identification of a fifty-two measure *cueca* as a *cueca campesina*, *cueca nortina*, or *cueca minera*, in opposition to the *urban cueca* (cf. http://culturapopulardechile.blogspot.com/2009/01/cueca-urbana-chilena.html and http://www.contenidoslocales.cl/sitio/6300/cueca-nortina-patrimonio-inmaterial-en-la-xv-region.

27. Quilapayún included a different version of it in their "*Antología*" (1998).

28. There were also various unpublished *cuecas* created by Héctor Pavez in exile (Bessière 1980: 240).

29. "La cueca urbana es canto de hombres. Más que juntarse a bailar, se juntan a competir en el canto. Competir en melodías y textos. Se forma una media rueda con no menos de cuatro cantores, de los cuales, *cada uno canta una estrofa del texto*. El que empieza a cantar o "saca" primero, es respetado como solista en esa estrofa y los demás hacen una *segunda voz en intervalo de tercera hacia abajo y paralela* ("llevar la de abajo")" (Alegría 1981: 125).

30. "El canto de la cueca brava genera una interesante alternancia de voces, la que se realiza en terceras paralelas; una primera voz y dos segundas comienzan cantando durante la copla; al inicio de la primera seguidilla, una de las segundas voces toma el lugar de la primera, la que pasa a segundear; en la segunda seguidilla (. . .) pasa a tomar la primera voz, la otra segunda y esta pasa a segundear. En el remate se vuelve a hacer el cambio de la primera seguidilla" (Loyola & Cádiz 2010: 123).

31. I would like to express my sincere acknowledgments to Daniel Añez, Daniel Larraín, and Felipe Verdugo who helped me to create an accurate transcription.

32. "[E]l baile fue injustamente despreciado como modo de comprensión del mundo y como soporte de ideas" (Bowen 2006, paragraph 33).

33. Something similar occurs with their "Cueca autobiográfica," also created in exile.

34. "En la primera etapa, nuestra creatividad se vio resentida por el activismo en que caímos por obra de las obligaciones políticas que no podíamos eludir. Como se sabe, el movimiento de solidaridad con Chile fue uno de los más activos y masivos que nuestra época haya conocido, tal vez sólo comparable al que despertó la guerra de Vietnam" (Carrasco 2003: 265).

Chapter Four

Modern Foundations of Uruguayan Popular Music

Abril Trigo

It's so good to have lived it, so I can tell the tale.

"Chiquillada" (José Carbajal 1967)[1]

Uruguayan Popular Music[2] is a relatively recent cultural phenomenon that was established in three phases. The 1960s (characterized by the revolutionary optimism inspired by the Cuban Revolution, the irreversible socio-political crisis of the no longer viable "Switzerland of America," and the emergence of the youth as a new cultural and political actor), witnessed the simultaneous development of a socially committed "protest song" doubly inspired in local rural folk and the overwhelming Argentine folkloric wave, and a largely derivative though locally adapted and widely eclectic, rock-and-roll. After the military coup of 1973, which imposed brutal political repression, cultural and artistic bans, and harsh media censorship, many musicians went into exile, while some were imprisoned and others went underground. By mid 1970s, a new generation of artists and musicians, inspired by their elders of the "committed" or "protest song" movement, had filled their shoes by developing a formidable space of cultural resistance that would be known as "canto popular," or "popular song." By the end of the 1970s, "canto popular" became increasingly experimental and gradually shifted from rural folk forms to urban folk genres, prominently the carnival rhythms of *murga* and *candombe*, variously fused with different shapes of rock and pop. The return in 1985 to liberal democracy, however restricted, opened the gates to a plethora of cultural manifestations while making palpable the consolidation of an original musical landscape. The process that had

97

started in the early 1960s had finally come to produce a distinctively Uruguayan musical identity.

In this chapter I will focus specifically on the first foundational moment,
between 1960 and 1973, when an outstanding generation of singers, musicians, and poets, part of a larger countercultural movement that set the stage
for the ulterior development of a left national front (the currently governing
Frente Amplio), coalesced under an extraordinary set of circumstances, inspired by the pioneering work of artists such as Víctor Santurio and Los
Carreteros, Osiris Rodríguez Castillos, Aníbal Sampayo, and Anselmo Grau,
and set the foundations of contemporary Uruguayan popular music. As the
musicologist Coriún Aharonián has stated, "The creative movement of the
1960s firmly established in Uruguay a taste for a popular music based on
local traditions that interacted freely with diverse influences while resisting
the colonial models imposed by transnational corporations" (Aharonián
2002: 199). I will focus on the popular music of primarily rural folk inspiration produced by Alfredo Zitarrosa, Daniel Viglietti, and the duo Los
Olimareños, integrated by Braulio López and José Luis Guerra, who are
indisputably the emblematic artists of this period. This will leave aside many
great musicians of the folk venue as well as the decidedly urban, middle-
class explorations in rock 'n roll, which will bear fruit in later years when
these foundations are already well established.

> I know in the town some people don't like me
> because I don't follow the laws of the bigwigs;
> and I despise other's trails/so I always open my own path.

"*Orejano*" (Serafín J. García and Los Olimareños 1962)[3]

1960. The Uruguayan musical market was dominated by foreign rhythms.
Bolero, Mexican ranchera, and tango filled the radio airwaves, beside the
Argentine folkloric wave, originally bred by the coalescence in Buenos Aires
of a massive working class of rural origins and Perón's populist national
politics, and developed after 1955 by the transnational record industry (Martins 1986: 17). As the rural teacher Rubén Lena, main composer and intellectual mentor of Los Olimareños, said, "We didn't have a song tradition or an
audience [. . .] We were dominated by North Argentine folk music, which in
the 1950s saturated the space, an influence that moved some people to explore other rhythms. . . . In that regard, the Argentine invasion was ultimately
a good thing" (Pellegrino 2009: 114). According to Carlos Martins, it is
unlikely that local precursors, like Amalia de la Vega, Sampayo, and
Rodríguez Castillos, whose repertoire was based on local rural folk and
influenced by the research of the musicologist Lauro Ayestarán, were much
affected by North Argentine folklore, although their later national recognition could be understood as a sort of side effect of the Argentine invasion.

Nevertheless, its influence in the young musicians to come to the stage in the 1960s is undeniable; their musical taste was shaped more by the models massively spread by the record and radio industries than by those less known local precursors (Martins 1986: 18). There was a craze for quartets, definitely not a local tradition, like Los Carreteros, Los Salteños, Los del Sur. Zitarrosa, as well as Los Olimareños and Viglietti, were under the spell of Atahualpa Yupanqui, Antonio Tormo, and Los Chalchaleros. Even such a folk icon as Víctor Lima composed mostly zambas, carnavalitos, and chacareras well into the 1960s, when he began to write milongas, polkas, and candombes (Lena, in Lima 1981: 12). Lena, a major inspirer of this musical renaissance, declared in 1965 that "[i]n Brazil, Argentina, Colombia, Venezuela, people live immersed in a robust folkloric world. In our country, where folk culture is very weak, that doesn't happen. Only the determination of a handful of artists will finally create a national folk repertoire" (Lena 1980: 48).

There was, of course, a distinguishable corpus of Uruguayan folk music, as Ayestarán had demonstrated, which due to ethnic and geopolitical histories, overlapped with other regional folk traditions, alongside four historical cycles: a Rio de la Plata cycle, shared with some Argentine provinces; a Northern cycle, shared with Southern Brazil; the traditional European songbook; and the music and dances of African heritage, to which we should add the Rio de la Plata modern tango cycle (Ayestarán 1967: 8; Martins 1986: 11). However, by the mid-twentieth century, the distribution and consumption of this local folk music was confined to limited circles and local venues, because media outlets, particularly radio, broadcasted only what was fashionable according to the tastes of Montevideo's audiences and the output of Buenos Aires' record industry. There was no national audience or a national market. Once again, Rubén Lena: "There were no songs, so we had to create them. But there was no audience for those songs, so we had to create it [. . .] We had to contribute to the creation of a national songbook, to the spiritual liberation of our people. I wanted the downtrodden to feel represented in those songs" (Pellegrino 2009: 57).

> Mire amigo no venga
> con esas cosas de las "custiones."
> Yo no le entiendo mucho
> discúlpeme, soy medio "bagual."
> Pero eso sí le digo
> no me interesan las "elesiones";
> los que no tienen plata
> van de alpargatas:
> todo sigue igual.

> *"Mire amigo"* ("Look My Friend") (Alfredo Zitarrosa 1965, in Forlán and Migliónico [1994: 49–50])[4]

Lena, who understood the socio-economic and cultural constraints hindering the development of a national popular music, had come to believe that if it couldn't be recovered, it had to be invented. That will be the task of the generation, and recover they did, though from a very critical understanding of folklore studies and the political manipulation of traditions that predates the postmodern critiques of the field. Anibal Sampayo, interviewed in 1966 by Zitarrosa, said,

> Look. . . . We don't do "folklore" but music with "folk projection." [. . .] Some people believe that dressing up as gauchos they are saving the traditions. That's grotesque. . . . Others talk about native genres, even though they haven't been around for a hundred years. [. . .] I sing to the woodcutters from the coast, the islanders, the forgotten ones. [. . .] Musical areas are never clearly defined, they crisscross and overlap, so we have to work upon this dual axis: the present and only afterward the past, "improving" traditions whenever is possible. . . . Never tie the hands of an artist. . . ." (Zitarrosa 2001: 150–153).[5]

Consequently, they would create a songbook and a musical canon, a new audience and a professional market, a social memory and a national musical identity "for a country that never had a distinctive musical personality" (Fabregat and Dabezies 1983: 18). It will be a complex and comprehensive creation, political indeed, but primarily esthetic, that will involve the lyrics and the music alike, and will determine the creation of a musical sensibility, deeply intertwined to the advance of social awareness and political motivation. The crucial move, in this regard, is the construction of a new musical market or, put it differently, the musical reeducation of existing audiences and the creation of new ones, the opening of spaces in a negligible media market, and the development of an alternative mode of production, circulation, and consumption of music.

Existing audiences of middle-aged people from the lower and middle classes, both in the cities and the countryside, had to be won back from the declining consumption of tangos and the conspicuous consumption of Argentine folklore and romantic *boleros*. This was done by competing head-on with media stars like Los Chalchaleros or Los Fronterizos, which explains why some of the first hits were brand-new zambas, such as "*A orillas del Olimar*" ("At the Shore of the Olimar"), by Los Olimareños, or "*Recordándote*" ("Remembering You") and "*Si te vas*," by Zitarrosa. However, these audiences were regained and reeducated by appealing to a new brand of lyrics, which revamped the old *gauchesca* formulae of social critique and "cantar opinando," by revitalizing old folk rhythms, almost unknown to most audiences, like the *chimarrita*, the *cielito*, the *vidalita*, and some forms of *milonga*, and even by inventing new ones, such as the *litoraleña*, cultivated by Sampayo from the *guarania* and other littoral rhythms, and the *serranera*, created by Lena in a bold transcultural move. But in addition to this reeducated old audience, a new audience was found: the culturally avid and politically demanding emergent youth, center of gravity of what in retrospect amounts to a cultural revolution that would transform the country, from literature and the arts to society and politics. The limits reached by the import substitution economic model, coupled to the decline of the Fordist regime of accumulation and the neocolonial world system, made visible the obsolescence of the country's democratic institutions. The lethargic Uruguayan society, torn between the utopian dreams of a socialist-nationalist revolution of continental scope and the harsh reality of authoritarian repression, will end up with a neofascist regime that will enforce the implementation of neoliberal policies and the insertion of the country in the global order. The dream will be defeated but the cultural revolution will go on.

> Some people have too much and some people have nothing
> and that's not by chance;
> if corn grows uneven/there must be a reason why.

"*La rastrojera*" (Marcos Velásquez 1964)[6]

Although several recordings were released in the early 1960s, such as the instantly successful first LP by Los Olimareños in 1962 and the refined album *Canciones folklóricas y seis impresiones para canto y guitarra* (*Folk Songs and Six Impressions for Singing and Guitar*) recorded by Viglietti in 1963, 1965 can be established as the year when the movement reached a massive audience, with the release of the first album by Los Olimareños and Zitarrosa's instant hits "*Milonga para una niña*" ("Milonga for a Little Girl") and "*Mire amigo*." As Zitarrosa himself put it, "Those records are the prehistory of national discography. . . . Since then, a market opened up" (Forlán 1994: 23). After that, a constant and abundant production, which sold an average of 30,000 copies per record (a huge figure considering the size of the market), became increasingly political and esthetically superior (Aharonian 2007a: 134).

Between 1965 and 1973 Viglietti produced five extraordinary albums: *Hombres de nuestra tierra* (*Men of our Land*) (1965), *Canciónes para el hombre nuevo* (*Songs for a New Man*) (1968), *Canto libre* (*Free Singing*) (1970), *Canciones chuecas* (1971), and *Daniel Viglietti y el Grupo de Experimentación Sonora de ICAIC*, reissued in Uruguay and elsewhere as *Trópicos* (1972–1973), plus several singles, reissues, and collaborations in collective works. After recording in Cuba *Canciones para el hombre nuevo*, which includes "*A desalambrar*" ("Tear Down the Wire Fences") and other radical anthems, he became a leftwing international star. In Uruguay he appealed mostly to urban middle-class students, intellectuals, artists, and political activists, due to his musical sophistication, as a subtle singer and a consummate guitar player, and his militant radical lyrics, which included many musicalizations of great poets, such as Nicolás Guillén, Federico García Lorca, Rafael Alberti, and César Vallejo, among others.

> Tear down the wire fences, tear them down!
> Because the land is ours,
> is yours, is theirs,
> It belongs to Pedro, María, Juan and José.

"*A desalambrar*" (Daniel Viglietti 1968, in Benedetti [2007: 183–184])[7]

Braulio López and Pepe Guerra did not have Viglietti's formal musical education. They had learned their trade playing in the brothels of the provincial city of Treinta y Tres, coached by traditional musicians, as Pepe Guerra tells (Darnauchans 1995: 11). Therefore, they were able to master a sound and a style that was at the same time rough and elaborated, with traditional resonances and modern arrangements, a precise amalgam of strong guttural singing and stroke-fingering guitar playing that appealed to vast audiences, mostly of the working classes, in the cities and the countryside. As Lena said, "The voices and guitars of Pepe and Braulio handle the most complex rhythms with amazing simplicity. . . . They are able to mimic innumerable voices, and that's only possible because they master the secrets of the instrument. . . Braulio's vibrant and metallic leading voice matches Pepe's deep and imaginative one to produce an inimitable sweat and sour texture" (Pellegrino 2009: 131–132). Los Olimareños were extremely productive, releasing a great number of records in Uruguay and Argentina. Their major albums during this period include *De cojinillo* (1965), *Quiero a la sombra de un ala* (1966), *Nuestra razón* (*Our Motive*) (1967), *Cielo del 69* (*Sky 69*) (1970), *Todos detrás de Momo* (1971), *¡Qué pena!* (1971), *Del templao* (1972), *Rumbo* (*Direction*) (1973), *¿No lo conoce a Juan?* (*Do You Know Juan?*) (1973), and *Cantar opinando* (1973).

> It's so good to go back home
> and mimic the music
> of the rain falling down/the tin roofs;
> to get filled with the smell of smoke,
> walk on the soft dirt,
> play with the dogs,
> and live in peace.

"*La sencillita*" ("The Simple One") (José Carbajal 1969)[8]

Since the release of its first record in 1965, Zitarrosa became a national celebrity. Well known in radio circles, since he had been a radio announcer for years, his songs were widely broadcasted, competing in the ratings with the Beatles and displacing from the charts the Argentine folkloric groups, in spite of having been greatly influenced by Argentine folklore, as he has repeatedly acknowledged and his first compositions demonstrate (Pellegrino 2003: 87).[9] His main records include *Canta Zitarrosa* (*Zitarrosa Sings*) (1966), *Del amor herido* (1967), *Yo sé quién soy* (*I Know Who I am*) (1968), *Zitarrosa/4* (1969), *Milonga madre* (*Mother Milonga*) (1970), *Coplas del canto* (*Stanzas of the Song*) (1971), and *Adagio en mi país* (*Adagio in My Country*) (1973). Most of these albums were released simultaneously in Uruguay and Argentina, and sometimes reproduced in other countries as well.

> No te olvides del pago
> si te vas pa' la ciudad
> *cuanti* más lejos te vayas
> más te tenés que acordar.
> Cierto que hay muchas cosas
> que se pueden olvidar
> pero algunas son olvidos
> y otras son cosas nomás.
>
> "*Pa'l que se va*" ("For the One Who Is Leaving") (Alfredo Zitarrosa 1967, in Forlán and Migliónico [1994: 54]).[10]

If the combined production of these artists coalesced into the formation of a national public and became even part of a continental artistic and political movement, individually they addressed different audiences. While Los Olimareños were popular idols in Uruguay, as their intensive recording demonstrates, but less known out of the country except in Argentina, and Viglietti had become a sort of cult singer among middle class, young, and politically radical urban audiences both in Uruguay and abroad, Zitarrosa was able to draw large audiences, urban and rural, in the country and abroad, particularly in Argentina. Despite their political differences (while all of them shared a certain anarchist penchant, as the political crisis unfold Zitarrosa affiliated to the Communist Party, while Los Olimareños and Viglietti took a different path, with the latter becoming a sort of musical spokesman of the MLN-Tupamaros—a famous guerrilla group of the country), this had to do less with their political affiliation and more with their esthetic options, their specific repertoires, and their different styles of singing and addressing their audiences. The popularity of Zitarrosa and Los Olimareños even defied political and ideological barriers, to the point that the military coup in June 27, 1973, was announced through the airwaves with the soundtrack of Los Olimareños' version of "*A don José*," a milonga by Rubén Lena dedicated to José Artigas, which generated, of course, a great deal of political confusion.[11] Many testimonials by people imprisoned during the dictatorship mention that guards, soldiers, and military officers habitually listened to banned singers and censured songs in prisons and military barracks.

> Ven a ese criollo rodear,
> rodear, rodear . . .
> Los paisanos le dicen,
> mi General . . .
> Va alumbrando con su voz
> la oscuridad,
> y hasta las piedras saben
> a dónde va.

"*A don José*" (Rubén Lena 1968, in Pellegrino [2009: 143])[12]

In addition to the musical reeducation of existing audiences and the creation of new ones, these musicians contributed to the development of a modern recording industry, relatively small but technically comparable to international standards. But most importantly perhaps, they opened new venues and explored alternative modes of production, circulation, and consumption of music. They performed in radio and TV shows, whenever possible, as well as *peñas* (folk clubs), social clubs, and the traditional carnival *tablados*, neighborhood stages raised-up during the carnival season. Zitarrosa, the most entrepreneurial and professional perhaps, produced many concerts and shows where many artists performed (singers, musicians, actors, dancers, from dissimilar genres like pop, flamenco, tango, jazz), and also opened a restaurant show that finally went bankrupt, with the intent of "defending the artists' rights to a fair economic compensation . . . without the mediation of exploitative traffickers and phony impresarios" (Erro 1996: 46). As he used to say, "Singing is a social work and deserves a fair remuneration. Uruguayan artists can and should live from their art" (Pellegrino 2003: 98). In the same vein, Los Olimareños opened a wine bar, where many artists performed, usually in a cooperative way. Viglietti, who had been in his youth, like Zitarrosa, a radio announcer, hosted a radio program, an activity he will maintain, with interruptions, during his exile in Europe, and after his return to Uruguay in 1984. In 1967, inspired by the Protest Song Conference, several artists founded the Center for the Protest Song, later known as Center for Uruguayan Popular Song, as a cooperative that organized concerts and other activities and promoted the unionization of musicians and artists. They also founded cooperative recording companies, such as Ediciones Ayuí-Tacuabé, which after four decades of existence, demonstrates "that alternatives to capitalist corporations as well as bureaucratic party-owned companies are possible, and that a culturally progressive nonprofit organization can survive not just in the capitalist milieu of the 1970s or the transnational globalization of recent years, but also under one of the worst military dictatorships"

(Aharonián 2002: 200). Thus, following Martins, the movement could be characterized as a phenomenon of alternative communication, because of its resistance to the esthetic postulates and ideological connotations of transnational pop culture, its close-knit articulation to larger social and political practices, and its rejection of vertical, monopolistic, commodified media control. An alternative culture, of course, which proposed also an alternative worldview (Martins 1986: 104). However, as political tensions worsened, all these professional and semi-professional venues and activities began to fade and be complemented or replaced by concerts in trade unions, cooperatives, and political rallies. Performance as political activism was paid for with professional tours and performances abroad.

> Los chuecos se junten bien juntos,
> bien juntos los pies,
> y luego caminen buscando la patria,
> la patria de todos, la patria Maciel,
> esta patria chueca que no han de torcer
> con duras cadenas los pies todos juntos
> hemos de vencer.

"*El chueco Maciel*" ("Maciel the Bowlegged") (Daniel Viglietti 1971, in Benedetti [2007: 193])[13]

Most of the critics concur in underlining the esthetic contribution of this foundational moment of Uruguayan popular music. Nevertheless, the national and international overheated political climate of the 1960s and the overtly political positions the artists were bound to take, have determined the prevalence of a slightly biased interpretation of the phenomenon. In my opinion, the truest and ultimately everlasting political value of this movement is also its cultural value, which rests on its remarkable esthetic originality. In other words, what really matters is that beyond historical contingencies and circumstantial politics, this group of artists so fully committed to their ideals and engaged with their times, were able to create a new national musical identity. As Aharonián has written, in the last decades of the twentieth century, Uruguay, one of the most Europeanized countries in Latin America, went through a curious process of resistance to colonialism. The usually boundless power of transnational corporations was confronted by a boom in local popular music which combined the search for an identity with the repudiation of the status quo, and a mass-oriented production eager to take esthetic risks (Aharonián 2007a: 134).

This supports Martins's thesis about how the cultural values shared by these artists "were closely linked to their aesthetic options, because these were opposed to mass media offerings on two levels: geocultural origin and quality. [. . .] It seems evident that what we separate out for analyzing as an 'aesthetic option' is in reality a part of a complex system in which the main motivator is political: the effort to propose active alternatives to what existed and was approved" (Martins and Dumpiérrez 1997: 243). Zitarrosa himself admitted in 1986 that "regarding esthetics, I am a formalist" (Salinas 2006: 36). This "esthetic option" resembles, of course, Walter Benjamin's notion on the politicizing of art (Benjamin 1968: 242), and taking into consideration the importance assigned to the message, it explains the generally high poetic quality of the lyrics: "Quality was greatly valued by most of the singers, especially where lyrics were concerned. They frequently set their music to lyrics written for them by poets, or used published poetry for the words of their songs" (Martins and Dumpiérrez 1997: 243).[14]

The emphasis on the verbal content and the poetic quality of the text led sometimes to a certain degree of privileging the lyrics over the music, and songs being appreciated according to their literariness, a misconception followed by some critics that fed three common fallacies regarding this period: that the message prevails over forms, the music services poetic lyrics, and politics neutralizes esthetics. It is true, as Washington Benavides, a poet amply musicalized by many musicians has written, that most artists composed their songs in the Franco-Spanish tradition of the "canción de texto," as sung poetry, which makes extremely complicated the literary status of the lyrics (quoted in Salinas 2006: 15). From a literary point of view all forms of oral poetry have always been regarded of a lower status, and by the same token, the musicalization of "high" poetry has been perceived with suspicion. The solution has been to distinguish between the literariness of the lyrics, deemed as written literature, and the instrumentality of the music, considered a communicative conduit. What is missing from this view is the fact that the song is a hybrid cultural and artistic artifact, a product of the amalgamation of both lyrics and music that is consumed through its auditory reception (Salinas 2006: 14). "A poem is an object made with words whose value resides exclusively on those words. . ." wrote Lena, "But when I read the lyrics of a song I know something is missing, the object is incomplete. . ." (Lena 2009: 106–107). The musical adaptation of a written poem filters the passage from one cultural milieu to another, involving other means of communication, receptive frameworks, and an entirely different mode of production. The meanings of a musicalized poem will necessarily differ from those of its written version. The transformation of a poem into a song involves its structure, but also its textual dimension and its status vis-à-vis its reader/ consumer and the community. It is another text, which acquires a surplus semantic value through additional coding—voice, performance, musical arrangements—in a new context of communication (Figueredo 2005: 15–17). Moreover, great poets and composers could be terrible performers of their compositions; on the other hand, "the most vulgar poem can transfigure itself and acquire a unique expressive dimension in the voice of the singer" (Zitarrosa 2001a: 26).

> En mi país, qué tristeza,
> la pobreza y el rencor.
> Dice mi padre que ya llegará
> desde el fondo del tiempo otro tiempo
> y me dice que el sol brillará
> sobre un pueblo que él sueña
> labrando su verde solar.

"*Adagio en mi país*" (Alfredo Zitarrosa 1973, in Forlán and Migliónico [1994: 84–85])[15]

It was a massive and experimental movement, where artistic and political risks were taken without following established formulas or hegemonic cliques, and despite its apparent uniformity, it was actually very mobile, heterogeneous, and self-transforming. This duality many times blurred the borders between popularity and elitism, notes Aharonián, folk formulas and experimentalism, alarming critics unfamiliar with the Uruguayan milieu. For instance, Viglietti's first two albums, *Canciones folklóricas y seis impresiones para canto y guitarra* (1963) and *Hombres de nuestra tierra* (1965), show his search for a personal voice able to solve the tension between folk music and his classical formation. Originally influenced by Yupanqui, he found local folk sounds putting to music the *costumbrista* portraits of the poet Juan Capagorry. However, the influence on Viglietti of folk music was always more intellectual than experiential and he gradually abandoned rural folk forms to explore new musical territories: "Even if sometimes I start from folk forms, I am so concerned with renovating them, that the folk style gets more and more diluted. In *Canciones chuecas* I wanted to explore with electronic instruments and sounds appealing to young people" (quoted in Pellegrino & Basilago 2002: 211). This cycle will close with *Trópicos*, recorded in Cuba in 1973, entirely composed by quasi pop versions of songs by the Cuban Nueva Trova and Brazilian *música popular brasileira*, with sophisticated arrangements by Leo Brouwer. This experimentalism will continue until his latest works, such as the splendid poetic craftsmanship accompanying the sometimes atonal and minimalist music of the album *Esdrújulo* (1993), which reminds of Vicente Huidobro's linguistic experiments.

This creativity is evident in the invention of new musical genres, as is the case of the litoraleña, created by Sampayo from related rhythms from the Uruguay River littoral, closely related to the Argentine provinces of Entre Ríos and Corrientes, and even to Paraguay, or the reinvention of old ones, like the chamarrita or chimarrita, a festive dance from the northern tip of Uruguay, Eastern Argentina, and southern Brazil, recovered by musicians like Carbajal and Zitarrosa. However, even more important in esthetic and cultural terms, is the serranera (in its two variants, a fast-paced polka-styled form, and a 6x8 form), and the media serranera (a slower, bolero-styled 4x4 form), both created by Rubén Lena and popularized by Los Olimareños. The serranera was born to capture the social landscape of the borderlands with Brazil, and accordingly Lena inspired himself in a danceable milonga very popular in the region among smugglers and peasants (Lena 2009: 66).

> Yo soy cantor de estos llanos
> donde el viento no reposa.
> En el Brasil castellano
> y aquí soy Zenobio Rosas.

"*Platonadas*" (Rubén Lena 1967, in Pellegrino [2009: 212]) [16]

While the milonga is, due to its structural plasticity and cultural resonances, the emblematic genre of Uruguayan popular music, the most radical experimentation involved the adaptation of two carnival musical genres, murga and candombe, confined at that time to the carnival ambit of street parades and neighborhood open stages, disdained by the middle classes as culturally vulgar. Candombe, which originated in the calls to dance among African slaves in colonial times, obtained national recognition as a subcultural practice since the institutionalization of carnival in the 1920s, alongside murgas, characteristically white, lower class ensembles of about twenty members who sang and danced popular songs with satirical lyrics. Candombe, according to Aharonián, cannot be apprehended as a musical form, because it encompass diverse musical products deeply engrained in the social and cultural framework of the "drums call" (llamada de tamboriles) of Montevideo's Afro-descendants. Both murga and candombe are musically defined by their characteristic rhythmic percussion (Aharonián 2007a: 106–108). Rubén Lena and José Carbajal were among the first to experiment with songs that bridged rural lyrics with urban carnival rhythms, a new sort of fusion that overcame the boundaries of folk music and opened popular music to a whole world of sounds, rhythms, and sensibilities. Some of the most accomplished songs of this period are murgas and candombes, and the most experimental album—largely misunderstood at that time—was *Todos detrás de momo*, produced by Los Olimareños and Lena, the first and only album to be completely structured, as a single piece, upon the esthetic, musical, and instrumental murga foundations. Of course, the public was not ready yet, and the album has never been reissued, although it has been regarded by critics and musicians as a masterpiece. It will take many years, a new generation, and the fusion with rock, to realize the crossover. The prominence of the esthetic option and the dual character of modern Uruguayan popular music as a mass-oriented movement with avant-gardist motivations, will flourish after the military coup, when a new generation of artists will resort to multiple esthetic strategies in order to dodge censorship, open new artistic venues, and resist political repression (Aharonián 2007a: 134–135). "*A redoblar*," by Rubén Olivera and Mauricio Ubal, will become in 1979 the hymn of resistance to the dictatorship; Jaime Roos's "*Brindis por Pierrot*," sung by the murga soloist Canario Luna, will finally make acceptable in 1985 the murga singing style beyond carnival boundaries.

> My dear, tough, fishermen people . . .
> keep your daily struggle of bread and work,
> because the drums pass, but misery stays!"
>
> "*A mi gente*" ("To My People") (José Carbajal 1969)[17]

The timely internationalization of what had begun as a local or national musical renaissance became both a political enticement and an ideological burden, insofar as it involved its international alignment with the Cuban Revolution, so the question of the more appropriate name for the movement got entwined to its artistic definition. Perhaps the problem started in 1967 at the first Encounter of Protest Song, organized by Casa de las Américas in Havana, Cuba, and attended by twenty-one Uruguayan artists (the largest delegation). Viglietti was a leading voice in the debates: "We Protest Song workers must be aware that songs, by nature, have an enormous capacity of communication with the masses. . . . In consequence, songs must become an instrument for the people, not a commodity for its alienation. We Protest Song workers have a responsibility to become better artists, because the struggle for artistic quality is in itself a revolutionary act" (quoted in Pellegrino 2002: 189). The appropriateness of the label Protest Song was a major issue. According to Pepe Guerra, the Uruguayans didn't like it (Darnauchans 1995: 33), and even Viglietti affirmed that "it would be more appropriate to speak of revolutionary song," though later in his career he will define it as "proposal song," or even "'human song,' because in spite of so much suffering, Latin America is full of joyful life. . ." (Pellegrino 2002: 239). Braulio López insists that he never liked labels such as "political song" or "engaged song": "A song is a song, and shows the needs of the people, human problems" (Arapí 1995: 20–21), and Zitarrosa has affirmed that "[a] protest song is not more necessary than a love song, nor a love song more beautiful than a rebel song" (Zitarrosa 2001a: 30). Finally, the issue will be settled in 1967 by José Carbajal "El Sabalero," in the title to his first album, *Canto popular*, or *Popular Song*. As he explained it in an interview, "[W]e needed to distinguish our music from Argentine folklore. On the one hand, if we said that our music was folklore, the audience would demand us to sound like Los Fronterizos; on the other hand, we did play folk music, but not in a traditional way. We played folk music for the present" (Martins 1986: 15–16). I concur with

Martins when he concludes that *"Popular Song* is definitely the best label for this production, whose music has been determined by 'local earlier influences,' and whose lyrics provide a social commentary or connote a demand for social change" (Martins 1986: 14).

> -Cantor que tiemble al cantar,
> no puede ser tan buen gallo.
> -Oigale al duro, oigalé,
> y menos ser uruguayo.
> -Ha cortao como pa' diez.
> -La garganta debe ser
> cerno de buena madera.
>
> -¡Ah! El que le cortó el ombligo
> conservará la tijera...
> -Como corazón de amigo.
>
> *"Nuestra razón"* (Rubén Lena 1967, in Pellegrino [2009: 209])[18]

"The Cuban Revolution, the reality and consciousness of underdevelopment, and the anti-imperialist struggle take us back to the times of Bartolomé Hidalgo," the anthropologist Daniel Vidart wrote in 1968, pointing out to one of the most salient features of the rising movement, the recovery of the *gauchesca* tradition of "cantar opinando": "The poet becomes a singer and enters into a dialogue, playing his guitar and singing his music, with an audience that demands a straightforward, radical, revolutionary proclamation. The protest song breaks into the interstices of social life convening hearts and minds" (Vidart 1968: 363). The artistic formula of "cantar opinando," or opinioned singing, which usually conveys a message of social critique, political protest, or individual lament through poetic singing, has characterized *gauchesca* poetry since its founding during the wars of independence in the early nineteenth century by Bartolomé Hidalgo, consequently canonized as "the poet of the motherland." The formula was later captured by José Hernández in the classic *Martín Fierro*: "I've known singers/who sing wonderfully;/but never risk giving an opinion/because they only sing for fun;/but I sing with an opinion/which is my way of singing."[19] In fact, the artistic formula of "cantar opinando" wasn't a recovery at all, or a discovery of the generation, who inherited it from their immediate precursors, the singer-poets of the 1950s and the living memory of fading *payadores*.

> Compañera,
> vendrán a preguntar por mí;
> si yo he sido, dónde estoy,
> si usted sabe adónde fue su marido.
> Usted levanta la vista,
> mira, calla, está pensando:

Pablo andará por la tierra,
su bandera enarbolando,
una bandera de trigo,
de pan y de vino,
levantando.
Por el camino, a los hombres
irá enseñando la libertad.

"*La canción de Pablo*" ("Pablo's Song") (Daniel Viglietti 1970, in Benedetti [2007: 189–190])[20]

Perhaps the best modern definition of "cantar opinando" is provided by Zitarrosa in an article published in 1970: "the singer who 'communicates' fulfills a collective social need. If we think about prevailing social injustice, the hunger of the many and their exploitation by the few [. . .] the relevance of the so called 'protest' or 'content' repertoires, so many times lacking in artistic merit, is completely understandable. . . ." (Zitarrosa 2001a: 29–30). The milonga complex provides, undoubtedly, the most malleable rhythms for the "cantar opinando" ballad format. Of remote African origins, the milonga, both music and dance, was at its height around 1880, associated with gauchesca literature and payada singing. There are two major forms of singable milongas, the milonga pampeana, lyrical and sentimental, and the milonga oriental, vigorous and accentuated, "more appropriate for epic subjects," according to the payador Carlos Molina (Aharonián 2007a: 36). Alongside twentieth century modernization processes, these rural forms seem to fade away, surviving as an urban dance alongside tango. However, due to its plasticity to accommodate emotions and narrations, the milonga will live a renaissance and become a pivotal genre in Uruguayan popular music. "In traditional milonga singing, the boundaries between song and recitative are very fluid, delivering the lyrics extremely well, especially in the long tirades, thus keeping the narrative tension and the audience's attention" (Aharonián 2007a: 39). Zitarrosa, unquestionably the most consummate milonga singer, admitted once that he couldn't compose anything but milongas, because of their cultural, ideological, experiential, and historical texture (Ibargoyen 2005: 62). Milonga, he used to say, is "Montevideo's blues" (Zitarrosa 2001a: 13).

Milonga madre cantando
te conocí yo no supe ni cuándo
sé que una tarde en un tango te pude oír
tarareándolo.
Madre milonga en tus brazos sentimentales
se fueron al mazo
taitas y yiros de paso
cuando tu amor les tanteó el corazón.

"*Milonga madre*" (Alfredo Zitarrosa 1970, in Forlán and Migliónico [1994: 75–76])[21]

Viglietti wrote in the back cover of *Canciones para el hombre nuevo,* "I need the lyrics. The historical and social circumstances demand me to speak out. Musical emotions and ideas are also important, but right now I need to communicate with suggestive, unraveling, moving words. Beautiful words like those of Vallejo and Lorca, or persuasive ones like those of a minor lyricist like me" (Benedetti 2007: 32). Viglietti's urgency expressed the urgency of the times, the sense of political emergency that pervaded much of the period's cultural production. The tense social and political climate, nationally and internationally, pushed many artists to speed up the production of "urgent songs," composed in a hurry with an explicit political message. A song, for Viglietti, can convey a simple counter-informational message, but always acts emotionally on the audience's affects, and therefore its meaning goes deeper, leaving affective resonances in the mind and the body (in Benedetti 2007: 83). For that reason, he warned against the slippery road to sheer propaganda: "The struggle has to be fought with both artistic rigor and political consciousness, because the facile communication of a political message can compromise the necessary unity of art and politics" (in Pellegrino & Basilago 2002: 212). The fulfillment of this collective social need explains the importance given to the lyrics and its communication.

Zitarrosa also thought extensively about it. He wrote that "[t]o communicate or not to communicate, that's a general law of the trade, . . ." but he also said that "effective communication between a good singer and his audience is conditioned by the social milieu, and hence it has a testimonial character, a precise cultural meaning when that particular singer and those songs are cultural products appropriate to said society. Even more so, they must be necessary, or they would be useless" (Zitarrosa 2001: 29 and 25). Consequently, "cantar opinando" involves a social responsibility, insofar as the artist is an agonist, in Unamuno's sense, a historical agent, and a cultural interpreter of his people. This is why, Zitarrosa adds, "at these difficult times, a popular artist carries a tough but unavoidable mission" (Zitarrosa 2001: 25; Salinas 2006: 40). Furthermore, at the core of the formula resides the artist's social representativeness, since "the singer is no more, no less than the indispensable medium in a social ritual. The instant a song touches the soul of the audience is simply magic. . ." (Pellegrino 2003: 135). This explains why the rhetorical figure of apostrophe, a main characteristic of gauchesco poetry that stresses the simultaneous levels of written, aural, and fictional communication (Trigo 2008), has been so widely used in popular song.

Mire doña Soledad,
póngase un poco a pensar,

doña Soledad,
qué es lo que quieren decir
con eso de la libertad.
Usted se puede morir,
eso es cuestión de salud,
pero no quiera saber
lo que le cuesta un ataúd.

"Doña Soledad" (Alfredo Zitarrosa 1968, in Forlán and Migliónico [1994: 45–46])[22]

Zitarrosa's awareness about the importance of style (in music, singing, and performance) allowed him to construct a persona whose cultural representativeness was inscribed in his body and acted out in and out of stage, from his always dark, formal and traditional dressing to the outmoded way of combing his hair; from his grim, concentrated facial expression to his tango-singer body posture; from his three or four guitars accompaniment to his deep, velvety voice of bass baritone. As told by himself and his biographers ("I want to interpret my country and my generation" [Pellegrino 2003: 130]), he will be always the bohemian night owl, the frustrated poet, the reluctant singer, the neurotic friend, the hypersensitive but rigorously professional performer prone to depression and alcoholism. All this led to some sort of mythology around his persona and his voice, best captured in this passage where Enrique Estrázulas tells us how he met the singer:

I saw him small and slow, with a self-assured, baritone voice of [. . .] an Uruguayan from the border, grandson of gaucho with Indian blood [. . .] It called my attention his ritual concentration on the guitar, as if he were alone. Also the silence around him. [. . .] Finally, the intimate, sad, charismatic singing rose up, and instantly I realized that I was listening to a popular singer with the voice of my country. He definitely was singing in "oriental style,"[23] with an inexplicable something inherent to him, that couldn't be learned anywhere, that couldn't be explained otherwise than by walking through life as an Uruguayan (Estrázulas 1984: 14).

Hoy siento que soy muy poco
como cantor y poeta.
Si nunca apliqué recetas
a mis canciones, tampoco,
ni más cuerdo ni más loco
que cualquier hombre prudente,
más de una vez fui inconsciente,
al ver que se me aplaudía,
de que en cada aplauso ardían
las manos de mucha gente.

"*Diez décimas de autocrítica*" ("Ten Stanzas for Self-criticism") (Alfredo Zitarrosa 1972, in Forlán and Migliónico [1994: 35–37])[24]

While Zitarrosa's formidable voice and self-assumed singing style "a la uruguaya,"[25] which he actually inherited from Amalia de la Vega and early tango singers but he had taken to the highest standards in the milonga genre, were natural assets for national representativeness, the apparently cruder style of Los Olimareños was not less representative, though in a different way. Under Lena's guidance, they assumed the symbolic and political representation, through the lyrics, the genres, and their singing style, of a local culture, peasant social strata, and a particular breadth of the popular (the life and lives of small towns, with their typical characters and local rituals), which curiously enough attained national popularity.

> A los hermanos Fuentes y al Rico Moreira,
> al Coco Brun y a Charquero, a don Gregorio y al Chilo,
> a Riaño y a Moriño,
> al Negro Bruno, a doña María y al Capincho Fernández
> y a toda esa gente que quiso un camino nuevo pa' su pago,
> pero no precisa un camino nuevo pa' llegar a mi memoria.

"*Isla Patrulla*" (Rubén Lena 1969, in Pellegrino [2009: 190])[26]

The recitative preamble to the milonga "*Isla Patrulla*," reminiscent of the payador tradition, provides a great example of the ordinary, local, intimate atmosphere created by the apostrophe addressed to locals, whose appeal to other audiences will be obviously based upon its poetic and connotational representativeness: in some way, the tiny and isolated hamlet Villa María Isabel (also known as Isla Patrulla, in reference to a small island where the police fought bands of smugglers), becomes the symbol of any hometown, or "patria chica." Braulio López's score and Los Olimareños's dialogic, hearty rendition is only surpassed, probably, by their own version of the polka "*De cojinillo*," a masterpiece that celebrates the picaresque environment of local brothels. Every quatrain is like a snapshot of a particular character.

> Cuando suena la acordeón en lo 'e Cachango
> y es asunto delicao,
> jiede a vino hasta con la boca cerrada
> y anda de ojo revoleao.
>
> . . .
> Y está el baile hasta la boca de parejas
> y hay más gente pa' dentrar,
> y te cobran quince reales a cara e' perro,
> sin derecho a protestar.

"*De cojinillo*" (Rubén Lena 1962, in Pellegrino [2009: 162–3])[27]

This intimate celebration of local customs is also the trademark of José Carbajal "El Sabalero," impressive performer and composer of several songs that received international acclaim, such as the milonga *"La sencillita,"* the murga *"A mi gente"* and the candombe *"Yacumenza,"* pioneering songs that incorporated carnival rhythms, the complex milonga/chimarrita *"El hombre del mameluco"* ("The Man of the Overall"), and the famous chimarrita *"Chiquillada."* But Los Olimareños, as well as Carbajal, didn't limit their politics to the subtle allusions of "costumbrista" pieces or the remembrance of legendary matreros, or outlaws. They also sung explicitly political songs, such as Carlos Puebla's homage to Che Guevara *"Hasta siempre,"* ("Farewell") or *"Cielo del 69,"* composed by Héctor Numa Moraes from a poem by Mario Benedetti, or the elegiac *"Milonga del fusilado,"* which reflects the somber pessimism of political defeat. In most cases, however, their politics was conveyed by poetic and symbolic means, many times by playing selected covers, or setting to music exemplary poems, such as *"Sentados sobre los muertos"* ("Seated over the Dead Ones") by Miguel Hernández, or adopting and adapting to the national taste Venezuelan traditional songs with intentional lyrics, mostly joropos, like *"Los dos gallos"* ("The Two Roosters") and *"El gavilán"* ("The Hawk"). Of course, the inclusion in their respective repertoires of songs, sounds and rhythms from other Latin American cultures is a hallmark of all these artists, who maintained close relations with progressive musicians from around the world and reached different segments of South America's markets. Zitarrosa's very first record (1965) included *"El camba,"* a Bolivian taquirari by Godofredo Núñez Chávez, and Viglietti's *"Canción para mi América"* (1963) begins, "Dale tu mano al indio/dale que te hará bien/y encontrarás el camino/como ayer yo lo encontré,"[28] which demonstrates how their cultural localism and social nationalism was deeply linked to a geopolitical and international Latin Americanism.

No other singer so clearly stood out as a political activist as Viglietti, who became a sort of cult reference for the radical youth. Unfairly, his enormous popularity was based many times more on ideological than on cultural or esthetic grounds, so up to a point, Viglietti's daring politics have obscured his sophisticated compositions and musical virtuosity. He had a strong following among middle-class students and young urban sectors, who also liked the Beatles, Georges Brassens, and Joan Manuel Serrat, which probably explains why Viglietti's songs, despite their unmistakable folk foundations, have a refined cosmopolitan flavor that spices his singing, musical arrangements, and guitar-playing style, all of which contributed to his international recognition.

> Yo quiero romper la vida,
> como cambiarla quisiera,
> ayúdeme compañero;

ayúdeme, no demore,
que una gota con ser poco
con otra se hace aguacero.

"*Milonga de andar lejos*" (Daniel Viglietti 1968, in Benedetti [2007: 185–186])[29]

Viglietti's development shows an increasing political radicalization, although, as Benedetti says, the early "*Canción para mi América*" summarizes his entire career: "La guitarra americana/peleando aprendió a cantar" (Benedetti 2007: 66).[30] With his third album, *Canciones para el hombre nuevo*, recorded in Cuba in 1968, the militant was born. The tension between the folk ballad singer and the classical musician is still there: one side of the album contains the politically oriented folk-inspired Latin-Americanist songs, while the other side contains exquisite, minimalist musicalizations of Spanish and Latin American poetry. "Yo quiero romper la vida,/como cambiarla quisiera" sings Viglietti, whose revolutionary passion goes well beyond revolutionary politics. As a convinced realist, he is truly demanding the impossible, and what began as social denunciation ended up in Che Guevara's ethics of the "new man" ("another way to imagine the future," he would say [Pellegrino & Basilago 2002: 194]), the guerrilla mystique, and his unwavering support to the MLN-Tupamaros (what he calls, "the Salerno commitment," after Jorge Salerno, a Tupamaro student leader and amateur musician killed in military action, some of whose compositions Viglietti would sing). "At that time there was a rare subjectivity in the air, because in a way the subject was the revolutionary process itself" (Benedetti 2007: 82–83). So, vehemently Viglietti declared his open support to the Tupamaros' armed struggle:

Ya no hay más secreto,
mi canto es del viento,
yo elijo que sea
todo movimiento.
. . .
La sangre de Túpac,
la sangre de Amaru,
la sangre que grita
libérate, hermano.

"*Solo digo compañeros*" (Daniel Viglietti 1971, in Benedetti [2007: 196–197])[31]

The albums *Canto libre* (1970) and *Canciones chuecas* (1971) belong to this Tupamaro period. The denunciation of social injustice gave way to the counter-information of political repression and young people's commitment to take arms. "*La canción de Pablo*" and "*Muchacha*" ("Young Woman") for instance, sing the eulogy of young guerrillas. This counter-informational and pedagogic function of art ("to raise unusual states of conscience in the audience"), is at the core of his notion of the "horsefly-singer," who must always be a critical and independent voice against power (Benedetti 2007: 83 and 97).

> La muchacha de mirada clara,
> cabello corto,
> la que salió en los diarios;
> no sé su nombre, no sé su nombre.
> Pero la nombro: primavera.
> Pero la veo: compañera.
> Pero yo digo: mujer entera.
> Pero yo grito: guerrillera.
>
> "*Muchacha*" (Daniel Viglietti 1971, in Benedetti [2007: 195])[32]

This defiant declaration placed him at the extreme left of the political spectrum and eventually will fire up a polemic with Zitarrosa that reflected strategic disagreements among the left, particularly between the Tupamaros, who were embarked in a guerrilla struggle, and the Communist Party, who endorsed a non-violent, electoral strategy of mass struggle. Zitarrosa's callous response in "*Diez décimas de autocrítica*," disdainfully alludes to Viglietti as a "charlatan," a reference that will be removed from future editions.[33] Although they were never close friends, they admired each other, and regardless of their mutually acknowledged artistic and political discrepancies, they would both agree with Zitarrosa's statement that "[a]rt should not be utilitarian nor plain entertainment. It is life, from its production to its enjoyment, even the political enjoyment of a work of art is always life . . ." (Ibargoyen 2005: 58).

By the end of 1972 the Tupamaros had already been militarily defeated, but the ascendance of neofascism was unstoppable. Finally, in June 1973 the remnants of the democratic institutions will be shut down. Most artists were banned, some imprisoned; many went into exile. Viglietti left the country in 1973, Braulio López in 1974 (and kept in prison in Argentina for a year), Zitarrosa in 1976, Pepe Guerra in 1978. They first tried Buenos Aires, but after the coup in Argentina in 1976, Viglietti settled in France, Zitarrosa in Spain and later Mexico, as did Los Olimareños. All of them returned to the country in 1984.

Their different experiences of exile would reflect, in a certain way, their respective ideological and esthetic positions. Viglietti's early departure, international recognition and cosmopolitan avant-gardism allowed him to adapt relatively well and maintain an intense range of activities, while Los Olimareños and Zitarrosa, feeling disconnected from their audiences and unable to set foot in the musical markets of Spain and Mexico, experienced different degrees of nostalgia, melancholy, and even depression. All of them fell into a state of creative paralysis and a profound ideological, esthetic, and existential crisis, in spite of which they were able to produce some of the most beautiful and powerful songs they ever made, such as Los Olimareños' *"Adiós mi barrio"* ("Good Bye to My Neighborhood"), a slow tempo murga version of a traditionally Montevidean tango from 1930, and *"Ta' llorando"* ("Is Crying") a melancholic elegy for the distant country, both from 1978, which distributed clandestinely in Uruguay epitomized exile;[34] and Zitarrosa's *"Stéfanie"* (1977), *"Candombe del olvido"* ("Candombe of Oblivion") (1979), and the ultimate masterpiece, *"Guitarra negra"* ("Black Guitar") (1977), a long prose poem, structured in chapters or movements, as a concerto, with a rhythmically complex musical accompaniment of Zitarrosa's classic guitars, orchestra and chorus. Upon their return to Uruguay in 1984, they found an entirely different country, and a new generation of artists filling the needs of a different audience. They were received like idols, but idols from the past, and they realized that the musical cycle they started in the early 1960s had come to an end. Contemporary Uruguayan popular music had already matured. They could move on, stick to the past, or leave the stage for good, as Zitarrosa will do in 1989.

> Cómo haré para tomarte en mis adentros, guitarra. . . . Cómo haré para que sientas mi torpe amor, mis ganas de sonarte entera y mía. . . . Cómo se toca tu carne de aire, tu oloroso tacto, tu corazón sin hambre, tu silencio en el puente, tu cuerda quinta, tu bordón macho y oscuro, tus parientes cantores, tus tres almas, conversadoras como niñas. . . . Cómo se puede amarte sin dolor, sin apuro, sin testigos, sin manos que te ofendan. . . . Cómo traspasarte mis hombres y mujeres bien queridos, guitarra; mis amores ajenos, mi certeza de amarte como pocos. . . Cómo entregarte todos esos nombres y esa sangre, sin inundar tu corazón de sombras, de temblores y muerte, de ceniza, de soledad y rabia, de silencio, de lágrimas idiotas. . . .
>
> *"Guitarra negra"* (Alfredo Zitarrosa 1977, in Forlán and Migliónico [1994: 90–94]).[35]

NOTES

My special thanks to Coriún Aharonián, for his careful reading and precise commentaries on this text.

1. The original lyrics of this song can be found on the Web at: http://www.cancioneros.com/nc/13566/2/chiquillada-jose-carbajal.
2. "Uruguayan Popular Music is the label I prefer to designate this cultural movement. It is the most comprehensive because it encompasses all forms of expressions produced in the country for a popular public. I share Elbio Rodríguez Barilari's provision to write it in capital

letters, to establish a difference with popular music produced in Uruguay but lacking in representational quality" (Martins 1986: 14).

3. The original lyrics of this song can be found on the Web at: http://www.cancioneros. com/nc/13666/2/orejano-o-el-orejano-serafin-jose-garcia-braulio-lopez-jose-luis-guerra.

4. "Look my friend, don't try/to confuse me with your gibberish./I don't understand,/sorry, I'm an ignorant./But I can tell you/I don't care about the elections,/we poor people/only wear espadrilles:/nothing will change."

5. Three decades later, Braulio López, member of Los Olimareños, would also define his work as "popular song with folk roots" (Arapí 1995: 37), in coincidence with Coriún Aharonián (2007a: 51).

6. The original lyrics of this song can be found on the Web at: http://www.cancioneros. com/nc/8544/0/la-rastrojera-marcos-velasquez.

7. The original lyrics of this song can be found on the Web at: http://www.cancioneros. com/aa/43/0/canciones-de-daniel-viglietti.

8. The original lyrics of this song can be found on the Web at: http://www.cancioneros. com/nc/13635/2/la-sencillita-jose-carbajal.

9. Zitarrosa was, for several years, a radio announcer in the Argentine province of Cordoba.

10. "Don't forget the hometown/if you go to the city/the farther you walk/the more you will remember./Sure, certain things/are forgettable/but some things are just forgotten/and others just things."

11. In 2003, the Congress passed a law declaring "*A don José*" "Uruguayan popular and cultural hymn."

12. "Do you see that man with people around him,/around him, around him . . . /His countrymen call him,/my General . . . /His voice illuminates/ the darkness,/and even the rocks understand/where he is going."

13. "Get the bowlegged all together,/put their feet together,/and walk in search of the motherland,/everybody's motherland, the motherland Maciel,/this bowlegged motherland they will not twist/our feet with chains all together/we shall overcome."

14. See Figueredo's chapter in this collection for a thorough account of this topic.

15. "In my country, so much sadness,/penury and rancor./My father says that/another time will come from the bottom of time/and the sun will shine/over a people he dreams/tilling their land."

16. "I am the singer of these plains/where the wind never rests./I am Zenobio Rosas/on this side and the other side of the border."

17. The original lyrics of this song can be found on the Web at: http://www.cancioneros. com/nc/13535/2/a-mi-gente-jose-carbajal.

18. "-The singer who's scared of singing,/cannot be such a good rooster./-Listen to the tough guy,/and even less be an Uruguayan./-You had dealt the cards great!//-The singer's throat has to be/made of good wood./-Ah! And the one who's cut it/should keep the scissors . . ./-As if it were the heart of a friend."

19. "Yo he conocido cantores/que era un gusto el escuchar;/mas no quieren opinar/y se divierten cantando;/pero yo canto opinando,/que es mi modo de cantar." (Hernández 1977: 261). For further elaboration on "cantar opinando," see Trigo 2008.

20. "Sister,/they will come asking for me;/if I've been, where am I,/if you know your husband's whereabouts./You slowly raise your eyes,/look, keep silence, think:/Pablo should be around the world,/flying his flag,/a flag of wheat,/bread and wine,/raising it high./Along the way/he will show people how to be free."

21. "Mother milonga, I found you while singing/I don't know when/but I know that I heard you/while singing a tango to myself./Mother milonga, thughs and hores/got redemption/in your sentimental embrace/when your love hit their hearts."

22. "Look Mrs. Soledad,/think just for a moment,/Mrs. Soledad,/what do they mean/with that talk about freedom./You can die anytime,/it depends on your health,/but you don't want to know/how much a coffin costs."

23. Oriental, actual national appellative for Uruguayans which evokes the heroic "Patria Vieja," or Old Motherland, in the national imaginary.

24. "Today I feel I am worthless/as a singer and a poet./I never used formulas/to write my songs,/but not being more sane or insane/than any judicious man,/I acted irresponsibly more than once,/when admired by the audience/I saw in those applauses/the hands of so many people."

25. In an interview published in 1970 in the Buenos Aires' magazine *Siete Días*, Zitarrosa said, "We share with Argentina milongas, vidalas, huellas, gatos, cifras. [. . .] I work over these foundations in a completely heterodox way, taking from here and there whatever I find useful. Roots don't matter; what really matters is the Uruguayan style of singing, recognizable everywhere" (Pellegrino 2003: 119).

26. "To the Fuentes brothers and Rico Moreira,/Coco Brun and Charquero, Mr. Gregorio and Chilo,/ Riaño and Moriño,/Bruno the Black, Mrs. María and Capincho Fernández/and all those people who wanted a new road for their hometown,/but do not need a new road to my heart."

27. "When the acordeon sounds in Cachango's place/it becomes very serious,/he stinks wine even with his mouth shut/and keeps rolling his eyes.//The ballroom is crowded/and there are people waiting at the door./They charge you without compassion/with no right to protest."

28. "Give your hand to the Indian/you will feel better/and you will find your way/as I found it yesterday."

29. "I want to smash life,/how much I want to change it,/please help me comrade;/hurry up, help me,/because a drop is very little/but with another becomes a torrent."

30. "The American guitar/learned to sing in the struggle."

31. "There is no more a secret,/my song belongs to the wind,/I decided that is/all movement.//The blood of Túpac,/the blood of Amaru,/the blood that is screaming/free yourself, my brother."

32. "The girl with clear look,/and short hair,/the one in the papers;/I don't know her name, I don't know it./But I call her: Spring./But I see her: Comrade./But I say: Woman./But I shout: Guerrilla."

33. The original lyrics can be found on the Web at: http://letras.mus.br/alfredo-zitarrosa/966280/.

34. "So many voices and gazes so dear / are no longer on the cafes, in the barbeques / others wandering disconsolately around the world. / Oh, my little country, my is 'crying.'"

35. "How could I take you inside me, guitar. . . . How could I make you feel my clumsy love, my desire to make you sound whole and mine. . . . How to play your flesh of air, your scented skin, your heart with no hunger, your silence in the bridge, your fifth string, your dark and macho bass string, your family singers, your three souls, talkative like girls. . . . How to love you without pain, without rush, without witnesses, without offensive hands. . . . How to hand over to you my most dear men and women, guitar; my distant loves, my certainty that I love you like nobody does. . . . How to hand over to you all those names, all that blood, without flooding your heart with ghosts, with horror and death, with ashes, with solitude and anger, with silence, with stupid tears. . . ."

Chapter Five

Popular Music and the Avant-garde in Uruguay

The Second Canto Popular *Generation in the 1970s*

Camila Juárez:
Translated by Peggy Westwell and Pablo Vila

In the mid-1970s a group of young musicians, commonly referred to as the second *Canto Popular* generation, begins writing songs conversant in different ways with both contemporary avant-garde music and genres popular in the *Río de la Plata* cultural milieu. Active between 1977 and 1985, these musicians cast a critical eye on political and cultural reality and act en bloc to oppose the military regime officially established in 1973.

In the present chapter I will examine the historic-political conditions making possible, within the broad-based *Canto Popular* movement of the 1970s, the emergence of a compositional strategy that apply techniques from so-called serious music to the writing of popular songs. In order to understand how this experimental mindset developed in young musicians like Leo Maslíah, Jorge Lazaroff, and Luis Trochón (the latter two members of the Los que iban cantando group), the modernizing on the institutional level in the field of music that begins in the 1960s in Uruguay will be analyzed. A prominent figure in this process is the composer Coriún Aharonián, cofounder of a series of important institutions such as the *Cursos Latinoamericanos de Música Contemporánea* (1971–1989).

THE POLITIZATION AND LATIN AMERICANIZATION
OF THE PRACTICE OF MUSIC

The compositional and discursive practices discussed below are framed by an ideological current of thought in which aesthetic renovation and political radicalization converge and are mutually reinforcing. The concept of "epoch," defined by Claudia Gilman as "the field of the possibility of the existence of a system of beliefs and the circulation of discourses and interventions" (2003: 19), is useful in this regard, as she views the 1960s and 1970s as a "temporal bloc" (2003: 33) in the course of which Left Latin-American culture becomes politically radicalized.

During this period Latin America experiences singular ideological transformations against a background of anti-colonial struggles in the so-called Third World, the Cold War in the world at large, and the political, economic, and cultural domination of the United States on the American continent. Other relevant factors are the emergence and failure of development policies in Latin American countries, and the hegemony within the Left of the principles sustained by the Cuban revolution (Jameson 1997; Gilman 2003; Marchesi 2006). The transcendental event of the era is the Cuban revolution in 1959, which serves as inflection point: from then on Left Latin American thought will compete with other ideological systems for intellectual hegemony. [1] This is the beginning of a generalized process of politization in the arts; immediate precursors in the field of music can be found in figures like Atahualpa Yupanqui (Argentina) and Violeta Parra (Chile). The focal point of discussion during this period is the Cuban case, which extends revolutionary hopes to all spheres of society, crystalizing the network of leftist ideas. International events such as the first *"Encuentro de la Canción Protesta"* (First Encounter of Protest Song) in Cuba in 1967 prompt many musicians to join Marxist social movements. [2] This initial *Encuentro* plays a key role in legitimizing the Cuban formula for protest songs committed to Latin Americanist and anti-imperialist political suppositions. [3] A number of musical currents linking protest and political commitment are born; one example is the first Uruguayan *Canto Popular* or *"Canción Protesta,"* arising in conjunction with the Latin American phenomenon called *Nueva Canción.*

In Uruguay social unrest and repressive practices infringing on civil liberties are on the rise in the 1960s. This internal situation, in conjunction with continent-wide political agitation, leads to the formation of peaceful and armed leftist groups professing a Marxist ideology in solidarity with Cuban interests. Organized at this juncture, the *Movimiento de Liberación Nacional Tupamaro* (MLN-T) becomes active in the 1960s. Likewise, protests by students and workers are increasingly frequent, culminating in the death of the student Liber Arce in 1968 (Rey Tristán 2002: 190; Markarián 2012: 13). Amid continuing repressive measures, the closing of newspapers, and the banning of left-wing political groups that "had supported the OLAS (*Organización Latinoamericana de Solidaridad*) platform" (Nercesián 2010),[4] President-elect Jorge Pacheco Areco takes office in late 1967. Anti-democratic forces accumulate power, increasing social polarization and tension between the guerrilla movement and the State.[5]

With strong support from the musical field, different leftist groups unite to form the *Frente Amplio* (Broad Front) in February 1971, thus rupturing the traditional bi-party dynamic in Uruguay.[6] The new party competes as third party in the presidential elections held in November of the same year, in which *Partido Colorado* (Red Party) candidate Juan María Bordaberry emerging as winner. Social turmoil and repressive measures increase. An authoritarian "civil-military" regime headed by Bordaberry takes power in 1973 and proceeds to dissolve Parliament, ban labor union activity, censure the press, suspend civil liberties, occupy the national university, pursue and jail members of the opposition, and suspend all political activity by banning political parties and social organizations.

In line with Luis E. González, Gerardo Caetano and José Rilla (2005) indicate three stages in this dictatorial period: the "commissarial dictatorship" (1973–1976) during which the regime attempts to "clean house" without presenting a political project of its own; the "foundational rehearsal" (1977–1980) during which it fails to construct a new political order; and the "democratic transition" (1981–1985) that follows the defeat of the government-sponsored constitutional reform in the 1980 plebiscite.

During the first stage President Juan María Bordaberry declares a state of siege in a speech, transmitted nationally on radio and television, in which he affirms his "democratic vocation" and "rejection of all ideologies of Marxist origin" (Caetano and Rilla 2005: 43–44). Conditions generated by the dictatorial regime force leading figures of the *Canción Protesta* movement like Daniel Viglietti, Alfredo Zitarrosa, and the Los Olimareños duo into exile,[7] leaving a cultural vacuum that affects the new generation of musicians. According to Abril Trigo, from that point on new cultural production will depend on the exiles on the one hand, and on the other, on the "insiles"—the new generation living under censorship in Uruguay (Trigo 1991: 217).[8] Elections scheduled for 1976 bring another round of negotiations between the Armed Forces and Bordaberry, who is replaced in June by Alberto Demicheli, who then cancels elections.

The second stage begins when Aparicio Méndez takes power on September 1, 1976, and attempts to found a "new order" that, in the end, fails. The plan involves deactivating political parties and legitimating the military regime by popular vote. In this same year the United States changes its policy and suspends military aid to Uruguay in the name of human rights. In August 1977 Méndez proposes "sanitizing" party leadership and holding a plebiscite to change the constitution in favor of the "foundational" regime. It is during this period of intense internal political activity that the emergence of a second *Canto Popular* generation becomes apparent with the appearance of the Los que iban cantando (Those who were going along singing) group.[9] Popular music encounters performed in public venues around Montevideo grow exponentially in number, attracting large crowds that turn them into veritable "political acts" (Aharonián 2007a: 26). Between 1977 and 1982 the musical movement becomes increasingly significant, with the incipient social mobilization gathering force in the early 1980s adding impetus. On November 30, 1980, more than 85 percent of the Uruguayan population cast their ballot, 57.9 percent of them voting against the constitutional change proposed by the Armed Forces (Caetano and Rilla 2005: 75). The decisive defeat of the plebiscite, leaving no doubt about the rejection of the de facto regime, marks a turning point that will culminate in the return of democracy in early 1985.

Little by little political parties retake the initiative during the "transitional dictatorship" stage. In September 1981 Lieutenant General Gregorio Álvarez is named "president of the transition," the first military officer to occupy the highest office (González 1983: 65).[10] In 1983 people take to the streets once again, with the Left reappearing at a massive demonstration at the Obelisk on November 27. In March 1984 Liber Seregni is released from prison, further strengthening and advancing the political initiative of opposition forces. During this period many *Canción de Protesta* figures return from exile, among them Viglietti, who is received with a multitudinous concert September 1, 1984. Opening up the government requires negotiations with political parties, including the Left. This process leads to what is known as the Naval Club Pact between military leaders and political parties that ends in the peaceful return to democracy. In November 1984 Red Party candidate Julio María Sanguinetti wins the presidential election. In March 1985 Uruguay returns to civilian rule after twelve years of military domination.

THE SECOND *CANTO POPULAR* GENERATION AND THE 1977 BOOM

Given the extreme heterogeneity of *Canto Popular*, whose members belong to two different generations, treating it as a single category is problematic: Initiated in the 1960s, the musical movement not only occupies an extended temporal span; it also comprises a variety of compositional traditions involving multiple genres that run from rock and folk to experimental music.[11]

In order to distinguish Uruguayan national music production from Argentine folk music, the term *canto popular* is instituted in 1969 following the release of an LP with the same name by José "*El Sabalero*" Carbajal (Martins 1986: 15; Rodríguez Barilari 1999: 99). The *Canto Popular* movement comes to identify the generation of the "*canción de protesta*" in Uruguay

(Fabregat and Dabezies 1983: 12–13; Donas and Milstein 2003: 18) that uses traditional folk forms of expression; representative figures include Daniel Viglietti, Alfredo Zitarrosa, José Luis Guerra and Braulio López (of the Los Olimareños duo), José Carbajal, and Héctor Numa Moraes, among others. In the Latin American context of the 1960s, the movement is categorized as part of the *Nueva Canción*, [12] a phenomenon seeking to revitalize national popular musical expressions exhibiting a commitment to social and political change (Yépez 2000–2001: 1076). This first *Canto Popular* generation is active in Uruguay until the military coup in 1973 drives the musicians into exile.

The next generation of musicians emerges in a country sunk in silence, which it breaks in 1977, inscribing its own identity on the movement. Under a full-fledged dictatorship, conditions for producing music have changed. The second *Canto Popular* generation is obliged to deal with both external and "self-censorship" (Maslíah 1987: 116), while at the same time functioning as a unified bloc in opposition to the military regime. This particular juncture brings together practitioners of different genres that include "juvenile sectors of the avant-garde" whose parameters of composition make possible experimentation from an "irreverent" perspective (Sosnowski 1987: 17). Examples of this current can be found in the compositions of Jorge Lazaroff, Luis Trochón, and especially, Leo Maslíah, who wrote songs "designed to do violence to consecrated aesthetic norms" (Trigo 1989: 106).

Consequently, one of the features of the new *Canto Popular* is generic heterogeneity. In the first book on the movement, titled *Aquí se canta: Canto popular 1977-1980,* Eduardo Darnauchans systematizes the differences:

> In the second half of the 1970s, an extremely wide gamut of formulations and proposals come together under the denomination "*canto popular*" that go from the least-orthodox survivors of the now-defunct national rock to the most traditional canons of singers linked to folk music, and including as well "*tangueces*"[tango-like music expressions], the Latin Americanist vein, and insertions of elements from the contemporary avant-garde into popular music (quoted in Capagorry and Rodríguez Barilari, 1980: 77)

However, another factor is the awareness of being part of a much broader movement opposing the dictatorship, which becomes evident in the many shows and "monster" concerts given from 1978 on, in which 1970s musicians of varied aesthetic allegiances share the same stage. [13] Indeed, Leo Maslíah indicates that he considers himself part of the "*nuevo canto popular,*" although with certain qualifications. For him the movement is a phenomenon that functions "as an alternative scenario in the absence of a free press" (quoted in Godoy 1985: 24), and constitutes a movement "only by virtue of the place it socially occupied, by the form it took in order to reach the public, by its relationship with the mass media. Taken together, this shapes a similar panorama that creates the image of a movement" (quoted in Godoy 1985: 23).

The second *Canto Popular* generation appears in 1977, considered the "year of resurgence" (Capagorry and Rodríguez Barilari 1980: 125), with appearances by groups like Los que iban cantando and musicians such as Leo Maslíah who, a year later, performs, along with Juan Peyrou and Luis Trochón, in the *Cinemateca Uruguaya*. The most important event of the year is the show given by Los que iban cantando at the *Café Concert Shakespeare & Co.* in Montevideo. The group, made up of Jorge Bonaldi, Jorge Lazaroff, Luis Trochón, Carlos da Silveira, and Jorge Galemire, later replaced by Jorge Di Pólito, enjoys great success in 1977: with two shows—"*Los que iban cantando*" and "*Los que iban cantando II*"—it goes from performing in a small locale to giving three performance a week in Auditorium 2 of the *Teatro Circular* in downtown Montevideo and cutting its first LP at the end of the year. This enthusiastic public response and the originality of the group, whose singular repertoire transcends without renouncing folk music, turn Los que iban cantando into the vanguard of the new popular musical movement. The group popularizes a particular aesthetic and political project featuring highly innovative music based on the "interaction of avant-garde elements and a strong Latin American identity" (Aharonián 2007a: 26). Moreover, the group's first recording becomes the top-selling LP that same year (Martins 1986: 37).

In addition to the Los que iban cantando phenomenon in 1977, *Canto Popular* as musical movement greatly expands its influence through a series of recurrent music events like the *Ciclo de música popular* in the *Alianza Francesa* and the folk song series *Canto Nuestro 1 & 2* in *La Cava del Virrey,* as well as similar shows in the Millington Drake auditorium, the *Café Concert Shakespeare & Co.,* and "in the YMCA, where a series of concerts called '*Canto para que estés*' (I sing so you will be here) is given in both the theater and the auditorium on the first floor" (Rodríguez Barilari 1977, December 30: 29).

In the limited press coverage given popular music in Uruguay at the time, the two predominant tendencies of the multi-generic *Canto Popular* movement are named: folk music and the urban popular song. Important figures from the former current include Carlos and Washington Benavides, Santiago Chalar, Carlos María Fossati, Mario Carrero, Juan Peyrou, Omar Romano, the humorist Carlos Cresci, and the Los Eduardos duo (Eduardo Lagos and Eduardo Larbanois), Los Zucará (Humberto Piñeiro and Julio González) and Los Hacheros (Anibal López and Rómulo Messones), among others. The urban tradition, to which Los que iban cantando belongs, is characterized by "the study and erudition provided by a university education that demands more of them and is more creative" (Segura 1977). In another article evaluating the musical scene in 1977, journalist Elbio Rodríguez Barilari points to the musical revitalization that has taken place, adding that record companies are offering new releases of "national music": Sondor specializes in folk music; dedicated to urban music, Ayuí released "the two best popular LPs"— *Candombe del 31* by Jaime Roos and *Los que iban cantando*; RCA released the Opa trio's first LP; Clave IEMSA rereleased *Musicasión 4-1/2* and launched the one and only LP recorded by El Kinto, prominent Uruguayan rock groups; Orfeo released *Universo*, and EDISA, *Contraviento* in 1978 on a new label[14] (Rodríguez Barilari 1977, 30: 29).

These early texts on *Canto Popular* written in the 1970s confirm the movement's dual approach: that led by the poet Washington Benavides from the county of Tacuarembó, and that of "*Núcleo Música Nueva*" (Fabregat and Dabezies 1983: 10) inspired by Coriún Aharonián. In other words, there is one current close to folk music with an emphasis on lyrics, and another defined by the use of experimental elements from avant-garde music.[15] With regard to the later, Hugo López Chirico states,

> The young, aesthetically and politically rebellious generation gathered around the *Núcleo Música Nueva de Montevideo* that, since 1966, played a fundamental role in introducing avant-garde tendencies into Uruguayan music. Their efforts were reinforced by the creation of the *Sociedad Uruguaya de Música Contemporánea* (1967), and the *Cursos Latinoamericanos de Música Contemporánea*. The driving force behind these innovations was Héctor Tosar, Coriún Aharonián, and Conrado Silva (López Chirico 2002: 609).

Young musicians like Fernando Cabrera, Carlos da Silveira, Leo Maslíah, and Elbio Rodríguez Barilari are active in the *Núcleo Música Nueva*, which is made up of avant-garde composers, many of whom combine this experience with popular music. This gives rise to popular songs with non-directional discourses in which the sense of lineal time vanishes, making way for reiterative—not mechanical—progressions (Aharonián 1993: 82); in addition to silences, other elements are austerity in the use of resources and "technical means," and the breaking down of the dichotomy between "art" and "popular" music (Aharonián 1993: 84; 2000: 4).

URUGUAYAN MUSIC: BETWEEN POPULAR SONGS AND THE AVANT-GARDE

The musical field is strongly incentivized in Uruguay in the 1960s, which is a key factor for understanding the subsequent interface between avant-garde and popular music. The set of new institutions that come into being at the time—*Núcleo Música Nueva, Sociedad Uruguaya de Música Contemporánea, Núcleo de Educación Musical, Editorial Tacuabé* and the *Cursos Latinoamericanos de Música Contemporánea*—become a veritable laboratory where the second *Canto Popular* generation hones its practice of music.

One of the criteria incorporated by young songwriters in the 1970s is the importance of a musical education for producing works with a "high level of creativity" (Aharonián 2007a: 26). This principle is inherited from the first *Canto Popular* generation born in the 1940s, some of whose members had classical music training. Two outstanding examples are Coriún Aharonián and Daniel Viglietti. The latter abandons a promising career as a classical guitarist in order to dedicate himself full time to writing protest music. In 1970 he and other musicians found the *Núcleo de Educación Musical* (NE-MUS), an "anti-conservatory" dedicated to the integral teaching of popular music (Ríos 1995: 136). Even during the dictatorship many new generation members receive training in NEMUS, which constitutes an important legacy of the first *Canto Popular* generation.[16] While firmly established in the field of avant-garde music, Coriún Aharonián maintains close contact with popular music, as evidenced by his seminars and writing, as well as his role in training young Uruguayan musicians. For both Viglietti and Aharonián the innovative use of experimental forms and techniques for raising awareness is a critical factor in writing songs with a political message (Milstein 2007: 55).

By making explicit the social and political role played by music, the first *"Encuentro de la Canción Protesta"* in Cuba in 1967 proves a defining moment in the development of the "Protest Song" movement. In the declaration that finalized the *Encuentro*, the "quality" of a song is also stressed, thus validating the value of musical training and innovative procedures:

> Protest song workers must be aware that, due to its particular nature, a song possesses enormous potential for communicating with the masses because it can break down barriers that, like illiteracy, make dialogue difficult between artists and the people. [. . .] Protest song workers have the duty of enhancing their tools of trade, given that the search for artistic excellence is in itself a revolutionary attitude ("Resolución final del Encuentro de la Canción Protesta" 1967: 143–144).

Following the *Encuentro* in Cuba, the *"Centro de la Canción Protesta"* is founded in Montevideo as a multi-disciplinary meeting place for poets, musicians, composers, educators, and so on. The fluidity of the interchange between popular and avant-garde music and politics in Uruguay during this period is noteworthy. In the words of Coriún Aharonián,

> There was a close, natural relationship among people from different areas of music. For example, in *Núcleo Música Nueva*, which is a group of avant-garde art musicians, one of the four founders is Daniel Viglietti. [. . .] There was also a certain complicity with other musicians like Los Olimareños, with whom we were very friendly. There was a political purpose in popular music that was

very important in Uruguay. There are meetings; we are seeking the same ends. For example, after the *"Encuentro de la Canción Protesta"* in Havana in 1967, the *Centro de la Canción Protesta* is founded in Montevideo, which had to change its name because of the repression. So the "CCP" became the *Centro de la Canción Popular*. My interests there were cultural and political. There were poets; Idea Vilariño and Juan Capagorry were there. There were *payadores* [folk musicians who improvise questions and answers in rhyme to guitar accompaniment], rockers, balladeers, folk singers. Nobody was in conflict with anybody, and we had discussions and held assemblies. In 1969 I gave a course called "What is mesomusic?" for popular musicians where I presented Vega's theory. It was more natural at that time for there to be horizontal links (Aharonián, interview with the author, May 4, 2008).

Both composer and musicologist, Aharonián studied under renown professors like Héctor Tosar and Lauro Ayestarán. Consequently, early on he becomes familiar with the category of "mesomusic" that, as outlined in 1965 by the Argentine musicologist Carlos Vega,[17] traces the limits of popular music, examining it from a Latin American perspective.[18] Vega proposes a tripartite system that differentiates popular or "mesomusic" from "superior music" on the one hand, and folk music on the other. Mesomusic is defined as "the set of creations whose function is to entertain (songs with or without lyrics), to accompany ballroom dancing, to be performed at shows, ceremonies, acts, classes, games, and so on, adopted or accepted by listeners in countries sharing modern conceptions of culture" (Vega 1979: 5).

For Aharonián the social function of "mesomusic" in Latin America is to provide "rootedness," a conceptualization that allows musical educators to "intelligently combat the pernicious aspects of the 'market'" (Aharonián 2004: 135) and exercise a direct influence on their particular environment. Starting in the mid-1970s, he himself, along with Graciela Paraskevaídis, offers private courses and seminars on contemporary avant-garde music that educate an entire generation of musicians.

Founding member of many of the new pre-dictatorship musical institutions existing to this day, Coriún Aharonián is instrumental in bringing postwar avant-garde music to Uruguay (Alencar Pinto 2003: 6). His trajectory begins when, while studying under Héctor Tosar, he and inquisitive fellow-students like Daniel Viglietti, Conrado Silva, and Ariel Martínez found the *Núcleo Música Nueva de Montevideo* in 1966[19] in order to familiarize Uruguayans with experimental concert music from abroad. In 1967 the *Sociedad Uruguaya de Música Contemporánea* (SUMC), the Uruguayan branch of the *Sociedad Internacional de Música Contemporánea (*SIMC) is born.[20]

In 1971 *Ediciones Tacuabé* and the *Cursos Latinoamericanos de Música Contemporánea*, two key institutions in developing and disseminating both avant-garde and *Canto Popular* musical production, are created. Founded by Viglietti and Aharonián, among others,[21] the former is a cooperative bringing under a single umbrella the *Tacuabé, Ayuí, Palma,* and *Ombú* record labels (Aharonián, 2007a: 30).[22] *Tacuabé* is dedicated exclusively to concert and *Ayuí* to popular music. From 1974 on the latter's catalogue includes recordings by many of the young musicians of the 1970s, including Leo Maslíah and Los que iban cantando (Aharonián 2002).

However, the essential institution for understanding the role of experimentation in popular music in the period under study is the *Cursos Latinoamericanos de Música Contemporánea* (CLAMC) presented once a year from 1971 to 1989. Co-founded by Coriún Aharonián and Héctor Tosar, the courses are a dual legacy from the *Centro Latinoamericano de Altos Estudios Musicales* (CLAEM) of the *Instituto Di Tella* in Buenos Aires on the one hand, and on the other, from European summer courses like the famous Darmstadt International Summer Course for New Music. Considered the incarnation of the international post-war musical vanguard in Latin America, CLAEM introduced technical innovations that modernized the field of music in the Río de la Plata area in particular, and in Latin American in general (Novoa 2007: 75–76) before closing its doors in 1971. The composers participating in CLAEM, which included Graciela Parakevaídis and Coriún Aharonián,[23] constitute the musical vanguard in Latin America from that point on (King 1985: 195).

CLAMC becomes a reality through the efforts of many composers and educators, including Héctor Tosar, Conrado Silva, Miguel Marozzi, and María Teresa Sande (Uruguay); Emilio Mendoza (Venezuela); José Maria Neves (Brazil), and Graciela Paraskevaídis (Argentina-Uruguay). The "team" in charge each year works out everything from organizational structure and administrative details to curriculum, course guidelines, and outside lecturers and teachers. Set up to be self-financing, intensive, and itinerant, CLAMC gives fifteen annual sets of courses during its seventeen years in existence: there are six in Brazil (São João del Rei, Itapira, Uberlandia, Tatuí, and Mendes); five in Uruguay (Cerro del Toro); two in Argentina (Buenos Aires); one in the Dominican Republic (Santiago de los Caballeros), and one in Venezuela (San Cristóbal). Two periods can be distinguished corresponding to who the president is and where the event takes place, the first under Héctor Tosar—1971–1977, and the second under José Maria Neves—1978–1989.[24] Comprising of ten to fifteen, ten-hour days, the courses are intensive and organized by specialties that include composition, interpretation and research, musicology, and teacher training. Students freely choose from offerings in the areas corresponding to their particular field of interest.

Course objectives are clear, reflecting the constellation of political ideas prevailing in the 1960s and 1970s, and catalogues evidence the importance given to compositional practice and musical training for young musicians. In a text closing the CLAMC cycle in 1988, Aharonián said, "The idea at the time was to invent or reinvent or redirect a structure that would be Latin

American; that gave the widest possible scope to music (art, popular, what was needed at the time); that provided training [. . .] at the highest 'international' level, and that didn't depend on any central or focal point of power" (Aharonián 2004: 142).

The institutional aim of CLAMC is to neutralize the isolation and lack of up-to-date technical training in order to shape critically minded generations in search of their Latin American identity. As a tool for defining what is Latin American, one premise permeating the fifteen courses is the need to better know "the present and its diverse tendencies in order to discuss and question them" (Aharonián 2004: 30). Consequently, the ultimate objective for composers is to produce authentic Latin American music within the extended occidental tradition, employing an "anthropophagic" approach.

Participating in this undertaking are salient intellectuals from Latin America and the world at large such as Luigi Nono,[25] Louis Andriessen, Helmut Lachenmann, Michel Philippot, Dieter Schnebel, Gordon Mumma, Christian Clozier, Julio Estrada, Héctor Tosar, Hans-Joachim Koellreutter, Oscar Bazán, Mariano Etkin, Gerardo Gandini, Eduardo Bértola, Graciela Paraskevaídis, Mesías Maiguashca, among many others. The fifteen CLAMC editions are conducted by around two hundred dedicated teachers and lecturers from all over Latin America, the United States, Canada, and Europe, and in some cases from Asia and Africa as well (Aharonián 2004: 143). The staff of teachers and lecturers comprises not only composers, many from the Di Tella generation, but also educators like Violeta Hemsy de Gainza, instrumentalists like Abel Carlevaro, writers like Eduardo Galeano and Noé Jitrik, philosophers like Héctor Massa, painters like Luis Felipe Noé, film directors like Leopoldo Torre Nilsson, and musicologists like Philip Tagg, Jorge Novati, and Irma Ruiz.

The broad scope of the subject matter covered in the *Cursos Latinoamericanos de Música Contemporánea* responds to the overriding objective of providing integral training to new generation of musicians, with the prime focus on Latin American reality. Course catalogues include classes on "Possibilities and perspectives of musicians in Latin America" (Etkin); "New Latin American music" (Aharonián, Asuar, Silva); "Culture and reality in Latin America" and "Latin America today" (Galeano), "The evolution of the electro-acoustic laboratory and its potential for Latin America" (von Reichenbach), "Problems in musical creation in Latin America" (Orellana); "Aspects of contemporary Latin American art music" (Paraskevaídis, Gómez, Duque, Cáceres, Rodríguez); "Popular art in América" (Puppo); "Popularizing works of music: a project for Latin America" (Milanesi), among others. Furthermore, special sessions are devoted to showing relevant films like "*La hora de los hornos*" (1968, Solanas and Getino); "*Fin de fiesta*" (1960, with music composed by Juan Carlos Paz), and "*Los siete locos*" (1973, directed by Torre Nilsson, with music composed by Mariano

Etkin). As evidenced above, students are trained in the latest techniques, and the courses "were also a forum for intense discussion [. . .] on what to do in Latin America" (Aharonián 2004: 143).

The two most relevant topics covered by CLAMC are the latest developments in electro-acoustic music,[26] and popular music—in which it can be verified the application of new techniques and technologies to popular song forms.

Training in post-war avant-garde music is not the only "contemporary" aspect of CLAMC however; another is the wide variety of genres and styles covered in seminars, discussions groups, and symposiums. Concerts and recitals of experimental music that include electro-acoustic, dodecaphonic, and aleatoric compositions figure in course catalogues, along with performances of prototypical musical and dramatic works of the twentieth century. Traditional types of folk and urban music (the latter in the form of tango and popular songs of different sorts), and so on, are also represented. Films are shown; dance and dramatic numbers are staged; mimes perform, and musical scores, texts, photos and paintings are exhibited. Thus, "It is not a question of so-called 'serious music,' but rather what occurred in these courses was the 'serious study of music' because the decision was taken—another prejudice vanquished—to integrate what is termed popular music into the program, and likewise indigenous and folk music" (Cáceres 1989: 47).

From its inception CLAMC is designed to encourage contact with different kinds of music; special emphasis is placed on establishing a dialogue between popular and experimental music. Examples of seminars and workshops led by Aharonián and talks he gives over the years on popular music are "Mesomusic" (1971, 1974), "The 'serious' composer and the mesomusical area in Latin America" (1972), "Approaches to a mesomusical analysis" (1976), "Proposals for a mesomusical analysis" (1978), "Kinds of music" (1982), "Mesomusical composition and Introduction to serious composition" (1985), and "Mesomusic, cultural identity and power" (1985), and "Popular composition" (1989).[27]

Coriún Aharonián's significant contribution to reflection on and the evolution of popular music in CLAMC is complemented by the efforts of the new generation of Uruguayan musicians attending first as students, and later as teachers.[28] This is the same generation that, as members of the *Canto Popular* movement, bursts on the scene in 1977 when the Los que iban cantando group begins performing in Montevideo. Members Carlos da Silveira and Luis Trochón participate in the fifth edition of CLAMC (1976) in Buenos Aires; Jorge Lazaroff and Luis Trochón attend the sixth (1977) after which the group is formally organized. Trochón remembers his first visit to the CLAMC:

[U]ntil I discover by chance a brochure (that obviously affected my life in all regards) about—if I remember rightly—the fifth *Curso Latinoamericano de Música Contemporánea* (1976) that took place at the Goethe Institute in Buenos Aires. It became evident that, when I read the words "contemporary music," I was very wrong about what they meant—I thought it would be popular music or rock or something like that. [. . .] So [. . .] the first day I said "What have I gotten into?" People with transfigured faces were listening to pieces in absolute silence and finding what it means to be a human being in the sounds . . . but I loved it, I got very enthusiastic. And it was there I got to know Coriún [Aharonián] (Trochón, interview with the author, June 26, 2009).

The first presentation of popular songs written by Uruguayan students takes place on January 6, 1977, during the sixth CLAMC. Called "Mesomusic: Student recital," it consists of compositions by Jorge Lazaroff and Luis Trochón, with the Venezuelan Delfín Pérez also performing. Da Silveira notes,

Then we went to the CLAMC in Buenos Aires in 1977, and there were Trochón and *el Choncho* (Jorge Lazaroff), who gave a recital at the Goethe at the end of the course. [. . .] When they returned to Montevideo, this whole scene (the forming of the Los que iban cantando group and what followed), already half-planned, was put into motion. Carlos Martins was behind it (Da Silveira, interview with the author July 2, 2009).[29]

In the eighth CLAMC (1979) Fernando Cabrera, Rubén Olivera, María Susana Celentano, Leo Maslíah, and Bernardo Aguerre present their "mesomusical pieces" on January 14, 1979, in a recital by CLAMC students for the community of São João del Rei as an example of what is being done in the courses. Some of them present art music pieces,[30] making clear the interrelation of the two traditions.

Starting in 1979, the young generation of Uruguayan musicians begins teaching in CLAMC. The first to go from student to teacher is Carlos da Silveira, who conducts workshops on electro-acoustic techniques, in addition to teaching popular music composition (1979, 1980, and 1986).[31] Active in both musical universes, he also symbolizes the relationship between popular and avant-garde music embodied by CLAMC in his workshop on electro-acoustic techniques. In 1979 there are two student recitals: "Young musicians from Uruguay and 'serious' music,"[32] and "Young Uruguayan musicians and mesomusic." On the program in the latter recital are pieces by Walter Venencio, Benjamín Medina, Danielda Rosa, Fernando Cabrera, and Jorge Lazaroff. Also presented was a number composed this same year and destined shortly to acquire added significance: "*A redoblar*" by Mauricio Ubal and Rubén Olivera comes to be considered the "hymn of resistance to the dictatorship" (Trigo 1991: 220; Aharonián 2009: 80) in Uruguay and announces the "no" vote in the 1980 plebiscite (Aharonián 2003: n.p.).[33]

In the *Cursos Latinoamericanos de Música Contemporánea* the link between music and politics is vital, indicating the close relationship binding
musical structure to a particular ideological position. Mauricio Ubal points
out that "a good song in the fullest sense was the best political instrument
that we could provide at that time" (López 2003: 136). In the 1970s a new
generation of songwriters is producing an experimental body of work in
technical and idiolectical terms, while at the same time, as committed leftists
their goal is to reach a broad audience. In this regard CLAMC also makes
participants aware that, by taking technical "risks" in music, they actively
manifest the need for social change, thus posing the question in aesthetic and
revolutionary terms. As indicated by Adolfo Sánchez Vázquez, "the political
problems that the artist poses have to be resolved artistically" (quoted on
Olivera 1986: 4),[34] giving voice to the subject of what the social implications
of art are. These musicians leave no doubt that it is "popular music" that has
the potential to bring new elements to the attention of the public at large,
making it possible to send a "message" that is both political and aesthetic.
And this message can be communicated in the new musical language of
twentieth century avant-garde music, bringing about the abolition of hierarchical distinctions between one kind of music and another (Nono 1985: 25
and Olivera 1986: 5).[35]

During the tenth edition of CLAMC (1981) a recital of "[t]he new popular
Uruguayan song" is given,[36] and the next year Rubén Olivera leads a seminar-workshop on "Musical education for adults through popular music."[37] In
1984 Luis Trochón gives seminars on "The creator in the area of the popular
song" and "The educator in the field of the popular song," while Jorge
Lazaroff gives a seminar titled *"Olla podrida"* (literally rotten pot, the name
of a popular stew): an analytic view of mesomusic." Worthy of note in this
CLAMC edition is the participation of the well-known musicologist Philip
Tagg, who holds seminars on "Mesomusical analysis" and "Proposals for an
analysis of popular music."[38] And mention should also be made of the
"Teachers' recitals" in which Luis Trochón and Jorge Lazaroff perform their
compositions for guitar and voice,[39] as well as the "Mesomusic seminar
students' recital" given by Lazaroff, Tagg, and Trochón.

In 1986 the largest number of second generation *Canto Popular* members
serve as teachers in CLAMC, which once again takes place in Cerro del
Toro, Uruguay. The list of educators includes Carlos da Silveira; Luis
Trochón; Rubén Olivera, who gives a seminar called "The 'political
song'";[40] Elbio Rodríguez Barilari, and Jaime Roos. In the last CLAMC
(1989), Guilherme de Alencar Pinto, Elbio Rodríguez Barilari, and Tato
Taborda give a seminar on "Creative problems in contemporary popular
music in Brazil and Uruguay."

While not represented until the ninth edition of CLAMC, where Carlos da
Silveira figures as teacher, second *Canto Popular* generation members start

performing their own songs in 1977. This confirms the hypothesis according to which 1977 is the key year in which these musicians begin to influence the field of popular music in Uruguay. As has been shown above, they have in common the experience and training received in CLAMC, as well as private lessons with Coriún Aharonián and Graciela Paraskevaídis in Montevideo.

CONCLUSION

The aim of this chapter has been to study the figures and institutions instrumental in shaping a generation of young Uruguayan musicians whose distinguishing compositional feature is bridging the gap between popular and twentieth-century avant-garde music. This type of musical production blurs the boundary line between so-called serious music—academic or concert—on the one hand, and popular music on the other, synthesizing the needs of an epoch in both, a multi-disciplinary aesthetic program in the field of music, and a Latin American–oriented political program aspiring to bring about social and economic change.

While this generation's aesthetic program promotes the interpenetration of genres by employing avant-garde techniques to break down the traditional limits of the popular song, the political program responds to a specific moment in time. The historical conditions making possible this sort of approximation between popular song and avant-garde music are registered in the context of political coercion experienced in Uruguay beginning in the late 1960s. The inclusion of a multiplicity of compositional strategies, a distinguishing feature of the Uruguayan *Canto Popular* in the 1970s, is indicative of a phenomenon defined less by genre boundaries than by the need for identification and agglutination to defend against a hegemonically determined social and political juncture.

It is in this sense that the second *Canto Popular* generation participates in the *Cursos Latinoamericanos de Música Contemporánea* (1971–1989), formalizing their relationship with a musical repertoire and aesthetic canons that have grown out of a program that is political as well. The canon from the 15 CLAMC editions list works whose innovative handling of musical techniques and forms, and commitment to the social movements sweeping the continent since the 1960s, is relevant in this regard. One aim of this chapter has been to delimit the canons of the Latin American music of this period that combines the post-war avant-garde tradition and popular music. And the ultimate objective has been to bring to light how music and politics converge in the *Canto Popular* movement of the 1970s.

DOCUMENTS

Programs CLAMC 1971–1986.

INTERVIEWS

Coriún Aharonián interviewed May 4, 2008, in Buenos Aires, Argentina.
Luis Trochón interviewed July 26, 2009, in Montevideo, Uruguay.
Carlos da Silveira interviewed July 2, 2009, in Montevideo, Uruguay.

NOTES

I want to thank Coriún Aharonián, Jorge Bonaldi (who allowed me to consult his copious archive), Carlos da Silveira, Luis Trochón, Leo Maslíah, Rubén Olivera, and Anna Veltfort for their generous contribution to the research for this chapter.

    1. For Frederic Jameson, "[i]t doesn't seem particularly problematic to mark the beginning of what would be called the 1960s in the Third World" (1997: 17), and he takes the Cuban Revolution as "the palpable demonstration that the revolution was not merely a historical concept or museum piece, but rather real and feasible" (23). To this list can also be added the African decolonization movement, the Algerian war, "the 'new black politics' and the civil rights movements that should be dated [. . .] in February 1960" (18).

    2. It should be pointed out that Peronism makes Argentina a special case.

    3. In this regard Aldo Marchesi states that the concept of imperialism is understood by means of the metaphor of a "history of looting," which lends itself to the idea of revolution as the only alternative for ending foreign domination and neutralizing possible internal conflicts on the continent. The author also points out that the relationship between political commitment and knowledge in the late 1960s "prevailed in an important cross-section of intellectuals in the Southern Cone" (2006: 2). Claudia Gilman adds that the concept of "commitment" was "one of the main aspects of the art of living the era" (Gilman 2003: 148–149).

    4. The *Organización Latinoamericana de Solidaridad* (OLAS) conference was held in Cuba July 31–August 10, 1967. In the opening speech, which centered on Latin America as revolutionary bloc of solidarity, two fundamental directives are established: armed revolution and Cuba as the driving force for anti-imperialist revolution in Latin America (Gilman 2003: 117). In an interview about his first visit to Cuba in 1967, Daniel Viglietti says "that it is also impressive, especially because of what is going on at that particular time, that it is tremendously strong; this is when Che has left Cuba, it's when the OLAS conference is taking place, and it is the moment of greatest strength of the guerrilla position in the tactic of the campesino [peasant] revolutionary. [. . .] In that year [1968] that whole Latin American perspective of the struggle awaiting us and how to carry it out is beginning to be worked out within its own sphere" (Benedetti 2007: 82).

    5. According to Gerardo Caetano and José Rilla, in September 1971 the military is charged by decree with conducting an "anti-subversive war" (Caetano and Rilla 2005: 42). Likewise, Clara Aldrighi states that, stimulated by United States policy, the politization of the Armed Forces dates from the large political demonstrations in 1968, "three years before the guerrilla offensive politically justified the institutional about-turn in 1971 from defense against external enemies [. . .] to defense against internal ones" (Aldrighi 2004: 36-37).

    6. The Broad Front is a coalition of left-wing parties that includes the Communist, Socialist, and Christian Democratic parties, as well as fractions of the traditional Red and White parties. Clara Aldrighi marks 1972 as a turning point when the U.S. government realizes the strength of the Broad Front and its potential to win the presidency in 1976: "That is why the primary political objective of the United States in Uruguay became impeding the election of a leftist coalition government" (Aldrighi 2004: 35).

7. For more information see Viglietti 1985.

8. Trigo adds that the term "insile" referring to "in-country exile" is a neologism created by Diego Pérez Pintos that "today is incorporated into the lexicon of the social sciences" (Trigo 1989: 114).

9. When this chapter was already on production a very important book about this group was published: Alencar Pinto 2013.

10. Unlike other cases such as Chile and Argentina, the visible head of government in Uruguay is a civilian from June 1973 to August 1981.

11. Terminology becomes problematized with the confirmation that, in addition to *canto popular*, there also exists a wide variety of other terms like "*canción popular*," "*canto*," "*nueva canción uruguaya*," "*nueva canción rioplatense*," "*the second canto popular*," the "*resurgence*" or "*rebirth*" of the *canto popular*, the "*Nuevo canto popular*," and so on, all used by authors that include Juan Capagorry and Elbio Rodríguez Barilari (1980); Elbio Rodríguez Barilari (1999); Aquiles Fabregat and Antonio Dabezies (1983); Carlos Alberto Martins (1986); Rubén Castillo (1983); María Figueredo (1999a); and Ernesto Donas and Denise Milstein (2003), among others.

12. Jane Tumas-Serna gives a panoramic continent-wide view of the "*Nueva Canción*" movement focused specifically on Chile, Brazil, Cuba, and the Latino communities in the United States (Tumas-Serna 1992: 143).

13. The first of these massive concerts takes place in the gymnasium of the *Colegio San Juan Bautista de Montevideo*, organized by agronomy students in early 1978 (Martins 1986: 40).

14. According to Coriún Aharonián, *Musicasión 4-1/2* was released by De la Planta in 1971. He also states that the first recording by *Contraviento* in 1978 "was released on the Phillips label, which belonged to EDISA (actually, it was one of the labels used by the *Palacio de la Música*, which, in turn, belonged to the Orfeo label)." Personal communication with the author, December 12, 2012.

15. In this sense Washington Benavides (1985: 16) underlines the importance of lyrics in songs he terms "text songs," and postulates his affiliation with French ballad singers (Georges Brassens, Jacques Brel), and the Catalonian and Spanish *nueva canción* (Serrat), among others.

16. Jorge Bonaldi, a young musician belonging to the Los que iban cantando group, says that Viglietti is "the only creator who remained attentive—and permeable—to the evolution of the next generation of singers, and with whom influences went both ways" (Bonaldi 2001: 48).

17. Carlos Vega presents his essay "Mesomusic: an essay on everybody's music" in 1965 at the Second Inter-American Musicology Conference in Bloomington, Indiana, in the United States. In Aharonián's view, "publishing a work on this subject was a brave move on the part of the official organ of the United States Society for Ethnomusicology" (Aharonián 2007b: 19). See also Aharonián 1997.

18. This is also confirmed by Richard Middleton, who, in his systemization of the concept of "popular music," affirms the existence of different ways of defining it in other languages and cultures. The point is illustrated precisely by "the trichotomy art/folk/mesomusic set down by the ethnomusicologist Carlos Vega" (Middleton 1990: 33).

19. The *Núcleo Música Nueva de Montevideo* "will become formalized as institution later on, in early 1968, with the incorporation of innumerable composers, performers, and just plain audiophiles" (Aharonián 1991: 54).

20. SUMC becomes affiliated with the International Society of Contemporary Music in 1974. Under the entry "Coriún Aharonián," Mary Ríos states that one of the positions Aharonián held in the institution was "co-founder (1967) and secretary general (1967–1982, 1985–1986)" (Ríos 1995: 36).

21. Founders were Daniel Viglietti, José Luis (Pepe) Guerra and Braulio López (members of the Los Olimareños duo), and Coriún Aharonián. They were later joined by María Teresa Sande, Edgardo Bello, and the actors Myriam Dibarboure and Dahd Sfeir (Aharonián 2002).

22. *Ediciones Tacuabé* collaborators include many popular musicians like Rubén Olivera, Jorge Bonaldi, Luis Trochón, Jorge Galemire, Francisco Rey, Guilherme Alencar Pinto, and Carlos da Silveira (an art music composer as well). Dedicated to art music are Fernando Condon and Graciela Paraskevaídis, together with Juan Graña, Mirtha Ducret, and Elena Sil-

veira. For a panoramic view of the historical development of discography in Uruguay, see Aharonián 2002.

23. The Argentine composer Graciela Paraskevaídis is a scholarship student in 1965–1966 during the center's second biennial, and Coriún Aharonián has a scholarship for 1969–1970 during the fourth. Aharonián "only used his scholarship until October 1969, at which time he left to study on a scholarship in France and Italy (Ginastera authorised him to return and complete his scholarship, but after Ginastera left, the scholarship was used for other ends during the financial crisis at the institute)" (Aharonián 1996: 100).

24. During the first CLAMC period, the courses take place in the Southern Cone, alternating between Uruguay and Argentina. The first four editions (1971, 1972, 1974, and 1975) are held at the International Campgrounds of the Latin American Confederation of the YMCA in Cerro del Toro, Uruguay. The fifth and sixth courses take place at the Goethe Institute in Buenos Aires in January, 1976 and 1977. During the second period courses are held in different cities in Brazil. In 1978 and 1979 the site is the Padre José María Xavier State Conservatory of Music in São João del Rei. The ninth course is located in Itapira (1980), the eleventh in Uberlandia (1982), the twelfth in Tatuí (1984), and the fifteenth in Mendes, all in Brazil. The tenth and thirteenth are held in the Dominican Republic (1981) and Venezuela (1985) respectively, while the fourteenth returns to Cerro del Toro, Uruguay (1986). On the permanent international staff when CLAMC closes are José Maria Neves (president since 1977); Coriún Aharonián (executive secretary since its founding); Graciela Paraskevaídis (1975–1989); Cergio Prudencio (1983–1989), and Conrado Silva (1973–1989). Other staff members at different times were Héctor Tosar (Uruguay) (president from CLAMC's founding until 1977); Miguel Marozzi, Margarita Luna, Emilio Mendoza, and María Teresa Sande. See Aharonián 2007c and CLAMC programs.

25. Convinced that artistic practice should be motivated by political considerations and that the composer should be familiar with the latest technological advances, Nono's discourse coincides with that of CLAMC organizers: "Everyone realized the need to analyze, surpass, and eradicate penetration, European and North American cultural domination, and imperialist colonization in order to bring to life, in music as well, a creative and original practice of one's own [. . .]" (Nono 1993: 407). For a comparison of the political positions as composers of Alberto Ginastera with Luigi Nono, see Buch 2002: 62–85.

26. A great many seminars, workshops, and recitals of electro-acoustical music are found in CLAMC course catalogues. The technological dimension is present from the start, continuing the interest in the subject generated by CLAEM in the *Instituto Di Tella*. One or two electro-acoustic laboratories are set up in each course so students can practice and update their technological know-how. A large number of teachers—Latin Americans, Europeans, and North Americans—known for their expertise in electronic techniques take part, including, among others, Fernando von Reichenbach, José Vicente Asuar, Francisco Kröpfl, José Ramón Maranzano, Conrado Silva, Eduardo Bértola, Luigi Nono, Konrad Boehmer, Gordon Mumma, Françoise Barrière, Christian Clozier, Dante Grela, Joaquín Orellana, Jorge Rapp, Mesías Maiguashca, Fernand Vandenbogaerde, Hilda Dianda, Dieter Kaufmann, Vania Dantas Leite, Leo Küpper, Michel Philippot, Micheline Coulombe Saint-Marcoux, Carlos da Silveira, James Montgomery, Folke Rabe, Pierre Boeswillwald, José Maria Neves, Coriún Aharonián, Eduardo Kusnir, Lars-Gunnar Bodin, Philippe Ménard, Ricardo Teruel, Julián Arena, Ariel Martínez, Wilhelm Zobl.

27. Likewise, in the early CLAMC editions there are performances such as "Singing on purpose" with Los Olimareños, Dahd Sfeir, and Daniel Viglietti, announced as a "show-collage" (1971); "Mesomusical recital" with the rock group Psiglo from Montevideo (1972); two concerts by the *payador* Carlos Molina, and one by the guitarist Agustín Carlevaro playing tangos (1974).

28. Collaborating as teachers and lecturers in CLAMC courses are young Uruguayan musicians Jorge Lazaroff (twelfth and fourteenth); Leo Maslíah (fourteenth); Rubén Olivera (eleventh and fourteenth); Carlos da Silveira (eighth, ninth, fourteenth); Luis Trochón (twelfth and fourteenth); Jaime Roos (fourteenth), and Elbio Rodríguez Barilari (ninth, fourteenth, and fifteenth).

29. The role played by Martins is very significant in the development of popular music in Uruguay in the 1970s. Starting in 1977 he organizes and presents many recitals and concerts such as the "Cycle of Popular Music" in the *Alianza Francesa* in Montevideo. Before that, Martins participates as lecturer in the fourth edition of CLAMC (1975) with talks on "Current Uruguayan popular music," "*Mesomusic* and its dissemination," and "The rock process." He is the first in the CLAMC courses to approach the subject of the broad-based appeal and relevance of popular music in Uruguay in the 1970s.

30. Notable among them are "*Cinco piezas cortas para piano*" (1978) composed and played by Leo Maslíah; "*Quichi 29*" (1978) by Fernando Condon; "*Siete*" (1978) by Bernardo Aguerre; "*Solo a dos voces*" (1978) by Elbio Rodríguez; "*Ventanía*" (1978) by Fernando Cabrera; and "*Piano, piano*" (1978–1979) by Carlos da Silveira (performed by Leo Maslíah).

31. In 1979 he gives a course on "electro-acoustic techniques" (along with Micheline Coulombe Saint-Marcoux) and one on "Arrangement and version in popular music"; in 1980 he assists Conrado Silva and James Montgomery in the seminar-workshop on "Initiation in electro-acoustic techniques," and gives a talk, along with Elbio Rodríguez Barilari, on "Popular music in Uruguay today"; in 1986 he and Conrado Silva again give workshops on "Electro-acoustic composition" and "Initiation in electro-acoustic techniques"; he also directs a workshop on "Popular composition," together with Jorge Lazaroff and Leo Maslíah.

32. With compositions by Felipe Silveira, Fernando Condon, Elbio Rodríguez, Carlos da Silveira, and Fernando Cabrera.

33. The song is first performed in Montevideo in September 1979 at a concert called "*Veterinaria canta*" in the *Palacio Peñarol*, with numerous versions appearing afterwards (Aharonián 2003: n.p).

34. Rubén Olivera takes this quote by Sánchez Vázquez from his book *Las ideas estéticas de Marx* (1965; Mexico: ERA), which was widely read by this generation.

35. See the influential and polemical article by Jorge Lazaroff titled "*¿?*" (1984), and the book titled *Un detective privado ante algunos problemas no del todo ajenos a la llamada "música popular"* by Leo Maslíah (1984). These are two examples of the theoretical basis of the new generation's aesthetic-ideological project.

36. With works and/or performances by Eduardo Darnauchans, the Los que iban cantando group, Jorge Lazaroff, Jorge Bonaldi, Luis Trochón, Jaime Roos, the "*Montresvideo*" group, Rubén Olivera, the "*Rumbo*" group, and Leo Maslíah.

37. He also performs the following songs for guitar and voice in the "Teachers recital": "*Tu carta*" (1980), "*Pájaros*" (1974), "*Al padre*" (1980), and "*Siglos*" (1980).

38. Likewise, on the flap of the program for the twelfth CLAMC edition, mention is made of the collaboration of the International Association of the Study of Popular Music (IASPM), founded in 1981 by, among others, Tagg. In the same year he is a co-organizer of the first International Conference on Popular Music Research in Amsterdam. In 1983 he co-organizes the second International Conference on Popular Music Research in Reggio Emilia, in one of whose important editions Coriún Aharonián participates. In 1984 Tagg is vice president of IASPM.

39. On January 3 Luis Trochón performs; on the program figure the following songs: "*De la propiedad que tiene el dinero*" (1981), "*Para Fabiana Ele*" (1983), "*Quien fue compañera*" (1982), "*Casi un ejercicio intelectual*" (1977), "*Parece de película*" (1982), "*Para qué tristeza*" (1982), "*A pura garganta*" (1981), "*En ese momento*" (1983), "*Lo nuestro*" (1982), "*Morocha*" (1981). On January Jorge Lazaroff performs, with the following songs on the program: "*El afilador*" (1978), "*Bares*" (1976), "*El corso*" (1982), "*Jugando a las escondidas*" (1981), "*Ley de probabilidades*" (1982), "*El rengo Zamora*" (1980), "*Ahí mar nomás*" (1982), "*Baile de más caras*" (1980), "*Los que iban cantando*" (1976), "*¿No serán zambas?*" (1983), "*Dos*" (1982), "*Barbaridad*" (1982), "*Darle de vuelta*" (1977).

40. This same year his article "*La Canción política*" is published in the magazine *La del taller* (Olivera 1986: 2–9); in it he examines the political and aesthetic thought of the generation dedicated to experimenting with the popular song.

Chapter Six

The Rhythm of Values: Poetry and Music in Uruguay, 1960–1985

Maria L. Figueredo

The interaction of music and literature as an authentic expression of cultural identity and social context in Latin America characterized the second half of the twentieth century in various countries of the region. The amplification and retraction of the dialogue between these two genres and the implications of those cycles for literary culture are borne out as a response, and at times a challenge, to those circumstances. The *ekphrastic*[1] exchange of poetry and music became as much a dialogue on the cultural values and the ideological climate of the time as a revitalization of the roots of cultural identity. This occurred in Uruguay within the wider contextual framework, not as a purely aesthetic search for innovation, but rather as a means to find voice for the values of a people who were searching to articulate their own philosophy following the destruction of the former European world order that had pre-dominated in the Latin American political imaginary. With the crumbling of that order in the 1940s, and as the effects of Cold War politics became pervasive across the region in the following decades, various groups within the national frontiers were considering their views of reality in dialogue with external and internal forces. This came to a head in Uruguay in 1973 when the CIA-backed military coup ruptured institutional governance, after which the situation became polarized and democratic consensus was challenged.

This chapter's title places emphasis on rhythm in terms of the representation of values rather than on rhythm as a characteristic of identity. The reason is clear: there is a deeper level of interpretation inherent in the first that can best grapple with the problematization (in the sense given to this term by Michael Foucault 2001: 170–173) of the concerns of the country beyond the notions of culture, popular or otherwise, that would have been previously created by a historically marked concept of the nation-state. It is well known that after romanticism the arts "became one of the chief ways in which nationalism sought to stimulate a sense of people's awareness of their national roots" (Cunningham and Reich 2002: vii). Could they not also be used to question a specific identification with the nation if the ruler of the state becomes a threat to the liberties of its people? What distinguishes a folksong that arises naturally from a certain time and place from one that is fabricated and/or imposed superficially as a symbol of a nation-state? Foucault would posit the test of such cultural productions against the question of truth, and upon the Greek notion of *parrhesia*, which he defines as akin to a "philosopher who speaks the truth, believes he is speaking the truth, and, more than that, also takes a risk (since the tyrant [against whom he is uttering his truth] may become angry, may punish him, may exile him, may kill him)" (2001: 14). What Roland Barthes termed "the grain of the voice" (1973) is the recognition of that authentic representation and truth are inseparably entwined. Whereas identity is constructed upon shared collective recognition of inherited socio-political and cultural history, values are moral precepts (truth claims about reality) that exist beyond specific time and space particularities and can be connected to individual interior interpretations as well as to exterior manifestations of the beliefs created by these values. How are these aspects represented if not in the body as site of meaning? For these reasons concrete geo-political markers come inevitably into play with the abstract concepts of the value system engendered.

As a vehicle for communicating a desire for or commentary about societal conditions, music is linked to the merging of action and perception, without having to pass through an intense analysis of the complex relationships it encapsulates. This trajectory is complex, of course. However, as Edward Said has posited, not all music can achieve a level of "elaboration" (2007: 263) that can speak to or for a society and its representatives' collective sense of belonging. What makes a musician remarkable for Said is one, such as Daniel Barenboim with whom he worked to create an orchestra of Arab and Israeli musicians, who

> brings a quasi-biological drive to the aesthetic project, gathering together so many strands, experiences, voices and urges in a contrapuntual web whose purpose in the end is to give all this diversity, all this utterance, all this complexity of sound and life the clarity and immediacy of a deeply human, yet transcendental presence. This is neither domination nor manipulation. It is elaboration as the ultimate form of expression and meaning. [. . .] [H]e makes one feel one's humanity and, yes, one's love and mortality as well, through an aesthetic experience that by means of a marvelously well-wrought sound connects the listeners to others, other selves, other musics, other utterances and experiences (Said 2007: 263).

The most authentic artists as collective meaning-bearers are "truth-tellers" (Foucault 2001: 14). Those who can voice their unique self-representation in a specific time and place while at the same time connect to others regardless of cultural origin.

Each artistic genre, in its own manner, articulates identity—and the values its expressions espouse—through the specific aspects of perception that are natural to it. Poetry, as Delmore Schwartz indicates

> by virtue of its rhythmic component, is . . . capable of mirroring inner feeling. But [on the other hand] there is a sense in which music, in its parameter of rhythm, does so more—shall I say—vividly. Poetry, in its turn, is more capable of directly embodying emotion that prose—the emotion in prose arising, rather, not directly out of the sensuous, the qualitative surface of the medium, but out of our conceptual grasp of the meanings conveyed by the conventional symbols. [I am aware that prose can be more or less rhythmic, but as rhythm becomes more and more important in prose, reaching the level which we encounter it in Joyce, we are apt to say that it approaches poetry.] Thus, poetry is an intermediate stage between prose and music. The meanings poetry shares with prose enable us to localize the attitudes and feelings conveyed purely by the sound and the rhythm (Berger 1994: 304).

Rhythm lies at the heart of experience and self-recognition. According to S. H. Burton, "Rhythm is a fundamental phenomenon of life, and it is poetry's dependence upon it that helps make poetry so powerful an influence in the lives of men" (cit. in Carvahlo da Silva 1989: 89). Music alone must use its rhythmic structure to organize and transmit its messages, and to create the center axis of its meaning. The power inherent in the interface of poetry and popular music is the way they complement their symbolic and semiotic strengths. T. S. Eliot (1942: 465) wrote that "the poet may gain much from the study of music . . . a poem, or a passage of a poem, may tend to realize itself first as a particular rhythm before it reaches expression in words" (cit. in Berger 1994: 310). Although both poetry and music rely more heavily on sound and rhythm for their nature than the other arts, poetry can communicate most clearly through language—thereby granting a collective understanding through ideas, while music engages the physical most clearly through sound and rhythm, thereby engaging collectively through action on the body.

When combined in song, music and poetry become one of the most powerful vehicles of identity, and when they are set to do so in a song, they enter into dialogue with the subset of values under debate. If rooted in the shared beliefs and values that have been tested through challenge, such as the fight for freedom or defense of human rights, the song can represent the truth claims of the self at a deeply personal and at a collective level by those who share the same values. Given the power of simultaneity, which can be seen as two-fold, a song that reaches this proportion in the public domain can exert influence: a) collectively, it can simultaneously mobilize large numbers of people; b) individually, it has the capacity to simultaneously engage various levels of experience and lead each us to receive its message(s) in ways we may not be fully analytically aware. Poetry's rhythmic components can be seen to achieve this also; quiet reading may be a solitary activity, but recitation as an art form, and one well regarded in the Uruguayan education system until the 1960s, comes even closer to demonstrate how poets sought to reach a wider audience since the rise of the mass media.

THE URUGUAYAN CASE STUDY

A case study providing empirical evidence of hybrid texts produced by poets and musicians during a period of significant socio-political crisis in Uruguay, particularly after 1960, allows us to explore the effect this has had on issues of distinguishing the values upon which identity is constructed. Although a small country of approximately three million inhabitants, two-thirds of whom reside in the capital, Uruguay's unique cultural expressions have characterized it as distinctly different from the geographical giants of Brazil and Argentina between which it was founded. It has historically harbored a different approach to the way it has integrated the original indigenous and African influences found on its soil, producing, for example (unlike Argentina, and more like Brazil and Cuba) distinct Afro-Uruguayan cultural art forms that thrive until today despite having often been marginalized by societal and religious norms in previous centuries (see Paez Villaró 2000 and Chasteen 2004), and surviving various attempts at being used for inauthentic nationalistic purposes.

The *República Oriental del Uruguay* was formed primarily on the acquisition of lands over time by the growth of population bases that expanded from the late 1770s into the nineteenth century. In 1778 Montevideo became "an insatiable draw" (Benvenuto 1967: 27) and by 1800 grew to over 30,685 inhabitants, in addition to the existing indigenous population and residents of the Misiones Orientales. The new Republic became independent on August 25, 1825, but its constitution took effect on July 18, 1830, at the end of a three-year war with Argentina. The country was built subsequently on the management of its agricultural lands and the influx of immigration facilitated by Uruguay's fluid social structure. Other factors that contributed to solidifying the strength of the country are evident by 1904, such as the ease of access to education, a continued insistence on integrating minorities in political participation, and sustained, vigorous promotion of the importance of the humanities to a vibrant society, with particular emphasis on the areas of philosophy, arts and letters (Benvenuto 1967: 99–101). These became hallmarks of the cultural heritage of the country, making it one of the most educated and economically stable in the region until the second half of the twentieth century. The constitution underwent subsequent revisions and amendments, with major reforms in 1966–1967 that ushered in a new level of uncertainty, coupled with the effects of external factors in the world wide context prevalent since the Cuban Missile crisis, cold war politics and U.S. incursions in Latin America.

The history of Uruguay had important repercussions for the way poetry was recontextualized in a song to reaffirm certain values. As mentioned above, its very social fabric rested on the vigor of education, arts, and critical thinking, as well as on the success of its agricultural resources, its "pago" in both senses of the term, as an endearing reflection of a sense of belonging, and its economic well-being.

This chapter takes a two-fold approach to account for the conditions in which the literary and the musical arts join and how they create responses to collective experience in times of challenging socio-political circumstances, such as those evident in Uruguay in the second half of the twentieth century. Although this chapter can address only some of the effects of these tendencies in Uruguay, more detailed accounts of how the interactions of poetry and music reflect artists responses to their contexts can be found in various studies: see Fabregat and Dabezies (1983), Martins (1986), Figueredo (1999b, 2001/2002, 2003, 2005, and 2011). Delving into the question of rhythm as the basis for the relationship of poetry and music, and for their power to communicate grounds the body's sense of itself and its place in the world. It also points to the interaction of the verbal and sound elements forming a cultural expression that seeks to represent the self as a source of what it values and to share that on a collective scale. Specific examples drawn from the case of Uruguay (based on primary research conducted on poetic texts set to music between 1960 and 1985),[2] establish the empirical basis for interpreting the phenomenon in greater detail.

RHYTHM AND IDENTITY: LYRICAL TRUTH-TELLING

Music's effects reach beyond a conceptual grasp of the message, thus its potential power exists in the way it communicates and expresses its structure through complex relationships between the composer, the interpreter, the listener, and society as a whole. And yet, these complexities need not be overtly understood. As a vehicle for communicating a desire for or commentary about societal conditions, music is linked to the merging of action and perception, without having to pass through an intense analysis of the complex relationships it encapsulates. This trajectory is complex, of course. Suffice to summarize, for our purposes here, some of the elements of the relation between music and societal construction. For example, in his research on the popular music of Argentina and Chile, Rodolfo Pino-Robles proposes that "[t]o speak of music and social change in the same breath, is to speak of a commitment of people exercising this form of art to the service of a social cause" (Pino-Robles 1999: 1). In this first level of human interaction music reflects an argument put forward by British socio-musicologist Simon Frith (1996) and the relation of popular music the community of its production creates, to a significant extent, the nature of the effect of popular music, regardless of its aesthetic value. Jon Garelick notes about Frith's view "that music's value is never merely inherent but always part of a larger social framework" (Garelick 1996: 1). As he underscores, it is this attribute that "begins to unravel music's mysterious power to move us, and to liberate. Our relationship to various musical genres, our willingness to 'try on' different musics as different social identities, helps *define* us" (Garelick 1996:1). At some point, we recognize the popular music of a place to which we feel a sense of belonging and that recognition is beyond an appreciation of the lyrics or even of the quality of the music; rather it communicates to us directly on the level of sound recognition of a particular identity, be it in the articulation of vocal style, rhythmic structure, or repetitions of certain melodic patterns, to name the most prominent features.

The web of sonic articulation of identity, cultural creation, and representation has been documented in several studies from various perspectives, and the performance or action-based manifestation of the values they are meant to communicate rests on the site of body for meaning. Citing evidence from Barthes, Nietzche, Bakhtin, Max Weber, and Schoenberg, Michael Chanan writes in his historical investigation into the social practices of Occident, that "music is always—among other things—an expression of actual or ideal social relations" (Chanan 1994: 11). The way music interacts with society was also explored by German philosopher, sociologist, and trained musician Theodor Adorno who found parallels between the structural composition of musical form and societal organization: "Musical forms are interiorizations of social structures . . . [and] social circumstances are expressed concretely in the *topos* of music" (Rothstein 1996: 28). This is especially true in moments of socio-political crises when the simultaneous and collective aspects of music serve the message proposed by socially engaged literary creation such as in the works of writers Mario Benedetti in Uruguay, Nicolás Guillén in Cuba, and Pablo Neruda in Chile. These poets understood that the musical and rhythmic elements are visceral communications of the cultural identity of a people. Benedetti often used the *cielito* form in his poetry and for his musical collaborations, and also referred to music as a vehicle for social commentary, such as in his collection of poems, *Letras de emergencia* (1977). Guillén published a collection of poems inspired by the Cuban *son* dance form. Neruda included waltz forms and the tango ("*Tango del viudo*"

["The Widow's Tango"]), for example, borrowing musical styles to *inspire* the rhythm and sound qualities of the text to invoke specific cultural resonances.

Protest music in Latin America comes from the experience of colonization and the subsequent development of society in the generations that followed. From the origins of these *creole* cultures, there was evidence of a new way of creating music. One of the most formidable influences on the forms of Latin American protest music known as the "New Songs" in the second half of the twentieth century comes from Cuba.[3] Murray Luft explains that this key relationship forged between popular song, lyrical poetry, and social commentary is also nurtured by political and social development in Latin America in the second part of the twentieth century. In particular he highlights the effects of Cold War politics and the increased polarization of ideologies, a context in which the effect of Cuba are keenly influential in the development of "New Songs" and their insistence on the verbal text's message linked with popular song forms:

> The Cuban Revolution of 1959 nourished the roots of Latin American protest music even more profoundly [than the music of Spanish Civil War (1936–1939)]. The voice of revolutionary Cuban singer Carlos Puebla, one of the troubadours in the old style, was popular in South America in the 1960s. During the 1970s, Cuba's socialist musical renaissance, known as the *Nueva Trova*, acquired a following among Bolivia's [and other Latin American nations'] progressive sectors increasingly opposed to de facto military regimes (Luft 1996: 10).

Cuban singer-songwriters most cited as examples of the *Nueva Trova* genre are Silvio Rodríguez, Noel Nicolla, and Pablo Milanés. The *Nueva Trova* in Cuba, as Luft aptly describes, "proved to be an exciting experiment in the construction of a Latin American musical tradition that was both politically progressive and esthetically pleasing" (1996: 11).

Similar phenomena began to appear across the region. In Brazil, it took the shape of a cornucopia of popular musical forms which came to be known as *Música Popular Brasileira: MPB*. According to Charles Perrone in his study of poetry and music in Brazilian cultural history, *Letras e Letras da MPB* (1988), "the presence of literary figures in the rise of the popular song is mentioned in the historical studies of literature as much as of popular music" (Perrone 1988: 16). Prominent among these artists were Elis Regina and her collaborations with poet Vinícius de Moraes and with bossa nova singer, guitarist, and composer Edu Lobo. Others included Chico Buarque, Maria Bethania, Milton Nascimento, Gal Costa, and Jorge Ben. Elements of social criticism and defense of social justice, as well as liberation on several social fronts from existing norms and prejudices, were themes that ran throughout MPB artists' work. Musically, it stemmed from bossa nova, whose roots in the heart of Brazilian samba and its link with its urban and non-urban expressions gave way to experimentation and innovation. Within the MPB, Caetano Veloso and Giberto Gil's *Tropicália* movement arose in the 1960s, whose salient feature was the fusion of elements of North American and European rock and new sound technologies, with the musical subgenres and Afro-Brazilian percussive techniques and religious/spiritual aspects of the Brazilian landscape. This fusion of interior and exterior elements never belied an undercurrent of Brazilian-ness that Perrone describes well in his study cited above.

When musicians and poets set out to look for authentic expressions of what it meant to be Cuban, Chilean, Mexican, Brazilian, Argentine, and so on, it was the popular forms of the arts, stemming from a natural expression of the *pueblo* (popular) where they found their inspiration. As we recalled, Nicolás Guillén's translation of the black culture of Cuba into such poetry as contained in *Motivos de Son* which appeared in 1930 (Guillén 1972: 25–32), and *Sóngoro Cosongo in* 1931 (Guillén 1972: 33–49), and other experiments like it, bridged the popular and literary forms of cultural expression as a means of taking stock of Cuba's true identity and struggle. However, it did not stop there. Beyond this was an emergent view to linking across nationalistic frontiers (from a postcolonial perspective) and aesthetic categorizations (eroding strict demarcations between "high" and "low" culture or between artistic genres). Guillén's poetry was later set to music by Cuban musicians such as Eliseo Grenet,[4] and subsequently became part of the repertoire for popular musicians all over Latin America, including Daniel Viglietti from Uruguay. For more detailed accounts of these complex histories, published at that time in music periodicals, see the following articles: Benavides (1980, 1982a, 1982b, 1982–1983, 1983a, 1983b, 1983c, 1983d, 1984, 1985), Caula (1983), Cunha, Dabezies, and Fabregat (1983), Darnauchans (1981), Giovanetti (1981, 1983, 1984), Lena (1984), Mántaras (1987a, 1987b, 1989), Rodríguez Barilari (1982, 1983a, 1983b, 1984a, 1984b, 1985), Sotelo (1982), and Viglietti (1985).

The literary and musical arts share a common heritage, and thus possess the ability to encapsulate social relations in symbolic form, especially when they depart from the oral traditions, such as in the poetry of the medieval troubadours, the minstrels, and the Arabic *jarchas*. As Charles Perrone states,

> The discussion naturally reverts back to the Middle ages, when all poetry was sung. [. . .] Literary textbooks generally attribute the music-poetic art of the *Provençal* troubadours and of the *trouvéres* of Northern France as the first manifestations of lyrical poetry. [. . .] The first collections of poetry from the Iberian Peninsula were songbooks organized by royalty to preserve the oral traditions of sung poetry. During the Renaissance, poetry began to evolve as an art independent of its musical accompaniment; however, the birth of coloni-

al literature in Brazil [and other Latin American countries] is marked by the medieval tradition (Perrone 1988: 16).

This was the case of the birth of literature in Uruguay, when Bartolomé Hidalgo (considered the first national poet) writes his verse in song. Using the form of the *cielito* he comments on the political climate of his day, highlighting the fight for independence. We see an example of this theme in the following verses: *"Cielito, cielo que sí, / no se necesitan Reyes / para gobernar los hombres / sino benéficas leyes"* (Cédar Viglietti 1968: 43), which state that there is no need of Kings to rule men, but rather beneficent laws. According to Ayestarán, this early form of Uruguayan music appears during the first wars of independence, and became a musical "symbol for the nascent nation, wrapped in an aura of liberty" (Ayestarán 1971: 111).[5] While the cielito can be said to have predominated in the cultural imaginary in the early history of Uruguay, it was later to be superseded by other forms, such as the milonga, in the twentieth century, although it does not disappear altogether and its power to comment on socio-political issues remained. Why did these forms do so and how do they communicate values in each time period?

The premises for a more detailed discussion of a Uruguayan case study are based on extensive field research[6] that I conducted in that country from 1992–1999, and upon which I have continued to build through analysis and field work. This has produced a catalogue of poems written by poets of diverse time periods and styles that entered the sphere of popular music through diverse types of musical collaboration and production. The majority of those poems set to music were registered between 1960[7] and 1985.[8] The greatest measurable production of texts in that group is from 1970 and 1982, the years that overlap with the years leading up to the military coup in 1973 and the ensuing rule of military dictatorship in Uruguay until the return of democratic government in 1985. A salient feature of the data of the corpus of poetic texts, which are set to music during those decades, appear to create a new phenomenon, thereby perhaps not creating a new literary tradition per se, but rather forging more overt ties between the reception and dialogue of the art forms. These musical settings of poetry did not possess historical antecedent in the country, that is not in the sense of uniting poetry and music in "artistic movements" (such as were seen in the case of Brazil, for instance); nevertheless, through its experiences with socio-political challenges in the second part of the twentieth century, and most intensely during the institutional crisis of 1973–1985, the phenomenon in Uruguay generates an aesthetic current with a strong focus on the poetic and literary quality of texts that merge with a resurgence in traditional and folkloric musical subgenres. After the dictatorship came to an end, the most concerted efforts to connect poetry with popular and/or protest music diminish in the sense of political and social commentary (Figueredo 1995: my interview of Kmaid), although much can be said to remain as echoes of the emphasis on lyric and its relationship to context that is yet to be explored more deeply in further studies (for example, Figueredo 2011).

The socio-political challenges and ideological questionings that were predominant in Uruguayan society after 1960 had an influence not only on the creation of an artistic phenomenon but also on its forms of expression. This resulted not only in an increased use of poetic texts of various historical periods (from Hidalgo to Herrera y Reissig to the contemporary authors at the time) in the new popular music, but also an increased willingness of some poets, such as Washington Benavides, Mario Benedetti, and Idea Vilariño to voluntarily compose texts for music. These texts reach a collective level of reinterpretation and ekphrastic exchange in conditions that differ from the original text and/or from the reception of written poetry. In this way, poetry and popular music together created a new space for a more active dialogue between the arts and society.

During the period between 1960 and 1985, Uruguay underwent a long political, economic, and social crisis. In this climate the guerilla movement of the Tupamaros and the creation of a new political party—the *Frente Amplio*—culminated in a military intervention in 1973. The population, already polarized into factions either for order or for social justice, became more firmly set in groups that were in favor of democracy or of the dictatorship. In this context, political persecution and censorship (after 1973) eventually led to exile for the majority of the best known artists of the time. Among those exiled were musicians Daniel Viglietti, Alfredo Zitarrosa, and the duo Los Olimareños, and writers such as Mario Benedetti, Juan Carlos Onetti, Cristina Peri Rossi, Martínez Moreno, Saúl Ibargoyen, and Eduardo Galeano.

For the new generation of artists that remained in Uruguay after 1973, the climate for their production had to contend with working under censorship and repressive conditions. Poet, musician, and critic, Leo Maslíah points out,

In the first years of the dictatorship, repression in the area of popular music didn't follow a geometrically coherent course. Perhaps its coherence derived from some other academic discipline. Two records by the group Patria Libre couldn't be issued as planned; neither could a 1974 title by Los Olimareños. But while Aníbal Sampayo was a prisoner at Libertad [prison], some of his records could still be found in record shops. [. . .] In 1975 Washington Carrasco's album *Antología de Canto Popular* came out. It contained little-known songs by well-known authors, all of whom had been banned [. . .]—Viglietti, Palacios, and Los Olimareños among others. Perhaps the fact that it was issued under a major label helped make that possible (Patria Libre records had been cut by a smaller record company). Intentional or not, however, the confusion caused by this kind of arbitrariness fit in well with attempts to dismantle the political and cultural opposition in other areas (Maslíah 1993: 112–113).

The discontinuities that characterized the official registration of poems set to music must be considered in light of the fluctuations in the conditions of censorship and regulation of artistic production at the level of public access. It is significant to note that many of the works were circulated by grassroots means or through other similar forms of distribution. Although numerically the poems that were registered set to music of the period under consideration (especially after 1977) are sporadic, this is not an indication of lesser creative efforts; it seems rather to point out that problematized access to audiences and the ability to track the popularity of certain groups who were listened to on bootleg or underground recordings circulated despite being officially censored. The years 1976 and 1977, according to Maslíah, witnessed a "gradual proliferation of new places to perform popular music—albeit with lyrics that bore little resemblance to those of the protest songs of previous years. This apparent easing of censorship may have had to do with the same optimism that would underlie the military's decision to submit their fascist draft constitution to a plebiscite in 1980" (Maslíah 1993: 133). Maslíah adds that, despite the measures taken by the regimen to control the production of certain cultural texts during the first years of the dictatorship, these regulations were lessened by the end of the 1970s and beginning of the 1980s:

> So it was that during those years—even as broadcasting of Joan Manuel Serrat's songs was prohibited in 1976 because of his participation in international festivals against the Uruguayan dictatorship—in a few 'peñas' (clubs) and theaters there was a resurgence of a type of popular music that came to be referred to as *canto popular*. At first the *canto popular* movement was not subject to any prior censorship; the dictatorship was at the height of its power, and its confidence in people's capacity for self-censorship was very great. The decay of the censors during the last two or three years of the dictatorship, by which time active opposition to the regime was widespread, [and] the inventiveness of musicians had proved influential in police circles as well (Maslíah 1993: 113–114).

The fluctuations in the application of censorship, as noted by Maslíah, made it very challenging on the one hand for musicians to know what to expect, or to plan for whether they would be permitted to perform. At the same time this encouraged increased inventiveness, even to be perceived in songs commissioned by police authorities to contravene the effects of other circulating popular musical forms; for the latter, the inherent contradictions between folkloric or traditional musical subgenres, associated with revolutionary acts of the past, would be co-opted by a reactionary or conservative message to counteract the effect of the musical vehicle's original connotations. Nevertheless, most of these songs did not experience a lasting reception in the public domain, nor did they possess poetic quality to warrant their insertion into the aesthetic public imaginary.

Near the end of the military rule in Uruguay, there was a significant increase in the number of poems set to music. As of 1982, there is a spike in the data signaled by the quantity of eighty-five poetic texts registered to have been set to music in that year alone. In the following year the number of texts fell to thirty-four. The decline continued until 1991; only one poem was registered as having been set to music that year. In 1994 the number increased to twenty-one, then declined until 1997.

THE DEFENSE OF VALUES THROUGH CULTURAL EXPRESSION

Two stages in the chronology of the phenomenon can be distinguished, based on the analysis of the research of the poems set to music in Uruguay from 1960 to 1985. In the first period (1960–1973), poetry adopts a more popular style, responding to a renovation in popular music and a focus on political autonomy and identity. This phase is a more generalized response to the socio-political crisis set within the international arena and amidst rising anti-imperial sentiments in certain sectors of Latin American society. In the second period (1973–1985), the situation generated by the military dictatorship intensifies the relation of poetry to music as a means of indirect protest within the country. This more local phenomenon includes experiences of exile of a large part of the artists prominent in the former period; the control of censorship; and issues of new democratization with which the new generation of popular musicians would have to contend.

During the first stage of the historical period under consideration (1960–1972), the musicians most associated with the setting of poetry to music are Daniel Viglietti, Alfredo Zitarrosa, the duo Los Olimareños (José Luis Guerra and Braulio López) and Santiago Chalar. In the second phase (1973–1985), these include the duos Cristina Fernández/Washington Carrasco and Eduardo Larbanois/Mario Carrero, as well as Eduardo Darnauchans, Esteban Klísich, Carlos Benavides, Héctor Numa Moraes, Grupo Vocal Universo (Washington Luzardo and Alfredo Percovich), Jorge Bonaldi, Abayubá Caraballo, and Rubén Olivera. To a lesser extent in quantitative terms, though with significant contributions during this period, Luis Cardozo, Pablo Estramín, Eduardo Lagos, Ruben Lena, Juan José de Mello, Julio Mora, and Edgar Rodríguez should be mentioned. Of the popular composers on this list (twenty-three artists or groups), fourteen were included in an index created by Mary Ríos (1995) to recognize thirty-two musicians who have made significant contributions to Uruguayan cultural history.

The corpus of poems set to music in the above two periods represents a total of 614 texts, as catalogued in the complete list produced from my research (1960–1985). Of these texts (listed by poet in the first instance), 362 texts are registered under the authorship of Washington Benavides such as

"*Cantor de estas tierras*" by Julio Mora (1979) and "*Décima de la paloma*" with E. Darnauchans (1978), and "*Como un jazmín del país*" and "*En el país de la cina cina*" with C. Benavides (1971 and 1976 respectively), and "*En horas duras*" with E. Labarnios (1976); seventy-four by Mario Benedetti such as "*Cielito del 69*" by Numa Moraes (1969), recorded by Los Olimareños; "*Corazón coraza*" by A. Favero, recorded by Darnauchans (1973); thirty by Idea Vilariño such as "*La canción y el poema*" by A. Zitarrosa and by Los Olimareños (both in 1974); twenty-seven by Líber Falco such as "*Ahora*" by Abel García (1976) and "*Canción por la España obrera*" by E. Darnauchans (1974); and twenty-six by Juana de Ibarbourou. The rest of the list of poetry-set-to-music includes authors Jorge Arbeleche with twenty-two poems, such as "*Estoy atado a esta tierra*" and "*Son muchachos*" (set to music by W. Carrasco and C. Fernández [1988]); Víctor Cunha (fourteen, such as "*El abismo*" and "*Yo tenía una canción*" by Numa Moraes [1988 and 1989 respectively]); Juan Cunha (eight, such as "*Hay un verdor*" by W. Carrasco [1996]); Circe Maia (seven, such as "*Los que iban cantando*" by Jorge Lazaroff [1981] and "*Otra voz canta*" by D. Viglietti, [1994]); Humberto Megget (seven); Amanda Berenguer (five); Estela Magnone (five); Julio Herrera y Reissig (three, such as "*La fuga*" by Carrasco [1996]); Álvaro Figueredo (three); Cecilia Prato (two); Delmira Agustini (one, "*Lo inefable*," Carrasco [1996]); Walter Ortiz y Ayala (one); Sara de Ibáñez (one); Romilo Risso (one); and Juan Zorrilla de San Martín (one). There are also gauchesque texts recorded by artists between 1960 and 1985, including poems by Wenseslao Varela (six), Serafín García (five), Yamandú Rodríguez (one), and Fernán Silva Valdés (two).

The Uruguayan phenomenon of poems set to popular music in the second half of the twentieth century allow us to identify the following implications of the texts and their significance to expressing cultural identity: (1) there is a predominant influence of the socio-political context in opening an interdisciplinary stream of projects linking literature and popular music; (2) poets and popular musicians prefer popular traditional structural forms for their works, promoting a continuous dialogue with the popular roots of culture in terms of identity and for defining the position of self in the world; (3) simultaneous and complicit engagement is achieved between poetry and popular song in Uruguay, and with a significant percentage of the Uruguayan public, as a result of certain challenging socio-cultural and political conditions; (4) a renewed place is secured for hybrid texts that reactivate the popular roots in literary history which had been less significant since the eighteenth century; and (5) literary criticism became more concerned with a consideration of the text and its ability to cross boundaries between genres—in particular this brought to the fore questions about transcending the strict division of genres to open the flow of the arts to greater renewal by new technologies of communication (radio, television, newspapers, and other more popular forms of mass media). Another considerable aspect is the effect on the work of art itself in terms of the new dimensions introduced to the "reading" of the poems in song form and their insertion into the popular oral tradition of the community. This popular tradition is carried in the musical subgenres of the song forms, which in Uruguay include the *milonga, chamarrita, cielito,* among others.

URUGUAYAN MUSICAL SUBGENRES AND POETRY IN SONG (1960–1985)

The diversity of musical styles to which poems were set to music manifest the heterogeneous character of the case study and the convergence of various tendencies that together promoted artistic creativity after 1960. All of the folkloric subgenres of the Uruguayan tradition are represented in the registered texts, along with musical forms that are amalgamations of the subgenres or forms based liberally on them. These musical forms are not neat categorizations, of course, but followed historical developments which can be traced back across what are now politically set borders. Nevertheless, since the time of the nation's birth, the musical subgenres that have become associated with Uruguay are identified in a groundbreaking musicological study by Lauro Ayestaran; this work appeared in print between 1944 and 1963, in various periodicals. The book was first published in 1967. In it Ayestarán traces the development of Uruguayan folklore, from indigenous influences that remained (chana-charrua, which disappeared in the nineteenth century); to the four main cycles of the formation of Uruguayan folkloric music: (1) country dances and songs (*la media cana, el cielito, el perico; la milonga, la cifra, and la vidalita; el estilo* and *la payada*. In this early stage it became evident that the foremost instrument of the music of the area was the guitar (Ayestarán 1971: 8–10); (2) Northern Song Forms: *la chamarrita, la Tirana, el carangueijo,* among others; (3) Classical European Songs: these were part of the inherited forms in Hispanic song that persisted in the new environment, and was preserved in its original form: children's songs with more than one hundred melodies, some dating from the eighteenth century— *villancicos, romances, rondas, arrullos* (1971: 11), a few of the nineteenth, but the majority are from earlier periods; among the romances, Ayestarán notes that there he identified thirty-two types (1971: 12); and (4) Afro-Uruguayan music, such as *el candombe* (1971: 12). There are examples such as the *candombe-beat* and the *canción* (song) represented in the poems set to music in Uruguay after 1960 that are variations and fusions of the fourth category.

The majority of the poems set to music from 1960 to 1985 are of the *canción* variety. From a total of approximately 415 poems set to music during that time, 60 percent can be classified as *canciones*. The registration of this term, according to AGADU's records, is used for compositions for which musicians do not have a more suitable denomination. Although not a highly specified subgenre, it nonetheless emphasizes the hibridity of styles prevalent at that time. As a result, although the musical compositions possessed predominantly folkloric overtones in the broadest sense of the term, the forms reactivated and experimented with traditional styles to infuse them with original and contemporary traits. A significant proportion of the *canciones* contained elements rooted in folkloric musical forms.

To illustrate, let us take a brief look at an example of a text such as these found in the poem by Idea Vilariño, "*La canción*," set to music by Alfredo Zitarrosa, with musical guitar accompaniment and a folkloric singing style. Regarding the rhythmic potential of Vilariño's poetry, according to Mexican poet Octavio Paz, in her work, "rhythm is not a measure: it a vision of the world" [my translation] ("*el ritmo no es medida; es visión del mundo*" (Crellis Secco 1990: 511). Alfredo Zitarrosa found inspiration for his composition appropriately titled "*La canción y el poema*" ("The Song and the Poem"), calling attention to the birth of the piece. The original nine verses of Vilariño's poem (published in *Canciones*, 1993a) become in Zitarrosa's musical text, the chorus (Vilariño 1993b: 73).[9] Around this nucleus he adds a framework of two new verses, comprised of eight lines each. The additions contextualize the core poem and set it off against heightened quotidian details. In this way, the original poem becomes the concentrated emotive center of the text. Another aspect that marks the transition from the verses to the chorus is a reference to the blend of voices mentioned. Thus the poet's voice fuses with that of the popular singer.

The remaining 40 percent of the texts contained in the Uruguayan case study correspond to clearly recognizable traditional forms. The *milonga*, with fifty-two texts, or 9 percent of the total, is the second-most highly represented subgenre after the *canción*. Following in descending order of quantitative importance, are the *chamarrita* (thirteen), *balada* (eleven), *candombe* (eleven), *polca* (seven), *vals* (five), *cielito* (three), *tango* (three), *schotis* (two), *gato* (two), *habanera* (two), *pericón* (two); and the following with one text each: the *afro-cubana*, *candombe-beat*, *chacarera*, *danza*, *fado*, *huella*, *marcha military*, *milonga-canción*, *ranchera*, *son*, *tango-canción*, and *zapateado*.

The *milonga* is the most powerful example. It resonated more strongly in the twentieth century Uruguayan cultural imaginary and is a vehicle for representing community, solidarity and justice. The insistence on popular oral cultural expressions as sources of identity and links to the past serve as keys to understanding the formation of Uruguayan identity. In part, these values are represented by the idealization of gauchesque life, which bring to the Uruguayan imaginary symbols of an innate noble justice, rebellion, and telluric belonging, even if these are fraught with political maneuvers and complex appropriations at various time in the late nineteenth and early twentieth centuries when the figure of the gaucho was adopted to romanticize or fictionalize national images.

One of the poets most associated with references to the art of the *payador,* or singing gaucho, and for his extensive collaboration with representatives of popular music in Uruguay is Washington Benavides. This poet, born in Tacuarembo, a region in the interior of the country, published in 1969 a book of poetry entitled *Las milongas.* This was to become his best-selling work, with two subsequent editions, the last one in 1993, which includes additional poems under the revised title *Las milongas y otras canciones.* In a critical study of this work, Ricardo Pallares explains, "[t]he title *Las milongas* alludes to a type of song and music that is very much ours, popular, adorned with scales and flourishes, and implicitly, alludes to a type of dance. Both of these aspects possess a diffusion and tradition that is as much urban as it is rural" [my translation] (Pallares 1992: 11). The last characteristic manifests the milonga's appeal as a musical symbol representing all of the country, making it the ideal vehicle for expression in popular Uruguayan culture.

As an example we can examine a *milonga* (poem) by Benavides analyzed by Pallares. Referring to a text *"Yo no soy de por aquí"* (I'm not from around here), published in *Las milongas* (1969), Pallares explains, "If the patrimonious land is an abbreviated and early form of the spirit of the Nation (in as much as it is an idiosyncratic trait present in River Plate literature of gauchesque origins), then this homeland is as much a sinecdoque as it is a harbinger of doubt. At the same time it signals that the doubt is reabsorbed in the desire pursuit of the spirit of the homeland. The first-person subject aspires to recuperate or define its sense of identity by returning its soul to its original place" (Pallares 1992: 17). The return aims to reassure the subject, while at the same time hides an unknown danger that must be faced. Many of Benavides's poems, such as this one, were to appear in the repertoire of the leading popular musicians of the time for their ability to fuse historical allusion and contemporary rebellion in the face of the socio-political dangers of the time and cultural threats from external forces.

In the same way, his collaborations with the young musicians of the day manifest confident interplay with other cultural expressions; the Tacuarembó Group in particular was inspired to a great extent on the Tropicalia movement in Brazil that fused Anglo-American rock sounds with the more traditional autochthonous subgenres of the region. The poem interpreted above was registered at AGADU as having been set to music by Daniel Viglietti in 1971, as a *"canción,"* which is interesting given the inspiration of the *milonga* subgenre inherent in the title of the collection where it appeared in print. The song does not appear on Viglietti's LP album released that year (*Canciones chuecas*). In that year Viglietti founded the independent record label

Ayuí/Tacuabé with fellow musicians Pepe Guerra, Braulio López (both components of the group Los Olimareños, formed in 1962) and classical composer and musicologist Coriún Aharonián to promote Uruguayan music. The following year "the number of records of Música Popular Uruguaya diminishes in number, as well as the number of recitals. The song themes become more politicized, there is a more general adoption of the use of Spanish language for the songs, and the public becomes more adept at reading between the lines of the lyrics" (Rios 1995: 26). The fact that this occurs the year leading up to the military coup is no mere coincidence. What is more difficult to assess is to what extent the relationship of poetry and music would have developed apart from these socio-political circumstances.

Fabregat and Dabezies suggest in 1983 that prior to the above-noted innovations in the 1970s "Uruguay did not possess a purely distinct cultural heritage in musical forms [and this] always swayed the balance in favor of the verbal texts of the compositions. And within these texts, exigency grew to the same degree as the situation improved. Even in the case of the *murgas*—the most popular and autochthonous musical genre—the *pueblo* required increasingly better texts. When in the [19]60s the interpreters were chosen for their ability to craft verses, in the face of the vacuous product imported from commercial firms, the option was clearly defined. Uruguayans had found, in their own way, a national identity" (Fabregat and Dabezies 1983: 19). Uruguayan poetry became a stronghold for the expression of that national identity, in general terms, but it would soon also bring to the fore a battle for the distinction of shared cultural values and to the debate on how to contribute to elevating the production of high quality of verbal texts for the *canciones populares* evident in the corpus of settings until 1990.

POETRY IN THE *CANTO POPULAR URUGUAYO*

By the late 1960s and throughout the 1970s poetry, thus, became more radically and profoundly integrated into the popular music of Latin America through the emergence of the "Nueva Canción," or "New Song," movement. In Uruguay this genre formed what became known as the *Canto Popular Uruguayo* (CPU). These "New Songs" manifested a predominant focus on the poetic force of the lyrics, which in turn fostered greater collaboration from poets, as well as musical structures that reinforced the communicative power of the lyrics.

The most represented poets in the total corpus of texts registered as set to music after 1960 are Benavides, Benedetti, and Vilariño; they were also the most willing to contribute texts as lyrics and they did so by composing these in close collaboration with musical artists. Other poets included in the body of poetic work set to music in this period are Delmira Agustini, Victor

Cunha, Líber Falco, Julio Herrera y Reissing, Juana de Ibarbourou, Circe Maia, and Osiris Rodríguez Castillos.

For Uruguayan poet Washington Benavides, the CPU and popular music in general represented a possible "defense of poetry" (Interview 1995) from the predominance of new forms of technology and art. The contemporary conscience of the crisis had its roots in the changes that began manifesting themselves in the 1940s and 1950s, and the effects of mass culture in the second half of the twentieth century, when a greater proportion of the public gained access to television, radio, audio and audio-visual reproductions, and more recently, technology associated with cyberspace. These aspects, combined with a more localized need to revalue the tradition of the Uruguayan trouboubador, the *payador*, or singing *gaucho* and guitarist, as a popular vein to support the autochthonous sense of identity and values of community.

HYBRID TEXTS AND CULTURAL HISTORY

What does the study of the relationship of poetry and popular music imply about the boundaries between these genres, and how does that relate to the value-generating process inherent in those forms? In other disciplinary terms of study, it is also interesting to examine whether a poem that is set to music is seen to belong subsequently only to the realm of music or can it still be considered literature? That is, what is the relationship of music and literature in this case? Why do these merged forms emerge at certain times? How does the study of the lyrics of popular songs fit into literary criticism? These are some of the more poignant issues that arise in this subject.

The *Princeton Encyclopedia of Poetry and Poetics* lists numerous ways that Anglo-American songs of the 1960s are related to modern poetry (Perrone 1988: 15). This also calls to the forefront the question of the survival of the lyrics of popular music, in this case rock music, on the printed page. Allen Ginsberg suggests, "Rock lyrics should be considered together with their music as a unique poetic construction: since many rock lyricists 'think not only in terms of the words but also in music simultaneously,' they in fact create a new genre of 'rhyming personal verse, realistic and imaginative' (980)" (my translation; Perrone 1988: 15). In Brazil, the effects of *Concrete Poetry* on the production of musical texts is one of the most notable advancements. By the same token, Brazilian literary critic Augusto de Campos stated in the late 1960s that the greatest innovations in poetry were being produced by the composers of MPB, or Popular Brazilian Music, so much so that it called the interest of literary critics and cultural analysts of the time (Perrone 1988: 15). In 1968, Augusto de Campos wrote *Balanço de Bossa,* for example, in which he studies the poetic discourse of the best-known composers. According to Charles Perrone, this critical anthology had important literary implications (Perrone 1988: 9). In his book, Augusto de Campos, a distinguished poet, translator, and literary critic, considered the popular songwriter Caetano Veloso the major poet of the new generation (De Campos 1974: 9).

Brazilian literary critic Haroldo de Campos also wrote about these musician-poets in an article for his book *América Latina en su literatura*. In a 1972 essay titled "Superación de los lenguajes exclusivos," he cites that during the twentieth century we witnessed the transcending (superación) of the former strict demarcation of genres (my translation). The prior exclusivity of languages, which he views as "a natural corollary of the regulating and normative conception that was the characteristic of 'classicism,' gave way to a reversal of this division toward an appreciation of hybrid constructions" (De Campos 1972: 279). Indeed, literary culture in the second half of the twentieth century dissolved the overly compartmentalized tendencies. Haroldo de Campos attributes this to "the Romantic revolution against the predominantly prohibitive character of the classic aesthetic norms and manifested itself above all . . . in the lexical camp" (my translation) as well as in syntactic structure more closely resembling colloquial language (De Campos 1972: 279). Thus, literary culture began to assimilate and integrate genres of various registers, joining texts that were previously considered "high culture" with those formerly categorized as "low culture" or "popular culture" and those parting form the "oral traditions"; the latter had been excluded from what de Campos calls the "patron-language." This was in large part influenced by the rise of the "mass-media" (De Campos 1972: 280), which, although we cannot delve into much detail here on this aspect, suffice to make reference to the press, the invention of the telegraph and its influence on the way news is communicated, its style of delivery, which closely resembles the oral cultures because it is not linear but rather "synesthetic, tactile, simultaneous and tribal" (De Campos 1972: 282). Thus the mass press, which Mallarmé was to call the "modern popular poem" due to its epic characteristics, and later its evolution and widespread contemporary electronic repercussions which Marshall McLuhan came to hail as a global influence on the transmission of cultural messages. According to McLuhan, "'hybridism' is a technique of discovery and creation, as he revealed in his studies of Mallarmé, Joyce and Poe. What is most telling of these hybrid forms is the exigency on a 'do-it-yourself' type participation of the reader/listener" (McLuhan 1995: 282). It is within this context of the movements of literary culture that the genres of poetry, literature, and popular music converge.

In Uruguay this was to awaken the latent values of liberty that first created its identity, but the artists had to do so without their works becoming "petrified" (Castillo Durante 2000: 160) as a thing of the past. Their relevance and agency as voices in the cultural dialogue depended on it.

CONCLUSION

The prominence of popular music in the domain of poetic production during the latter half of the twentieth century can be attributed to the socio-political context. The significant increase in the number of collaborations between poetry and music in the case of Uruguay could be argued to have led "to the development of a new social reaction . . . or to the challenges posed by certain processes" (Foucault 2001: 172). In this way, in Foucaultian terms, the "problematization is not an effect or consequence of a historical context or situation, but is an answer given by definite individuals (although you may find this same answer given in a series of texts, and at a certain point the answer may become so general that it also becomes anonymous" (Foucault 2001: 172). The socio-political conditions did not in themselves create the aesthetic responses; rather these were more detectable at a time when the country was seeking to redefine itself from within and in its relation to the world. The simultaneous creation of poets and musicians across styles and influences gave rise to a reactivation of the lyrical expression of the oral traditions and the creative social awareness of colloquial forms of language to inspire innovations in literary forms.

Many of the poets and musicians who were exiled during the second phase of military rule in Uruguay did not fully reintegrate into the Uruguayan socio-political arena after the return to democratic government in 1985. Instead many chose to continue to reside in other countries and were able to forge new cultural resonances across shared values with other artists. Mario Benedetti, for example, resided in Spain for many years; for a time he wrote in his poetry about the process of "desexilio" or of the problematized process of returning to a sense of belonging to a culture and a country after such traumatic experiences. The dialogue continues today, and much more could be discussed. Benedetti's poetry, as one example only, continues to serve as an emblem of certain ideological debates that stemmed from the second half of the twentieth century in Uruguay and that continued to be remembered in song. Daniel Viglietti still performs their collaborations. They had traveled together to take part in various international presentations since the launch of their work "*A dos voces*." With music by Viglietti and poetry by Benedetti, the performances also included musical settings and recitations of poems by Viglietti and Circe Maia. "*A dos voces*" was first presented in Mexico in 1978. Latin American, Canadian, and European dates since then expanded the reach of the work beyond its original borders. Recent performances have occurred in Uruguay, even after the death of Benedetti in 2009, and in Canada in 2013. This attests to the ability of these voices to manifest what Said had described earlier in the capacity for authentic artistic expression to cross cultural boundaries along shared values and beyond the space and time in which they were created. Far from limiting the conclusions to the selected case study, the analysis serves to extrapolate at least some of the conclusions to other comparable cases.

NOTES

1. *Ekphrastic,* from Greek, *ekfrasis:* art from other art, as poems inspired by paintings or photographs, or songs inspired from poems. The musical equivalent of *ekphrasis* is a relatively recent phenomenon; for a further review of this topic see Siglind Bruhn (2001). In particular, Bruhn distinguishes between Program music which "narrates or paints, suggests or represents scenes or stories (and by extension events or characters) that enter the music from the composer's mind," whereas Musical ekphrasis "narrates or paints stories or scenes created by an artist *other* than the composer of the music and in another artistic medium. Furthermore, musical ekphrasis typically relates not only to the content of the poetically or pictorially conveyed source text but usually also to one of the aspects distinguishing the mode of primary representation—its style, its form, its mood, or a conspicuous arrangement of details. [. . .] Program music represents, while musical ekphrasis re-presents."

2. For a more detailed analysis and description of the related Latin American context and Uruguay in this regard, please see my doctoral dissertation (Figueredo 1999a). This research originated from my interest in the relation between poetry and music in Latin America as a twentieth century phenomenon in the work of poets such as Cesar Vallejo, Alvaro Figueredo, Pablo Neruda, Nicolas Guillén, Gabriela Mistral, and Mario Benedetti, to name a few. However, after an initial stage of field research undertaken from 1994 to 1994 in Uruguay (Montevideo, Pan de Azúcar, and Punta del Este) and in Brazil (Sao Paulo, Rio de Janeiro, and Brasilia), a specifically Uruguayan case study with ties to the 1960s developments in Brazil surfaced. Ivan Kmaid (1995), also a journalist and poet, believed strongly that the phenomenon of poetry set to music in Uruguay had reached a critical mass that was timely to study. According to Kmaid, this phenomenon, such as had been done in Brazil about waves of interaction between poets and musicians, was beginning to be perceptible as such a "movement" or a "tendency" in a similar way in Uruguay.

3. This statement works a little bit different in the Argentine case, because the militant song in this country starts in 1944 and is well underway in the 1950s, before the Cuban revolution.

4. In the 1950s, Horacio Guarany (one of the founders of the militant song movement in Argentina) also musicalized Guillen's poems. One of them, *"No sé porque piensas tú [soldado que te odio yo],"* became quite famous and was recorded not only by Guarany, but also by some of the most popular singers of the time.

5. Although primarily a dance, as were most of original forms of Uruguay's folkloric repertoire, the "cielo" often assumed a lyrical form that was meant only to be sung. Such are the "Cielitos" a musical form that developed in Uruguay between 1813 and 1850, during the first wars of Independence. One of the original and most prominent musicologists of Uruguay, Lauro Ayestarán (1913–1966) commented, in his description of this musical subgenre, that "for us it is born wrapped in an aura of liberty" (my translation; 1971: 111).

6. One of the principal sources of data for this study was the *Asociación General de Autores del Uruguay (AGADU),* a society which administers the copyrights of authors of the country. Founded in 1929, AGADU represents approximately 6,000 authors (Ríos 1995: 131).

7. Until the 1960s there is no market for Uruguayan popular music; it is in this decade that greater access emerges for a wider audience. The year that divides the two stages of the phenomenon is the same as that of the coup d'etat on June 27, 1973 (Ríos 1995: 26).

8. The end of the phenomenon in 1985 coincides with its chronological trajectory, reflecting a change in conditions affecting the reception of the poems set to music. In 1984, "elections were held for the first time since the de facto period, resulting in the election of Dr. Julio María Sanguinetti as President of the Republic" (Ríos 1995: 29). A democratic government was reinstated in 1985.

9. For complete text of the poem in its song setting, and a sound file of the same, see Gabriel Tuya's Blog, http://elgatoutopico.blogspot.ca/2008/05/la-cancion-y-el-poema-idea-vilario.html.

Chapter Seven

Atahualpa Yupanqui

The Latin American Precursor of the Militant Song Movement

Carlos Molinero and Pablo Vila

Well before the militant song movement became a force for social change in Argentina in particular, and Latin America in general, Atahualpa Yupanqui was writing and singing songs that, in hindsight, were laying the groundwork for it. In this chapter we will chronicle Yupanqui's foundational role by following his trajectory from the late 1930s and early 1940s to the early 1970s; we will also analyze the sharp twists and turns his career took, with special emphasis on his conflictive relationship with the concept of "protest song" as applied to his artistic production. In a word, the part Yupanqui played in pioneering the militant song, and the conceptual strictures he placed on it, had decisive consequences for the development of a movement that would spread continent-wide.

As precursor, Yupanqui's primary contribution to the Latin American militant song movement is two-fold: he introduced important themes that would be developed over time, and he provided the sense of mission essential to any movement, musical or otherwise. For reasons of space, out of Yupanqui's vast repertoire, we have singled out for discussion the two themes that, in our view, were landmarks in the subsequent militant song movement: the vindication of actors previously made invisible by the power structure (above all, Argentina's indigenous population), and critical commentary on the socio-political conditions of his time.

PRECEDENTS

Although, in general, the social question was never absent from *Criollismo* or popular criollo culture in Argentina,[1] as exemplified by its importance in *Martín Fierro* (ca. 1870), as well as in the *Criollista Discourse* (see Prieto 1988 and Ludmer [1988] 2012), it was treated very differently in the nineteenth century than will be the case in the militant song of the second half of the twentieth century.

Folklore as a cultural phenomenon did not merit serious consideration until 1910. Centennial generation intellectuals sought it out in order to reaffirm the rural origins of nationhood in the face of the massive entry of European immigrants that had altered Argentina's socio-demographic profile, and the levers of political power as well. Through their efforts, the culture (and within it, the music) of the rural subaltern class came to be candidly viewed as an ingenuous whole comprising everyone living on the land; the resulting undifferentiated cultural composite of landowner and peon became the authentic expression of the real Argentina, which suited land owners fine. Yupanqui changed this mindset (Molinero 2011: 133). And this made him the cornerstone of the militant song movement to be analyzed below. As militant, irrespective of any particular socio-political affiliation (he was a member of the Communist Party from 1945–1952), Yupanqui made his mark early in the field of music, going on to exercise unparalleled influence in the course of a lifetime not only as musician, but also as writer, journalist, and filmmaker. This "multimedial" approach (also begun precociously) mirrored the image that Yupanqui sought to project in his own life, where man and artist, intellectual and man of action, essence and appearance, are inseparable parts of one and the same integral reality. He did not see his defense of Argentina's indo-criollo roots, and his fight for the underdog and national cultural as contradictory, although they might seem so in retrospect. Rather, for him they constituted a historically coherent image of an Argentine essence to be simultaneously defended and changed.

VINDICATING INDIGENOUS ARGENTINES

In a short article entitled "Indigenous Recital in Phoenix Radio" published in the magazine *Sintonía* on April 6, 1935, a person by the name of "Atahualpa Tupanqui" is described as follows: "A pleasing—and infrequent—musical recital is what the performer Atahualpa Tupanqui has offered on the Phoenix radio station. Indigenous music has not been fully represented until the magnificent pianist Argentino Valle revealed it with his moving interpretations." This may be one of the first references in print to Atahualpa as performer. Preceding considerably the commercial release of his first recordings in

1941, it also antedates the non-commercial recordings he made in 1936 for Néctar Yerba, when three of his records were given as a bonus for buying a certain amount of the product. Of interest is the title of the article, which encapsulates what is, in our view, one of the principal hallmarks of the "Yupanqui effect" in popular Argentine and Latin American music: the vindication of indigenous themes in popular music.

Yupanqui introduced significant innovations in the folklore of his epoch that, among the most important, include the vindication of the Indian, the social question, and deregionalization of the music repertoire (Molinero 2011: 137). However, they were not perceived as groundbreaking at the time. We will first examine how he deals with the vindication of the Indian in his music.

It is important to keep in mind that the attempt (real and symbolic) to annihilate the gaucho, launched by the ruling elite (and its organic intellectuals) under the banner of "civilization or barbarism," was followed by an attack of nativist fever affecting the next generation, who felt that "they were losing the nation" as a result of the onslaught of European immigrants who, it is worth noting, were not the kind of Europeans (more precisely, the praised Northern Europeans) their forerunners imagined were going to migrate to Argentina. Thus, while gaucho-inspired literature is in vogue, a revival of the folk genre is also underway in the field of music; both are seen as representative of the "true nation," by which is meant the flatlands of the gauchos, not the cities where workers—many of them socialists and anarchists at the time—lived. During the first three decades of the twentieth century there are quite explicit government-sponsored attempts to this end in the field of music: the musician and musicologist Andrés Chazarreta is promoted by Leopoldo Lugones in his lectures on *El Payador* (1916) early on, and supported and praised by Ricardo Rojas (University of Buenos Aires President in the late 1920s) when he later performed in Buenos Aires, while popular expressions of the same movement include the rural repertoire of Gardel-Razzano, among other examples.

But the center of gravity of this effort to revive nativist culture and the government support (primarily symbolic) it receives is the gaucho, not the Indian: the campesino or field hand is seen as the "natural" ally of the landowner, who pays his wages and whose patrimony he defends against raids by the Indians, the true "outsiders" in this discursive-political structure. Shrouded in silence, the Indian as such does not figure in criollo folk songs. If required to synthesize what are we talking about in a single example, it would be the *"Zamba de la Tolderia"* ("Zamba of the Indian Camp") by Buenaventura Luna, where, in his battle against the Indian, the gaucho is the hero, and the Indian a savage who "burns houses and steals women." In short, at this point in time, the Indian is either invisible or a savage.

This is precisely what Atahualpa Yupanqui is going to change. Beginning with his pseudonym and the social actor he chooses to address, Atahualpa distinguishes himself from the folk music of his day. By selecting a first and last name belonging to Inca emperors, Atahualpa issues a clear challenge to the criollo folklore in vogue at the time. Totally different from figures like Chazarreta, who keeps his own last name, or Eusebio de Jesús Dojorti Roco (the second-to-last name a deformation of "Daugherty" that occurred after the British invasion and the need for the family to settle in the provinces), who takes the name of "Buenaventura Luna," at only thirteen years of age Héctor Roberto Chavero adopts an indigenous name in an epoch when vindicating the Indian was nothing if not quixotic. It won't be until thirty years later in the mid- and late 1950s that, with the appearance of Horacio Guarany, Los Huanca Hua, Los Cantores de Quilla Huasi, among others, there is a certain proliferation of indigenous stage names in the world of folk music.

Yupanqui's first songs, composed and recorded in the 1930s and early 1940s, aim in the same direction: many of them depict figures from what Atahualpa called "the landscape of the Ande": paisanos of indigenous origin (usually Kolla or Calchaquí) who, like migrant workers, come down from "their hills" to the flatlands to harvest crops in northeastern Argentina, usually cane fields in the provinces of Tucumán and Salta. As Yolanda Fabiola Orquera (2008) reminds us, between 1936 and 1944 Yupanqui records four songs directly linked to the topic under discussion: *"Caminito del indio"* ("Indian Trail") (the first song he ever composed, in 1928); *"Ahí andamos, señor!"* ("And This Is the Way We Are Doing, Sir"); *"Vidala del cañaveral"* ("Vidala of the Reedbed"); and *"La viajerita"* ("The Little Traveler"),

> [. . .] that around 1937 was sung by cane cutters en route to the furrows of sugarcane [. . .] many of those singing it had had to leave the hills where they live to work in the cane fields. The repeated references to the obligatory exile and the loneliness is associated with the constitutive "sorrow" of the yupanquian poetic subject. [. . .] For its part, the place of origin is described as what is not contaminated. [. . .] This allows the subject to reaffirm himself in the flatlands that are foreign to him [. . .] this is the same meaning that is found in the initial verses of *"Piedra y camino"* ("Stone and Road"): "From the hill I go down /road and stone" [. . .] the subject of these stories lets us know that, despite his loneliness, his isolation, and the "sorrows" he suffers, the relationship he maintains with his ancestral environment is harmonious [. . .] (Orquera 2008: 195).

This *"indo-criollismo"* was a constant in his first creative period, not only in his music, but also in his performances and written works. It permeates *Cerro Bayo*, his first book and a case in point:

> The voice of the quena was always sad: the Quechuan farm worker used it as a talisman for forgetting. Indians accompanied the death of the sun with the

music of quenas. All the peoples of Latin America confided to their reed flute their sorrows and their dreams. They lightened the soul, mitigated torture, cauterized pain. The song of the quena is the only treasure left to the man of the land. Because the other treasures passed into the hands of the usurper. Even the language was lost. Because without organization rebellion is useless. Condorkanki in Perú, Pilltipico in Homahuaca, Juan Calachaquí in the valleys of Tucma already paid for their inexperience and their rash urgency. And far away, in the south, the heroisms of Catriel, Calfú-curá, Cacique Benancio and Chillahué are becoming blurred (Yupanqui [1947] 1967: 27).

In other words, the quena covers the forgetting of a race that unites in its defeat Peru, Homahuaca, and the Mapuche south. Defeat caused only (or primarily) by lack of organization and inexperience in anticipating what was to come.

In *El Canto del Viento* (in 1965 now) Yupanqui says that only subalterns, "cane-cutting arms, of obscure destiny" and nature are the preserve of immaterial history (the "*hechizada bolsa del viento*" or spellbound bag of wind). Meaning all truth that is sung can be revived as weapon (given that it is a "*punta de flecha*" or "arrowhead," an Indian weapon, of "*un adiós bagualero*" or bagualian goodbye) with the playing of Indian flutes in order that, after the pain is conquered, it may be (this is its destiny) transfigured, becoming sonorous dignity. And so the story continues, returning to the wind of recommencing history.

A more concrete example of Yupanqui's vindication of the Indian is his scathing criticism of the Peronist government, published in the Communist Party daily *La Hora* under the title "Letter to the Kollas," for not responding to the Raid for Peace when, in 1946, indigenous Argentines marched on Buenos Aires seeking redress for the confiscation of their land (paradoxically, marchers had been warmly received upon arrival). In the letter Yupanqui, according to Orquera (2008), affirms his subjectivity on the basis of his imaginary conjunction with the Kolla Indian, which is the enunciative position he assumes to describe the scene when the Raid reaches downtown Buenos Aires. Indeed, by not limiting himself to making Indians visible, here Yupanqui goes slightly beyond his position in his songs to imaginarily take his place alongside them as the voice that represents and incarnates indigenous Argentines: "Although all the voices fall drowned out, bought off, debased or bored, my voice, the voice of my dark song, that of the free verse of this guitar of mine that knows about roads and distress, will always be your voice, the voice of your hill, that of the open, desolate bleak upland, that of the fierce jungle" (Valko 2007: 129)

All this not only makes Yupanqui unique in the cultural milieu of the 1930s and 1940s—the thematic vindication of indigenous people will not reappear in Argentine folk music until the mid-1960s (and then it will be expressed differently, due to the Americanist vision derived from the militancy of the time). His viewpoint was also at odds with the Peronist interpellation of poor people (its constituency, the "pueblo") as "*descamisados o cabecitas*" (shirtless or dark-skinned): even in Peronist terms, if not included among the categories of campesino, peon, rural day laborer or urban worker, the indigenous Argentine fell outside the scope of the discourse sustaining its political project.

What is interesting is that all these events (his songs, his criticism of Perón's government management of the Kolla rally, and the like) unfold within the framework of Yupanqui's own pro-indigenous vision that, viewed retrospectively, is itself full of symbolic contradictions. Indeed, given the originality of his position, this was all but inevitable, and, more importantly, for him indigenous and criollo are not contradictory terms, because he sees the indigenous world as the natural, necessary precedent for the criollo's own, not as its enemy. In that regard, for instance, his first recordings were made under the auspices of the "El Mangruyo Traditionalist Group" in 1936 (where "mangruyo" is precisely the element of the fort's architecture whose role is precisely to warn the soldiers of the arrival of Indian raids); for a firm marketing yerba mate (an industry whose origin is based on an indigenous custom, but which is certainly not known for respecting the rights of indigenous workers). And Yupanqui performed in public dressed like a gaucho from the pampas, eschewing garments linked to any indigenous tribe, from the beginning until well-advanced in his career; and the incongruences go on and on. The obvious conclusion is that Atahualpa synthesized in his person currents present in a society with multiple fault lines: born in the province of Buenos Aires, he signed with a name recalling Incan aristocrats; he studied classical guitar and sang songs originating in criollo genres that vindicated indigenous Argentines; his second and last marriage was to a French-Canadian concert pianist, Antoinette Paule Pepin Fitzpatrick, double gold medal winner at the Conservatory of Cannes, and his hyper-cultured wife coauthored (under the pseudonym Pablo del Cerro) some of his most beautiful songs such as "*El alazán*" ("The Sorrel") and "*Indiecito dormido*" ("The Dormant Little Indian").

Similar contradictions also plagued the Peronist government. After massively casting their ballot for Perón, indigenous people found there was really no place for them as such in party discourse and policy. This very much despite the fact that Perón seemed unaware of the problem, as reflected in the anecdote describing his first meeting with Yupanqui, when Perón said, "With that Indian face of yours, how could you not be a Peronist?" Our focusing on the indigenous theme for analysis should not be taken to mean, however, that it was his most important contribution to the field of popular music. Other innovations include adding poetic complexity to the genre, which aligns him more closely with certain poets from the 1950s, such as Castilla, Dávalos, Perdiguero, Petrocelli, Tejada Gómez, and Lima Quintana, among others, than with his contemporaries in the 1930s and 1940s; his *"El arriero va"* ("The Drover Goes") can also be pointed to as the first militant song in the genre; to name just a few. On the contrary, our objective is to draw attention to an aspect of Yupanqui's trajectory that has been treated only in passing to date, although studies like those by Yolanda Fabiola Orquera (not surprisingly from the province of Tucumán) have begun to give the topic the importance it deserves:

> [W]hat Yupanqui did during the initial stage of his career was work from an indo-criollo perception of reality. [. . .] His contribution signifies a notable change, since he feels he knows the experiential ambience of those he is going to represent, taking on their way of feeling, believing, and hoping. [. . .] His voice becomes the catalyst that lifts the indigenous worldview out of its solitude and isolation, placing it in the amplified circuit of the cultural industry (Orquera 2008: 199).

Yupanqui saw himself as "the singer of forgotten arts." Notwithstanding the complexities discussed above, in the 1930s and 1940s he was one of the few voices vindicating what might be described as "the subaltern of the subaltern"; in essence, what he accomplished was to give a "voice" to this figure in urban environments. In this he distinguished him from both Peronism, which had great difficulty in incorporating the Indian qua Indian into its discourse, as mentioned above, and from the folk music that preceded and was contemporaneous with him until, at least, the mid-1960s. Before Yupanqui arrived on the scene—and for at least thirty years after—the Indian in folk music was depicted, like in the history books, as a savage synonymous with raids, barbarism, and bloodshed. *"Zamba de la toldería,"* with its image of "atavistic savagery" in the terms of Kaliman (2004: 76), is emblematic in this regard. By contrast, in Atahualpa's work, the Indian is viewed as "wise ancestor," as someone natural and uncontaminated but forgotten who must be rescued from oblivion. The reason being because he was the preeminent source of mystery and teachings for the musician himself (Yupanqui 1965a):

La guitarra fue a los indios	The guitar went to the Indians
para aprender su misterio	To learn their mystery
y volvió al pueblo, más honda	And came back to people, deeper
de tanto beber silencio	From drinking so much silence.

Yet someone who is neither seen nor heard cannot be integrated into a project for nationhood. Yupanqui makes constant reference to "silence" when speaking of the Indian and his "Ande." Silence as wisdom, as speaking little but wisely, but also meaning things "they know that we don't know."

This leads Atahualpa to denounce the silence to which the indigenous voice is subjected in terms of the "silencing of silence," of keeping its wisdom silent; yet at one and the same time his mandate is, on the contrary, to "listen to the silence" and learn from it as a source for unveiling mysteries. Thus, the obligatory first step is the recognition of his (the Indian is mostly male in Yupanqui's account) value due to his subject position being an Indian, not a rural wage earner or day laborer. And this is the point of departure for pursuing indigenous vindications that include, primarily, the right to (and respect for) the land Indians occupy, as Yupanqui suggests in *"Camino del indio"*: *"sendero coya sembrao de piedras, antes que en la montaña la Pachamama se ensombreciera"* (Indian path seeded with stones, before the Pachamama in the mountain becomes somber). If recognition of indigenous Argentines as such is Yupanqui's first legacy to the militant song movement, his preoccupation with the social conditions of his time is the next.

CRITICALLY COMMENTING ON THE SOCIO-POLITICAL CONDITIONS OF HIS TIME

Ask an Argentine to name the first "protest song" in their country, and the answer will almost always be *"El arriero va"* written by Atahualpa Yupanqui in 1944. This "common sense" assumption about the genre is worth examining because, strictly speaking, a number of songs written earlier could easily qualify as "protest songs" as well. One candidate might be *"Guerra a la Burguesía"* ("War on the Bourgeoisie"), an anarchist tango from the early 1900s. Or refining the search to the first popular protest song—*"Guerra a la Burguesía"* was quite obscure—the tango *"Pan"* ("Bread"), sung by Carlos Gardel in the late 1920s, would qualify. Further refining the distinction to the first popular protest song still remembered today (not many people remember *"Pan"*), Discépolo's *"Cambalache"* ("Junk Shop") and *"Yira, Yira"* ("And Goes and Go") (two very popular tangos from the 1930s) precede *"El arriero va,"* and most Argentines know at least some of the lyrics.

So the question remains: why *"El arriero va"*? A definitive response is beyond the scope of this chapter, but the short answer would be that Argentines automatically link the militant song movement to folk music, which would make *"El arriero va,"* the first folk song with social criticism, the first "protest song," effectively bypassing the aforementioned tangos, despite their quite poignant critical comments on the social conditions of their time.

Examined against the backdrop of the folk music that preceded it, *"El arriero va"* brought about a marked shift that may explain why it would tend to be identified tout court as the first militant song ever. Yet this makes the choice no less noteworthy, given the fact that the "protest" is limited to just two verses of a song that does not otherwise seem militant at all. Nevertheless, on the basis of these two verses "*El arriero va*" was deemed "revolutionary" back in 1944. The lines in question clearly caught on and became a rallying cry, striking a blow at the dominant view of the supposed poetic innocence and naiveté surrounding the campesino, his music, and his relationship with the landowner. The traditional peaceful panorama, depicted in folk music as reconciling the two parties, was regarded as the undisputed essence of Argentine nationhood at the time. With two verses, Yupanqui takes aim, points out, and denounces the unnamed distinction differentiating the rural "cohabitants"—landowner and laborer—that together produce the wealth and traditions inherent in this national essence. He accomplishes this with a spatial metaphor: while landowner and laborer appear to share the same road under equal conditions, a sharper eye reveals two very different things traveling down a single path.

In the song, a drover reflects on his life and sorrows, turning his eye, in the two verses in question, to society at large, where he observes that if "*las penas y las vaquitas, van por la misma senda. . . . Las penas son de nosotros/ Las vaquitas son ajenas*" (Sorrows and cattle, they go down the same path/ The sorrows are ours/The cattle are someone else's). Atahualpa explained on different occasions (not always in the same way) that he adapted something he heard a paisano say, which conveniently turns the verses into the projection or reflection of a reality taken from folklore; the two lines then become the expression of an implicit social criticism already held by rural inhabitants, not "placed there" by some politicized intellectual "stranger" protesting "from the outside" what is done to an "other." In this way, Yupanqui in the guise of "just another vernacular intellectual" simply articulates and spreads a preexisting social concern, albeit not unwittingly.

The interesting thing about "*El arriero va*" is that, in large part, it repeats the (usually) bucolic portrayal of agrarian life rendered standard by his predecessors. However, into this pastoral terrain, Atahualpa introduces the refrain he has heard ("gathered," collected and adapted to the rhyme scheme, that Atahualpa says he repeats, almost to the letter, as taken "from the people"). And with it he fixes a single, apparently minimal, but key idea: in contradiction to the hegemonic version current at the time of an "essential" Argentina linked to gaucho and countryside (itself mounted to counteract the opposite version of a "non-essential/alien Argentina awash with European immigrants") that equated them, drover and landowner are not the same thing.

The one and the other are part of the agrarian world. Just as the drover is an inevitable part of the other, for the owners of the cattle; for the drover, those owners are "the other." And this is what caught on.[2] It is the first noteworthy contested presentation of gaucho's reality as subaltern in Argentine folk music, recognizing himself as different (and, by the same token, inferior) and not an integral part of the hegemonic collective imaginary. The distinction as such is brought to the attention of the listener. Without displacing pastoralism, essentialism or any other of the many "isms" surrounding folk music at the time, what was sought—and amply achieved—was the inclusion of a social topic in a folk song.

But if we compare the songwriter's version of what the drover said with what Yupanqui actually wrote in the best-known refrain in Argentine folk music, his assertion of "only having reflected" what he heard is misleading. At least two variations exist of the drover's words. One is found in *Tierra que Anda* ([1948] 2006), where a couple of *anteños* (people from Anta region, Tucuman province) greet a cattle drover they pass going downhill: "How's it going Udilón?" "Like a well-worn joke," the drover "replies with the last two verses of a local stanza":

"¡Fieras pobrezas pasando	Having hard times
Y ajenas vacas tropiando!"	And driving somebody else's cattle

Another more credible version, with more details on the protagonists, figures in an interview with Yupanqui published in the newspaper *La Opinión*, October 14, 1973, and reproduced by Galasso (2009). In it the local gamekeeper is invited to eat a deer he poached; Antonio—"don Anto"—Fernández says he doesn't have time and, when asked what his hurry is, answers,

"es que tengo que andar nomás	I gotta be on my way
Ajenas culpas pagando	Gotta pay for somebody else's sins
Y ajenas vacas arriando"	Gotta drive somebody else's cattle

The changes made from the stanza heard to the song's lyrics are not innocent: the aim goes well beyond the desire for "folk" authenticity proclaimed by the composer. It also belies his pretention of only "representing" a social criticism already voiced by the "natives." In fact, in *"El arriero va"* Yupanqui is doing precisely what he will later criticize militant songwriters in the 1960s for doing: putting in the mouths of popular actors his own political position instead of merely "representing" an opinion already held by "natives." Thus, while in Fernández's refrain, sins are associated with sorrows, in *"El arriero va,"* sorrows and cattle are separate, and there is no doubt as to which belongs to whom in the social universe the drover lives in. By contrast, both sins and cattle are alien in Fernández's refrain, while in Yupanqui's song, on the road sorrows and cattle go together, but when divided up, the drover is left with the worst.

In our view, this justifies applying Farred's definition of vernacular intellectual to Yupanqui (Farred 2003). His ability to "elucidate what is ideological and animate what is political" that we have exemplified with this inaugural song—there will be others—is the means he uses to produce (rather than reproduce) a "subaltern" voice that resists, subverts, reconfigures, and has an impact on the dominant discourse (i.e., the vernacular). This dominant discourse first imposed silence on folk music and then reified it as ingenuous, making it politically malleable by anchoring it to a particular, very biased image of the past. Even if unsought, which it was not, the rupture occasioned by Yupanqui with the refrain under discussion reconfigured the dominant discourses, the consequences of which can be seen in the folk music that followed. In this sense "*El arriero va*" is not an "isolated" case in Yupanqui's repertoire as will be shown below. However, placing at the center of the scene "a campesino who sings" (and is not "sung about"), and who also conjures up in the listener identificatory pleasure and ideological resistance, is the beginning of something truly new in the folk genre.

To reiterate, Yupanqui does not see his innovations as affecting folk music. In his *Canto del Viento*, and more concretely, in his manifesto titled *Destino del Canto*, he reinforces his message that the singer's function is to return to the wind wayward shreds, "renewed" perhaps, that have been received from the same wind (symbolic and immaterial image of a natural people). And the one who does this will be "the one chosen by the earth," about whom he says,

> Sí; la tierra señala a sus elegidos.
> Y al llegar el final, tendrán su premio, nadie los nombrará, serán lo "anónimo,"
> pero ninguna tumba guardará su canto.

> Yes; the earth indicates who the chosen are.
> And when the end comes, they will have their recompense, no one will name them, they will be "anonymous,"
> but no tomb will hold their song . . . (Yupanqui 1965a)

And on this road toward producing an audible subaltern voice, Atahualpa's socio-political innovations continued. In practice, the following years were rich in "iconoclastic" production. Three outstanding examples between 1944 and 1965 are "*Las Preguntitas*" ("The Little Questions"), "*El pintor*" ("The Painter") and "*El poeta*" ("The Poet"). In point of fact these compositions were written between 1945 and 1953, as were the poem "Basta ya" and other more "inflammatory" verses that seem close to being political manifestos for the Communist Party,[3] which he joined during this period,[4] and not examples of "independent" poetic production.[5] It is difficult to establish when these compositions were first heard. Censored by the Peronist government during these years, Yupanqui was obliged to perform and record abroad.[6] Nevertheless, according to available information, those songs were recorded in France and Uruguay on singles and compilations, and, for sure, were made while Yupanqui was a member of the Communist Party, and, due to censorship, it meant that the recordings were not played on the radio or distributed in Argentina until Yupanqui left the Party, and probably not until after the fall of Peronism. When recorded by Jorge Cafrune well into the 1960s, "*El pintor*" and "*El poeta*" gained a wide audience and helped launch the signature decade of the militant folk song in Argentina (to be covered in the next chapter of this book).

In "*El pintor*," for example, Yupanqui rebukes the politically uncommitted artist, making clear his own position when he criticizes those who portray the social reality of rural Argentines as merely "picturesque" or *costumbrista* and imbued with the romanticized realism that colored folk music at the time. For Yupanqui, rather than "filter" reality, the artist should reflect it whole. In that regard he admonishes the painter that, although he was thinking he was doing a good thing, he only painted the putative protagonist of the song (characterized as a poor peasant), "from the outside," because he didn't care to take a look at him from the inside. In the next stanza the peasant wonders when will a painter come "who paints what I feel." The last stanzas go back to the initial claim that the painter was a bad one because, yes, poor people like the protagonist are part of the landscape; and yes, they are singing, but under their colorful ponchos, their stomach is empty. The painter was a bad one "since he only painted my poncho/and forgot about my hunger."

The song is a pledge in favor of the "honest" representation of subalterns' daily life, something that, for Atahualpa, was not characteristic of the artists of his day. The song itself is just such an honest representation, placing in the foreground precisely what the painter "forgot" to portray: the empty stomach under the campesino's colorful poncho.

A different criticism of the conventional folk perspective is advanced in "*El poeta*." The function of the artist is to act explicitly as head (vanguard) and source of support for the actual people, which means he must abandon the ivory tower and humbly take his place among them.[7] Once part of the people, the poet must do what was required of the painter in the previous song: honestly portray subalterns and their struggle for survival.

Tú crees que eres distinto,	You think you're different,
porque te dicen poeta,	because they call you a poet,
y tienes un mundo aparte,	and you live in your own world,
más allá de las estrellas.	beyond the stars.
De tanto mirar la luna,	From so much looking at the moon,
ya nada sabes mirar	you don't know how to look at anything now

Eres como un pobre ciego	You're like a poor blind man
que no sabe a dónde va	who doesn't know where he's going.
Vete a mirar los mineros,	Go look at the miners,
los hombres en el trigal,	the men in the wheat field,
y cántale a los que luchan,	And sing to those who fight
por un pedazo de pan.	for a crust of bread.

It is interesting to note that in this song "looking at the moon" symbolizes a distancing from reality for Yupanqui who, a short time later (after leaving the Communist Party) will become wildly popular with the song "*Luna tucumana*" ("Tucuman Moon") although (possibly for the same reason), he clearly states in the later composition that he doesn't sing to the moon "*porque alumbra nada mas*" (only because it sheds light). Living and creating in "*El poeta*" means having a political commitment and, as an artist, suffering and working for, in the name and as one of the people. The artist must not be an isolated entity, but instead an integral part of the reality from where, as subaltern and creative person, he talks, acts, and writes.

Poeta de ciertas rimas	Poeta of certain rhymes
vete a vivir a la selva	go live in the jungle,
y aprenderás muchas cosas,	and you will learn a lot of things,
del hachero y sus miserias.	from the woodcutter and his miseries.
Vive junto con el pueblo	Live with the people:
no lo mires desde afuera,	don't look at them from the outside,
que lo primero es ser hombre,	man comes first,
y lo segundo, poeta.	and second, the poet.

The clear ideological stance characterizing Yupanqui's seven years in the Communist Party is expressed even more caustically en "*Las preguntitas,*" where the target is religion as "opium of the people," one of the main leitmotifs in Communist ideology. In this song Atahualpa points out how, for three generations, God was not someone his putative family could rely on. Furthermore, if God was related to anyone, it would be to the boss, not his family.

Un día yo pregunté:	One day I asked:
"Abuelo, ¿dónde está Dios?"	"Grandfather, where is God?"
Mi abuelo se puso triste	My grandfather got sad

y nada me respondió.	and didn't say anything.
Mi abuelo murió en los campos	My grandfather died in the fields,
sin rezo ni confesión	with neither prayers nor confession
y lo enterraron los indios,	and the Indians buried him,
flauta de caña y tambor.	reed flute and drum.

The first member of his alleged family abandoned by God is his grandfather, who died working in the fields and was buried outside the Catholic tradition by the "natural" owners of the land, the Indians, in accordance with their traditional burial rites instead. In the following verse it was his father who was deserted by God and ended up dying unprotected in a mine without medical attention.

Al tiempo yo pregunté	After a while I asked,
"Padre, ¿qué sabes de Dios?"	"Father, what do you know about God?"
Mi padre se puso serio	My father got serious
y nada me respondió.	and didn't say anything.
Mi padre murió en la mina	My father died in the mine,
sin doctor ni protección	with neither doctor nor protection
color de sangre minera	the color of miners' blood
tiene el oro del patrón	is on the boss's gold.

In this stanza, Atahualpa goes a step further in his criticism of the social conditions governing his father's life: not only did his father die in the mine without medical attention, there is also the implication that he died from overwork in order to make the mine owner rich, and that God did nothing to avoid it. In the last stanza Yupanqui moves on to his fictitious brother's experience with God:

Mi hermano vive en los montes	My brother lives in the scrublands
y no conoce una flor.	and doesn't know a flower.
Sudor, malaria y serpiente	Sweat, malaria and snakes
es la vida del leñador.	is the life of the woodcutter.
Y que naide le pregunte	And let nobody ask him
si sabe dónde está Dios.	if he knows where God is.
Por su casa no ha pasado	Such an important gentleman

tan important señor . . .   hasn't passed by his house . . .

Thus, if dying (over) working in the fields was the destiny of his grandfather, and suffering the same fate in the mine that of his father, his brother's will surely be to die in the scrublands; the other thing family members have in common is the absence of any help from God to modify such a destiny. However, the implication in the case of the father that God might be on the mine owner's side is made explicit in the next stanza when Atahualpa affirms that God doesn't frequent humble houses like his brother's, preferring rich people's dwellings.

The last stanza is a reflection on religion in general drawn from the experience of his putative family:

Yo canto por los caminos	I sing on the road
y cuando estoy en prisión.	and when I'm in prison
Oigo la voz del pueblo	I hear the voice of the people
que canta mejor que yo.	who sing better than me.
Hay un asunto en la tierra	There's an issue on earth
más importante que Dios	more important than God
y es que naide escupa sangre	which is that nobody should spit blood
pa' que otro viva mejor.	so that another lives better.
Que Dios vela por los hombres,	Whether God looks out for men,
tal vez sí, o tal vez no,	maybe yes, maybe no,
pero es seguro que almuerza	but there's no doubt he lunches
en la mesa del patrón.	at the boss's table.

As can be seen in this stanza, during this period of Atahualpa's career, the song itself does not appear as protagonist (as will be the case in later more radical militancies); instead, it plays a supporting role as means of expression and weapon in battle. The song that rises from below is better than music originating in a "superior" stratum ("the voice of the people that sing better than me"). And this message from the people says more "important" things than God does (such as "nobody should spit blood so that another lives better"); also, there is an image of God (clearly identifiable with the Catholic Church) according to which, though he may look after everyone, he "lunches at the boss's table." The degree of militancy here is far greater than in *"El arriero va"* where, written only six years earlier, the innovation was simply introducing the social question, as discussed above. Having moved considerably beyond including a social issue in a pastorally oriented folk song, Yupanqui now makes social criticism the motive for and protagonist of the song, its message and purpose. However, the song is not yet the protagonist of change, the catalyst for revolution.

And this idea of "going well beyond" his previous production is also applicable to how "*Las Preguntitas*" is positioned with regard to popular songs of any genre. Our point here is that, out of the mere handful of songs that criticize religion, most people remember only two: "*Las Preguntitas*" and "*Parte de la Religion*" ("Part of Religion") (composed in the mid-1980s by Charly Garcia). In this regard "*Las Preguntitas*" is not only unparalleled in its time, but extraordinary in Argentine popular music in general as well.

Although militant songs are only one part of Yupanqui's vast, rich, multifaceted musical universe, their temporal evolution, which flourished during his membership in the Communist Party and ebbed when he left it in 1952, is remarkable. Yet these compositions did not become widely known until the 1960s, when the composer himself had already moved on. Indeed, this belated resignification coincided neither with his nor the CP's position at the time. In declarations reinforcing his similitude to Farred's "vernacular" intellectual, Yupanqui minimized the importance of these songs and their practitioners: "Dissident singers, who call themselves men of the earth and don't know how to dig, plant seeds or milk a cow, don't interest me (interview in "*La Vanguardia Española*" published in 1974 and cited in Boasso 2006: 178); he reiterated: "I have written 1200 songs, and it is always these that are mentioned to start a conversation" (Boasso 2006: 178). For Yupanqui his message is in all his songs, not just a few, which leads him to scold his interviewers for not having read his literary works. In the period under study, his demand is for an integral commitment, according to which the artist should dress, act, and live like the campesino, the people in whom his message originates and to whom it is directed.

The four songs analyzed above do not, of course, exhaust Yupanqui's militant repertoire. Other songs gained importance when recorded by members of the militant song movement in other Latin American countries, as was the case with "*Basta Ya*" ("Enough Already"), which was recorded by Ángel Parra, (Orquera 2008) and later Quilapayún, in Chile:

Se acerca la madrugada	Dawn is coming
los gallos están cantando	the cocks are crowing
compadre están anunciando	*compadre* they're announcing
que se acerca la jornada.	that the new day is coming

[. . .]

El Yanqui vive en palacio	The Yanqui lives in a palace

Yo vivo en un barracón	I live in a shack
Como es posible que viva	How can it be that
El yanqui mejor que yo	the yanqui lives better than me?
¡Basta ya! ¡Basta ya!	Enough already! Enough already!
¡basta ya que el yanqui mande!	Enough already that the yanqui is boss!

The theme of certainty regarding the future appears here, anticipating a familiar topic in militant songs of the 1960s and 1970s, especially during the most radicalized period in the first half of the 1970s. Also present is the thematic duality of the happiness in the song in order to bear the sadness of life found in "*El arriero va*" and "*Los ejes de mi carreta*" ("The Axes of My Wagon"), among others, where the song strengthens resistance: "*Triste vida la del carretero/ que anda por esos cañaverales/sabiendo que su vida es un destierro/se alegra con sus cantares*" (Sad is the life of the wagoner/ who goes around these sugar-cane fields/knowing that his life is an exile, he cheers himself up with his songs). The ironclad nature of Yupanqui's political message during his CP period is evident here.

Atahualpa's most explicit, integrative message relating to the militant song is found in his first and best-known long work, *El Payador Perseguido* ("The Persecuted Payador [Troubadour]") which, according to the songwriter, was begun in the early post-World War II period, although it wouldn't be recorded and become known until the 1960s. In it his two thematic innovations—Indianism and social criticism—are on full display. Not unintentionally, its name—*El Payador Perseguido* or persecuted verse singer—mirrors how Yupanqui saw himself: Atahualpa develops a veritable "re-elaboration" of his life in this long musicalized conversation. In our view, this work is overture and coda, impulse and anchor, for his militant song period. For Yupanqui, if we take into account his previous and subsequent artistic production, it is a coda, that is, a closing of the chapter of his most deeply felt experiences relating politics to song in order to move on to a more tradition-oriented stage in his work. For his listeners and the musicians he inspired, however, it is an overture, opening up the path to follow. In name and subject matter, the work refers back to two well-known Argentine literary classics Yupanqui was undoubtedly familiar with—*Martín Fierro* (both parts) and *El Payador* by Leopoldo Lugones.

Because *El Payador Perseguido* was written over a long period of time, it mixes different ideological stances, some belonging to Yupanqui's membership in the Communist Party, and some to his post-communist posture. In both cases, however, Yupanqui advances a social and political perspective that clearly distances him from his model, *Martín Fierro*. In the latter, for instance, any economic damage the gaucho suffers is inflicted by storekeepers or a legal system that robs him of his property, not low wages. By contrast, in Yupanqui's work, surplus value is the cause of misfortune. There is no paradise lost to be recovered, but instead, a long-standing inherited state of affairs that must be changed. Whether written during or after Yupanqui's time in the Communist Party—the long period spent writing *El Payador Perseguido* makes this a logical question—the work undoubtedly reflects the Marxist perspective of its author.

Pena sobre pena y pena	Sorrow over sorrow and sorrows
hacen que uno pegue el grito.	make one cry out.
La arena es un puñadito [. . .]	Sand is a small fistful [. . .]
pero hay montañas de arena	but there are mountains of sand.
[. . .] *El trabajo es cosa buena,*	[. . .] Work is a good thing
es lo mejor de la vida;	it's the best thing in life
pero la vida es perdida	but life is lost
trabajando en campo ajeno.	working someone else's field.
Unos trabajan de trueno	Some work by thunder
Y es para otros la llovida	And it's rain for others
Estoy con los de mi lao	I'm with those at my side
cinchando tuitos parejos	pushing all together and evenly
pa' hacer nuevo lo que es viejo	to make new what is old
y verlo al mundo cambiao	and see the world changed.

Within this framework (that is repeated in different ways throughout *El Payador Perseguido*) the landowner is not "just one of the guys," a peer who rewards a good worker with a drink as occurs in *Martín Fierro* by José Hernández; here he is a boss who consciously exploits his hired hands because he considers them socially inferior: "*El estanciero presume/de gauchismo y arrogancia/él cree que es extravagancia/que su peón viva mejor/mas, no sabe ese señor/que por su peón tiene estancia*" (The landowner feigns/gauchismo and arrogance/he thinks it is an extravagance/that his peon live better/but this gentleman is unaware that/he has a ranch because of his peon).

With the line "feign *gauchismo,*" Yupanqui denounces the cult, established by intellectuals and landowners in the early twentieth century, to the body and culture of rural inhabitants that made the gaucho the essence of nationhood because of his identification with an ingenuous version of an uncontaminated natural world. So while this view dominated folk music and

Martín Fierro as national epic and founding work of Argentine literature, Yupanqui accomplished in *El Payador Perseguido* what he had done in *"El arriero va"*: he broke the link. He speaks from the perspective of the peon to the peon, fully aware of the virtues of and social conditions surrounding his protagonist. And from the perspective of the peon to the peon, the reality of rural life looks very different from what the landowner sees.

Probably owing to the long gestation period of the poem, this anti-capitalist stance is toned down, however, when the *payador* says *"Aquel que tenga sus reales/hace muy bien en cuidarlos;/Pero si quiere aumentarlos/que a la ley no se haga el sordo"* (Someone who has money/is wise to take care of it;/But if he wants to increase it/let him not be deaf to the law). Here Yupanqui criticizes not capitalism but rather its excesses. In our view, ideological shifts like this one clearly reflect the artist's own trajectory during the decades when *El Payador Perseguido* was being written; his joining and then somewhat turbulently leaving the Communist Party is significant in this regard.

Notwithstanding what he have pointed out above, the history of rebellion, persecution, significance and legacy that this work transpires is perhaps made much more unambiguous in the printed version of the poem (Yupanqui 2003), which contains some new, added, verses. Such stanzas (though not without contradictions) explicitly restate Yupanqui's social concern, and the function of the singer ("to sing giving opinions") displayed from the beginning of his artistic production:

Si uno pulsa la guitarra	If one plays the guitar
Pa' cantar coplas de amor	To sing love songs
de potros, de domador	or about colts, or horse breakers
del cielo y las estrellas	or heaven and the stars
dicen ¡Que cosa más bella,	they say How beautiful it is!
si canta que es un primor!	he sings like an angel!
Pero si uno como Fierro	But if like Martin Fierro, one
por ahí se larga opinando	happens to give opinions
el pobre se va acercando	the poor gather round
con las orejas alertas	with their ears perked up
y el rico bicha la puerta	and the rich man spies at the door
¡y se aleja reculando!	and backs off in a hurry!

Regarding the two pillars of yupanquian production that we have been analyzing in this chapter—the visibilization of the indigenous world and the social question—the former is not a central concern in *El Payador Persegui-*

do (which goes to show the temporal scope of and variety of interests in his work), but neither is it absent. For example, the following is how Yupanqui introduces himself:

Gente de pata en el suelo	People with bare feet on the ground
fueron mis antepasados	were my ancestors
criollos de cuatro provincias	criollos from four provinces
y con indios mesturaos	mixed up with Indians
Nunca se buscó dotor,	A doctor was never called,
Pues se curaban con yuyos	since they cured themselves with herbs
O escuchando los murmullos	or listening to the murmurs
De un estilo de mi flor	of a traditional song

Yet there is no doubt that, with more than 20 out of the poem's 132 stanzas devoted to them, social concerns impregnate the entire work. And, not by chance, we also find in this work a reiteration of the anticlerical theme glimpsed in "*Las preguntitas*":

El trabajo es cosa buena,	Work is a good thing
es lo mejor de la vida	it's the best thing in life
pero la vida es perdida	but life is lost
trabajando en campo ajeno	working in someone else'e field
[. . .] *y le juro, créamelo*	[. . .] and I swear, believe me
que yo pensé con tristeza	it made me sad to think it
Dios por aquí . . . no pasó.	God hasn't passed by here.

This denunciation is made in the name of Atahualpa as just another criollo worker, a right he has because he identifies himself as one of them. This position gave him enormous symbolic capital among fellow-folk-musicians (of whom he would demand that they "know how to rope a horse"): "*Y pa' los pobres cantaba/Lo que a ellos les pasaba/También me pasaba a mí*" (And for the poor he sang/what was happening to them/was happening to me too). For Yupanqui, this is what folk songs were: neither whim of city-dwellers nor trade for making a living, musician as worker was the "authentic" expression of a valid, experiential reality. The function of the song as vehicle for protest, as decodification of meaning and differentiation of the poor man's song from the rich man's, with which it coexists, is forcefully legitimized in *El Payador Perseguido*. Songs must have a social mission. This imperative will find an echo in fellow artists as an extension of *Martín Fierro*.

Yupanqui is careful, however, to passionately affirm that complete political independence must accompany the fulfilling of this social function if the paisano is to be authentically represented, the prerequisite for the validity of the singer. Yupanqui's break with the Communist Party is pristinely painted in *El Payador Perseguido*:

pa' que cambiaran las cosas,	in order to change things
busqué rumbo . . . y me perdí,	I looked for a way . . . and got lost,
al tiempo cuenta me di	in time I realized it
y agarré por buen camino	and got on the right road
antes que nada . . . argentino	above all . . . Argentine
y a mi bandera seguí.	and followed my flag.
El cantor debe ser libre	The singer must be free
Pa' desarrollar su cencia	To develop his science
Sin buscar la convenencia	Without looking for convenience
Ni alistarse con padrinos	or signing up with godfathers
De esos oscuros caminos	of those dark roads
Yo ya tengo la esperencia	I have already had the experience.

Equally and symmetrically transparent is Yupanqui's independence from Peronism (and his time in jail):

Yo no canto a los tiranos	I don't sing to tyrants
ni por orden del patrón	not under orders from the boss
el pillo y el trapalón	the rascal, and the swindler
que se arreglen por su lao	can fend for themselves
con payadores comprados	with bought *payadores*
y cantores de salón	and drawing-room singers
Por la fuerza de mi canto	Because of the strength of my song
conozco celda y penal	I know cell and jail
con fiereza sin igual	with unequaled ferocity
Más de una vez fui golpeao	I was beat up more than once
Y al calabozo tirao	And thrown in jail

| *como tarro al basural* | like a can on the garbage dump |

Among the stanzas not originally recorded but included in the printed text are the following, the first dealing in general terms with the political problem of corruption (which Yupanqui imputed primarily to Peronism), and the second where his self-esteem does not prevent him from ratifying his birthright as first militant songwriter:

Los malos se van alzando	Bad people are pocketing
Todo lo que hallan por áhi	Everything they find lying around
Como los granos de máiz	Like kernels of corn
siembran los peores ejemplos	they plant the worst examples
y se viene abajo el templo	and the temple is falling down
de la decencia en el páis	of decency in the country.
Hoy que ha salido un poquito	Today a little
De sol p'al trabajador	Sun has come out for the worker
No falta más de un cantor	A singer is no longer lacking
Que lo cante libremente	that sings freely to him
Pero sabe mucha gente	But many people know
Que primero canté yo	That I sang first.

His message is couched in the traditionalist and "essentialistic" terms that are seen as a feature of the language "of the countryside," with its reminiscences of illiteracy alongside the wisdom of the ages, spoken by the simple paisano (who carries the country in his heart):

Si alguien me dice señor [. . .]	If somebody calls me sir [. . .]
Agradezco el homenaje,	I'm grateful for the homage
Mas soy gaucho entre el gauchaje	But I'm just another gaucho
Y soy nada entre los sabios	And I'm nothing among wise men
Y son para mí los agravios	And those for me are the wrongs
Que le hacen al paisanaje	That are done to country folk
[. . .] *Yo he caminao por el mundo*	[. . .] I've walked the world over
He cruzao tierras y mares	I've crossed lands and seas
Sin fronteras que me pare	Without borders to stop me
Y en cualesquiera guarida,	And in any old lair

Yo he cantao, tierra querida,	I´ve sung, dear country,
Tus dichas y tus pesares	Your blessings and misfortunes
Menos mal que llevo adentro	Thank goodness I carry inside me
Lo que la tierra me dio	What the land gave me
-Patria, raza, o qué se yo-,	-Country, race, or what-have-you-,
Pero que me iba salvando	But that was saving me
Y así seguí caminando	And that's how I kept on walking
Por los caminos de Dios	on God's roads

What is definitively reaffirmed is the anonymous destiny of the folk song: the objective is to be the folklore of the future, with rebelliousness in plain sight openly challenging the powers that be. Always traveling, the song should leave a trace as "trading mark" and ultimate self-reference while making its way around the world. So even after death, the songwriter only asks to be remembered, in the anonymity of song or popular memory, as "an Argentine." However, Yupanqui actually seeks (and achieves) greater pre-eminence over time as example for other singers and, in the beginning, for introducing the denunciation into folk music. This patriarchally drawn path he followed as identity and direction, leaving and arriving, can be found in other yupanquian works.

Siempre canté estremecido	I always sang shaken by
las penas del paisanaje	the sorrows of the paisano
la explotación y el ultraje	the exploitation and outrage
de mis hermanos queridos	of my dear brothers
Y aunque me quiten la vida	And although they take my life
O engrillen mi libertad	or handcuff my liberty
O aunque chamusquen quizás	or although they maybe burn
Mi guitarra en los fogones	my guitar on bonfires
Han de vivir mis canciones	My songs are going to live
En el alma de los demás	in the soul of the others.
¡No me nuembren, que es pecao	Don't say my name, it's a sin
Y no comenten mis trinos!	And don't comment on my trills!
Yo me voy con mi destino	I go with my destiny
Pa'l lao donde el sol se pierde	Off into the sunset

| *¡Tal vez alguno se acuerde* | Maybe somebody remembers |
| *que aquí cantó un argentino!* | that an Argentine sang here! |

In summary, taken as a whole, the works of Yupanqui are the expression of and mandate for a folk song that should have opinions but not be "militant" (linked to political parties, even when in the opposition); even less should it have dealings with tyrants (i.e., the government). The singer's independence (a value clearly harking back to Leopoldo Lugones) is only compatible with anonymity as the objective of his songs. Achieving this is the fundamental proof of his identity with the stated subject, the people. This is why, within Yupanqui's own cycle, *El Payador Perseguido* constitutes closure. Other artists, who (identifying themselves with "social concerns" in an era of inaugurations) followed his message, privileged the part advocating opinions over that urging non-militancy. This leads us to the conclusion that the closure of a cycle for Yupanqui served, paradoxically, as the overture of the cycle of his successors. Indeed, what follows is the inflexion that, in 1965, inaugurated the militant decade par excellence in Argentine folk music.

That *El Payador Perseguido* closed a cycle in Yupanqui's trajectory is well illustrated by his position regarding the "protest song" movement of his time. In that regard, by the late 1960s and early 1970s, Yupanqui saw himself and his work as well beyond the "protest song" movement, which was becoming increasingly popular; this led him to advance very negative comments about it. Here it is important to note that, if on the one hand, the "protest" song movement of the 1960s and 1970s considered Atahualpa as precursor, the form the protest songs themselves took was not taken from the yupanquian songbook. Specifically, in his work "the absence of a call to rebellion or the promulgation of a collective group of opposition to dominant sectors can be noted" (Kaliman 2004: 93). However, Yupanqui was clearly a driving force behind the factors stimulating the interest in folk music among "enlightened" musicians in the 1960s. He becomes a paradigm for intellectuals who attempt to articulate their creative practice so as to attract the popular masses to revolutionary causes (or incite in them the desire to bring about social change). This paradigmatic role he played with his songs, articles,[8] literary works, and even cinema. But he also spoke out on several occasions against being labeled "protest" singer, declaring that his sole aim was to express "the feelings of the Argentine paisano." He maintained this position in the 1970s in debates with the "upstarts lacking campesino authenticity," extending his criticism to include those who wanted to hold up the "message" as supreme, converting themselves into leaders of the collectivity they supposedly represented. As he put it,

I don't believe in professional protest song singers. Someone who wants to put music to his political pamphlets and shout them out in public, let him do it. But he isn't an artist. I am an artist who sings the things, the problems of my time. I tell truths common to everyone . . . I don't believe in "the protesters." That is too easy. My songs are different [. . .] being a professional protester seems false to me. I think one must make poetry and set down one's times, [. . .], portray one's epoch (Declarations to *Extra*, March 1971, in Galasso 2009: 160).

Or, in *Provincia de Canarias*, May 5, 1981, Atahualpa states,

[P]rotest about what and why? When one says "the sorrows are ours, the cattle are someone else's," this doesn't go against the owner of the cattle. The destiny of this human being (the drover) is what interests me, his interior destiny. That doesn't make me a protester, but rather someone who knows a great truth that can't be pawed by someone who listens to me, the young man in the café or the leftist of the moment (Boasso 2006: 178).

What is paradoxical about Yupanqui's effect on Argentine music is that his legacy will multiply in stages as it spreads several decades later in the works of artists he criticizes extraordinarily harshly for, either being "protest song singers," or for distancing themselves from the essence of folk music in musical terms. In this sense, Yupanqui had absolutely no compassion for the new generation of folk singers who, nevertheless, greatly contributed to the spread and continued popularity of his poetic and musical works. And this phenomenon is the basis for considering him (Molinero 2011: 133) both driving force and anchor of the militant song movement in Argentina and America in the twentieth century.

In this regard, Yupanqui described Quilapayún (one of the main Chilean disseminators of his work), as impersonating "a truckload of Peronists" with their protest songs. And in the magazine *Folklore*, the most important in its genre, he spoke of the 1960s generation of folk musicians and their music as follows: "Just as there are laws to prevent the illegal practice of medicine, there needs to be thought up a kind of *spiritual police to prevent these attacks on the spiritual health of the popular masses [sic]*. What would happen to public health if, instead of doctors, the field was full of quacks?" (in "*¿Que piensa Atahualpa Yupanqui de los nuevos valores de la canción?*" No. 89, March 9, 1965, italics ours).

Although the verbal broadside quoted above is self-sustaining, Yupanqui goes on to contextualize it in the course of the article: "The majority of young people singing folk and quasi-folk songs today sing irresponsibly. Deforming the moral and spiritual face of the country cannot be tolerated. They have every right to do as they please, but if that tendency means deforming the spiritual physiognomy of our people, I am against that tendency." And to the comparison of Quilapayún to "a truck full of Peronists,"

Yupanqui added reflections on other folk groups: El Cuarteto Vocal Zupay—
"Are you the ones that paved my 'Indian Trail'?"—in reference to the sophisticated vocal arrangement the group made of the song; and Los Huanca
Huá—"One sings and four make fun of him behind his back." Counterbal-
ancing these criticisms was the observation that "The Farías Gómez are the
only ones that put mustard on the barbequed meat . . . and make it taste
good," before continuing with remarks about Daniel Toro—"he's going to
wake up my little Indian"—in allusion to the potency of Toro's vocal version
of "*Indiecito dormido*"; and Manolo Juárez—"not even in my worst night-
mares would I have imagined an arrangement like the one you made for
'*Piedra y camino.*'" However, these comments cease to be humorous, to be a
reflection of a way of life and art that he proclaimed most fully in "*Mi Tierra
te están cambiando*" ("My Land are Changing You")—"*o te han disfrazao
que es peor, ¡Amalaya, que se ruempa pa' siempre mi corazon*" (or they have
disguised you, which is worse, oh, my God, my heart is breaking forever).
This comes to its extreme expression with some "re-qualification" (down-
ward, to put it mildly) of Larralde and Cafrune, two faithful followers of his
style of folk music who were touring Europe at the time:

> Paul Segés . . . disdains the craze for protest songs elaborated comfortably
> from the outside [. . . on the other hand] Cafrune, Larralde, and many others,
> from a traditional point of view, are only rookies. They get around, but haven't
> yet been born as standard bearers of a tradition. They compose what in my
> country has come to be called "radiophone fauna." I'm about to affirm that
> none has read more than 50 books. And without thinking, without meditating,
> without learning, you can't sing folk music. Yet it's a way of earning a living
> that I respect [. . .] none of them means anything to the culture of my country,
> which is the most important thing. [. . .] In no way do I consider them my
> disciples, and if this were the case, I would give them a zero in all subjects.
> [. . .] They are not prepared to transmit popular culture.

Nevertheless, it is precisely the ones that "paved his Indian Trail" or "woke
up the little Indian" that will fulfill the yupanquian legacy. On the one hand,
they brought the indigenous theme to the forefront in popular music (Víctor
Heredia, Rubén Patagonia, León Gieco making Gerónima Sequeida known
on his LP *De Ushuaia hasta La Quiaca*, among others); they also carried the
militant song with social content to its logical extreme (El Cuarteto Vocal
Zupay, Los Trovadores, El Quinteto Tiempo, among others).

So when Roberto Chavero (Atahualpa Yupanqui's son) gives Víctor
Heredia around seventy unpublished poems by his father to musicalize, the
latter, in a highly unusual gesture, tells him the task cannot depend on a
single individual but must be shared out among other musicians; homage to
Yupanqui must be done with "different voices, different colors, different
seasons of the year" (Javier Rombouts, *Clarín*, October 22, 1998). To carry

out the project, Heredia convoked six other musicians (León Gieco, Fito Páez, Pedro Aznar, Divididos, Jairo, Alberto Cortés, Peteco Carabajal, and Teresa Parodi), four of them national rock authors, two ballad singers like Heredia himself, and only two folk singers. It is worth noting that none of these musicians belonged to the musical movement to which Yupanqui always believed he did: traditional folklore. As Heredia aptly recalls about Yupanqui, "[H]e didn't like electronic music at all, for him there was only one guitar and it was acoustic. That's why we can do it now that he is sleeping. If he weren't, for sure he'd come at night and pull our feet," (Javier Rombout, *Clarín,* Oct. 22, 1998).

Yet old Atahualpa just might think twice before pulling any feet. After being jailed and tortured during the first Peronist government, he saw fit to rethink his anti-Peronism during the last years of his life (after resigning from—or being thrown out of the Communist party in 1952–1953—it's not clear which—Peronism had received him with open arms, naming him "favorite son of Tucumán and pride of working class people" [Orquera 2008], and he had received a gold medal from the National Congress in 1954). So it is within the realm of possibility that, in light of the vitality of national rock in representing "lo Argentino" (the truly Argentine) at the turn of the last century, although assuredly not plugging in, Yupanqui would at least understand the rockers (despite not sharing their taste and criticizing how they make music). For their part, Fito Páez, León Gieco, Pedro Aznar (who on Pat Metheny's LP *Letter from Home* sang the anonymous vidala "*Ay por qué Dios me daría*" collected by Leda Valladares), and Divididos paid him the homage he so well deserved with rock versions of his poems where "the Indian as Indian" occupies a privileged position, together with the social question: if not his model (formal and substantive) as a whole, the essence of what he left "in the shreds of the wind" drew a following, and as he himself would say, was gathered up by "the boys going round the valley . . ."[9] in Argentina and all of America.

NOTES

1. We use the term "criollismo" in the sense given by Prieto when he analyzes the process of evolution of Argentine society following the amendments made by the 1980s generation. Mass immigration and basic schooling implied mass access to reading, which would propel the popularity of cheap brochures and newspapers. This would occur in the late nineteenth century and the first decade of the twentieth century, entailing the popularity of creoles based novels in which their protagonists were mostly marginal or disgraced. "Juan Moreira" and "*Hormiga Negra*" ([Black Ant]; as before the Martín Fierro) were emblematic cases. Prieto consider that literature somehow constituted a form of civilization, which affected the mentality and behavior of its readers, provided evidence of identification and contributed to the establishment of customs, including the formation of "centros criollos" (Creole centers; clubs that promoted rural customs in cities, particularly in Buenos Aires) where young people reproduced the rural atmosphere that guaranteed the acquisition of a sense of nationality necessary to survive the

"metropolitan confusion" and "xenophobic outbreaks," socializing "in the ritual homage of myths of literary origin" (Prieto 1988: 146).

2. As the song became popular, especially among the more politicized sectors of Argentine society (members of the Socialist and Communist Parties, for example), the words were changed (". . . the sorrows are ours, the cattle are Anchorena's") in an attempt to make its revolutionary content more manifest (above and beyond the wishes of the composer) by directly naming one of the most conspicuous representatives of the landowning oligarchy in Argentina (the real cattle owners), the Anchorena family.

3. Atahualpa justifies joining the Communist Party as follows: "I know communism can achieve the affirmation of man and popular consciousness in order to live, without myths in the face of the reality of the earth and the future of the country, an industrious and worthy existence. (. . .) I have joined the Communist Party in order to improve myself as an American artist and dedicate my efforts to the good of my Country." (*Orientación*, No. 448, June 23, 1948, quoted in Flores Vassella and García Martínez 2012).

4. Throughout the history of the folk genre in Argentina there has been a close relationship between its leading figures and the Communist Party. A brief list of artists who were members of, or close to, the CP is evidence of the importance of the link between song and party: Atahualpa Yupanqui, Horacio Guarany, Armando Tejada Gómez, Hamlet Lima Quintana, Tito Francia, Oscar Matus, Mercedes Sosa, César Isella, Víctor Heredia, Quinteto Tiempo, Los Trovadores, Ricardo Romero of Los Tucu Tucu, Los Andariegos, Chito Zeballos, Moncho Mieres, and so forth.

5. Other poems in the same style and from the same period ("*En el Tolima*" and "*Meta Bala*"—put to music later on by Ángel Parra in Chile—show the importance of Atahualpa's poetry to other militant songwriters in the Southern Cone.

6. Yupanqui was censored several times during his prolific career. The first time was under the Peronist government (between 1947 and 1953, when not only was he banned from the radio and prohibited from performing live, but he was also jailed eight times). When Perón fell, the military dictatorship that succeeded him censored Yupanqui for the social content of his songs and his proximity to Peronism in 1953. Censorship was lifted in 1958, and his music could be played in public. During the 1976–1983 dictatorship he was censored yet again. The early periods of censorship, imposed more because of his anti-Peronist declarations than for the content of his songs, extended to the very mention of his name on the radio (thus, the verse at the end of *El Payador Perseguido* that says "don´t name me/it's a sin . . ."), anticipating what the Libertadora Revolution would do when the military banned the public mention of Perón. Yupanqui tells an amusing anecdote in this regard: "Remember that it was a sin to name me on the radio? The thing lasted nine years'. For example, if somebody sang "*Camino del indio*," they said: 'by an anonymous composer'. [. . .] About this business of the prohibition to say my name ('46-'55), I've got a funny story. Once I arrive by car in Cruz del Eje (Córdoba) and I go to a club for a barbeque with some friends. People recognized me and pointed to me, but I played dumb. There was a little local orchestra that played tangos. This was in '48. Then suddenly they played "*Viene clareando*," a *zamba* with my verses, and, so as not to break the law, the master of ceremonies—the guy was sharp—said: 'The zamba we have played belongs to an anonymous author . . . who honors us with his presence'" (Interview with Leo Sala in the magazine *Gente*, May 1970).

7. In the Communist Party newspaper (*La Hora*, No. 1204, December 30, 1945, p. 6) he expressed it in politically current and pre-electorally militant terms: "I want to ask popular musicians and singers if we must continue singing rural and urban traditions that speak of mountain ridges and pampas . . . while in the streets of our cities democratic youth is being gunned down by anti-liberty hordes. I want to know if our painters must continue putting on their canvases aristocratic hands and elegant madonnas and children at the beach, and landscapes from Córdoba, the Delta, and quebracho groves, while Argentine women heroically resist the abuses of the mob that abominates culture."

On the other hand, in *Orientación*, No. 450, July 7, 1948, there is a poem that incites the subject (precisely the man from the mountains, the indigenous protagonist of the majority of Yupanqui's songs at the time) to join the songs and unite in the songs to rebel. This "protagonism of the song" will be another of the thematic mainstays characterizing "militancy" in song in the 1960s and 1970s.

Allá lejos (¡y tan cerca!) en otras montañas ||
(Far away [and so near] in other mountains)
hay hombres que levantan la copla de una patria libre
(there are men raising the song of a free country)
con idiomas dulces y rebelados, con acentos fraternales y firmes[. . .]
(with sweet, rebeled languages, with fraternal and firm accents)
Y nosotros cantaremos la baguala de la libertad
(And we will sing the *baguala* of liberty)
[. . .] *desde la cumbre de todos los puños levantados*
(from the summit of all raised fists)
bajará un viento feliz y florecerá la plenitud del campo.
(a happy wind will blow down and make flower the plenitude of the fields).
Mira cómo crecen los ríos
(Look how the rivers grow)
¿no sientes dentro tuyo como crece la sangre?
(Don't you feel inside you how the blood grows?)
Ya amanece sobre el mundo compañero.
(Day is dawning over the world comrade)
Mira tu campo, las piedras y el potrero.
(Look at your field, the stones and the pasture)
Mira bien dentro tuyo.
(Look well inside you)
Y dime la primera palabra para nuestra canción
(And tell me the first word of our song)

8. A role that coexisted with that of insuring the untouchable "essence" of the song. Specifically, regarding the political value of the "boring bagualas" he wrote, "what they fail to understand, or to say, is that these verses *tickle the people*, they wake them up, they present *human problems* and end up *ruining the digestion of the provincial landowner* who comes near to listen to a couple of little *zambas* before going to the cabaret" (*Orientación* 460, September 1, 1948; italics ours). Yupanqui also ratified his essentialist function and the corresponding need for a "spiritual police." In this regard, he put limits on the desire to use festive dances to make folklore popular: "happiness always competes with vulgarity, and joy has nothing to do with the shout that almost always comes out of a *white throat half-choked by a hard collar* (. . .) "A patriotic duty *demands the greatest control* over these manifestations. The song, the pure Argentine song, from any region, has *authentic values and expresses an exalted, lasting sentiment*" (*Orientación* 501, August 10, 1949; italics ours).
9. Concept used by Yupanqui in "*El canto del viento.*"

Chapter Eight

A Brief History of the Militant Song Movement in Argentina

Carlos Molinero and Pablo Vila

Compared to the other national cases covered in this book, the Argentine militant song movement not only started earlier (the 1940s instead of the 1960s), influencing other Southern Cone movements and even the Cuban Nueva Trova, but also shows a political variance absent both in Uruguay and Chile. In terms of time-lines, most analysts accept that Yupanqui's "*El Arriero Va*" ("The Drover Goes"), composed in 1944, can be considered the first militant folk song of the Southern Cone. As it was shown in the previous chapter, "*El Arriero va*" started an entire production of militant songs by Yupanqui that, paradoxically, almost entirely stopped precisely when the movement was in full throttle in the mid-1960s everywhere (see Yupanqui 2008). But not only Yupanqui was composing militant songs well before his counterparts in Chile and Uruguay, but also Horacio Guarany was doing the same in the second half of 1950s (although Guarany continued doing it until the mid-1970s).

MILITANT SONG MOVEMENT: AN INTRODUCTION

Due to the extension and complexity of the phenomenon (covering ideologically diverse periods and sectors over thirty years), our overview of the trajectory of the militant song in the second and third quarters of the twentieth century needs to be cursory.[1] During the initial period (1944–1965) Atahualpa Yupanqui pioneers the incorporation of socio-political themes into the folk music repertoire, which is taken up later by Horacio Guarany. Their influence is expanded by the collective efforts in the province of Mendoza (in western Argentina) of a group made up of Oscar Matus, Armando Tejada

Gómez, Tito Francia, and Mercedes Sosa, among others. This *Movimiento del Nuevo Cancionero* (New Song or Songbook Movement)[2] inspired like-minded groups throughout Latin America. Thus a new period was inaugurated, termed the "militant decade" by Molinero (2011), when a growing number of artists—not only from the left—used the folk song to express their ideas; partisan positions became increasingly radicalized, leading to the adoption of concrete political proposals.

In terms of political variance the militant song movements in Chile and Uruguay were both linked to the left. Sure, different musicians and composers had their political sympathies in different parties of the left spectrum, but, nonetheless, all of them considered themselves "leftists." A different scenario characterizes the militant song movement in Argentina, where their practitioners can be widely allocated from right to left in the political palimpsest.

Figures representing the permutations of nationalism in Argentina were Roberto Rimoldi Fraga, Hernán Figueroa Reyes, Oscar Valles, Omar Moreno Palacios, Argentino Luna, among others. An increasingly heated debate among nationalists, Peronists, and more or less radicalized leftists was conducted within the folk genre regarding what the essence of Argentine nationhood was, what a viable model for the future of Argentina was, and how to get there. Participants were eventually silenced by the censorship imposed during the "Triple A" period and continued by the military dictatorship that followed in 1976.[3]

Even among those who promoted some kind of "social change" loosely linked to various versions of socialism (the subject matter of this chapter, which, for reasons of space, cannot deal with the "right wing" part of the movement), their political affiliations were quite varied and (as it is the case in many aspects of Argentine society) the main reason is the impact of Peronism in Argentina's history. In this regard, while the members of the El Nuevo Cancionero identified themselves as leftists and, most of them, were even affiliated to the Communist Party, other very important actors of the movement identified themselves as "Peronists."

We will try to shed some light in this complex story, following some of the most important manifestations of the militant song movement in Argentina. If, for obvious reasons the bulk of the chapter will be dedicated to El Nuevo Cancionero, we will also address other organic manifestations that, somehow, developed outside the sphere of influence of the Nuevo Cancionero, such as the group of peronist artists that were involved in the "*Cancionero de la Liberación*" ("Liberation Songbook").

Looking at the entire century, the path of music with folk roots in Argentina is quite paradoxical. Initially identified as the representation of the past that still exists in the present, moved from being despised at the end of the nineteenth century as "the backward past," and "uncivilized" to be heralded as the "truer representation of the country" by the 1920s (Molinero 2011). In that condition, already during the 1960s folk boom (see Vila 1982), innovative artists considered it as a projection of the everyday (a present to last), while the militant song representatives, especially between 1965 and 1975, saw it as anticipatory and propitiatory of an impending change (the future, today). Thus, folk music moved for these artists from mere "representation" of the past in the present, to a "political weapon" to bring the future now (a future that, according to the lore of the time, was "scientifically" predicted as "socialist"). Of course, this move was not automatic and took a while to materialize, but by the end of the 1960s and the beginning of the 1970s such a move was in full throttle. In between, what Molinero (2011) called "the militant Decalogue" was, step by step, being developed. The Decalogue included *Indigenismo* (vindicating indigenous people), *Americanism* (the search for the union of all Latin American people), *historical reinterpretation* of the Argentine past, *hope* (or even certainty) for a better future, *social change*, *fighting pacifism*, *popular leadership*, the immortality of the freedom fighter, (a kind of *unreligious religiosity*), and the primordial *role of the song* in the revolutionary transformation. In different degrees, and with different weights in diverse artists, most of these topics were present in the songs of the militant movement, above all between 1966 and 1975, concluding with a political proposal.

HORACIO GUARANY: A MILITANT SINGER WELL BEFORE A MILITANT SONG MOVEMENT

By the end of the 1940s Guarany was the singer of a well-known folk group (the Herminio Giménez band—which performed mostly Paraguayan songs without any political content), whose members were Paraguayan exiles living in Argentina, and some of them (most prominently José Asunción Flores—highly admired by Guarany) members of the Paraguayan Communist Party, party that Guarany joined in 1955. After some party discussion about Guarany's membership affiliation, the Argentine Communist Party claimed and Guarany moved to the Argentine branch of the political organization. After a trip to the Soviet Union in 1957 (a country that captivated Guarany) sent by the Communist Party to represent Argentina in the "International Festival for Peace and Friendship," Horacio started to write many songs with clear political messages, well attuned to the CP's ideology of the time. However, Guarany claims that he was already composing songs and poems with political content since the late 1940s and early 1950s (Interview, May 2010; see also Guarany 2002).

As we are going to see repeated in the case of the Nuevo Cancionero Movement, the early artistic activities of Guarany were facilitated by some Jewish community organizations and representatives. Many of those organizations and representatives functioned as "satellites" of the Communist Party. In the case of Guarany, his first steps as a soloist were expedited by Mr. Zeligman (a CP member who represented several folk artists at the time), who was instrumental in recording Guarany's first demo "*Guitarra de medianoche*" ("Midnight Guitar"), and Julio Epstein (director of National Radio and Alegro Records), who produced his first recordings after hearing the demo (Interview with Guarany, May 2010). Jewish cultural institutions, many of them linked to ICUF (Idisher Cultur Farband [Federation of Jewish Cultural Institutions]), provided manpower and theaters (most prominently the IFT Theater in Buenos Aires) for those artists to perform. When some of those artists (like Guarany, Mercedes Sosa, César Isella, and Víctor Heredia, for instance) became very popular, they gradually withdrew from acting in those venues and moved to regular commercial venues instead. Some other CP artists, less popular, continued to perform in ICUF venues their entire careers. In short, somehow ICUF functioned, in relation to popular music, as the "unofficial" cultural branch of the CP, whose influence merits a specific study.

More than any other member of the leftist branch of the militant song movement (except for the brief stint of Yupanqui as a party member in the late 1940s, and some compositions of the José Podestá group) Guarany represents the classic role of "official singer of the party." Not only because he was always present in CP congresses, celebrations and the like (usually explicitly admitting his liaison with the CP), but also because his lyric production was very closely related to what the CP was advocating at different points in time; and still, even more importantly, because his performances were sometimes more reminiscent of a political leader than those of a popular singer. Taking all this into account, it is not by chance that he was one of the first composers in Latin America to put music to poems written by noted Cuban poet Nicolás Guillén, doing so at the peak of the Cuban Revolution, and precisely putting music to a poem that was asking Cuban soldiers to join forces with the guerrillas in the Caribbean country: "*No sé por qué piensas tú*" ("I don't know way you think so"):

No sé por qué piensas tú	I don't know why you soldier think
soldado que te odio yo,	that I hate you
si somos la misma cosa	if We are the same thing
tú y yo.	You and me
Tú eres pobre, lo soy yo	You are poor, me too
soy de abajo, lo eres tú.	I belong to the lower sectors of society, you too

De dónde has sacado tú	Where did you get soldier
soldado que te odio yo.	That I hate you.
Me duele que a veces tú	It hurts me that, sometimes
te olvides de quién soy yo,	you forget who I am,
caramba, si yo soy tú	gee, I am you
lo mismo que tú eres yo.	In the same way that you are me
Pero no por eso yo	But this is not a reason why
he de malquererte tú,	I am going to hate you
si somos la misma cosa	if we are the same thing
tú y yo.	You and me.
Ya nos veremos tú y yo	We are going to see each other
juntos en la misma calle,	together in the same path
hombro con hombro tú y yo	shoulder by shoulder you and me
sin odio ni yo ni tú,	without animosity, neither you, nor me
pero sabiendo tú y yo	But knowing, both of us
a donde vamos yo y tú,	where are we going to go
de donde has sacado tú	Where did you get
soldado que te odio yo.	Soldier that I hate you.

We can draw many more examples of this kind from his very extensive career, that is, songs that were quite "appropriate" for the CP political program of the time and prone to be used as "fighting slogans" by the Party: "*Milonga del Soldado*" ("Soldier's Milonga"), "*La voz de los pájaros de Hiroshima*" ("The Voice of Hiroshima's Birds"), "*Luche y luche*" ("Fight and Fight"), "*Coplera del Prisionero*" ("Song of the Prisoner"), "*Yo soy el dueño de todo*" ("I Am the Owner of Everything"), "*Si se calla el cantor*" ("If the Singer Becomes Silent"), and so on. Let's start our brief analysis with the opening stanzas of "*Luche y luche*," where the frontiers between political slogans and song lyrics are completely blurred because the first part of the song is a verbatim quotation of political slogans sang at political rallies in the 1970s. More precisely, the first coming from some workers' mobilizations in Tucuman (Interview with Guarany, May 2010: "I composed that song because in Tucuman I heard 'people who hear this, join the fight.' I took the lyrics from there"): "People who hear this, join the fight."

The next stanza, asking for *people united, so never defeated*, were widely sung in leftist political rallies in Chile and Argentina in the late 1960s and early 1970s (and also recorded by Quilapayún in its song "*El pueblo unido, jamás será vencido*" in 1973), and eventually became a political slogan for the left not only in Latin America but everywhere in the world. We think that it is very difficult to find such a direct connection between party politics and popular songs than in "*Luche y luche*," where, directly, without any type of "poetic" mediation, several political slogans enter a song. For sure it is impossible in any other artistic production on the left wing of the militant song movement, and only present in the "*canciones coyunturales*" (situational songs) of the José Podestá peronist group, which, different from Guarany's intentions, didn't expect any "artistic afterlife" for their songs. And Guarany is completely aware of this, and clearly differentiates his artistic production from the more "aesthetically oriented" production of other representatives of the left wing militant song movement: ". . . Víctor Heredia wrote with a degree of poeticalness different from mine. Mine was closer to political sloganeering, more rudimentary. Víctor wrote songs that said a lot. Isella too" (Interview, May 2010). Defining his songs as "being like a political pamphlet" (*panfletarias*) is a very good way to account for the "politically situated" character of his songs.

Without the extreme conflation of music and politics shown by "*Luche y Luche*," "*Coplera del Prisionero*," "*Yo soy el dueño de todo*," and "*Si se calla el cantor*" can be characterized too as part of a repertoire of an "official party singer." "*Yo soy el dueño de todo*" clearly shows how, in 1971, early on in the first years of radicalization, a very explicit example of a "revealing" denunciation becoming a veiled threat of direct action appears in a song by Guarany. The lyrics revolve around the need to reverse ownership of the means of production.

The generically anonymous protagonist of the song "will get tired" and, without any apparent mediation, let loose "the flames" (metaphor for revolution in many songs of the time). The image of surplus value is explicit (when he says he makes the chair but doesn't have any place to sit down), as is the seed of protest for overexploitation (he doesn't even have the right to get tired). The real innovation here is the latent announcement of the day when revolution, no longer just a hope for the future, takes the form of spreading flames.

In point of fact, H. Guarany is the musician who, over the course of the militant decade, incorporated into his repertoire the greatest percentage of compositions in which the singer is protagonist and the song "objectified," to some extent, as the driving force for social change.

One notable example is *"Si se calla el cantor,"* which can easily fit the description of "protagonism set to song." In this case the song is no longer in the hands and at the service of the militant; rather it is the essence of the struggle, with the singer emitting its self-referential function. In fact, according to Guarany, the origin of the song is a precise act of censorship he suffered in the early 1970s:

> **Guarany**: Once we arrived in Orán and an hour before the concert, a military officer in charge: "no, you can't perform," he tells me. And I had to leave Orán, having to pay all the musicians. There were hundreds of these prohibitions. Then I wrote *"Si se calla el cantor."* Everybody told me: Don't talk! Why do you talk, stupid? But if the singer who has a microphone doesn't talk, then what kind of singer are you? So I wrote *"Si se calla el cantor"* (Interview, May 2010).

"Si se calla el cantor" unequivocally praises the singer, while at the same time indicating the road to be followed by the listeners:

> "If the singer is silenced, life is silent, because life itself is one long song, if the singer is silenced, hope, light and happiness die of fear."

> *"Si se calla el cantor/, calla la vida/, porque la vida misma es toda un canto/, si se calla el cantor/ muere de espanto/ la esperanza, la luz y la alegría."*

The troubadour-like function of the singer is elevated to that of protester, or better yet, union leader ("longshoremen cross themselves: who will fight for our wages!") of those "who have no voice," the subaltern, the poor. The category of singer is intended to establish its own meaning: it connotes impeccable conduct, protest, integrity, and dignity. By contrast, if these conditions are not met, the function of the singer is betrayed. "Singers don't know how to dodge, they will never keep quiet in the face of a crime." This unity of the singer with a vital, popular essence and the struggle is portrayed in the final verse; vibrant and declamatory, it seems to say that the singer *is* life: "If the singer is silenced . . . life is silent."

In terms of our conceptualization of Guarany as an "official Party singer," he himself recognized that he used certain doses of self-censorship to avoid navigating waters he knew the CP didn't like him to sail. In this regard he even went farther than the José Podestá 's lyric production:

> **Molinero**: Did the CP ever ask you to write some song or did they ever censor one of your songs?

Guarany: Not directly, but. . . they let you know. And a lot of things I never wrote for fear they would censor me. For example, a love song: "our love was forbidden and God commanded it to be punished." And how can I put God in? I can't say God, they're going to give me crap. So: "our love was forbidden, your God commanded it to be punished." (laughter) But many things like that, I wanted to write but didn't because they would censure me. They are very intelligent, they don't tell you not to do it. (Interview, May 2010)

If music interpellates people from very different angles and many times in conflicting ways (through its sound, lyrics, performances, and what people say about music (Vila, forthcoming), Guarany's central role in the militant song movement is related not only to what kind of songs he composed and sung, but also (and perhaps more importantly) on how he performed them. Thus, and above all in the first part of his career, because he is a pioneer in that regard, a significant contribution to the evolution of folk song militancy is attitudinal. With his lofty, in-your-face stance and the tough macho attitude visible in certain LP covers and titles of his songs, symbolically speaking Guarany was more Juan Moreira or the first Martín Fierro (iconic rebellious gauchos and outlaws in Argentine literature) than Atahualpa Yupanqui.

Looking at his role from the point of view of the present Guarany comments the following:

Guarany: If I'm the people's singer, I have to act like a people's singer. If I were a union leader I would organize mass meetings for . . , right? But I was a singer. So I began to write songs and sing them on the stage because I understood that, in the first place, it was a way of justifying the honor it was for me to be loved by my people and be told I was the people's singer. I had to respond, if I didn't, I would be stealing something that wasn't mine. I put my balls on the line and sang what the pueblo couldn't say. I had a microphone, I had an audience, I even had a certain immunity because I was known, I was famous. So I had to act that way. (Interview, May 2010)

Guarany posits his stance as if he didn't have any other choice: he had the chance of using a microphone he believed that his public persona allowed him certain power he equated with "immunity" (which history proved it was only in his imagination, considering the several murder attempts he suffered); and, wanting to deserve the title of "people's singer," he expressed what "people couldn't say." When he wants to illustrate the kind of message he was advancing at that time, he recited to us a poem in which issues of silenced voices, social exploitation, economic deprivation, censorship, the guitar as a weapon, and the like occupy center stage. And this is so because

Guarany truly believes that the song has a very important role (albeit limited) in relation to social change and revolution.

Guarany: Songs raise consciousness, incentivize rebellious feelings, but revolutions don't come about through songs.

Molinero: In other words, they weren't a weapon for making a revolution.

Guarany: No, no. They incentivize, stimulate. At least those who are fighting like Agustín Tosco when I wrote "*Qué tristeza tendrán. . .*" ("How sad they will be . . . ") for him, they are stimulated, they feel good, at least somebody says I'm right or supports me or is with me. Songs stimulate. But the revolution . . . [isn't made only with songs]. (Interview, May 2010)

Interestingly enough his first answer addresses how militant songs stimulate militant leaders, not the rank and file. All in all, reassurance or reaffirmation among militants at the most. Agustin Tosco was a well-known trade union leader of the 1960s and 1970s, and Guarany knows how important the song he composed in his honor was for him.

He composes about topics he feels important, topics he thinks are important for people's lives as well, above all to improve their lives. That is the role he wants to play: to stimulate people to think about those topics. But that is also the limit he sees for himself. Social revolution is in people's hands, not at the mercy of his voice. If this is so, it is not coincidental that he had a very negative evaluation of the outcome of the militant song movement he was a very important part of. According to Guarany the militant song movement was fruitless, it didn't stimulate any revolution (as he thought it was going to); the world is as bad (or worse) than it was in the 1960s and 1970s. However, in the last instance, Guarany does not think that the culprit is the militant song, but the "soil" in which the song was planted: "I'm praised for what I say. But they don't imitate me. What a pity . . . the world's in very bad shape. [. . .] The seed fell on rotten soil, poorly-tilled soil" (Interview, May 2010). The "soil" was not well toiled for the militant song to fructify. Here the "soil" is the metaphor Guarany uses for "the people," in particular "people's fear" (while not people's knowledge). In that way Guarany can address, simultaneously, in very negative terms the outcome of the militant song movement in general, but positively his role on it and, most importantly, he can also attempt to "rescue" the "people" for its potential role in promoting change.

THE NUEVO CANCIONERO MOVEMENT

By most accounts the NCM (and his heritage) is, with Yupanqui, the most recognizable face of the militant song movement in Argentina.[4] The difference with Yupanqui is that the NCM was a group encompassing several poets and musicians, and that they produced the only formal militant "manifesto" of the period (the José Podestá's comment on the back of the LP *Cancionero de la Liberación* cannot be truly be named a "manifesto").

Interestingly enough, the movement (as a movement and, in particular, its manifesto) was not well known at the time. Its impact was retrospective and, paradoxically, came as a result of the cumulative efforts of its main exponents as individuals, not as a group. Having been born in the Mendoza province and signed by poets and composers who were not national figures at the time, its first impact was only local (with the regional music of Cuyo). That is the reason why even singer/composers who (politically and artistically) could be considered "natural" allies of the movement were totally unaware of its existence until the late 1960s.

> **Guarany**: I never knew about them at that time. I knew nothing about it. And I believe it was a fabrication, an aspiration, because it never had any projection. Tejada and Matus, Mercedes's husband, and somebody else talked about it but it never really came into being. (Interview, May 2010)

*****

> **Poggini** (main agent for Communist artists): This had taken place in Mendoza. But not a word had reached here (Buenos Aires up to 1972, the era of the Report on the Nuevo Cancionero). Besides, all the singers and artists who had participated in the NCM were totally unknown here (at the time), here people only knew Los Chalchaleros and Daniel Toro. Not the members of the MNC. (Interview, May 2010)

Given its retrospective importance in Latin America, although with less repercussion in Buenos Aires at the time, the obvious question is what was the aim of the Nuevo Cancionero? The movement's opening declaration, presented in public on February 11, 1963, gives a preliminary idea. The primary aim was deregionalization (a single, useful kind of folk music for the entire country).

In an earlier stage of the folk song in Argentina, the manifesto claims, the aim was for folklore to show "how things had been in the beginning," but now it was time to confront the need for a second, higher stage, since stagnation would be alien to the *blood* and *destiny* of the people. According to the manifesto, the process would lead to consciousness-raising throughout Argentina, "real and continent-wide," part of the fight against those who wanted to deform this essence/objective that had been taken up by the NCM in order to accompany the struggles and lives of the people. The aspiration was to create something artistically new rather than to continue collecting/reproducing the spontaneous popular production.

In the Manifesto the creative preoccupation must include "the people, their historic circumstances and their landscape." The function of the Nuevo Cancionero is to serve as a kind of "enlightening," interpretative watchtower or lighthouse for determining and distinguishing between good from evil. To this end, "It will discard, reject, and denounce to the public, through enlightening analysis in each case, all coarse, subaltern production." The NCM proclaimed itself the critical vanguard for ascertaining the quality and meaning of songs. In a certain sense, the last sentence of the Manifesto sums up its basic premise: we are going to change art so that it accompanies the life and struggles of the people, thus placing the accent on the future more than on the past (the latter the legitimating factor of "folklore" up to that time). And this is the real revolution in "folklore." What is popular is contained within the people through their destiny (obviously open to a still undetermined historical and political evolution) rather than through their traditions.

The ethos emanating from the Manifesto is made manifest in songs written in its initial period such as *"Zamba del Riego"* ("Irrigation Zamba," by Matus and Tejada Gómez). The perspective is that of a worker laboring in someone else's vineyard (just as Maestro Yupanqui's cattle were someone else's), who now, additionally, is waiting for the arrival (with no mention of how it will come about) of the "people's grape harvest," expressed as festival and also property. *"Coplera del viento"* ("Wind coplera") by the same composers, is a *tonada* (folk song from the Cuyo region) in which the wind is presented as unseen and ubiquitous, moving and pushing things like an ideology. It doesn't "walk just to walk," in the same way that you don't sing just to sing: the reason you do it is "to push the others." The promoters of this "moving" (in other words, the process of ideological pushing) are identified as persecuted, although the futility of the oppression is made clear, since "no one can stop" the ideological wind now.

"Coplera del viento"
("Wind coplera")

I am singing to the wind	I had a friend close by,
and not just to sing	heart of the dovecote
just as the wind	they saw wind in his eyes
doesn't walk just to walk	they didn't let him pass.
I am blood in movement	They don't know that the wind

and he is a landscape that goes, goes,   nobody can stop it, he goes, goes.
goes
I like to walk in the wind
and it's because I like to walk,
pushed by winds
and pushing the others.

Ando cantándole al viento   *Tuve un amigo aquí cerca,*
y no sólo por cantar   *corazón de palomar*
del mismo modo que el viento   *le vieron viento en los ojos*
no anda por andar nomás.   *no lo dejaron pasar.*
Yo soy sangre en movimiento   *Ellos no saben que al viento*
y él es paisaje que va, va, va.   *nadie lo puede atajar, va, va.*
Me gusta andar en el viento
y es porque me gusta andar,
empujado por los vientos
y empujando a los demás.

"*Zambita de Los Humildes*" ("Humble People's Zamba") the first open collaboration between Matus and Tejada Gómez written before the Manifesto,
aims at instilling endurance in the downtrodden of the earth. If the poor are
obliged to "wait for hope" (because the time has not yet come, but it will
eventually arrive), it is preferable to "wait for it singing."

A good example of the initial objectives of the NCM is "*Los oficios del
Pedro Changa*" ("The Different Jobs of Pedro the Migrant Worker"), a comprehensive work composed in 1967 and interpreted by Armando Tejada
Gómez and Los Trovadores that fulfills comprehensively and quite literally
the "requirements" set forth in the Manifesto: high quality and relating the
realities of the people without musical or thematic regionalism. A closer
examination reveals that the role of song and singer are also present, as well
as the value of consciousness-raising in preparing the way for the future. The
subaltern as protagonist appears in the form of all the regional iterations of
the migrant worker; the different kinds of work he does give rise to the music
and texts read by Armando Tejada Gómez himself. The problem of the
migrant worker is viewed as inherent to an unjust social structure; after
crossing the different geographical regions and chronicling the work done in
each, the irrefutable need for change is confirmed. At the end of this musical

rite of passage, two changes have been registered: the migrant worker has become a singer, and the victim of injustice an actor fighting for change.

Three levels of meaning are posed in this trajectory. The first two are the initiation of both the migrant worker and the composer himself, the latter who reflects himself in the song and is preparing to return at the end of the song:

"already suspecting that there is something in all this that isn't working/no matter how hard he tries/and that his hands have gotten as broad as the map."

("ya sospechando que hay algo en todo esto que no anda/por más que él ponga el hombro/ y que sus manos le hayan quedado anchas como el mapa.")

"*Los oficios del Pedro Changa*" ("The Different Jobs of Pedro the Migrant Worker")

But at a third, more important level, both author and protagonist make way for the listener, the real target of the rite of passage, the one the song pretends will be able to discover "what is going on" (to discover himself as exploited) and, in the process, will justify the narrator as the vanguard and *primus inter pares* among the proponents of change. For that purpose each song details a different phase of the migrant worker's trajectory (gather corn, load ships in the port of Rosario, harvest wheat in Pehuajo and yerba mate in Misiones, . . . cut cane in Tucumán, and pick grapes in Mendoza). However, "unemployment" is also considered a job.

In sharp contrast to the traditional image in folklore, unemployment is an innovative element in the musical work trajectory. From the methodological perspective of the NCM in 1967, structural unemployment is not singled out to be acted upon; rather, it is intended to only be mentally reflected upon. Later on, in the radicalized 1970s, this will change and the call will be for action, not reflection. Still affirming the need for intellectual awakening and consciousness-raising, Tejada does not postulate "come down my road or you are in the wrong," but rather "we'll all go together, you and me." Los Trovadores, progressively raising the emotional temperature with their exultant musical accompaniment, prepare the way for the Chorale referred to in the title. Not coincidentally, the militant message of the song is declared in the brief, explicit final verse: "Now I sing all I have walked and learned/ But I don't sing alone, since every day a child awakens in my guitar."

The narrator is no longer a migrant worker; now he is a singer with a mission, a destiny, and with him the song becomes liberating. The apparent mission of this kind of song is to awaken consciousness with its guitar, or, in the narrator's words, "awaken a child," an ingenuous, fertile, uncontaminated image of the future. The people, as a child, are awakened with his song. One would be hard-pressed to find a more categorically beautiful metaphor to characterize the body of Tejada's work.

THE MOVEMENT'S IMPACT

NCM compositions (more than the movement itself) moved younger inter-preters musically and poetically, with its members becoming a source of inspiration for the militant decade. Víctor Heredia describes NCM's impact as follows (see also Heredia 2007):

> **Heredia**: (Viglietti and Zitarrosa . . .) didn't come along until 1968-69. What there was were the great composers who expressed in one way or another what the Nuevo Cancionero Manifesto was. My first record, *Gritando Esperanzas* (*Screaming Hopes*) comes from there. What I mean is that the majority of composers that I choose to sing their songs were them. Ramón Ayala ("*El mensú*," "*Cachapecero*"), Tejada Gómez. I was the first to record "*Canción para un niño en la calle*" ("Song for a Kid Living in the Streets") for example. (Interview, June 2010)

NCM composers and singers also exercised great influence in other coun-tries:

> **Molinero:** Who would you say influenced other countries' protest songs most? I mean did Argentina influence Chile, Uruguay, or did Uruguay or Chile influence Argentina? Who came first, who came later?

> **Pino**[5]: (Argentina and especially . . .) the Cosquín festival (that. . .) was very important. It influenced everybody else and neighboring countries.

> **Poggini:** I (. . . too) think Argentina influenced the other countries. In my view, especially, fundamentally, vocal groups, . . . right? Because of their aesthetic form. Like what happens with Cuba is the same. When we go to Cuba, the new Trova Cuban was just beginning to grow, and they were amazed by our way to treat musically poetic lyrics. Because not even the Uruguayans wrote music that paralleled the poetry like that, the music was like an accompaniment (. . .), it was a singing poem.

> **Pino**: Here poetic lyrics got a musical treatment that was very far . . . superior . . . I mean, the way of singing of the vocal groups of the time: there was a school. And at that time we had the best poets in America in popular music. We sang poems.

> **Poggini:** I still remember when we were in Cuba what Silvio Rodríguez said, "it's fantastic, it's really nice to hear your music without words." He said that. (Interview, May 2010)

SECOND STAGE: 1966–1975 OR "THE MILITANT DECADE"

During this decade there was phenomenal growth in the number and message intensity of politically oriented social songs, in line with the general socio-political evolution of the times. Preliminary efforts described above converged to produce the greatest concentration of militant songs and singers ever seen either before or after.

Although more and more artists are writing and singing songs with social content during the first half of the decade (1966–1970), the essential concern is still to legitimate this socio-political content or "decalogue" within the folk movement. By 1970, however, this stage is considered as accomplished. With this subject matter now an "integral part" of folk music, specific strategies for bringing about social change come into play. The second half of the decade (1971–1975) is characterized by increased radicalization in which the musicians involved seek to put their music at the service of a particular political program. Rather than "waiting for hope," they proclaim the time has come to begin constructing change. At the end of the decade simply musicalizing the topics of concern to the "left" (indigenism, inequality, a brighter future, etc.) falls short. A specific proposal for how to achieve these goals must now be aligned with the political alternatives articulated at the time. The term "protest" gains popularity during this period. In 1975 a third turning point is reached when, for extra-musical reasons such as the appearance of the Triple A paramilitary group and the subsequent military coup on March 24, 1976, this vector of the folk song is silenced.

Singers like Jorge Cafrune and Mercedes Sosa, and singer-songwriters like Víctor Heredia and César Isella (who throw in his lot with the Nuevo Cancionero from 1969 on) represent this tendency. Other artists that should be mentioned in this regard are Chango Farías Gómez (one of the truly innovative and original Argentine folk musicians), Chito Zeballos, Marián Farías Gómez, Moncho Mieres, and Daniel Toro, among soloists. Groups aligned to this trend include El Quinteto Tiempo, Las Voces Blancas, El Cuarteto Vocal Zupay, and El Dúo Salteño, as well as Los Trovadores. Degrees of political commitment among groups varied, as did political orientation, although CP membership predominated.

The spread of popular music "with content" leads, in parallel, to a certain preponderance of interpreters over songwriters; the singers form their own relationship with a circle of followers, singing and selecting songs written by others, which makes both the message and how it is received of interest. Music, interpretation, and literary content appear inseparable during this markedly innovative decade. That means that, artists like Chango Farías Gómez, known for his creative musicalizations, are on equal footing with NCM musicians, and virtuoso lyric writers.

In an era when politically committed artists proliferated, although feminism was not a prime concern, two women did stand out, one from within the political sphere centered around the Communist Party, and the other from the ranks of Peronism. The former, Mercedes Sosa, standard bearer and iconic voice of the NCM (and consequently emblematic of the Argentine CP) became world-renown; although lesser known, the latter, Marián Farías Gómez is, as Vila correctly determined, a hinge joining Peronism and Communism in Argentine folk music.

MERCEDES SOSA, THE VOICE

As was the case with Guarany, the greatest hits of Mercedes Sosa, the symbol of militancy in the period under analysis, were non-militant. This by no means detracts from (but rather illuminates) the value of her more political songs. In this regard, it is worth mentioning the title of her first LP, *Yo no canto por cantar* (*I Don't Sing for Its Own Sake*) a ringing declaration of principle.

The objective of the following necessarily abbreviated synthesis is to examine certain relevant aspects of her trajectory (for a thorough biography see Braceli 2003). Esteemed as a singer who built her career around a superlative voice, Mercedes is also an artist whose specific political orientation nurtured the growth of the militant song movement. Examined chronologically, her recordings reveal a growing number of increasingly mordant songs in the course of the militant decade. The LP *Hermano* (*Brother*) recorded in 1966, for example, includes a single "social" song, "*Zamba del Chaguanco*." In 1967 in *Para cantarle a mi gente* (*To Sing to My People*) the number doubles: "*Canción para un niño en la calle*" and "*Canción para despertar a un negrito*" ("Song to Wake Up a Little Black Child," a song by Isella and Guillén that postulates that the final destiny of the master should be the fire: "*¡muera en la brasa!*").

In the second half of the decade there is no doubt about the rise in militancy among musicians in general, and in Mercedes's recordings in particular. This is no accident. The year 1969 is significant politically as the year of the Cordobazo, but also when "*Canción con Todos*" ("Song with Everybody") is composed. At this point the Argentine Revolution of General Onganía is severely weakened, General Aramburu is subsequently kidnapped by the Peronist guerilla movement Montoneros, which, together with two other armed groups, E.R.P. and F.A.R., become increasingly active. The idea of lifting the ban on the Peronist party and calling elections, implying the eventual return to power of its leader, is the order of the day, while at the same time guerrilla activity becomes more and more radical. This brings about a change in the spirit (and the songs) of militants and the society at large. The nature of the "political" songs themselves is transformed by these events. Whether to accept guerrilla methodology as the means for a revolutionary destiny becomes a topic of debate. This change is visible on the covers of Mercedes's LPs, where her initial serious visage in close-up gives way to an image of her convoking multitudes with arms held high (in the style of Horacio Guarany).

The LP *El grito de la tierra* (*The Cry of the Earth*) from 1969 includes "*Canción con todos*" and "*Fundamento coplero*" ("Singing Manifesto"), which as the name implies, makes explicit the raison d'etre of a song: all or nothing; militant or not at all. It is no longer a question of incorporating rebellious themes into folk music; now the objective is to exclude all else. The protagonist is the song, and the one who sings it will be seen as "actor" of history.

Now the function of a song is no longer to "wait for hope." The song now knows, and men and women do too, that hunger exists for a reason with a long history, and is the child of the poor and their struggle. But above all, they know that power is predestined to revert to the people. An unmitigated struggle is proposed that should make the oppressor tremble, and lead to the construction of a new man from the light cast by the oppressed who will achieve "redemption." In sum, an idealization in favor of openly militant songs. On the LP *Hasta la victoria* (*Until Victory*) is found "*Plegaria a un Labrador*" ("Prayer to a Peasant") by Víctor Jara, an extraordinary example of non-religious religiosity and of the flourishing circulation of militant songs among Chileans, Uruguayans and Argentines.

In 1973 Mercedes records *Traigo un pueblo en mi voz* (*I Bring People in My Voice*) that includes "*Hermano dame tu mano*" ("Brother, Give Me Your Hand"), "*Triunfo agrario*" ("Agrarian Triumph"), "*Cuando tenga la tierra*" ("When the Land Belongs to Me"), and "*Si un hijo quieren de mí*" ("If They Want a Child from Me"), among others. Subject matter and militancy are explicit in "*Triunfo Agrario*" (which is also sung in the show *El Cóndor Vuelve*).

> This is a triumph, mother, but without triumph. . . /the large estate hurts us in our bones./This is the land, father, that you trod,/my song has not yet rescued it./When will the day come, I ask when/on the sterile land/ all the dispossessed workers come planting seeds?/The way the wind blows has to change like the dice, if you don't change everything, nothing changes!
>
> *Éste es un triunfo, madre, pero sin triunfo. . . /nos duele hasta los huesos el latifundio./Ésta es la tierra, padre, que vos pisabas,/todavía mi canto no la rescata./¿Y cuándo será el día, pregunto cuándo/que por la tierra estéril vengan sembrando/todos los campesinos desalojados?./¡Hay que dar vuelta el viento como la taba, el que no cambia todo, no cambia nada!*
>
> "*Triunfo agrario*" ("Agrarian Triumph")

The keys to the period of radicalization are not hard to find in the lyrics of this song: explicit political terminology is used ("latifundio" or large estate is a non-rural, non-criollo or agricultural term); the song is the protagonist ("my song has not yet rescued it"); urgency ("when will the day come," the people are no longer waiting for a revolution "that is on its way" or that "we will make on a given day"), and ideological opposition to the reformism attributed to Peronism ("if you don't change everything, nothing changes"). It also shows the militant interaction between song and political actors. The final stanza will be used from then on as an almost obligatory "common sense" refrain to combat gradualism (a distinction established by Marxism as essential in combatting "Peronist reformism").

This increase in the quantity of militant songs and intensity of their revolutionary content in Mercedes Sosa's recordings over this decade is representative of the general course of the genre.

MARIÁN FARÍAS GÓMEZ: COMMITMENT AND CONSTANCY

Joining Los Huanca Huá when only nineteen years old established for life her profile of political and musical "group member." She recorded the *Misa Criolla* with Los Huanca Huá, something that would have been impossible for Mercedes Sosa to do at that time (she did record it near the end of her career). However, Marián Farías Gómez was always a Catholic ("but anticlerical") precisely because she was "very Peronist." The song *"Romance de María Pueblo"* ("Romance of Mary People") written by her mother (Pocha Barros) and interpreted by Marián, is a good example of where she positioned herself.

The "good/companion/comrade" in these songs has a life after death: he or she will live on in the people, a nicely functional guarantee of immortality for somebody who decides to be a militant. In the song under discussion a rank and file female worker, unappreciated and with little to make her happy, is described: heels always worn down/wage worker all her life/nobody watches her pass by/María among a hundred Marías (*los tacos siempre gastados/a jornal toda la vida./nadie la mira pasar/María entre cien Marías*).

She is precisely the person who will be vindicated, for being a social activist, for having a common dignity, not particularly a militant one: When they talked about the strike/María wasn't afraid/If they shot to kill, they didn't think about María/María, María Pueblo, how lonely she was dying! (*Cuando hablaron de la huelga/no tuvo miedo María./Si tiraron a matar, no pensaron en María/ María, María Pueblo, ¡que solita se moría . . . !*)

Like a good revolutionary she "wasn't afraid"; like a good "comrade" she went on strike, she was killed, and that is why she will be reborn in the paradise of those who fight. She will be admired by everyone. That is why:

Some day she will be born again through happiness;/everyone will see you pass by/María Pueblo, María . . . /all four Sundays will be María's/ Sundays to go with God,/ for María to live (*Alguna vez volverá /a nacer por alegría; / todos te verán pasar/María Pueblo, María . . . /de cada cuatro domingos/ todos serán de María/ domingos de andar con Dios,/ para que viva María*).

The message is clear: supporting a strike, meaning concretely trade unions (the veritable "backbone" of Peronism) but combatants (not like "the union bureaucracy," which brought the message close to the left) not only "isn't bad" and "is dangerous"; it means that the maximum risk one can assume (death) is compensated for by glory and recognition.

Her friendship with Tejada Gómez and Lima Quintana, two excellent, popular Communist poets, determined her connecting role:

Marián: Armando was an extraordinary, fascinating guy. . . There is a very short poem that is the one I like best which says: "my mother, who was so creole, that put in the pot . . . love." That's . . . . He is so much like Federico García Lorca, they are guys you read and nothing else is important to you. And being his friend taught me a whole lot of things, for example, that I was never going to be a Communist, I ended up being convinced. And I told him so. But we loved each other anyway, really, he was . . . (Interview, May 2010)

Tejada's dogmatism (an expression of his practice as Communist at the time) rather than his ideological orientation was the source of conflict. Her presence (synthetically delineated in our analysis of "*María Pueblo*") on opposite sides of the "ideological divide" among musicians pushing for revolutionary change makes it possible to identify Marián as "hinge" joining sung Marxism and musical Peronism.

Putting collective interests before individual ones was her choice in life and art. This opened the way for integrating ideologies that were widely divergent during this period.

Marián: This way of being is what led me to think that me being a kind of hinge as you said existed with everyone, with Communists, with Peronists. Not with the others because we never paid much attention to each other, never with the other ideologies. In general, I navigated in both, among Communist friends with whom I did the shows, and Peronists, even though perhaps very few of them proposed putting on shows. I have always liked teamwork. It seems much more valuable to me to perform in something like a collective show on the stage rather than simply going to sing alone in a recital. (Interview, May 2010)

CANCIONERO DECALOGUE

A series of recurrent topics, first introduced into the folk music milieu by militant artists, spread and gained intensity in the course of the decade discussed above. Applying the term "decalogue" to them is meant to indicate a certain structural tendency or "formula" (to achieve effects through repetition) present in the poetics of protest of the period. By way of example, we will examine certain of the decalogue's characteristics in the show "*El Cóndor Vuelve*" ("The Condor Returns") that César Isella, Armando Tejada Gómez, and Los Trovadores put on in the IFT theater in Buenos Aires from June through August 1973 (from the inauguration of H. J. Cámpora as president of Argentina to the fall of S. Allende in Chile), which has been described as a sort of "Runa Marxism as militant decalogue" (Molinero 2011).

The show did not come to light by chance. César Isella notes that "a very good artistic and ideological chemistry existed among us. In fact, we used this same strength to support militant cultural movements in Argentina and neighboring countries. Those songs served at times as a source of inspiration for mobilizations and a lighthouse for those attracted to the new political and social movements." (Isella 2006: 133). The apparent subject-protagonist of the show is collective (an ancestral runa that traverses time), and is waiting for a vanguard. But the real mediator during the trajectory is not a political leader or idea; *the protagonist is the song itself,* which throughout the ages has accompanied, come to the aid of, comforted, and at times awakened the people. And, completely reversing the song's prior function of "making the wait pleasant" in "*Zambita de los Humildes*," now it can only be interpreted as rebellious:

> Because subjugated and humiliated for long years/And also betrayed for a long time/we only know how to sing in the sense of rebellion and struggle,/because he who is silent consents./ He who sings, doesn't . . .
>
> *Así como sometidos y humillados largamente/Y también, largamente traicionados/no sabemos cantar sino en sentido de rebelión y lucha,/porque el que calla otorga./ El que canta, no. . .*
>
> "*El Cóndor Vuelve*" ("The Condor Returns")

The militant singer is not only necessary. The declaration here is that the only reason to sing is to bring about rebellion and struggle. The zenith of the radicalization cycle has been reached. The song must be militant, or it does not exist as a song.

Sharing its name with the name of the show, the last song is exemplary in this regard: it enumerates the militant decalogue almost in its entirety. The militant is the one who should occupy the stage, if for no other reason to indicate that immortality is his reward for dying in the struggle. Thus the show reaches its culmination by finally providing the listener with a solution. *El Condor Vuelve . . .* to a revolutionary America.

"El Cóndor Vuelve"
("The Condor Returns")

There goes Gen. Sandino
And the Ecuador
traces the hot map
of Nicaragua in my heart

With Prestes I am the column
of the coffee plantation
And I go with Camilo Torres
Che people in Arms, Che gale

Artigas takes this blood
Where the light
becomes Fidel, and finds
that Guemes takes care of the Southern Cross

Allende [beyond as well in Spanish] the Andes
the sun returns
And America is this blood
through which liberation goes.

The Condor returns
From High Peru
This time there will be no Guayaquil
The entire South has to unite
In a shout

Liberty, Land and bread
Liberty Liberty!!!!

Ahí va el General Sandino
Y el Ecuador
Dibuja el mapa caliente
De Nicaragua en mi corazón

Con Prestes soy la columna
Del Cafetal
Y voy con Camilo Torres
Che pueblo en Armas, Che vendaval

Artigas toma esta sangre
Donde la luz
Se vuelve Fidel, y encuentra

Que Güemes cuida la Cruz del Sur

Allende la cordillera
regresa el sol
Y América es esta sangre
Por donde va la liberación.

Vuelve el Cóndor
Del Alto Perú
Esta vuelta no habrá Guayaquil
Hay que unir todo el Sur
En un grito

Libertad, Tierra y pan
Libertad Libertad!!!!

The end, with *"Canción con Todos"* as encore incorporated as almost an integral part, is neither coincidental nor out of place. It condenses and completes the meaning of the work.

"El Cóndor Vuelve" summarizes the totality of militant topics, going one step beyond *"Los Oficios del Pedro Changa,"* surpassing the requirements of the "Nuevo Cancionero Manifesto," while representing a new way of understanding the song as well. It no longer suffices to posit meaningful testimony as a way of "not hiding" the part played by paisanos in the struggle, their "suffering and sorrows." Here that is the only reason for the artist to embark on a struggle that had (and will have) *desaparecidos* (missing people, actually killed by the military) who don't die if they are in the song, because of the certainty of a future that is ratified by what is going on today. The reversal of meaning is now complete, and the singer no longer "permits himself" a militancy; all things considered, the militancy is what permits its own song. One doesn't know, one mustn't sing in any sense other than that of rebellion and struggle. It is the road of the future: That is why:

> Our song will always arise to set dignity on its feet. They will surely want our soul again but we will take away their ill-begotten land. They will surely want our song but we will take away the gold oil and tin they steal from the ground. They will surely want our sweat again. But from the hurricanes of fury the people will come out singing and fighting protecting the flight of their condor [. . . and] we will be a torrent of the growing life of peoples . . .
>
> *"El Cóndor Vuelve"* ("The Condor Returns")

The singer, protagonist of dignity, cultural resistance, and struggle responds and takes the lead in agrarian expropriation: *they will want our soul or song, we will take the land.* That is why *"Cuando Tenga la Tierra"* "those that fight will have it, the teachers, the workers." And in the *"Triunfo Agrario"*: "the one who doesn't change everything, changes nothing." These songs are not in the show by accident. Neither is oil or gold. The people, the singer affirms, will come out fighting yet singing, while protecting their condor's flight (image of the vanguard and, at the same time of history being recuperated), and that is when "we will be a torrent" of life.

EL *CANCIONERO DE LA LIBERACIÓN* (THE LIBERATION SONGBOOK)

While the actors we have been analyzing so far belong to the "classic Left," (if such a thing ever had existed), due to their political adscription to the Socialist or Communist Party, in a country like Argentina, in which a very important part of the "leftist agenda" (social change, redistribution of income, anti-imperialist stances and popular political participation among others) was carried out by the Peronist movement, it is not by chance to find many members of the militant song movement who identify themselves as "Peronists."

Because Peronism was prohibited to participate in democratic elections from 1955 to 1973 (and while allowed, the party won the elections and the military intervened to cancel the results, or/and institute a military-guided regime—as happened in 1962–1963 and 1965–1966), most of its political endeavors occurred outside the democratic system of political parties, above all trade unions. However, in the late 1960s, a new political actor became central to Peronism's attempts to return to power: the peronist youth; and, within these newly arrived, a central role was played by its left win: "la Juventud Peronista" or JP, and its guerrilla arms, Fuerzas Armadas Peronistas (Peronist Armed Forces), Montoneros, Descamisados, and Fuerzas Armadas Revolucionarias (Revolutionary Armed Forces). If the idea in the 1960s was that: "there is no revolution without songs," it is not by chance that this political actor also developed its own variant of militant songs, whose characteristics are very different from those of the more traditional left wing of the militant song movement.

THE JOSÉ PODESTÁ GROUP

Much of what happened with the Peronist leg of the militant song movement in Argentina in the late 1960s and early 1970s has to do with the activities of Oscar Rovito, a well-known film and theater actor who, by those years nearly abandons his acting career to be highly involved in the political movement that tried to bring back Perón from exile. As part of such political movement, many artists (mostly actors and musicians—and many "actors-turned-musicians" like Rovito himself and Marilina Ross) were involve in diverse cultural endeavors that tried to help, from that particular cultural sphere, the return of Peronism to power.

With Juan Carlos Gené (a very-well-known actor and theater director), Rovito decides to launch (with the collaboration of many respected musicians, actors, and actresses, such as Piero, Marilina Ross, Chango Farías Gómez, Emilio Alfaro, Carlos Carella, Leonor Benedetto, and Paulino Andrada) the "Centro de Cultura Nacional José Podestá" (National Culture Center José Podestá). A very important part of the activities of the José Podestá were theatrical performances in which songs alluding to the political topics being addressed were sung, songs that were composed by the different members of the group. After a couple of years performing those theatrical events here and there, they decide to stage the songs as a "stand-alone" performance in a trade union auditorium, the Luz y Fuerza theater in July 1973. Piero (at the time a very successful commercial singer) was quite instrumental in the production of both, the event itself, and the recording of the event that gave birth to the *Cancionero de la liberación* LP (which was recorded using RCA recording equipment—Piero's company), with songs like "*El Chamamé del Tío*" ("Uncle's Chamamé" by Juan Carlos Gené -Alejandro Mayol), "*La Calle de la Cárcel*" ("The Street of the Jail" by Marilina Ross–María Maristany), "*La matanza del basural*" ("The Slaughter of the Landfill" by Daniel Barberis), "*Para el pueblo lo que es del pueblo*" ("For the People What Rightfully Belongs to Them" by Piero), and so on.

Here the group states their revolutionary compromise with the Cámpora and Perón's governments and, more importantly, takes sides in the Peronist internal struggle of the time, that between "*la patria socialista*" (the socialist homeland) (vindicated by the JP and the rest of the left wing of the movement) and "*la patria peronista*" (the peronist homeland) (vindicated by the center and right wings of the movement): the José Podestá explicitly fights for "*la patria socialista*" and claims that it is Perón himself who is pushing the movement in that direction.

The edition of the LP was financed in what Rovito terms "a militant way,"[6] that is, the record was sold in advance to prospective buyers (militants of different Peronist organizations, family and friends) in order to cover its production cost. The concert and the record were really the swan song of the José Podestá group, because many of its members became part of the Peronist government (Juan Carlos Gené went to the National Culture Secretariat, Carlos Carella to National Radio and Rovito to the Buenos Aires city administration) and their cultural activities suffered because of that. As the confrontation between Perón and the Peronist left wing hegemonic group Montoneros escalated (above all when Montoneros assassinated José Ignacio Rucci—Perón's most important trade union ally—only days after Perón won the presidency with more than 60 percent of the popular vote) the José Podestá could not overcome the internal debate and confrontation that ensued

(Rucci's assassination meant the fracture of the Peronist left wing between those who continued supporting Montoneros regardless of the crime, and those who considered that guerrilla tactics had to change when not only there is a democratic government in power, but, more importantly, when that democratic government is led by your own political party) and, step by step, diluted its presence in the cultural scenario of the period and, eventually, disappeared. According to Rovito, what happened is this: "wounds were opened that at another time would have been surmounted by enthusiasm."

In that regard Rovito claims that the kind of militant song they advocated and performed was very important in the construction and popularization of the political messages linked to the return of Perón to power. In particular he talks about the "power of the popular song to affect people's state of mind, their spirit."

> This mobilizing power, this power to convoke. . . this power that frequently enlightens. Not because you put yourself in a pretentious vanguard position, far from it. But sometimes things expressed in the simple poetry of a song. . . that reach. . . that tug on people's heartstrings, explain much more than an erudite speech on a particular set of problems, right? (Interview, May 2010)

His statement above is important for several reasons. On the one hand, because it talks about the "enlightening power" of the song. In this regard, the popular song is viewed as the perfect vehicle to combine the rational message of a political position with the emotional component (*"la fibra íntima de la gente"*) that can, first, make it easier to understand a particular stance; and second, and more importantly, can eventually transform a partisan slogan into social and political action. On the other hand, Rovito's statement wants to differentiate his position from the one he (correctly—as we saw in our discussion of the Nuevo Cancionero movement) adjudicates to the militant singers linked to the left, that is, their "vanguard" position regarding the popular masses. Later in the interview Rovito elaborates on this point: "The songs we sang aimed at being an answer to what was happening to people. Far from wanting to make an interpellation or tell people what to do, what we were looking for was to take things people depended on or were familiar to them and transform these things into this kind of artistic expression."

In this regard, Rovito goes deeper in his criticism of the Nuevo Cancionero movement: their songs did not want to "illuminate" people who, somehow, were ignorant of what happened with their lives and what was the real origin of their subordination. Instead, their songs' starting and ending point was what already people knew about them and their socio-economic situation, but transformed into an artistic expression.

This stance regarding the "enlightened" attitude of many representatives of the leftist wing of the militant song movement spills toward their aesthetic choices as well, which, from the point of view of the José Podestá group, is characterized as too intellectual, "less closer to the fiber . . . to the popular sensibility," than their own musical production.

In other words, they were not apologetic for the "directly political" message of their songs, which could be discredited as "*panfletaria*" (a political pamphlet, instead of an artistic song). On the contrary, they were composing those songs out of the urgency of a real struggle for power. This is central in the following dialogue:

> **Rovito**: Another type of song [he refers here to songs linked to the Nuevo Cancionero Movement] of this kind. . . a protest song that sought to be an end in itself. What I mean is that both poetically and musically . . . it took for granted what, on the other hand, every creative person aspires to in this sense . . . in . . . in finding a way to make it lasting, to make it transcend epochs and particular junctures. This spirit wasn't in us. You had to do it, you had to do it. If it lasts, if it continues, doesn't continue, wasn't an issue that concerned us. And neither did we worry too much . . . about polishing lyrics . . . like saying: "no, look, this is too obvious. Here I think we have to find another metaphor. . ." [Laughter] See what I mean? . . . This wasn't among our motivations when writing those songs and doing those things, you see.

> **Vila**: Your perspective was more immediate.

> **Rovito**: We thought about it in correspondence with what reality and our own sensations were bringing to our attention. It wasn't that we, as composers or writers, were trying to elaborate something that aspired to a certain transcendence that went beyond singing to people and with people . . . or to the people and with the people as [they used to say at that time]. (Interview, May 2010)

This goes well beyond a mere aesthetic choice. We think that it marks the difference between singing to a revolution far away and one in which my party can only be a secondary actor (the Communist Party most of the NCM belonged to was only a very minority actor in Argentina, never involved in any real political contest, nor behind any major guerrilla group), than singing to a revolution that is occurring right now and one in which my party (a movement in this case) is a principal actor. In this regard, this difference puts the José Podestá group much closer to the Chilean New Song movement, than to the Argentine Nuevo Cancionero. It is not by chance then that "songs for the political moment," or "circumstantial songs" ("*Canciones urgentes*" [Urgent Songs] in the tradition of Silvio Rodriguez and the Cuban Nueva Trova) were the trademark of both, while the Nuevo Cancionero strived for more "poetically mediated" (song which could transcend the passage of time, in Rovito's terms) political songs. At the same time, it is no coincidence that Horacio Guarany and his "politically direct" songs were never truly considered a part of the NCM. Additionally, while in the case of Guarany the *"canciones panfletarias"* (songs as political pamphlets) are only a very small part of his militant production (and his militant production a small part of his entire oeuvre), in the case of the José Podestá group, all of their songs (at least all of those they wrote under the banner of the group, because some authors—Piero and Marilina Ross prominently—had artistic careers outside of the group) are "songs for the political moment," or "circumstantial songs" (*"canciones coyunturales"* in Spanish).

Rovito is completely aware that their politico-aesthetic choices had important repercussions to the after-life of the songs they composed at that moment:

> Except in the case of Piero, *"Para el Pueblo lo que es del Pueblo,"* I don't think there is any song that you can say today that it can last . . . that it will even stay in people's heads [as a song].

It is not by chance that a similar opaque destiny accompanied most of the *"canciones panfletarias"* composed by Horacio Guarany (who remembers today *"Luche y Luche"*?), but not his other songs and most of the ones composed by the NCM.

But what about the songs of the Liberation Songbook? Let's start for the one most people still remember, *"Para el pueblo, lo que es del pueblo."*

> Liberty was a matter
> badly handled by three
> Liberty was an Admiral
> General or Brigadier
>
> *Libertad era un asunto*
> *Mal manejado por tres*
> *Libertad era almirante*
> *General o brigadier*

This is a direct criticism of the military government that ruled Argentina between 1966 and 1973: they didn't know how to democratically govern the country.

> For the people
> What rightfully belongs to the people
> Because the people earned it
> For the people
> What rightfully belongs to the people
> For the people liberation

Para el pueblo
Lo que es del pueblo
Porque el pueblo se lo ganó
Para el pueblo
Lo que es del pueblo
Para el pueblo liberación

Here the song points out that if liberation is coming (something that rightfully belongs to people), it is not because somebody gave it to them for free, but they conquered it by a long struggle.

Eating well was very rare
Eating little was normal
To eat was subversive
for the military officer

Comer bien era muy raro
Comer poco era normal
Comer era subversivo
Para el señor militar

According to the lyrics the mere act of eating well (something unusual under military rule) was considered subversive by the military.

It was a violent act
Popular happiness
The people are patient
said a general

Era un acto de violencia
La alegría popular
El pueblo tiene paciencia
Dijo un señor general

In the same fashion, if eating was subversive, for the military, people's happiness was subversive as well.

To study was a sin
Knowledge was clandestine
Because when the people know
A brigadier does not fool them

Estudiar era un pecado
Clandestino era saber
Porque cuando el pueblo sabe
No lo engaña un brigadier

To study was a sin, and to know clandestine, but, according to Piero, when people know, they cannot be fooled by an Air Force Brigadier General.

> We will prohibit hope
> And it is prohibited to be born
> Won't It be too much Admiral?
> Not at all Coronel

> *Prohibiremos la esperanza*
> *Y prohibido está nacer*
> *No será mucho almirante?*
> *faltaba más coronel!!*

The next stanza mocks a dialogue between an admiral and a colonel. They claim they will prohibit hope and won't allow anybody to be born. To such an order the colonel asks, "Mr. Admiral, perhaps we went too far on this, what do you think?" The admiral answers: "Not at all."

> They put the country on the auction block
> And they made a bad deal
> They broke it in pieces
> And now it has to be put back together again

> *Y al país lo remataron*
> *Y lo remataron mal*
> *Lo partieron en pedazos*
> *Y ahora hay que volverlo a armar*

The next verse is about what the military did to the country while in power. Piero uses the expression "*remataron*" here, which is polisemic, because it can mean "they put the country in an auction" (meaning that the military sold the country to the best offer), but, at the same time "*remataron*" can mean that the military "killed the country." In any case, claiming that "*lo remataron mal*" Piero stresses that the end result was a disaster because they broke the country in small pieces and the people have the arduous task of putting all those small pieces together again.

> And now the people are in the street
> To look out for and defend
> This country we won
> It must be liberated

> *Y ahora el pueblo está en la calle*
> *A cuidar y a defender*
> *Esta patria que ganamos*
> *Liberada debe ser*

The last stanza is a celebration of people's triumph over the dictatorship. On the one hand, Piero celebrates that people have taken over the streets to accomplish two different things: on the one hand, to defend the country they took over from the military. On the other hand, and more importantly, to liberate the country from the socio-economic forces (which go well beyond the military) that sustain people's subordination.

The other songs of the Cancionero address the different aspects of the peronist struggle to return to power, mixing the ups and downs of such an endeavor. For example, "The Street of the Jail" refers to the people who were incarcerated by the military for their political ideas. The song takes issue with the topic from the point of view of the family members of those incarcerated who, at least, have the "*esperanza de poder verlos . . . un ratito*" (have the hope of seeing them, at least for just a moment). "*Curas del Tercer Mundo*" ("Third World Priests") is a vindication of those Catholic priests who, adhering to the Liberation Theology doctrine, were quite instrumental in the struggle against injustice in Argentina. One of the most important members of the movement, Carlos Mugica, was assassinated by the triple AAA (Anti-Communist Argentine Alliance) in May 1974. The song "The Slaughter of the Landfill" refers to a massacre of peronist militants by the military in 1956. The "Uncle's Chamamé" is a song dedicated to Héctor Cámpora (whose nickname was "uncle," because Perón was the "Viejo" [father/oldman]), Perón's personal delegate while in exile and the person who he designated as the presidential candidate for the Peronist Party in 1973. Cámpora was a close ally of the Peronist left wing and adored by their militants. The song stresses Cámpora's loyalty to Perón, claiming that through his loyalty and honesty, his jealousy complying with Perón's mandates, was the one who "*con nobleza y lealtad, obró con fidelidad al Pueblo y al Movimiento*" (with nobility and loyalty, acted with fidelity to the People and the Movement). "*Triunfo del Cuero*" ("Leather's Triumph") is a song addressing Perón's courage to return to Argentina when the military (who hated him) were still in power. Showing the "situational song" approach to its extreme, the title of the song refers to something that only some people who lived in the early 1970 still remember, that is, when General Lanusse (at that time de facto military president of Argentina) challenged Perón to return to the country if "*le da el cuero*" (a colloquial Argentine expression for "if he has the courage"). Because Perón eventually returned (i.e., "*le dió el cuero*" [he was courageous enough]), the authors of the song titled it "*El triunfo del cuero.*" The last song of the LP is "*El Pueblo Peronista*" ("The Peronist People"). It was also called, at its time, "The Peronist Anthem," because of its peculiar musical and poetic structure, which resembles parts of the Argentine national anthem. As we can see, quite circumstantial songs.

PERSISTENCE

Then the Triple A and the Process came, and "the song" had to go into exile or die. During that period rigorous censorship and self-censorship were the order of the day. Marián and Pino talk about it:

Pino: Look, we felt awful. Because we were threatened, censored, banned, what can I say? everything . . . and we felt bad because it got to such an extreme point that the words "poor," "day wage," "worker" were prohibited in a song (. . .) and the worst was the self-censorship because (. . .) look, we recorded la *"Zamba de Juan Panadero"* ("Juan Baker's zamba") that says that at night Juan Panadero left "his door open for the poor" [to be able to take bread for free] (. . . and they objected or asked) "if we can't change the word 'poor' for 'anybody,' and it wasn't the same . . ." (Interview, May 2010)

***

Marián: I was really out of the country for five years because I couldn't return. And in those five years I grew more than what it might have taken here much longer, because it's difficult to live in exile, you know. Horacio (Guarany) with (Héctor) Alterio did a marvelous job over there, they found out that someone was going, they didn't ask what party they belonged to, they went and waited for them. And if they already knew from here who was going, they looked for a place where they could live, tried to get them a job. We saw a lot of each other until one day I decided to make friends with the Spaniards because exile was very hard. Among us it was very hard. We cried every day. You didn't have much time during the day to think about being exiled. At night, when you returned home was when you bit the pillow and cried because you didn't want to be in Spain, you wanted to be here. And besides, one thing is to go because you want to and another to go because you have to. And to see your friends, see Marilina, see "Tano" Piero, so many people so unjustly . . . for being artists who followed an ideology. None of us was a guerrilla, we didn't have a weapon in our hands, we didn't kill anyone. It was hard. But you grow, you grow. I grew a lot in five years. (Interview, May 2010)

Prior to the coup, the artists had made a weapon of the militant folk song, which was recognized by their enemies, who granted the folk song a privileged position in the subsequent repression. As a consequence "commitment" migrated from folk music to other genres, and when it returned, it was transformed. But it didn't disappear, its persistence is evident in Teresa Parodi, Peteco Carabajal, Antonio Tarragó Ros, Enrique Llopis, Raly Barrionuevo, and so many others, albeit with different characteristics than in the period studied.

In summary, we can say that what made it possible for the militant song to scale the heights so rapidly (in five to seven years) during this period of revolutionary centrifugation was the political situation in general, and in particular in the field of folklore, the implicit rupture in how the nature of the popular essence was conceived. Locating it more in the future than in the past, and embodying it more in the subaltern than in agrarian rural life meant it was "logical" to project onto the genre (appropriate potential representative of nationhood in music), what was imagined and considered ideal in political life. And this occurred in an era when opting for the subaltern meant opting for revolution (albeit with variants, given the peronist phenomenon in Argentina), which successively over time came to be the only certainty. The same interpretation was made by the military during the Process, and they treated folklore accordingly.

The legacy left by the militant song was recognized not only by its enemies, but also by the artists involved in the movement (despite Guarany's opinion to the contrary). For example, Marián Farías Gómez has this to say about her role:

Marián: I was very young and thought we could change the world, and I made the mistake of . . .

Molinero: That you could change it with a song or that with a song you collaborate with the revolution . . .

Marián: (laughter) Because what is most direct for people . . . is a song. It is much easier to reach a person through a song than if that person reads a book where you show him what is happening. It is much more direct because, besides, you reach the heart right away or you don't reach it at all. (Interview, May 2010)

Víctor Heredia enlarges upon this, going into the consequences.

Heredia: Out of innocence, you felt you could make a difference; that is to say that every song you wrote was going to be heard, was going to be analyzed, and was going to serve those who accessed to that message.

Molinero: How?

Heredia: Through consciousness-raising at first. Like a book. Reading it could help establish a new consciousness.

Molinero: Did you think it was a weapon?

Heredia: We all thought it was. It was a weapon loaded with future, that's what it was.

Molinero: What effect did the song have, didn't it have, should it have had?

Heredia: We're standing now in the future we proposed in that epoch. When Latin American unity was talked about, and the need to unite Latin America, the peoples that were only united by horror, today our peoples are united by democratic governments. I am absolutely convinced that all literature, all art, cinema and culture honorably represented those expectations and accompanied them. I don't know if songs were a driving force behind this, but they accompanied it with absolute nobility and posed what newspapers denied, that is very consciously . . .

Molinero: Was the song a herald?

Heredia: Yes, that's exactly right, it was a herald, what the newspapers denied, it transmitted. And I'm not only convinced of that, but I believe that a song means the same thing today, if that wasn't the case, I wouldn't write it. What I have some doubts about is if the impact would be as rapid as what we believed in those days. I feel today that if I shoot a poem, and this poem is a weapon that must arrive someplace, it's going to take a little bit longer (Laughter).

Molinero: Is it a bottle in the ocean?

Heredia: In a river, but I write with the certainty that at some point someone is going to find it.

Molinero: It's not a stone that causes an avalanche.

Heredia: Exactly, it's like a bottle someone is going to find and take the top off of, and it's going to help on the journey. (Interview, June 2010)

Isella explains the consequences as follows:

Molinero: What fruit did these songs bear?

Isella: A lot, a whole lot, and a lot politically on the continent. The death of Mercedes Sosa brought beautifully out in the open the message of continental leaders. Among others, the most lucid of all: Arias, the Nobel Prize winner who was president of Costa Rica. He published a beautiful homage to Mercedes Sosa in *Clarín* (. . .) And the speeches many give in both Brazil and Chile. . . . Look how two presidents of Chile from the same party as Allende turned out to be brilliant politicians, and the country functioned brilliantly, and Allende, who brought the same idea, only at a different time, was destroyed. Well, the circumstances, the times, the song was present. Culture, I can't lock myself up in the song because painters were there, the dance, poetry, writing, music, the cinema was there (. . .) the song helped to raise consciousness. The message was given by the poet, the musician, and the messenger, the one who carried the message, was the one and only voice of Mercedes. I introduced "*Canción con todos,*" Willy Bascuñan took me to President Frei's house in '69. When we performed in Viña del Mar, one night they invited us to eat with President Frei, with the father of the one who [became president in the 1990s] . . . and it was incredible because afterwards I sang to the son when he came to the presidents' meeting [post-Pinochet, in which . . .] Fidel [Castro] was there, Felipe González, King Juan Carlos. And I told him that I sang that song for the first time in his father's house. "I was very small," the Chilean said. "You weren't that small because if you were, you wouldn't be president now [the king answered]." (Laughter). It was fantastic. Armando and I said: if the Popular Unity wins, brother, we swear to go unannounced to Santiago and write a song. We wrote "*Hombre en el tiempo*" in a peña that belonged to some kids from Mendoza, the Talquenca brothers. (Interview, May 2010)

And thus it was that, effectively recognized (by enemies and contemporary political actors that grew up with these songs), despite divergent views regarding their legacy, the Argentine Militant Song had a continent-wide influence, its richness and amplitude testifying to the intensity and seriousness of song writers and singers in the majority of cases.

NOTES

1. We are not analyzing, for instance, a very important actor in this story, the oeuvre "*Zafra*" ("Sugar Harvest"), written by Ariel Petrocelli and the Nuñez brothers in 1966, which is a prominent (and beautiful) example of the vibrancy of the movement in Northwest Argentina.

2. In English "*cancionero*" can be translated as either "song" or "songbook." To make translation issues even more complicated, in the colloquial use of the terms by the members of the movement itself, sometimes they appear to even refer to the idea of singing, but other times to the idea of a collection of songs. Illa Carrillo Rodríguez prefers to use "New Songbook," since the *cancionero*—as canonic repertoire, cultural object, and link to early twentieth-century folklore—was a conceptual keystone of this movement. We prefer to keep the meaning more open and, from now on, will use the Spanish term.

3. The Triple AAA, that is, the Alianza Anticomunista Argentina (Anti-communist Argentine Alliance) was a paramilitary group linked to José López Rega, Social Welfare minister of the Peronist government of the early 1970s.

4. For an excellent analysis of the Nuevo Cancionero Movement see García 2006 and Gravano 1985.

5. Carlos Pino is a prominent member of Los Trovadores.
6. All the quotes from Rovito come from an interview we had with him in May 2010.

Chapter Nine

The Revolutionary Patria and Its New (Wo)Men

Gendered Tropes of Political Agency and Popular Identity in Argentine Folk Music of the Long 1960s

Illa Carrillo Rodríguez

The socially and politically committed music movements that flourished throughout the Americas from the 1950s to the 1970s critically engaged with the continent's national folksong traditions, putting them to work in the articulation of a "popular-revolutionary" voice and identity. Even though this version of identity was fraught with highly gendered representations of political agency, the question of how these music movements (and the left-wing culture that encompassed them) contended with issues of gender remains largely unexamined. The discussion that follows posits such gendered modes of enacting "popular" and "revolutionary" identities as crucial sites of political signification in which key elements of the sixties' utopian imagination crystallized.[1] By examining a repertoire of songs that emanated from different sectors of Argentina's folk-music milieu and 1960s New Left culture,[2] I will evaluate the ways in which the gender paradigms conveyed by this repertoire made possible, but also disavowed, certain political subjectivities.

The first part of my discussion considers two currents of 1960s and 1970s folk music production as distinct artistic iterations of popular-revolutionary identities that wrestled with the issue of representing the "authentic" *pueblo*[3] and, thereby, with the difficulties of enacting a politically committed aesthetic praxis. My discussion moves back and forth from an analysis of the figurations of popular-revolutionary subjectivities in Argentina's *Nuevo Cancionero* (New Songbook) Movement and in a contemporaneous Latin American New Song repertoire, to a consideration of how these subjectivities were represented in a "militant" musical narrative (the cantata *Montoneros*) that stemmed from the official cultural program of an armed political organization.

The focus of the second part of my discussion is on the gender and political paradigms that recur in these representations of the revolutionary *pueblo*. Here, I enlarge my scope of analysis by examining the tropes of femininity and masculinity through which other, less overtly politicized sectors of Argentina's folksong milieu articulated musical narratives of nationhood that evoked the figure of the guerrilla. These narratives, which reference the nineteenth century's struggles for independence and subsequent civil wars, are shaped by that historical moment's discursive and ideological traditions and, thus, bear the traces of deeply rooted assumptions about gender and nationhood.

In the final part of my discussion, I trace the persistence of these narratives' underlying gender and political paradigms in 1970s cultural artifacts like the cantata *Montoneros*. In what ways, I ask, do these paradigms partake in the configuration of the early 1970s' dominant model of *militancia* (militantism)? To what extent do this model of revolutionary agency and its musical representations unsettle normative political, aesthetic, and gender regimes? My discussion of the tense dialogue that these musical narratives entertained with political praxis and historical discourse seeks precisely to interrogate the ways in which 1960s cultural production not only reflected, but fundamentally partook of, the configuration of polysemous, often equivocal models of revolutionary agency.

THE *NUEVO CANCIONERO* MOVEMENT
AND PARTISAN FOLK MUSIC

Argentina's *Nuevo Cancionero* Movement (henceforth NCM) played a key role in the articulation of an "authentically popular" locus of enunciation by producing a folksong repertoire that focused on the *pueblo*'s travails, rather than on the bucolic landscapes and idealized peasants of folklore's "paradigma clásico" (Díaz 2009; classical paradigm), which had been wed, throughout the first half of the twentieth century, to the conservative ideology of Argentina's political and economic elites. As Díaz (2009: 222–223) has shown, both emerging and institutionalized leftist ideologies, especially the Communist Party's conception of folklore, underlay central aspects of the NCM: its recourse to the genre of the manifesto to introduce its historiographic, aesthetic, and political ideas; its representation of the *pueblo* in a sociological guise (as workers); and its understanding of folklore, not as a fixed repertoire of cultural practices anchored in a romanticized past, but as a vital expression and political instrument of the people's ongoing struggles.

The public reception of the NCM as a leftist cultural movement was reinforced by the political affiliation of many artists who subscribed to its 1963 manifesto, of whom the most audible and visible was Communist Party member Mercedes Sosa.[4] Notwithstanding such associations to left-wing organizations, the songs authored and composed by leading NCM figures, such as Armando Tejada Gómez and César Isella, were not conceived as chants for political campaigns and rallies or as the musical synthesis of an official party line.

Other musicians who also participated in Argentina's folk music circuit and shared some of the NCM's ideas did engage, however, in the composition, recording, and performance of a partisan repertoire, a practice that was more widespread in Chile, where prominent *Nueva Canción* (New Song) artists—for example, Víctor Jara, the groups Quilapayún and Inti-Illimani, Sergio Ortega, Luis Advis—composed and performed chants and songs for Salvador Allende's 1970 presidential campaign and the Popular Unity government (1970–1973). The cantata *Montoneros*, which the Argentine folk group Huerque Mapu[5] recorded in 1973 for the leftist Peronist guerrilla group Montoneros, is an example of this "militant" repertoire, although the songs that composed the cantata never reached the broad audience nor attained the level of popularity of partisan anthems like *"Venceremos"* (Claudio Iturra and Sergio Ortega, "We Will Triumph")[6] and *"El pueblo unido jamás sera vencido"* (Quilapayún and Sergio Ortega, "The People United Will Never Be Defeated"). Indeed, while these and other Chilean New Song anthems went on to become standards of cosmopolitan left-wing music culture, Huerque Mapu's cantata never circulated far beyond Peronist militant circles.[7]

Insofar as this musical epic emanated from a cultural initiative undertaken by the Montonero leadership during and immediately after the short-lived government of Peronist President Héctor Cámpora (May 25 to July 13, 1973), the way in which aesthetics and politics are intertwined in the cantata is not analogous to the NCM artists' conception of the relationship between music and political commitment. This significant difference, however, does not situate *Montoneros* and the NCM's heterogeneous repertoire in impervious artistic and political cultures. Rather, such distinct modes of contending with the relationship between art and politics stemmed from a common "structure of feeling" (Williams 1985: 132–133), within which three ideas held pride of place: the notion that art could (and should) be put to work in the construction of a utopian, emotive form of politics; the construal of political praxis as a potential site of *poiesis*; and the belief that a "popular-revolutionary" locus of enunciation would emerge from the tension between, and creative articulation of, politics and music (especially folk genres). As different artists grappled with this tension, they conceived and performed multiple figurations of the "popular."

REIMAGINING THE *PUEBLO* AND
REWRITING PERONIST HISTORY

Of the Montoneros, Richard Gillespie has written that their capacity for
mobilizing large crowds was rooted, less in the coherence of their political
project, than in "the emotive appeal of Montonero rallies and marches, with
all their colour, chanting, and drum-beating, with their exuberance, their
sense of power and solidarity, and their sheer arrogance" (1982: 137).[8] Composed and recorded between October and December 1973, under the vigilant
auspices of the Montonero leadership (Marchini 2008: 155–158), the cantata
Montoneros endeavored to capture the sense of power and solidarity that
characterized those marches and rallies, as well as to render their playful
exuberance politically and historically meaningful. This was done by inscribing documentary sound recordings of Montonero rallies within a highly
structured, overarching narrative-musical work: the cantata, a form of vocal
music that the Chilean group Quilapayún had popularized through its 1970
performance of Luis Advis Vitaglich's cantata *Santa María de Iquique* during the second Chilean New Song Festival (Advis Vitaglich 1999: 1078–79).
Marchini (2008: 155) attributes to the Montonero leadership the idea of
reconstructing the history of the Peronist Left's struggles through an elab-
orate musical production that would transcend the repertoire of songs and
slogans spontaneously crafted and chanted during the organization's public
gatherings. However, it was the folk group Huerque Mapu's decision to
articulate this history through the cantata's narrative and musical aesthetic or,
to be more precise, through the version of that aesthetic most closely associated with Chilean New Song.

Advis Vitaglich characterizes Chilean New Song's versions of the cantata
as complex theatrical-dramatic texts that,

> *exigieron una variante inédita en las estructuras musicales. Así nacerían*
> *secuencias extensas que, al modo de la tradición docta, se desplegaban medi-*
> *ante la alternancia de partes habladas (relatos) y cantadas (canciones de-*
> *sprendidas formalmente del modelo originario), incluyendo desarrollos in-*
> *strumentales (preludios, interludios) de contextura más libre y hasta*
> *parabólica*[9] (1999: 1079).

Much of the cantata's appeal for musicians in the "enlightened" folksong
milieu of the 1960s and 1970s[10] rested, indeed, on this vocal tradition's
eclectic, extensive, all-encompassing architecture, which enabled them to
combine contrasting narrative and musical forms: harmonic textures derived
from European art music, with melodic and rhythmic elements inspired in the
Latin American folksong tradition; this tradition's imagery of love, with
amorous tropes steeped in the modernist aesthetic; and festive songs, struc-

tured according to the strict metric patterns of folk genres, with long historiographic texts following no rhyme scheme.

In the early 1970s, the recourse to this modality of the cantata had distinct cultural connotations, for Chilean New Song and the cantata *Santa María de Iquique* operated as politically and historically charged texts that synthesized important aspects of the Latin American New Left's revolutionary aesthetic, in particular its project of reconstructing the continent's popular history through the articulation of elements of high culture with the folk traditions of the Latin American masses. In *Montoneros*, the intermingling of these aesthetic elements and traditions is put to work in producing a totalizing epic that endeavors to conflate two figurations of the "popular": the Peronist masses and the *pueblo montonero*. This conflation of popular tropes is sonically performed by intercalating an eclectic set of poetic voices and musical styles throughout the cantata's ten parts,[11] which narrate significant events in the history of the Peronist Left's struggle against the *pueblo*'s enemies.

"*Memoria de los basurales (el Aramburazo)*" ("Memory of the Dumping Grounds [the *Aramburazo*]"), the cantata's first part, focuses on the Montoneros' foundational politico-military feat: the 1970 *Aramburazo*, that is, the judgment and execution of General Aramburu, Argentina's de facto President from 1955 to 1958.[12] Aramburu was held responsible by Peronists, not only for his participation in the 1955 coup against Juan Domingo Perón, but also for "spiriting the body of Eva Perón out of Argentina in 1956 and [. . .] for the illegal execution of twenty-seven Peronists in June of the same year" (Gillespie 1982: 91).[13] The sonic representation of this episode is divided into nine sections, each of which is dominated by a different narrative voice and structure.

In the second section of "*Memoria de los basurales (el Aramburazo)*" (henceforth "*Aramburazo*"), the voice of an omniscient male narrator tells Peronism's history from a foundational present (Aramburu's execution), which figures as the *telos* of a series of events connected to 1960s revolutionary culture, rather than to the Peronist movement *stricto sensu*. The mythical figures and moments of Peronism are subsumed into another political lineage: that of mid-twentieth-century revolution, a genealogy within which Peronism appears as a local avatar.

1970. The Peronist *pueblo* suffers the dictatorship of imperialist boots and monopolies, but it starts to prepare its response: a new stage in the long resistance that started in 1955, when the oligarchic minorities overthrew Perón.

In 1969 the *Cordobazo* [student-worker protest movement in the city of Córdoba] explodes.

Sometime later, other popular uprisings set the Patria alight.

Meanwhile, the 1960s usher in the definitive awakening of the *pueblos* of the Third World.

The Cuban Revolution is a light that lives on.
Camilo Torres in Colombia and Che's heroic death in Bolivia come together
as signs in the path to Latin American liberation.
Here, in our land, that path has its own name, which the people decided to give
to it with their blood and combat: Peronist Movement.

(Huerque Mapu et al. 1973: "*Aramburazo*")[14]

Even though Perón's leadership is acknowledged and the traditional slogans in his honor are repeated throughout the cantata, his name operates as a
readily available signifier that the *pueblo* appropriated to name "its blood and
combat." Perón's centrality within the epic of the national-popular movement is, thus, displaced by another, more abstract repository of political
affects, the *pueblo*, which 1960s left-wing movements construed as the fertile
terrain where the seeds of Guevara's *Hombre Nuevo* (New Man) would
flourish.

In the final section of "*Aramburazo*," the Montoneros appear center-
stage, as heirs of the long struggle for the emancipation of a nation whose
ontological status is clearly defined: the "authentic" Argentina, whose birth
(liberation) the *pueblo montonero* will usher in, is the Socialist Patria embodied by the New Man that the Cuban Revolution engendered.

The time has come; it is here, *compañero*.

. . . .

Patria in ashes,
Patria of the New Man,
It was born in a night of the *pueblo montonero*,
it inseminated the land and blazed in revolution.

(Huerque Mapu et al. 1973: "*Aramburazo*")

THE *PUEBLO*, FROM WORKER TO REVOLUTIONARY

In the NCM's foundational repertoire,[15] the *pueblo* was not assimilated to the
Peronist masses; it was embodied by anonymous men (rarely women) whose
identity was defined by their occupation, rather than their political partisan-
ship. The sugar cane worker, cotton grower, and lumberman of this early
repertoire were some of the figures around which lyricists like Tejada Gómez
and Ramón Ayala elaborated a telluric poetics of the *pueblo*'s lived experiences and misfortunes. In the late 1960s, especially after Che Guevara's
execution in 1967, another avatar of the *pueblo*—the New Man—was incorporated into this repertoire of popular subjectivities. Lyricists associated to
the NCM and other Latin American New Song movements represented this
revolutionary figuration of the "popular" through a recurrent set of military,
religious, and amorous tropes. In widely circulated songs like Rubén Ortiz's
"*Zamba del 'Che'*" ("Che's" Zamba) and Daniel Viglietti's "*Canción del*

hombre nuevo" (Song of the New Man),[16] the tropology of the New Man was dominated by images of the guerrilla as saint or Christ and of war and *militancia* as poetic, even erotic, experiences.[17] The revolutionary combatant's emblematic weapon, the rifle, was often juxtaposed to, and conflated with, "feminine" symbols of love (flowers, hearts) and instruments of artistic and manual labor (the guitar, the voice, the worker's arm), thereby appearing as an artifact of political, sentimental, and aesthetic *poiesis*.[18]

> When song is useless
> Because bread is missing from the table
> I don't know whether to give you my heart,
> my voice, a flower, or a rifle.
>
> . . . .
>
> but [man] only lives if he gives himself
> in a flower, or a rifle.
>
> . . . .
>
> Because it is time to start
> I give my arm and my song
> and if my arm is nothing,
> just like song is nothing,
> I will go out and die for love,
> your twenty years and a rifle.

(Palombo and Sánchez 2009: lines 1–4, 7–8, 27–32)[19]

Through the aestheticization of guerrilla warfare and the figuration of *militancia* as an ethos of love, the folk and New Song repertoires of the late 1960s and early 1970s contributed to the production and circulation of revolutionary political desire.

GENDERED PARADIGMS OF POLITICAL AGENCY IN NARRATIVES OF REVOLUTION AND NATIONHOOD

Scholars of the Latin American 1960s have noted that this period's utopian impulse was set in motion and sustained by a gendered economy of desire that oscillated between pleasure and discipline, hedonism and asceticism, the "feminine" discourse of love and the "masculine" discourse of organized politics. The tensions that resulted from this libidinal economy crystallized in ambivalent cultural and political trends. Thus, as Zolov (2008) has argued, the relationship between the counterculture's bohemian, pacifist mores and the New Left's cult of discipline and militarism was tense, yet porous. This permeability gave rise to new modes of femininity and masculinity that reciprocally appropriated the attributes associated to the opposite gender's normative identity.

In her reading of the economy of desire that underpins Che Guevara's writing, Sorensen characterizes Guevara—that is, "the construct derived from the myth and the writer" (2007: 28)—as the embodiment of a new masculine social identity situated "in the interstices between strength and weakness, . . . [a masculinity] less epic in its actual achievements than in . . . the longing to reach them" (2007: 37–38). Even though this emerging identity claimed for itself the attributes of an idealized femininity (i.e., physical frailty, self-sacrifice, *tendresse*), it did not entail the subversion of the phallocratic political order but, rather, its reformulation in homoerotic terms.[20] The forms of homosociality unleashed by this reformulation were scrupulously kept in check by the discursive and ideological apparatuses of left-wing politico-military organizations, which tended to articulate (homo)erotic desire as political brotherhood and camaraderie. Thus, the language of sentimentality entered 1960s political discourse in sublimated forms: through the ideals of *compañerismo* and solidarity and the concomitant narrativization of warfare as political romance.

This apparent romanticization of political discourse and ideology, far from evacuating normative versions of male identity from the narrative of revolution, endowed them with an auratic quality discernible in songs that metaphorized the New Man as a sacred source of (en)light(enment), among them some of the most popular anthems of Latin American leftist culture: Carlos Puebla's *"Hasta siempre"* ("Until Forever"), Daniel Viglietti's *"Cruz de luz"* ("Cross of Light"), and Aníbal Sampayo's *"Hasta la victoria"* ("To Victory").[21] *"Hasta siempre"* and *"Cruz de luz"* pay homage, respectively, to Che Guevara and Camilo Torres, two of the guerrillas who best embodied the period's paradigm of revolutionary agency. While *"Hasta la victoria"* does not explicitly reference a guerrilla figure, the song's poetic persona, who calls himself Ramón, describes his actions in terms that echo those used in *"Hasta siempre"* and *"Cruz de luz"* to portray Guevara and Torres. Like the guerrillas in these songs, Ramón bears a powerful light that illuminates different forms of oppression and, thereby, kindles a desire for justice and fires up revolt. Described through both soothing and unsettling tropes, the poetic personae who convey this light appear, at once, as the incarnation of revolutionary love (Puebla 1970), as unbridled forces of nature—for example, as a gale in *"Hasta la victoria"* (Sampayo 1972: line 8)—and as lucid, self-possessed agents of liberation, whose omniscience and courage allow them to triumph over death (Puebla 1970; Viglietti 1969: *"Cruz de luz"*).

Though inscribed in the romance of revolution, these enlightened figures and the political project they represented bore the traces of the liberal-modern myth of masculinity, which figured the ideal male as an iteration of modernization's paradigmatic body politic: the well-administered, rational, progress-driven bourgeois state.[22] Rigorous, ascetic, and morally incorruptible, the New Man embodied by the likes of Che Guevara and Camilo Torres was, thus, caught between the teleological exigencies of a developmentalist modality of revolution and the sentimental "excesses" of a romantic-religious aesthetic.[23] As the decade wore on and left-wing political culture became increasingly militarized, the preoccupation with containing these excesses, often associated with a negative image of femininity, moved to the center of revolutionary politics.

In the cantata *Montoneros*, the realm of subjective emotions appears as a "feminized" locus of potential political dissipation that the militant must transcend in order to become a revolutionary New Man. "Fernando y Gustavo," the cantata's third part, articulates the Montoneros' official conception of *militancia* through a poetic voice that "speaks" for two of the organization's heroes: Fernando Abal Medina and Gustavo Ramus, who died in a confrontation with police forces in 1970 (Gillespie 1982: 97–98). This poetic voice describes death as the consummation of revolutionary love and, thereby, as the *telos* of the Montoneros' militaristic understanding of *militancia*:

> If I am to die tomorrow
> you must know that when I fall,
> my brothers,
> it will be because of love and not bullets
> even if you find me wounded.
>
> (Huerque Mapu et al. 1973: "*Fernando y Gustavo*")

In this conception of *militancia*, the consummation of (political) affects entails forgoing the "objects" of individual, prosaic love, in order to fully embrace revolutionary commitment. Thus, "*Fernando y Gustavo*" evokes these guerrilla commanders as young men who

> *abandoned everything*
> dying because they were Peronists.
> . . . .
> *[They] probably left young girls behind,*
> *loves in a corner.*
> And dreams they must have dreamt
> wandering lost streets.
>
> (Huerque Mapu et al. 1973: "*Fernando y Gustavo*"; emphasis mine)

In this hagiographic song, the girls who are "left behind" represent a realm of subjective emotions that is evoked, in autobiographical accounts of revolutionary militantism, through references to different forms of intimacy and love, very often to filial and parental relationships. In these accounts, as in "Fernando y Gustavo," the references to both familial and amorous ties conjure up a "mundane" domestic sphere—traditionally construed as feminine—that many militants felt compelled, and would eventually be forced, to subordinate to "higher" revolutionary duties and ideals.[24]

Many of the "prosaic" women evoked in *"Fernando y Gustavo"* (and in other contemporaneous songs) as the object of a male militant's love were also active participants in the revolutionary undertakings of the 1960s and 1970s. However, they were seldom the subject of these idealized representations of insurrectionary belligerency, in which the resilient male guerrilla generally incarnated the paradigm of revolutionary agency.[25] *"Juana Azurduy"* (Luna and Ramírez 1991) was one of the few songs of this period that represented revolutionary courage through a female historical figure. First recorded by Mercedes Sosa for the 1969 album *Mujeres argentinas* (*Argentine Women*), this tribute to the female guerrilla who fought against the Spanish forces in the early nineteenth-century wars of independence was appropriated by many leftist militants as an anti-imperialist anthem through which they could connect their struggle against late twentieth-century neocolonialism to a broader genealogy of liberation. Although *"Juana Azurduy"* was authored by Félix Luna, a historian who had few ideological affinities with the political culture that construed the song as an insurrectionary call to arms, its lyrics represent the origins of the Argentine nation as a revolutionary uprising, thus bringing together two major objects of political desire of 1960s leftist culture: the guerrilla and the nation, feminized as Patria and conceived as the repository of political sovereignty.

The protonational body politic is feminized in this song through a set of poetic clichés that conflate Azurduy's biography/body with the geography/history of the "incipient Patria" (Luna and Ramírez 1991: line 9). Azurduy is described as an "Amazon of liberty" (line 26); the "land up in arms that becomes woman" (line 25); and the "flower of Upper Peru" (line 2), a South American region that the song's lyrics identify with the revolt against Spanish rule led by Tupac Amaru in the late eighteenth century: "In Upper Peru / the echo still names / Tupac Amaru" (lines 22–24). These telluric representations of Juana Azurduy—and the inscription of her poetic persona in an epic of liberation that is Latin Americanist *avant la lettre*—are intercalated with a call to arms in which belligerency is, as in the folk and New Song repertoire discussed before, both feminized and aestheticized:

> The cannon thunders,
> lend me your rifle
> because the revolution
> arrives with the scent of jasmine.
>
> (Luna and Ramírez 1991: lines 17–20)

Metonymically associated to Azurduy, the scent of flowers evoked in the song's chorus figures revolution as a feminine, ethereal endeavor from which warfare's vicissitudes—of which the real Azurduy and her family were victims—are absent.

Woman is, thus, brought into this narrative of nationhood and revolution, not as a real subject, but as the trope of a virtuous body politic through which the battle over the Patria's essence is waged. In the album *Mujeres argentinas*, of which "*Juana Azurduy*" was one of the most popular songs, the feminine largely operates as the idealized reservoir of patriotic values. The virtues of nationhood embodied by the album's female characters are systematically poised against more or less threatening avatars of cultural and political alterity, from which the Argentine Republic (or proto-Republic) must be safeguarded: the Spanish enemy in "*Juana Azurduy*"; the early nineteenth-century English invaders in "*Manuela la tucumana*" ("Manuela of Tucumán"); the undomesticated land and "savage" denizens of the Chaco region in "*Gringa chaqueña*" ("*Gringa* [Female European Immigrant] of the Chaco Region"); and illiteracy, that inveterate foe of modernization and liberal culture, in "*Rosarito Vera, maestra*" ("Rosarito Vera, Teacher").

Scholarship on the gender inscriptions of narratives of nationhood has made familiar the notion that the disembodiment of woman and her concomitant allegorization as virtuous Patria (or as protector of the Patria's integrity) is a common discursive gesture that ideologically sustains these narratives.[26] Different, often opposing, currents of Argentina's 1960s folk music milieu put to work the format of the *ciclo integral* (integral cycle) in the construction of epics that focused on the heroic figures of different historiographic schools.[27] Notwithstanding the divergent historiographic perspectives deployed in these musical cycles, the "feminine" is (re)iterated as the repository of an unwavering passion for a male hero who embodies the "authentic" *pueblo* and, thereby, the Patria. In *Juan Lavalle*, the struggle for the Unitarian Patria is represented as an all-male undertaking in which the presence of the feminine is only authorized in the form of an innocent, unquestioning girl-woman: a noble savage of sorts called Damasita Boedo. Portrayed more as a self-sacrificing *mater dolorosa* than as Lavalle's sentimental and political partner, Damasita embodies, indeed, a primitive mode of devotion associated to the realm of "feminine," private passions. The masculinist counterpart of this atavistic dimension of fidelity is an ethos of loyalty that Lavalle's followers couch in the language of revolutionary ideals—"¡Libertad o muerte!" (Sábato and Falú 1965; Liberty or death!)—and patriotism. The object of both modes of loyalty and desire is the same: Lavalle's decaying corpse, which is figured as both an incarnation of the fraught body politic and the (phallic) beacon of a utopian community of men.

> . . . *[Los ciento setenta hombres y una mujer] no cejarán hasta que el cuerpo de su General tenga descanso digno y sagrado. Esta decisión se yergue como una fortaleza solitaria entre aquellas derruidas torres de [la] adolescencia [del alférez Celedonio Olmos]. Entre las ruinas, Celedonio Olmos ha descubierto finalmente algo por lo que todavía vale la pena sufrir y morir: aquella*

comunión entre hombres, aquel pacto entre derrotados. Una sola torre, sí,
pero refulgente e indestructible.[28] (Sábato and Falú 1965)

Even though Luna's lyrics do not represent Juana Azurduy as the vessel of male desire, some elements of this figuration of the feminine, which structure Sábato's portrayal of the Unitarian guerrilla brotherhood, undergird Leopoldo Torre Nilsson's representation of Juana Azurduy in the film *Güemes, la tierra en armas* (Güemes, the Land Up in Arms), one of the cultural artifacts through which Ramírez and Luna's song circulated in the early 1970s. In this historical epic that narrates the deeds of the eponymous caudillo of Salta and his peasant guerrilla army, Azurduy appears as a loyal soldier who rescues the head of her murdered husband from the Spanish enemy and, through that act of courage, sets an example for her troops and ensures the continuity of the struggle for independence. It is in honor of these feats that Güemes attributes to her the rank of Lieutenant Coronel in a sequence of the film that is set to the music of *"Juana Azurduy"* (Torre Nilsson 2008). This sequence is visually narrated through a series of medium close and big close-up shots that juxtapose the austere countenance of a self-contained Azurduy (Mercedes Sosa), dressed in military attire, and a virile, bearded Güemes (Alfredo Alcón), whose physical appearance was probably reminiscent, in the early 1970s, of the Cuban revolutionaries' demeanor. In this sequence, Azurduy appears as a resilient woman whose entry into the political brotherhood of the embryonic Patria entails donning the sartorial symbols of a quintessential (military) masculinity and sublimating "feminine," private emotions—the pain for her husband's and children's deaths—into a masculinist, patriotic ethos of courage. Although the trope of the self-sacrificial *mater dolorosa* underlies this figuration of the feminine, another epochal paradigm of womanhood is at play in this representation: that of the masculinized *compañera*, which 1960s leftist discourses and pop culture had transformed into an object of desire.

The "Evita Montonera" of early 1970s left-wing Peronism operated as the charismatic synthesis of these figurations of the feminine. The cantata *Montoneros* conjures up this Janus-faced Eva Perón but also registers a subtle, though significant, shift in the form and function of the Evita myth in the Montoneros' discursive apparatus. In the cantata, Eva's political judgment is invoked in the form of a Manichean discourse—opposing traitors and true Peronists—through which the ethos and genealogy of authentic Peronism and patriotism are charted. In *"Pueblo Peronista"* ("Peronist *Pueblo"*), the cantata's eighth part, this moral genealogy is introduced by a documentary recording of one of the most popular and effective Montonero slogans: *"Si Evita viviera, sería Montonera"* (If Evita were alive, she would be a Montonera). This documentary intertext, which posits the Montoneros as the heirs of Eva's political legacy, prefigures their claim to a moral higher ground; a claim that is explicitly formulated in the second section of "*Pueblo Peronista.*" Accompanied by the sound of *bombo* drums and the collective chanting of the Montonero slogan, the voice of an omniscient male narrator intervenes in this section of the phonographic narrative invested with the authority of Eva's words: "Those who give their lives and those who negotiate. Those who are loyal to General Perón and those who conciliated [with the anti-Peronist political regime] for so many years. *Evita had already said it*: the shirtless and those who are willing to compromise. The Peronist people and the traitors" (Huerque Mapu et al. 1973: "*Pueblo Peronista*"; emphasis mine). Such an arrogation of her voice and persona is reiterated in the cantata's sixth part, "*El Combate de Ferreyra*" ("The Combat of Ferreyra"), by the same narrator, who invokes her sententious pronouncements as prescient dictums that dissipate the ambiguities and uncertainties of the cantata's extradiegetic present (post-Cámpora Argentina).[29] "While the conciliatory trade union bureaucracies sealed pacts with, and made concessions to, the dictatorship, the Revolutionary Armed Forces and the Montoneros have entered the heart of the people. They are part of what Evita announced: Peronism will be revolutionary or it will be nothing" (Huerque Mapu et al. 1973: "*El Combate de Ferreyra*").

The invocation of Eva's words to confirm the "authentic" (i.e., revolutionary) nature of Peronism is a self-legitimating gesture that characterized the Montonero discursive apparatus, especially in 1973.[30] In the genealogy of the *Patria Montonera*, the figure of Eva Perón generally appeared in the double guise that the historiography of "civilization" had rendered barbaric: as the subject/object of unrestricted love and the shrewd agent of organized politics; as the embodiment of the passion-driven masses and their clever organizer; as impetuous lover and astute Stateswoman. However, the disruptive potential of these transgressive combinations was contained within the Montoneros' narrative of *militancia*, in which subjective emotions, associated with the feminine and the irrational, were displaced to the "masculine" sphere of politics and, thereby, endowed with heroic, patriotic connotations. This particular narrativization of the Evita myth insists on the political dimension of her love for Perón: that very "feminine" of feelings was, indeed, interpreted and appropriated by 1960s youth as a political ideal, and the melodramatic language of sentimentality through which she expressed this subjective emotion was apprehended as political discourse.[31] Through this decodification of the Peronist romance, thousands of young Argentines in their teens and twenties negotiated a transition that Guevara's teleological model of a novel humanity had rendered desirable: the "transition from individual passions, such as love, to the collective and social dimensions of the state" (Sorensen 2007: 27).

The emphasis on the political dimension of Eva's love for her husband not only enabled the reformulation of traditional Peronism in the terms of

1960s revolutionary culture; it also implied a subtle modification of the Evita myth within left-wing Peronism, which the cantata registers in its mise-en-scène of Eva's words as exclusively political rhetoric. This modification entailed a shift in focus that rendered Perón's discourse of compromise and consensus virtually inaudible, as Eva's uncompromising, dichotomous formulations grew more visible and audible in the Montoneros' iconography, publications, and marches. Certain sectors of the Peronist Left continued to produce and disseminate the traditional, hyper-feminized representations of Evita, in which she was predictably portrayed as Perón's loyal, loving wife and the embodiment of the *descamisados'* passion for their leader. However, other sectors increasingly foregrounded the infallibility of her political judgment and relegated to the background her declarations of boundless love for her husband, as well as Perón's legendary political lucidity and pragmatism. Thus, in keeping with a discursive strategy deployed by the Montoneros and allied sectors of the Peronist Youth throughout the second half of 1973, the cantata largely evacuates Perón as the model of political agency and patriotic masculinity. In the vacant space left by "el Viejo" (the Old Man), Evita Montonera emerges as a fully revolutionary, masculinized *compañera*: indeed, as the Peronist incarnation of the New (Montonero) Man and, thereby, as the link between socialist and Peronist nationhoods. [32] On one hand, this representation of Eva Perón was instrumental in the Montoneros' struggle for legitimacy and power in a crucial year (1973), during which the tensions between the New Man of the *Patria Montonera* and the Peronist nation's *pater familias* (Perón) started to surface. On the other hand, I submit that this masculinized avatar of the Evita myth, which "left behind" a certain aesthetics of love and loyalty, constituted a model of *militancia* that sought to resolve the tension between the private realm of subjectivity and the public sphere of politics by positing a revolutionary identity capable of encompassing both individual and collective forms of commitment.

This model of *militancia* is eulogized in *"Juan Pablo Maestre,"* the fifth part of the cantata *Montoneros*, which references the illegal kidnapping of two FAR militants on July 13, 1971, by the dictatorship's security agents (Lipcovich 2006). In the introduction to this part of the cantata, recited by an omniscient male narrator, the love relationship between Juan Pablo Maestre, who was assassinated on that date, and Mirta Misetich, who was "permanently disappeared," is represented as the expression of a profound sense of solidarity that is inextricably connected—indeed, subordinated—to a totalizing revolutionary praxis.

> Juan Pablo Maestre and Mirta Misetich . . . are murdered in cold blood by the armed commandos of the *anti-Patria*. . . . [B]oth of them die: in a conjunction of love and militantism. . . . We might imagine that, on that last night, she spoke to her *compañero* or remembered, as never before, that phrase: in a

revolution, one either triumphs or dies. (Huerque Mapu et al. 1973: "*Juan Pablo Maestre*")

Here, woman appears as the voice and rigorous guardian of a dichotomous, absolutist conception of *militancia*, in which the only alternatives are victory or death. Her words echo the Manichean rhetoric of the Evita Montonera that the cantata profusely references. In these echoes, it is possible to discern not only the figures of the masculinized *compañera* and the abnegated female guardian of the virtuous Patria, but also the consolidation of a paradigm of *militancia*[33] that both women and men found difficult to sustain as the increasingly violent repression and militarization of political life in the mid-1970s transformed the utopian longings of the 1960s into profoundly dystopian experiences.

MILITANCIA AS A TOTALIZING POLITICAL AND AESTHETIC PRACTICE

In spite of its absolutist underpinnings, the promise of an all-inclusive revolutionary identity, at work in this model of *militancia*, contained an intensely empowering dimension that fuelled much of the cultural production and political practices of the 1960s and 1970s. Thus, the figurations of revolutionary agency that appear in the musical artifacts I have discussed were, in many cases, shaped by this unifying, totalizing impulse, which demanded of many cultural actors that they reformulate the existing divisions between, and definitions of, aesthetics and politics. An analysis of the gender inscriptions of these artifacts enables us to better understand, as I have endeavored to do, how musical figurations of revolution constitute forms of rupture, but also of continuity, with normative political, aesthetic, and gender regimes. Considered through this prism, the modality of the cantata chosen to represent the history of the Montoneros appears, not only as an all-encompassing architecture that facilitates the articulation of an eclectic set of narrative and musical idioms, but also as a totalizing, epic form that subordinates the "minor," "inarticulate" cultural production—for example, festive chants, *murga* songs[34]—of *militantes de base* to the rules of organized (political and aesthetic) discourse. The totalizing gesture implicit in this aesthetic form is, I argue, connected to the masculinist, teleological narrative of revolutionary transcendence that underlies the models of *militancia* extolled in *Montoneros* and in such Latin American New Song standards as "*Canción del hombre nuevo*" and "*Hasta siempre*."

The feminized New Man and masculinized Evita Montonera that emerge as quintessential symbols of this model of *militancia* appear to unsettle normative gender identities, insofar as they displace the attributes of paradigmatic femininity to the realm of the masculine and, conversely, masculinize the site of the feminine. However, these seemingly novel political identities do not evacuate the canonical gender regimes that structure the masculine/ feminine dyad: that is, the feminine as the impotent site of love and self-sacrifice and the masculine as the empowered locus of discipline, reason, and transcendence. The recurrent tropes of revolutionary agency in the cantata *Montoneros* and part of the Latin American New Song repertoire tend, in fact, to replicate this binary construction and the hierarchy of values attached to each of the terms in the masculine/feminine dyad. Indeed, by focusing on the death in combat of a handful of guerrilla leaders, whether it be Che Guevara or a Montonero commander, this musical repertoire often posits military prowess and death as the *telos* of *militancia*, thus implicitly construing other, more mundane forms of activism as a "feminine," incomplete political praxis and identity that both men and women must shed if they are to become truly revolutionary agents.

NOTES

1. Following Terán (1991), Gilman (2003), Sorensen (2007), and Zolov (2008), I consider the "sixties" as a constellation of cultural and political formations and sensibilities, rather than a discrete ten-year period. In Argentina, a possible periodization of the long 1960s would encompass the "Post/Anti-Peronist" second half of the 1950s, when important cultural institutions like the National Fund for the Arts (FNA) and the Di Tella Institute were created, and the years 1971–1974, marked by intense political and artistic activity and experimentation.

2. The concept of the New Left encompasses multifarious ideologies and practices that, in the case of Argentina, have been analyzed in detail by Terán (1991) and Sigal (1996). For a review of recent research on the concept and history of the New Left, see Zolov (2008).

3. Two highly polysemous terms, of difficult translation, are central to my analysis: *pueblo* and *compañera/o*. Though they may be translated as "people" and "comrade," respectively, I have chosen to use the Spanish terms in italics. It is worth noting that the term *pueblo*, which has various social and cultural connotations in political parlance, is frequently associated with the lower socio-economic strata, though not exclusively with the working classes. In 1960s political and popular culture, the term *compañera/o* could refer to a political comrade or love partner.

4. The list of artists who subscribed to the NCM's manifesto appears in Tejada Gómez et al. (2003).

5. In 1973, Huerque Mapu's members were: Hebe Rosell (vocals, guitar, flute, *quena*, percussion); Naldo Labrín (guitar, *tiple*, *charango*); Tacún Lazarte (guitar, *charango*, percussion); Ricardo Munich (cello, flute, *quena*, *sikus*, percussion, choirs); and Lucio Navarro (vocals, *tiple*, *cuatro*, *charango*) (Portorrico 2004: 204).

6. The version of *"Venceremos,"* with lyrics by Claudio Iturra, "became [Salvador] Allende's [1970] campaign song" (Morris 1986: 121). Víctor Jara also wrote pro–Popular Unity lyrics for this song. Both versions are available online at http://www.quilapayun.com/canciones/venceremos.html.

7. After left-wing Peronist militants' brief stint in power in 1973–1974 and especially following the military coup of 1976, this cantata, like many other expressions of Montonero culture, "went underground" or into exile along with the organization's members. However, these circumstances do not account, in and of themselves, for the cantata's reduced circulation in Argentina and abroad. Its limited impact was due, in part, to the political specificity of the figures and events it referenced, a characteristic that set it apart from less culturally idiosyncratic partisan songs like *"El pueblo unido jamás será vencido,"* which could be easily appropriat-

ed by heterogeneous sectors of the left. The cantata's precise references to Montonero culture were further compounded by their rootedness in a broader political and cultural movement—Peronism—that does not neatly fit into cosmopolitan left/right categories. Hence, while Western European leftist culture readily assimilated Chilean New Song's political universe, its reception of left-wing Peronism often oscillated between circumspection and confusion.

8. Based on this premise, Gillespie concludes that

> [a]dhesion to the Montoneros' front organizations often expressed a desire for change, but one which was inarticulate and confused [. . .]: a smallish minority became cadres, . . . while the vast majority did little more than contribute bodies and voices at the mass events plus stamina and enthusiasm during National Reconstruction [1973–1974] social work projects. (1982: 137)

While Gillespie's critique of the Montoneros' undemocratic power structure is largely accurate, "the absence of mechanisms for rank-and-file participation in the elaboration of policy" (Gillespie 1982: 138) did not prevent the organization's sympathizers and *militantes de base* (rank-and-file militants) from debating policy. Many of these debates arose from, and took place during, their work "in the field," that is, building schools, carrying out literacy campaigns, and organizing rallies. Far from being inarticulate forms of political activism, such work and the cultural production that came out of it (publications, chants, visual artwork) were key formative experiences through which the Montoneros' rank and file developed political analyses of the leadership's guiding principles and course of action. These analyses sometimes evolved into well-documented, lucid internal critiques that laid the groundwork for the emergence of dissident groups.

9. [. . .] required novel variants in the musical structures. Thus, long sequences emerged; as in the art music tradition, these sequences unfolded through the alternation of spoken parts (narratives) and sung sections (songs that were formally detached from the original model), including instrumental developments (preludes, interludes) with a freer, even parabolic contexture.

Unless otherwise noted, all translations are my own.

10. Kaliman (2010: 298–302) uses the concept of "identidad ilustrada" (enlightened identity) to describe the cultural background—partially rooted in institutionalized forms of high art—of a group of social actors (performers, lyricists, musicians, amateurs, and fans) who transformed the field of Argentine folk music in the 1960s.

11. Throughout the cantata, Huerque Mapu included genres and instruments that evoked different folk and popular music traditions (e.g., the tango, jazz, sung *milonga*, and highland Andean music idioms).

12. By late 1973, the organization known as Montoneros comprised not only the homonymous group that kidnapped and executed Aramburu in 1970, but also the Revolutionary Armed Forces (FAR) and Los Descamisados (The Shirtless). The fusion of these three groups, under the banner of the "original" Montoneros, was formalized in 1972–1973, shortly before the cantata was recorded. Thus, the theme of unity among armed Peronist organizations figures prominently in the cantata. Even though these organizations' process of unification had been fraught with tensions, the cantata glosses over the competition and heated discussion among them, focusing instead on their most renowned militants' courage and commitment. Hence, while the *Aramburazo* is given pride of place in *"Memoria de los basurales,"* other military operations, carried out jointly or independently by the FAR, Descamisados, and the Peronist Armed Forces (FAP), are also extolled throughout the cantata, especially in its fourth and sixth parts ("*Garín*" and "*El Combate de Ferreyra*," respectively).

13. This illegal execution is metonymically evoked in the title "*Memoria de los basurales,*" through the reference to the *basurales* (dumping grounds) where several of the shootings took place.

14. The original version, in Spanish, of the narratives and lyrics of *Montoneros* is available online at http://www.elortiba.org/huerque.html.

246 Illa Carrillo Rodríguez

15. This repertoire was performed and popularized by many folk music artists, among them César Isella, Los Trovadores, Víctor Heredia, and Mercedes Sosa. On the latter's recorded performances of the NCM's repertoire, see Carrillo Rodríguez (2010).

16. Recorded versions of these songs can be found, respectively, in Jara (1969) and Viglietti (1969).

17. The poetic voice in *"Zamba del 'Che'"* speaks of anonymous peasants who refer to Guevara as "Saint Ernesto." In *"Canción del hombre nuevo,"* revolutionary struggle is portrayed as an act of collective *poiesis* and love; those who partake in this act draw from Guevara's physical and symbolic attributes to engender a new man whose feelings of love crystallize as revolt and whose voice takes on the form of a battle cry. The lyrics of these and other quoted songs are available online at http://www.cancioneros.com.

18. The conflation of war's artifacts with the hand and guitar is a recurrent discursive operation in late 1960s and early 1970s popular music, even in songs written by lyricists who were not ideologically close to leftist sectors, like Marcos and Paulo Sérgio Valle. For an interesting account of the influence of the political events of 1968 on their song *"Guitarra enluarada,"* which also assimilates war's artifacts with the instruments of artistic and manual labor, see Ridenti (2009: 219).

19. Here and elsewhere, the numbered line references are to the verses in the order in which they are performed in the cited version of the song.

20. On the ways in which Guevara's conception of the revolutionary New Man made use of "feminine" attributes, see Rodríguez (1996: 49–61).

21. Recorded versions of these songs can be found, respectively, in Puebla (1970), Viglietti (1969), and Sampayo (1972).

22. An illuminating analysis of the common (masculinist) ideology that structures both modernism and modernization can be found in Huyssen (1986: 55–62).

23. On the developmentalist underpinnings of Guevara's construal of revolutionary transformation, see Saldaña-Portillo (2003: 63–90) and Zolov (2008: 67–69).

24. Through an insightful analysis of letters written by ERP (People's Revolutionary Army) and Montonero militants to their loved ones, Ana Longoni (2007: 175–81) charts the ascendancy, in mid-1970s Argentina, of this ethos of *militancia*, which was tensely poised between political commitment and familial responsibilities. Female militants' autobiographical accounts, such as those that appear in the documentary film *Montoneros, una historia* (Di Tella 1995) and La Lopre's prison diary (2006), show that this tension played out in a gendered division of domestic and political labor that largely disempowered women and reinforced the antithetical categories at work in the period's dominant conception of *militancia*: that is, public/private, collective/individual, revolutionary/bourgeois, militarism/antimilitarism, patriotic/unpatriotic, hero/traitor.

25. Even though some female militants, like Montoneros founder Norma Arrostito, commanded respect and admiration, the revolutionary pantheon was nonetheless dominated by male combatants, and the leadership positions of the major insurgent organizations—the Montoneros and the ERP—were primarily held by men.

26. For comprehensive analyses of gendered figurations of Argentine nationhood in a corpus of nineteenth- and twentieth-century cultural texts, see Masiello (1992) and Taylor (1997).

27. Some of the period's musical narratives that had recourse to folk literary and musical genres to articulate historical narratives of nationhood were: *Vida y muerte de don Juan Manuel de Rosas* (1969; *Life and Death of Don Juan Manuel de Rosas*), by the vocal group Los Montoneros (also known as Los Federales); *Los caudillos: Cantata* (1966; *The Caudillos: Cantata*) and *Mujeres argentinas*, both by Félix Luna and Ariel Ramírez; and *Romance de la muerte de Juan Lavalle* (1965; *Romance of the Death of Juan Lavalle*)—henceforth *Juan Lavalle*—by Ernesto Sábato and Eduardo Falú. The aesthetic and historiographic differences among these integral cycles deserve a nuanced analysis that is outside the scope of my discussion. An overview of the relationship between Argentina's Revisionist historiographic school and the folk music milieu can be found in Stortini (2004: 98–101).

28. [. . .] [The one hundred and seventy men and one woman] will continue relentlessly until the corpse of their General rests in dignified and sacred repose. This decision rises like a solitary fortress among those towers in ruins of [the] adolescence [of Second

Lieutenant Celedonio Olmos]. Among the ruins, Celedonio Olmos has finally discovered something for which it still worth suffering and dying: that communion among men, that pact among the vanquished. A single tower, yes, but resplendent and indestructible.

29. In October 1973, Perón publicly sided with the Montoneros' enemies: the Peronist Right and the "conciliatory" union bureaucracy, which he saw as a strategic ally in the implementation of a multi-sector Social Pact. Perón's public disavowal of the Montoneros was ostensibly motivated by the assassination of labor union chief José I. Rucci, for which the organization was thought to be responsible (Gillespie 1982: 165). Carried out only a few days after Perón's sweeping victory in the September 1973 presidential election, Rucci's execution was also condemned by many Montonero militants and sympathizers who were critical of the organization's increasingly seditious logic and open contempt of Perón's authority and government. Though Rucci's assassination alone does not fully account for internal divisions within the organization, it operated as a catalyst for the rupture of dissident sectors that wished to remain loyal to Perón and sought to extricate themselves from both the Montoneros' militaristic structure and the escalation of violence promoted by right-wing Peronist groups. Branded as "the left in disguise" by the latter, as "traitors" by the Montoneros (Montero 2008: 14), and as "obsequious to Perón" by certain commentators (Gillespie 1982: 138), the Loyalist Tendency that emerged from this schism represented a consensual, "ambiguous" form of political activism, which questioned the certainties conveyed by totalizing, sectarian narratives of revolution, counterrevolution, and *militancia*. For a nuanced discussion of the conception of loyalty that underlay this tendency and its political vicissitudes in mid-1970s Argentina, see Montero (2008).

30. For a detailed analysis of the ways in which the Peronist Youth and the Montoneros used Eva Perón's image and discourse in their 1973 publications, see Sigal and Verón (2004: 202–213).

31. This reading of Eva's passion for Perón was neither completely novel nor unfounded for, as John Kraniauskas observes, she had passionately forged and performed an aesthetics of sentimentality in which "subjective feelings became organising forces, that is, political affects" (2001: 148).

32. Since the late 1940s, Eva Perón's "masculine" traits—symbolized by her inflammatory rhetoric and bellicose body language—had been construed by various anti-Evita sectors, among them Perón's early clerical and military allies, as violent incursions into the sphere of politics that unsettled established social/gender roles and, thereby, national/patriarchal order. Rather than evacuate those traits from their representations of Eva, the Montoneros divested them of their deviant overtones and articulated them with elements drawn from official Peronist history, popular Peronist hagiographies, and 1960s youth and revolutionary culture. The Montoneros' early uses of this syncretic Evita did not seek to undermine Perón's role as ideologue and strategist. However, in 1973, as they increasingly emphasized her ideological influence in, and struggle against the "traitors" within, the Peronist movement, another version of the Evita Montonera emerged: one that bore the traces of *evitismo*, the polemical Eva Perón cult, which in its leftist, anti-Peronist variant exalted Evita for her pro-plebeian combat and distinguished her from the fascist and bourgeois sectors within Peronism and from Perón himself.

33. While not all political groups, militants, and intellectuals subscribed to this paradigm, important sectors of the New Left validated, in different ways, the bureaucratization and militarization of political culture and the consequent reformulation of the ethos and praxis of *militancia*. Militants formulate their anxiety about, and critique of, this process in the autobiographical narratives and testimonial accounts found in La Lopre (2006), Gelman and Mero (1987), and Di Tella (1995).

34. The *murga* is a choral, theatrical, musical, and choreographic practice associated to Carnival festivities. The *bombo* drum and other percussive instruments are central to its sonic aesthetic. Some examples of Montonero *murga* songs, composed by neighborhood *militantes de base*, can be found in Baschetti (2000).

References

Acevedo, Nano. 1995. *Los ojos de la memoria*. Santiago: Cantoral.

Advis, Luis. 1984. "Carta a Eduardo Carrasco, 15 de marzo 1984." In Archivo Eduardo Carrasco. http:// www.quilapayun.com. Accessed December 28, 2007.

———. 1998. "Historia y características de la Nueva Canción Chilena." Pp. 28–41 in *Clásicos de la música popular chilena, Volumen II, 1960–1973 Raíz Folclórica*, edited by Luis Advis and Juan Pablo González. Santiago: Ediciones Universidad Católica de Chile.

———. 1999. *Santa María de Iquique, Cantata Popular* [Partituras]. Santiago: División de Cultura del Ministerio de Educación y Sociedad Chilena del Derecho de Autor—SCD.

Advis Vitaglich, Luis. 1999. "Nueva canción. II. Chile." Pp. 1077–80 in *Diccionario de la música española e hispanoamericana*, Volume 7, edited by Emilio Casares Rodicio, José López-Calo, and Ismael Fernández de la Cuesta. Madrid: Sociedad General de Autores y Editores.

Adorno, Teodoro. 2003. *Filosofía de la nueva música. Obra completa, 12*. Madrid: Akal.

Adorno, Teodoro and Max Horkheimer. 1994. *Dialéctica de la Ilustración*, 3rd ed. Madrid: Trotta.

Aguirre González, Francisco Javier. 1977. "Significado literario y alcance político de la nueva canción chilena." *Cuadernos Hispanoamericanos* 328: 5–31.

Aharonián, Coriún. 1991. *Héctor Tosar, compositor uruguayo*. Montevideo: Trilce.

———. 1993. "Tendencias en la música culta latinoamericana joven." Pp. 80–84 in *VI Encontro Nacional da ANPPOM, ANAIS*. San Pablo, Brazil.

———. 1996. "El Centro Latinoamericano de Altos Estudios Musicales: En búsqueda de una documentación escamoteada." *Revista del Instituto Superior de Música* No. 5. Santa Fe: Universidad del Litoral, 97–101.

———. 1997. "Carlos Vega y la teorí de la música popular: Un enfoque latinoamericano en un ensayo pionero." *Revista Musical Chilena* 51 (188): 61–74.

———. 2000. "An Approach to Compositional Trends in Latin America." *Leonardo Music Journal* 10: 3–5.

———. 2002. "Technology for the Resistance: A Latin American Case." *Latin American Music Review* 23 (2): 195–205. http://www.latinoamerica-musica.net/sociedad/aharonian/technology-en.html.

———. 2003. *CD Canciones de la resistencia*. Uruguay 1977–1982, No. 1. Montevideo: Ayuí. A/E 234 CD.

———. 2004. *Educación, arte, música*. Montevideo: Tacuabé.

———. 2007a. *Músicas populares del Uruguay*. Montevideo: Universidad de la República.

———. 2007b. "Palabras previas." Pp. 13–20 in *Vega, Carlos: Estudios para los orígenes del tango argentino*, edited by Coriún Aharonián. Buenos Aires: Educa.

249

―――. 2007c. "Resumen de los quince cursos latinoamericanos de música contemporánea." http://www.latinoamerica-musica.net/informes/cursos.html.

―――. 2009. "La enseñanza institucional terciaria y las música populares." *Revista Musical Chilena* 211: 66–83.

Albornoz, César. 1999. "El tiempo del volar de las palomas." Pp. 310–319 in *Música popular en América latina, Actas del II Congreso Latinoamericano IASPM,* edited by Rodrigo Torres. Santiago: Fondart.

―――. 2005. "La Cultura en la Unidad Popular: Porque esta vez no se trata de cambiar un Presidente." Pp. 147–176 in *Cuando hicimos historia: La experiencia de la Unidad Popular,* edited by Julio Pinto. Santiago: LOM.

Aldrighi, Clara. 2004. "La injerencia de Estados Unidos en el proceso hacia el golpe de estado." Pp. 35–50 in *El presente de la dictadura: Estudios y reflexiones a 30 años del golpe de Estado en Uruguay,* edited by Aldo Marchesi, Varia Markarian, Álvaro Rico, and Jaime Yaffé. Montevideo: Trilce.

Alegría, Julio R. 1981. "La cueca urbana o cueca 'chilenera.'" *Araucaria de Chile* 14: 125–135.

Alencar Pinto, Guilherme de. 2003. "Años dorados: Siete apuntes sobre la música uruguaya." *Brecha,* July 11: 6–7.

Alencar Pinto, Guilherme de. 2013. *Los que iban cantando: Detrás de las voces.* Montevideo Ediciones del TUMP (Taller Uruguayo de Música Popular).

Allende, Salvador. 1973. Last words. Retrieved from http://www.youtube.com/watch?v= 3BxYT9DbwzA.

Anderson, Benedict. 1983. *Imagined Communities.* London: Verso.

Antezana, Luis. 2003. "Desplazamientos poéticos y 'Mass Media.'" *Revista de Crítica Literaria Latinoamericana* 29 (58): 25–38.

Arapí, Tabaré. 1995. *Desde afuera del área con Braulio López.* Montevideo: Ediciones del Clú de Amargueando.

Araucaria de Chile. 1978. Editorial, 5–7.

Arenas, Desiderio (editor) 2012. *Advis en cuatro movimientos y un epílogo.* Santiago: Sociedad Chilena del Derecho de Autor (SCD).

Arriagada, Genaro. 1988. *Pinochet: The Politics of Power.* Boston: Unwin-Hyman.

Asuar, José Vicente. 1973. "Cursos Latinoamericanos de Música Contemporánea en Uruguay." *Revista Musical Chilena.* Año XXVII, No. 123–124. Santiago de Chile. Universidad de Chile, julio/diciembre: 79.

Augé, Marc. 2007. *Por una antropología de la movilidad.* Barcelona: Gedisa.

Ayestarán, Lauro. 1971. *El folklore musical uruguayo,* 2nd ed. Montevideo: Arca.

Barthes, Roland. 1973. *Le plaisir du texte.* Paris: Editions du Seuil.

Barraza, Fernando. 1972. *La Nueva Canción Chilena.* Santiago: Quimantú.

Barr-Mejel, Patrick. 2009. "Hippismo a la chilena: Juventud y heterodoxia cultural en un contexto transnacional (1970–1973)." Pp. 305–325 in *Ampliando Miradas: Chile y su historia en tiempo global,* edited by Fernando Purcell and Alfredo Riquelme. Santiago: RIL.

Barros-Lémez, Alvaro. 1983. "Uruguay: Una literatura sin fronteras." *Revista de Crítica Literaria Latinoamericana* 9 (17): 195–206.

Baschetti, Roberto, comp. 2000. *Campana de palo: Antología de poemas, relatos y canciones de 35 años de lucha 1955–1990.* La Plata: De La Campana.

BBC News. June 4, 2009. Chilean singer Jara is exhumed. Retrieved from http://news.bbc.co. uk/2/hi/americas/8084201.stm.

Becerra-Schmidt, Gustavo. 1985. "La música culta y la Nueva Canción Chilena." *Literatura Chilena: Creación y crítica* 33–34: 14–21.

―――. 1998. "Rol de la musicología en la globalización de la cultura". *Revista Musical Chilena* 52 (190): 36–54.

Benavides, Washington. 1969. *Las milongas.* Montevideo: Ediciones de la Banda Oriental, Siete Poetas hispanoamericanos.

―――. 1980. "La búsqueda de un canto popular sin adulteraciones." *Opinar,* November 27: 22.

―――. 1982a. "La canción de texto, las letras, la poesía." *Propuesta* 1.4: 40–41.

————. 1982b. "Sobre el canto historicista." *Propuesta* 1.2: 38–39.

————. 1982–1983. "La *canción de texto* española." *Propuesta* 1.5: 44–45.

————. 1983a. "El canto popular uruguayo vuelto libro." *Propuesta* 1.11: 42–43.

————. 1983b. "Definiciones: Canto Popular." *Canto Popular* 1.1: 9.

————. 1983c. "Prehistoria del canto popular." *Propuesta* 1.7: 48–49.

————. 1983d. "El público del canto popular." *Canto Popular* 1.2: 26.

————. 1984. "Los Olimareños: Una breve y definitiva historia." *Nueva Viola* 1.1: 35–37.

————. 1985. "Apuntes sobre la cuestión textual en el canto popular uruguayo." *La del taller* No. 2. Montevideo: Talleres Latinoamericanos de Música Popular, febrero/marzo: 16–19.

————. 1993. *Las milongas y otras canciones.* 5th ed. Montevideo: Ediciones de la Banda Oriental, SietePoetas hispanoamericanos.

————. 1995. Interview with Maria L. Figueredo. Montevideo: August 5.

————. 2001. "Praga/Toledo." *Hispamérica* 30 (89): 67–68.

Benedetti, Mario. 1973. *Letras de Emergencia.* Buenos Aires: Editorial Alfa.

————. *Letras de emergencia (1969-1973).* Mexico: Nueva Imagen.

————. 1974. *Daniel Viglietti.* Madrid: Ediciones Jucar.

————. 2007. *Daniel Viglietti, desalambrando.* Buenos Aires: Seix Barral.

Benedetti, Mario and Daniel Viglietti. 1994. *A dos voces I y II.* Madrid: Orfeo (CDO 047–2)

————. 1994. *A dos voces.* Montevideo: Alfaguara.

Benjamin, Walter. 1968. "The Work of Art in the Age of Mechanical Reproduction." *Illumina-tions.* New York: Schocken Books.

Benmayor, Rina. 1981. "La 'Nueva Trova': New Cuban Song." *Latin American Music Review / Revista de Música Latinoamericana* 2 (1): 11–44.

Benvenuto, Luis Carlos. 1967. *Breve Historia del Uruguay.* Montevideo: Arca.

Berger, Arthur. 1994. "Music as Imitation." Pp. 302–312 in *Perspectives on Musical Aethes-tics,* edited by John Rahn. New York: W. W. Norton & Company.

Bessière, Bernard. 1980. *La Nouvelle Chanson Chilienne en exil.* Toulouse: Éditions d'Aujourd'hui.

La Bicicleta. 1982. Canciones de Eduardo Peralta, 17–18.

Bitar, Sergio. 2009. *Dawson, Isla 10,* 12th ed. Santiago: Pehuén.

Boasso, Fernando. 2006. *Tierra que anda.* Buenos Aires: Corregidor.

Bodiford, James Ryan. 2007. "Imagining 'el pueblo': Pan-Latin American Subaltern Solidarity and the Music of Nueva Cancion." Michigan State University, Masters Thesis.

Bonaldi, Jorge. 1985. "El canto popular uruguayo." *Música: Revista del Real Conservatorio Superior de Música* 106 : 4–12.

————. 2001. *¿Se muere la canción? 8 informes sobre la canción popular uruguaya, 1977–2000.* Montevideo: Edición del autor.

Bonnefoy, Pascale. December 28, 2012. Eight are charged with Chilean singer's 1973 murder after military coup. *New York Times* online. Retrieved from http://www.nytimes.com/2012/12/29/world/americas/eight-charged-with-victor-jaras-1973-murder-in-chile.html?_r=0.

Bowen Silva, Martín. 2008. "El proyecto sociocultural de la izquierda chilena durante la Uni-dad Popular: Crítica, verdad e inmunología política." *Nuevo Mundo Mundos Nuevos, De-bates.* URL: http://nuevomundo.revues.org/13732. Accessed January 30, 2012.

Boyle, Catherine and Gina Canepa. 1987. "Violeta Parra and Los Jaivas: Unequal Discourse or Successful Integration?" *Popular Music* 6 (2) : 235–240.

Braceli, Rodolfo. 2003. *Mercedes Sosa: La Negra.* Buenos Aires: Sudamericana.

Bravo Chiappe, Gabriela and Cristian González Farfán. 2009. *Ecos del tiempo subterráneo: Las peñas en Santiago durante el régimen militar (1973–1983).* Santiago: LOM.

Bruhn, Siglind. 2001. "A Concert of Paintings: 'Musical Ekphrasis' in the Twentieth Century." *Poetics Today* 22 (3): 551–605. Accessed January 10, 2011. http://muse.jhu.edu/lo-gin?auth=0&type=summary&url=/journals/poetics_today/v022/22.3bruhn.html.

Buch, Esteban. 2002. "Ginastera y Nono: Encuentros y variantes." *Revista del Instituto Superior de Música* No. 9. Santa Fe: Universidad del Litoral: 62–84.

Cáceres, Eduardo. 1989. "Los Cursos Latinoamericanos de Música Contemporánea—Una al-ternativa diferente." *Revista Musical Chilena* 172: 46–84.

252   *References*

Caetano, Gerardo and José Rilla. 2005 [1987]. *Breve historia de la dictadura (1973–1985).* Montevideo: Ediciones de la Banda Oriental.

Caimán Barbudo. 1972. La identidad cultural, 3–5.

Calle 13. 2011. Latinoamérica—Viña del Mar 2011—HD. Retrieved from http://www.youtube.com/watch?v=stutWBY35yw.

Campos, Augusto de. 1974. *Balanço da Bossa e outras bossas.* 2nd ed. São Paulo: Perspectiva.

Campos, Haroldo de. 1972. "Superación de los lenguajes exclusivos." Pp. 279–300 in *América Latina en su cultura,* edited by César Fernández Moreno. París: Siglo Veintiuno Editores S.A.

Campra, Rosalba. 2004. "En busca del gaucho perdido." *Revista de Crítica Literaria Latinoamericana* 30 (60): 311–332.

Cancioneros. Diario digital de música de autor. http://www.cancioneros.com

Cánepa-Hurtado, Gina. 1983. "La canción de lucha en Violeta Parra y su ubicación en el complejo cultural chileno entre los años 1960 a 1973: Esbozo de sus antecedentes sociohistóricos y categorización de los fenómenos culturales atingentes." *Revista de Crítica Literaria Latinoamericana* 9 (17): 147–170.

Capagorry, Juan and Elbio Rodríguez Barilari. 1980. *Aquí se canta. Canto popular 1977–1980.* Montevideo: Arca.

Carabineros de Chile. July 31, 1978. Acta de Notificación a Juan Osvaldo Larrea García. *Mimeo.*

Carbajal, José "El Sabalero." 1969. *Canto popular.* Montevideo: Orfeo ULP 90518.

Carmona, Alejandra. April 15, 2013. "Habla el hombre que salvó a Víctor Jara de ser un desaparecido." *El Mostrador.* Retrieved from http://www.elmostrador.cl/noticias/pais/2013/04/15/habla-el-hombre-que-salvo-a-victor-jara-de-ser-un-desaparecido/.

Carrasco, Eduardo. 1995. "La evolución formal." Pp. 109–113 in *Música popular chilena 20 años: 1970-1990* , edited by A. Godoy and J. P. González. Santiago: Ministerio de Educación.

———. 1999. "Canción popular y política." Pp. 63–70 in *Música popular en América latina: Actas del II Congreso Latinoamericano IASPM,* edited by Rodrigo Torres. Santiago: Fondart.

———. 2003a. *La revolución y las estrellas,* 2nd ed. Santiago: RiL.

———. 2003b. "Exilio musical en Francia." *Revista Musical Chilena,* Año LVII (199): 74–77. Retrieved from http://www.quilapayun.com/diario/exiliomusical.html.

———. 2007. *Cancionario.* Santiago: Archipielago.

Carrillo Rodríguez, Illa. 2010. "Latinoamericana de Tucumán: Mercedes Sosa y los itinerarios de la música popular argentina en la larga década del sesenta." Pp. 239–263 in *Ese Ardiente Jardín de la República: Formación y desarticulación de un "campo" cultural: Tucumán, 1880–1975,* edited by Fabiola Orquera. Córdoba: Alción Editora.

Carvalho da Silva, Domingos. 1989. *Uma Teoria do Poema.* 2nd ed. Rio de Janeiro: Civilização Brasileira.

Castillo, Rubén and Carlos Muñoz. 1983. "Las artes del espectáculo." *El Uruguay de nuestro tiempo: Tomo 9.* Montevideo: CLAEH (Centro Latinoamericano de Economía Humana) / Auspicio de CLACSO.

Castillo Durante, Daniel. 2000. *Los vertederos de la postmodernidad: Literatura, cultura y sociedad en América Latina.* México, D.F.: Dovehouse Editions Canada, Universidad Nacional Autónoma de México.

Caula, Nelson. 1983. "Destino del canto (popular)." *Canto Popular* 1 (1): 38.

Chanan, Michael. 1994. *Musica Practica: The Social Practice of Western Music from Gregorian Chant to Postmodernism.* New York: Verso.

Chaparro, Moisés, José Seves, and David Spener. 2013. *Canto de las estrellas: Un homenaje a Víctor Jara.* Santiago: Ceibo.

Chasteen, John. 2004. *National Rhythms, African Roots: The Deep History of Latin American Popular Dance.* Albuquerque: University of New Mexico Press.

Chilcote, Ronald H. and Joel Edelstein. 1974. *Latin America: The Struggle with Dependency and Beyond.* Cambridge, MA: Schenkman.

Cifuentes Seves, Luis. 2000. *Fragmentos de un sueño: Inti-Illimani y la generación de los 60.* Retrieved from http://www.cancioneros.com/co/3792/2/apendice-ii-el-poder-de-los-suenos-por-luis-cifuentes-seves.

Claro Valdés, Samuel, Carmen Peña, and María Isabel Quevedo. 1994. *Chilena, o, cueca tradicional: De acuerdo con las enseñanzas de Don Fernando González Marabolí.* Santiago: Universidad Católica de Chile.

Clouzet, Jean. 1975. *La Nouvelle Chanson Chilienne.* Paris: Seghers.

Colectivo Cantata Rock. 2012. Retrieved from http://www.myspace.com/cantatarock.

Constable, Pamela and Arturo Valenzuela. 1991. *A Nation of Enemies: Chile under Pinochet.* New York: W. W. Norton & Company.

Contardo, Oscar and Macarena García. 2009. *La era ochentera: Tevé, pop y under en el Chile de los ochenta.* Santiago: Ediciones B.

Cooperativa. December 26, 2012. Justicia procesó a ocho ex militares por asesinato de Víctor Jara. Retrieved from http://www.cooperativa.cl/noticias/pais/judicial/justicia-proceso-a-ocho-ex-militares-por-asesinato-de-victor-jara/2012-12-28/113320.html.

Corrado, Omar. 1992. "Posibilidades intertextuales del dispositivo musical." Pp. 33–51 in *Migraciones de Sentidos: Tres enfoques sobre lo intertextual,* edited by Omar Corrado, Raquel Kreichman, and Jorge Malachevsky. Santa Fe: Universidad Nacional del Litoral, Centro de Publicaciones.

Costa Garcia, Tânia da. 2009. "Canción popular, nacionalismo, consumo y política en Chile entre los años 40 y 60." *Revista Musical Chilena* 63 (212): 11–28.

Coulon, Jorge. 1995. "Inti-Illimani." Pp. 99–101 in *Música popular chilena 20 años: 1970-1990,* edited by A. Godoy and J. P. González. Santiago: Ministerio de Educación.

———. 2009. *La sonrisa de Víctor Jara.* Santiago: USACH.

Crellis Secco, Susana. 1990. *Idea Vilariño: Poesía e identidad.* México: Universidad Nacional Autónoma de México.

Cruz, Francisco. 1983. "Música popular no comercial" (Working paper). Santiago: CENECA.

Cunha, Victor, Antonio Dabezies, and Alfonso Lessa. 1982. "Cuando el canto es popular (y además uruguayo)." *Opción* 1 (13): 41–49.

Cunningham, Lawrence and John Reich. 2002. *Culture and Values: A Survey of the Humanities,* 5th ed. Toronto: Wadsworth.

Dabezies, Antonio and Aquiles Fabregat. 1983. *Canto popular uruguayo.* Buenos Aires: Editorial El Juglar.

Darnauchans, Eduardo. 1981. "Últimas opciones." *Música popular* 1 (1): 4.

———. 1995. *Un viejo guerrero en tiempos de paz: Reportaje a Pepe Guerra.* Montevideo: Ediciones del Clú de Amargueando.

Díaz, Claudio F. 2009. *Variaciones sobre el "ser nacional": Una aproximación sociodiscursiva al "folklore" argentino.* Córdoba: Ediciones Recovecos.

Díaz Inostroza, Patricia. n.d. *El canto nuevo de Chile: Un legado musical.* Creative Commons.

Dibam (Dirección de bibliotecas, archivos y Museos). n.d. Masacre de la escuela Santa María de Iquique. Retrieved from http://www.memoriachilena.cl/temas/index.asp?id_ut=masacre delaescuelasantamariadeiquique.

Discos Alerce. 1977. *El canto nuevo* [LP]. ALP-220.

———. 1978. *La gran noche del folklore* [LP]. FOL-8006.

Di Tella, Andrés (director). 1995. *Montoneros, una historia.* New York: Latin American Video Archives. Videocassette (VHS).

Donas, Ernesto and Denise Milstein. 2003. *Cantando la ciudad.* Montevideo: Nordan Comunidad.

Donoso Fritz, Karen. 2009. "Por el arte-vida del pueblo: Debates en torno al folclore en Chile 1973–1990." *Revista Musical Chilena* 63 (212): 29–50.

Dorat Guerra, Carlos and Mauricio Weibel Barahona. 2012. *Asociación ilícita: Los archivos secretos de la dictadura.* Santiago: Ceibo.

Dorfman, Ariel. 1998. *Heading South, Looking North: A Memoir.* London: Hodder & Stoughton.

Drake, Paul W. and Iván Jaksić. 1991. "Introduction: Transformation and Transition in Chile, 1982–1990." Pp. 1–17 in *The Struggle for democracy in Chile, 1982–1990*, edited by P. W. Drake and I. Jaksić. Lincoln: University of Nebraska.

Dubuc, Tamar. 2008. "Uncovering the Subject Dimension of the Musical Artefact: Reconsiderations on Nueva Cancion Chilena (New Chilean Song) as Practiced by Victor Jara." University of Ottawa, Masters Thesis.

Eliot, T. S. 1942. "The Music of Poetry." *Partisan Review* 9 (6): 465.

Errázuriz, Luis Hernán and Gonzalo Leiva Quijada. 2012. *El golpe estético: Dictadura militar en Chile 1973–1989*. Santiago: Ocho Libros.

Erro, Eduardo. 1996. *Alfredo Zitarrosa: Su historia "casi" oficial*. Montevideo: Arca.

Escárate, Héctor. 1995. "El rock chileno." Pp. 145–161 in *Música popular chilena 20 años: 1970–1990* edited by A. Godoy and J. P. González. Santiago: Ministerio de Educación.

Escárate, Tito. 1993. *Frutos del país: Historia del rock chileno*. Santiago: Triunfo.

Escobar, Ticio. 2008. *El mito del arte y el mito del pueblo: Cuestiones sobre arte popular*. Santiago: Metales Pesados.

Estrázulas, Enrique. 1977. *El cantor de la flor en la boca*. Madrid: Sedmay.

——. 1984. *Zitarrosa: cantar en uruguayo*. Montevideo: Banda Oriental.

Fabbri, Franco. 2006. "Tipos, categorías, géneros musicales: ¿Hace falta una teoría?" Paper presented at VII Congreso de la Asociación Internacional para el Estudio de la Música Popular (IASPM-AL). Casa de las Américas, La Habana, Cuba [Translated by Marta García Quiñones].

Fabregat, Aquiles and Antonio Dabezies. 1983. *Canto Popular Uruguayo*. Buenos Aires: Editorial El Juglar.

Fairley, Jan. 1984. "La nueva canción latinoamericana." *Bulletin of Latin American Research* 3 (2): 107–115.

——. 1985. "Annotated Bibliography of Latin American Popular Music with Particular Reference to Chile and to *nueva canción*." *Popular Music* 5: 305–356.

——. 1989. "Analysing Performance: Narrative and Ideology in Concerts by ¡Karaxú!" *Popular Music* 8 (1): 1–30.

Farred, Grant. 2003. *What's My Name?: Black Vernacular Intellectuals*. Minnesota: University of Minnesota Press.

Figueredo, María. 1999a. "Poesía y musicalización popular: Selección y recepción del texto poético en forma musicalizada: el caso uruguayo, 1960–1985." University of Toronto, PhD thesis.

——. 1999b. "Entre la poesía oral y la escrita: La canción y la cultura literaria." "La inscripción de la oralidad en las culturas latinoamericanas" [The Inscription of Orality in Latin American Cultures]. *Estudios hispánicos en la red*. http://www.ucalgary.ca/gimenez/revista.htm.

——. 2001–2002. "El eterno retorno entre la poesía y el canto popular: Uruguay, 1960–1985." *Revista Canadiense de Estudios Hispánicos* 26 (1–2): 299–321.

——. 2003. "The Latin American Song as an Alternative Voice in the New World Order." Pp. 178–200 in Yovanovich, *The New World Order: Corporate Agenda and Parallel Reality*. Kingston: McGill-Queen's University Press.

——. 2005. *Poesía y canto popular: Su convergencia en el siglo XX: Uruguay, 1960–1985*. Montevideo: Linardi y Risso.

——. 2011. "'Canto de madre': La revuelta femenina a flor de piel en el Canto Popular Uruguayo del dúo Washington Carrasco y Cristina Fernández." *Cuadernos de Música, Artes Visuales y Artes Escénicas* 6 (1): 53–64.

Flores Vassella, Schubert and Héctor García Martínez. 2012. *Hombres y Caminos-Yupanqui, afiliado comunista*. Rosario, Argentina: Fundación Ross.

Florit, Andrés. 2007 (July 10). "Nueva versión de la Cantata de Santa María: No hacen falta palabras: Egresados estrenan adaptación instrumental de la obra de Luis Advis." In *Archivo Chile–Historia Político Social-Movimiento Popular*, Centro de Estudios Miguel Enríquez CEME. Accessed December 8, 2011, http://www.archivochile.com/Historia_de_Chile/stama2/5/stamamusic00005.pdf.

Forlán Lamarque, Raúl and Jorge Migliónico. 1994. *Zitarrosa: La memoria profunda.* Montevideo: La República.

Frith, Simon. 1996. *Performing Rites: On the Value of Popular Music.* Cambridge, MA: Harvard University Press.

———. 2001. "Hacia una estética de la música popular." Pp. 345–413 in *Las culturas musicales,* edited by Francisco Cruces. Madrid: Trotta.

Foucault, Michael. 2001. *Fearless Speech,* edited by Joseph Pearson. Los Angeles: Semiotext(s).

Fundación Violeta Parra. 2008. Retrieved from http://www.violetaparra.cl/.

Gabriel Tuya Blog. 2008. "La cancion y el poema (Idea Vilariño y Zitarrosa)." *El gato utópico.* Accessed January 4, 2012,http://elgatoutopico.blogspot.ca/2008/05/la-cancion-y-el-poema-idea-vilario.html.

Galasso, Norberto. 2009. *Atahualpa Yupanqui, el Canto de la Patria Profunda.* Buenos Aires: Colihue.

Gallegos, Álvaro. 2006. "Apuntes estéticos sobre la música de Luis Advis." *Revista Musical Chilena* 55 (206): 97–101.

García, Fernando and Rodrigo Torres. 1999. "Gustavo Becerra-Schmith, Compositor, pedagogo y musicólogo." Diccionario de Música Española e Hispanoamericana. Madrid, Instituto de las Artes Escénicas y de la Música INAEM, Ministerio de Educación y Cultura de España. Accessed August, 23, 2011, http://www.gbecerra.scd.cl/bio.htm.

García, María Inés. 2006. *El Nuevo Cancionero: Aproximación a una expresión de modernismo en Mendoza.* Mendoza: Universidad de Cuyo.

García, Marisol. 2006a. La banda sonora de los '80: Centro Estudios Miguel Enríquez. Retrieved from http://www.archivochile.com/Dictadura_militar/muertepin8/muertepin8_0053.pdf.

———. 2006b. La música chilena bajo Pinochet. Retrived from http://solgarcia.wordpress.com/2006/12/19/242/.

García, Ricardo. 1973. "La Nueva Canción Chilena también vencerá." *Ramona* 2 (27): 27–31.

García Robles, Hugo. 1969. *El cantar opinando.* Montevideo: Alfa.

Garelick, Jon. 1996. "Sound effects: One Pop-Music Critic's Deep-Think Analysis: We are How We Listen." *Reviews.* The Phoenix Media/Communication Group October. Accessed January 16, 2012. http://www.bostonphoenix.com/alt1/archive/books/reviews/10-96/FRITH.html.

Garretón, Manuel Antonio. 1991. "The Political Opposition and the Party System under the Military Regime." Pp. 211–250 in *The Struggle for democracy in Chile, 1982–1990,* edited by P. W. Drake and I. Jaksić. Lincoln: University of Nebraska.

Garrido, Pablo. 1979. *Historial de la cueca.* Valparaíso: Ediciones Universitarias de Valparaíso.

———. 1976. *Biografía de la cueca.* Santiago: Editorial Nascimento.

Gavagnin, Stefano. 1986. "A proposito dei complessi cileni: Note sul linguaggio e sulla discografia dei gruppi della 'Nueva Canción Chilena.'" *Rivista Italiana di Musicologia* 21 (2): 300–335.

Gelman, Juan and Roberto Mero. 1987. *Conversaciones con Juan Gelman: Contraderrota, Montoneros y la revolución perdida.* Buenos Aires: Editorial Contrapunto.

Genette, Gérard. 1989. *Palimpsestos: La literatura en segundo grado.* Madrid: Taurus.

Gillespie, Richard. 1982. *Soldiers of Perón: Argentina's Montoneros.* Oxford: Clarendon Press.

Gilman, Claudia. 2003. *Entre la pluma y el fusil: Debates y dilemas del escritor revolucionario en América Latina.* Buenos Aires: Siglo XXI.

Giovanetti, Hugo. 1981. "Washington Benavides y el Canto Popular uruguayo." *Plural* 132: 56–61.

———. 1983. "Grupo Universo, el 10 en el Atenas." *Canto Popular* 1 (2): 6.

———. 1984. "Antirrutina: Labarnois-Carrero." *Nueva Viola* 1 (1): 46.

Godoy, Alvaro. April–May 1981. "El Nuevo Canto Chileno: En la senda de Violeta." *La Bicicleta.*

———. 1984. "Payo Grondona: A un año de volver." *La Bicicleta* 45: 19–20.

————. 1985. "Leo Maslíah, del canto popular uruguayo: Todo así, siempre igual." *La Bicicleta*, a. 7, No. 60: 22–24.

González, Jorge, Rodolfo Norambuena, and Arturo Opaso. 2008. "La Cantata popular chilena: Un producto artístico inclasificable." *Patrimonio Cultural* 13 (49): 28–29.

González, Juan Pablo. 1989. "'Inti-Illimani' and the Artistic Treatment of Folklore." *Latin American Music Review / Revista de Música Latinoamericana* 10 (2): 267–286.

————. 1997. "Cristalización genérica en la música popular chilena de los años sesenta." *Revista Transcultural de Música / Transcultural Music Review* 3, second article. ISSN: 1697-0101. Accessed August 8, 2011.

————. 1999. "Cristalización genérica en la Música Popular Chilena de los años sesenta." Pp. 365–374 in *Música popular en América latina, Actas del II Congreso Latinoamericano IASPM*, edited by Rodrigo Torres. Santiago: Fondart.

————. 2013. *Pensar la música desde América Latina.* Santiago: Universidad Alberto Hurtado.

González, Juan Pablo, Oscar Ohlsen, and Claudio Rolle. 2009. *Historia social de la música popular en Chile 1950–1970.* Santiago: Ediciones Universidad Católica.

González, Luis E. 1983. "Uruguay, 1980–1981: An Unexpected Opening." *Latin American Research Review* 18 (3): 63–76.

Gonzalez, Mike. 1987. "April in Managua: The Central American Peace Concert." LM9NSC 001 (1984). *Popular Music* 6 (2): 247–249.

González, Mónica. 2012. *La Conjura: Los mil y un días del golpe.* Edición actualizada. Santiago: Catalonia.

González Bermejo, Ernesto. August 1975. "Isabel Parra: Enemiga del olvido y la desesperanza." *Crisis:* 47–49.

González, Sergio. 2007.*Ofrenda a una masacre: Claves e indicios de la emancipación pampina de 1907.* Santiago: LOM.

Gravano, Ariel. 1985. *El silencio y la porfía.* Buenos Aires: Corregidor.

Guarany, Horacio. 2002. *Memorias del Canto-casi una biografía.* Buenos Aires: Sudamericana.

Guerrero, Juliana. 2010. "La risa y la insurgencia en las cantatas de Sudamérica." Paper presented at the XIX Conferencia de la AAM and XV Jornadas Argentinas de Musicología, Córdoba, Argentina, August 14.

Guillén, Nicolás. 1972. *Antología mayor.* México, D.F.: Juan Pablos Editor.

Haitsma, Marjanne. 1980. *El tamboril se olvida y la miseria no. La nueva Canción Popular Uruguaya entre 1960 y 1973.* Utrecht: Instituto de Estudios Hispánicos, Portugueses e Iberoamericanos, Universidad de Utrecht.

Hammer, Stephan. 1998. "Wolf Biermann, Wie man Verse macht und Lieder. Eine Poetik in acht Gängen. Köln, Kiepenheuer & Witsch, 1997. 287 S." *Jahrbuch für Volksliedforschung*, 43 : 178–180.

Hatten, Robert. 2006. "El puesto de la intertextualidad en los estudios musicales." *Criterios* (32): 211–219.

Heredia, Víctor. 2007. *La Canción Verdadera.* La Plata: Cántaro Editores.

Hernández, José. 1977. *La vuelta de Martín Fierro,* in *Poesía gauchesca.* Caracas: Biblioteca Ayacucho.

Herreros, Francisco. 2007. "Una historia dentro de la historia: Entrevista a Rodolfo Parada, director artístico de Quilapayún." *El Siglo*, No. 1.366 (9.066): 28–29, September 21.

Hite, Katherine. 2000. *When the Romance Ended: Leaders of the Chilean Left, 1968–1998.* New York: Columbia University Press.

Hoy. May 6–12, 1981. "Escollos en el camino," 44.

Huerque Mapu, Hernán Juárez, Rodolfo González, and Anonymous. 1973. *Montoneros,* by Huerque Mapu. Ediciones Lealtad/ELV 1001, 33⅓ rpm.

Hutnyk, John. 2000. *Critique of Exotica: Music, Politics and the Culture Industry.* London: Pluto Press.

Huyssen, Andreas. 1986. *After the Great Divide: Modernism, Mass Culture, Postmodernism.* Bloomington: Indiana University Press.

Ibargoyen, Saúl. 2005. *Alfredo Zitarrosa: La voz de adentro.* Montevideo: Fundación Zitarrosa.

Illapu. 2012. Historia. Retrieved from http://www.illapu.cl/historia/.
International Herald Tribune. October 9, 1981. "Chile Bars Rock Group as 'Marxist Activists,'" 5.
Inti-Illimani. 2013. Inti-Illimani en Mendoza, marzo 1985. Retrieved from http://www. youtube.com/watch?v=NENbFDS4Slw.
Inti-Illimani Histórico. 2013. Historia. Retrieved from http://intiillimani.org/index.php/en/ historia.
Isella, César. 2006. *50 años de simples cosas*. Buenos Aires: Sudamericana.
Jameson, Frederic. 1997 [1984]. *Periodizar los 60*. Córdoba: Alción Editora.
Jara, Joan. 1984. *Victor: An Unfinished Song*. New York: Ticknor & Fields.
———. 2007. *Víctor, un canto inconcluso*. Santiago: LOM.
Jara, Víctor. 1969. *Pongo en tus manos abiertas*. Jota Jota/JJL-03, 33⅓ rpm.
Jordán, Laura. 2009. "Música y clandestinidad en dictadura: La represión, la circulación de músicas de resistencia y el casete clandestino." *Revista Musical Chilena* 63 (212): 77–102.
———. 2010. "La musique des Chiliens exilés à Montréal pendant la dictature (1973-1989): La création musicale et la réception des auditeurs dans l'exil." Université de Montréal, Masters Thesis.
Juárez Cossio, Camila. 2012. "Experimentación en la canción rioplatense (1977–2000)." Facultad de Filosofía y Letras, Universidad de Buenos Aires, Phd Thesis.
Justicia Para Víctor. 2013. Retrieved from http://www.justiciaparavictor.cl/wp/.
Kaliman, Ricardo. 2004. *Alhajita es tu canto—el capital simbólico de Atahualpa Yupanqui*. Córdoba: Editorial Comunicarte.
———. 2010. "El canto de la dicha verdadera: Pueblo y utopía en letras del folklore de los '60 y '70 en Tucumán." Pp. 295–318 in *Ese Ardiente Jardín de la República: Formación y desarticulación de un "campo" cultural: Tucumán, 1880–1975*, edited by Fabiola Orquera. Córdoba: Alción Editora.
Karmy, Eileen. 2012. "Ecos de un tiempo distante: La Cantata Popular Santa María de Iquique (Luis Advis – Quilapayún) y sus resignificaciones sociales a 40 años de su estreno." Universidad de Chile, Masters Thesis.
Klísich, Esteban. 1985. *Un campo blanco*. Montevideo: Ediciones Ayuí-Tacuabé.
———. 1995. *Donde cayó el avión*. Montevideo: Ediciones Ayuí-Tacuabé.
Kmaid, Ivan. 1995. Interview with Maria L. Figueredo. Montevideo: August 3.
Knudsen, Jan Sverre. 2006. *Those That Fly Without Wings: Music and Dance in a Chilean Immigrant Community*. Oslo: Acta Humaniora.
Kraniauskas, John. 2001. "Porno-Revolution: *El fiord* and the Eva-Peronist State." *Angelaki* 6 (1): 145–153. doi:10.1080/713650371.
King, John. 1985. *El Di Tella y el desarrollo cultural argentino en la década del sesenta*. Buenos Aires: Ediciones de Arte Gaglianone.
Lacasse, Serge. 2005. "La musique populaire comme discours phongraphique: Fondements d'une démarche d'analyse." *Musicologies* 2: 23–39.
La Lopre. 2006. *Memorias de una presa política, 1975–1979*. Buenos Aires: Grupo Editorial Norma.
Largo Farías, René. 1977. *La Nueva Canción Chilena*. México: Cuadernos de casa Chile.
Lazaroff, Jorge. 1984. "*¿?*" Pp. 10–12 in *La del taller*, No. 1. Montevideo: Talleres Latinoamericanos de Música Popular.
Lena, Rubén. 1980. *Las cuerdas añadidas*. Montevideo: Ediciones de la Banda Oriental.
———. 1982. *Vagabundeos y canciones de Zenobio Rosas*. Montevideo: Ediciones de la Banda Oriental.
———. 1984. "Poesía y música en democracia: I." *Nueva Viola* 1 (4): 38.
———. 2009 [1993]. *Meditaciones. Memorias de un maestro*, 2nd ed. Montevideo: Banda Oriental.
———. 1984. Comp. *Cancionero de Los Olimareños*. Montevideo: Ediciones de la Banda Oriental.
———. 1994. *Rubén Lena. Canciones*. Montevideo: Ministerio de Educación y Cultura.
Lewis, Bart. 1980. "The Political Act in Mario Benedetti's 'Con y sin nostalgia' (With and Without Nostalgia)." *Latin American Literary Review* 9 (17): 28–36.

Lima, Víctor. 1981. *Cancionero*. Prólogo de Rubén Lena. Montevideo: Banda Oriental.

Linn, Karen. 1984. "Chilean Nueva Canción: A Political Popular Music Genre." *Pacific Review of Ethnomusicology* 1: 57–64.

Lipcovich, Pedro. 2006. "Mirta Misetich: el valor y la piedad." In "Suplemento aniversario: Los que no fueron tapa: 19 años de *Página/12*," supplement, *Página/12*, May 26. http://www.pagina12.com.ar/especiales/19aniversario/18.htm.

Longoni, Ana. 2007. *Traiciones: La figura del traidor en los relatos acerca de los sobrevivientes de la represión.* Buenos Aires: Grupo Editorial Norma.

López, Roberto. 2003. *Mauricio Ubal con la raíz a la intemperie.* Montevideo: Cangrejo Solar.

López Cano, Rubén. 2005. "Más allá de la intertextualidad: Tópicos musicales, esquemas narrativos, ironía y cinismo en la hibridación musical de la era global." *Nassarre: Revista aragonesa de musicología* 21. Accessed July 26, 2008, http://www.lopezcano.net.

López Cano, Rubén. 2011. "Lo original de la versión. De la ontología a la pragmática de la versión en la música popular urbana." *Consensus* 16. Accessed December 1, 2011, http://www.lopezcano.net.

López Chirico, Hugo. 2002. "Uruguay. III. La música culta a partir de 1960." Pp. 609–610 in *Diccionario de la Música Española e Hispanoamericana*, Volume 10, edited by Emilio Casares Rodicio. Madrid: Sociedad General de Autores y Editores.

Loyola, Margot and Osvaldo Cádiz. 2010. *La Cueca: Danza de la vida y de la muerte.* Valparaíso: Ediciones Universitarias de Valparaíso.

Lubetkin, Julio (ed.). n.d. *La nueva canción chilena: Ieri, oggi, domani.* Rome: O.N.A.E.

Ludmer, Josefina. 2012 [1988]. *El género gauchesco: Un tratado sobre la patria.* Buenos Aires: Eterna Cadencia.

Luft, Murray. 1996. "Latin American Protest Music: What Happened to the New Songs?" *Bulletin de musique folklorique canadienne* 30 (3): 10–26.

Lugones, Leopoldo. 1972 [1916]. *El Payador.* Buenos Aires: Huemul.

Luna, Félix and Ariel Ramírez. 1991. "Juana Azurduy." In *Mujeres argentinas.* Vocal performance by Mercedes Sosa. PolyGram Discos S.A./Polydor 501 509-2, compact disc. Originally released in 1969.

Mancini, Leonardo. 2002. "Franklin Thon Núñez." *Revista Musical Chilena* 56 (198): 119–120.

Manns, Patricio. 1986. *Violeta Parra: La guitarra indócil.* Concepción: Ediciones Literatura Americana Reunida.

———. 1995. *Patricio Manns en Chile* [CD]. Alerce CDAL 0234.

———. 2004. *Cantología.* Santiago: Catalonia.

Mántaras Loedel, Graciela. 1987a. *Caminos de la nueva poesía (1973–1988).* (Separata) Escritura XII, Caracas: Ananco Ediciones 23–24.

———. 1987b. "Uruguay: Resistencia y después." *Revista Casa de las Américas* 161: 3–10.

———. 1989. *Contra el silencio: Poesía uruguaya, 1973–1988.* Montevideo; Túpac Amaru Editorial.

Manuel, Peter. 1990. *Popular Musics of the Non-Western World: An Introductory Survey.* Oxford: Oxford University Press.

Marchesi, Aldo. 2006. "Imaginación política del antiimperialismo: Intelectuales y política en el Cono Sur a fines de los sesenta." *Estudios Interdisciplinarios de América Latina y el Caribe* 17 (1): 1–18.

Marchini, M. Darío. 2008. *No toquen: Músicos populares, gobierno y sociedad / De la utopía a la persecución y las listas negras en la Argentina 1960–1983.* Buenos Aires: Catálogos.

Markarian, Vania. 2012. *El 68 uruguayo: El movimiento estudiantil entre molotovs y música beat.* Bernal: Universidad Nacional de Quilmes.

Martí, Josep. 1995. "La idea de la 'relevancia social' aplicada al estudio del fenómeno musical." *Trans-Revista Transcultural de Música* 1: 7 article. Accessed August 26, 2008, http://www.sibetrans.com/trans/a301/la-idea-de-relevancia-social-aplicada-al-estudio-del-fenomeno-musical.

———. 2000. *Más allá del arte: La música como generadora de realidades sociales.* Barcelona: Deriba.

Martínez Reverete, Javier. 1976. *Violeta del pueblo.* Madrid: Visor.

Martins, Carlos Alberto. 1986. *Música Popular Uruguaya, 1973–1982: Un fenómeno de comunicación alternativa.* Montevideo: Centro Latinoamericano de Economía Humana (CLAEH). Ediciones de la Banda Oriental.

Martins, Carlos Alberto, Catherine Boyle, and Mike González. 1988. "Popular Music as Alternative Communication: Uruguay, 1973–1982." *Popular Music* 7 (1): 77–94.

Martins, Carlos Alberto and Carlos Dumpiérrez. 1997. "Uruguayan Popular Music: Notes on Recent History." Pp. 239–252 in *Whose Master's Voice?: The Development of Popular Music in Thirteen Cultures,* edited by Alison J. Ewbank and Fouli T. Papageorgiou. Westport: Greenwood Press.

Masiello, Francine. 1992. *Between Civilization and Barbarism: Women, Nation, and Literary Culture in Modern Argentina.* Lincoln: University of Nebraska Press.

Maslíah, Leo. 1984. *Un detective privado ante algunos problemas no del todo ajenos a la llamada "música popular": Ilustraciones Sergio Kern.* Rosario: Taller Argentino de Música Popular (Cuadernos del TAMP).

————. 1987. "La música popular: Censura y represión." Pp. 113–125 in *Represión, exilio y democracia: La cultura uruguaya,* edited by Saúl Sosnowski. Montevideo: Universidad de Maryland—Ediciones de la Banda Oriental.

————. 1993. "Popular Music: Censorship and Repression." Pp. 108–119 in *Repression, Exile, and Democracy: Uruguayan Culture,,* edited by Saul Sosnowski and Louise B. Popkin (Trad. Louise B. Popkin). London: Duke University Press.

Maza, Gonzalo. December 13, 2011. "No fue nada malo: 900 mil espectadores para el cine chileno en el 2011." *El Mostrador.* Retrived from http://www.elmostrador.cl/opinion/2011/12/13/no-fue-nada-malo-900-mil-espectadores-para-el-cine-chileno-en-el-2011/.

McLuhan, Marshall. 1995. "Understanding Media." Pp. 149–179 in *Essential McLuhan,* edited by Eric McLuhan. Concord, Ontario: House of Anansi Press Limited.

Medeiros Silva, Carla de. 2006. "A Nova Canção Chilena (1964–1970) E a busca por uma cultura popular." Paper presented at Usos do passado. XII Encontro regional de história. Niterói, Brasil.

Mellac, Régine. 1974. *Chants libres d'Amérique latine: La rose qui pleure.* Paris: Cerf.

El Mercurio. August 13, 1981. Ricardo García en libertad incondicional, 10c.

El Mercurio Internacional. September 8–14, 1984. Entregada lista de personas con prohibición de ingreso, 1–2.

Merino, Luis. 2004. "Luis Advis Vitaglic (1935–2004)." *Revista Musical Chilena* 58 (202): 6–8.

Middleton, Richard. 1990. *Studying popular music.* Milton Keynes: Open University Press.

Milstein, Denise. 2007. "Protest and Counterculture under Authoritarianism: Uruguayan and Brazilian Musical Movements in the 1960s." Columbia University, PhD Thesis.

Miranda, Soledad and Horacio Salinas. 2002. "Ritmos y tiempos de América: Entrevista con Horacio Salinas." *Guaraguao* 6 (15): 102–112.

Miró-Cortez, Carlos. 1976. "VI Festival de la Canción Política, Berlin 7-14 Febrero 1976." *Studia Musicologica Academiae Scientiarum Hungaricae* 18 (1/4): 367–375.

Molina Johnson, Carlos. n.d. *Chile: Los militares y la política.* Santiago: Estado Mayor General del Ejército.

Molinero, Carlos. 2011. *Militancia de la canción: Política en el canto folklórico de la Argentina (1944/1975).* Buenos Aires: De Aquí a la Vuelta.

Montero, Ana Soledad. 2008. "Héroes, ortodoxos, disidentes y traidores: Los avatares de la Juventud Peronista Lealtad (1973–1976)." Working Paper, Red Interdisciplinaria de Estudios sobre Historia Reciente (RIEHR), Argentina. http://www.riehr.com.ar/archivos/Investigacion/Publicacion_RIEHR._Montero_Ana_Soledad[1].pdf.

Moore, Robin. 2003. "Transformations in Cuban Nueva trova, 1965–1995." *Ethnomusicology* 47 (1): 1–41.

Morris, Nancy. 1986. "Canto Porque es Necesario Cantar: The New Song Movement in Chile, 1973–1983." *Latin American Research Review* 21 (2): 117–136.

————. 2006. "Las peregrinaciones del Gitano exiliado: La correspondencia de Osvaldo Rodríguez." Pp. 149–165 in *Exiliados, emigrados y retornados: Chilenos en América y Europa, 1973-2004,* edited by J. del Pozo Artigas. Santiago: RiL.

Muñoz, Heraldo. 2008. *The Dictator's Shadow: Life under Augusto Pinochet.* New York: Basic Books.

Museo de la Memoria y Los Derechos Humanos. 2013. http://www.museodelamemoria.cl/.

Music-bazaar. 2013. Canción protesta: Casa de las Américas/Cuba (1967). Retrieved from http://www.music-bazaar.com/spanish-music/albums/view/id/73766/name/Cancion-Protesta-Casa-De-Las-Americas-Cuba.

MúsicaPopular.cl. 2012. DICAP. Retrieved from http://www.musicapopular.cl/3.0/index2.php?action=U2VsbG9ERQ==&var=MTM=.

La Nación. June 4, 2009. Restos de Víctor Jara llevados al Médico Legal. Retrieved from http://www.lanacion.cl/restos-de-victor-jara-llevados-al-medico-legal/noticias/2009-06-04/132612.htmlO.

Nazabay, Hamid. 2009. *Osiris Rodríguez Castillos: Pionero del Canto Popular Uruguayo.* Rosario: FONAM.

Nercesián, Inés. 2010. "La política en armas y las armas en política. Surgimiento de la lucha armada en Brasil, Uruguay y Chile 1950–1970." Universidad de Buenos Aires, PhD Thesis.

Nono, Luigi. 1985. "Saludo a los trabajadores de la cultura de Chile." Pp. 25–26 in *La del taller* No. 2. Montevideo: Talleres Latinoamericanos de Música Popular, febrero/marzo.

———. 1993 [1972]. "Cours Latino-américain de Musique Contemporaine." Pp. 406–411 in *Écrits: Réunis, preséntés et annotés par Laurent Feneyrou.* Paris: Christian Bourgois Ed.

Norambuena, Rodolfo. 2008. "Análisis teórico práctico de las cantatas populares chilenas." Paper presented in the meeting "Cantatas populares chilenas," Música, Universidad Metropolitana de Ciencias de la Educación, Santiago, November 27.

Novoa, Laura. 2007. "Proyecto de renovación estética en el campo musical argentino y latinoamericano durante la década del sesenta: El Centro Latinoamericano de Altos Estudios Musicales (CLAEM)." *Revista Argentina de Musicología* 8: 69–87.

Odeon. September 28, 1973. Autocensura a la industria fonográfica. *Mimeo.*

Los Olimareños. 1962. *Los Olimareños.* Montevideo: Antar PLP 5044.

———. 1993 [1970]. *Cielo del 69.* Buenos Aires: EMI/Sondor, ULP 90543.

———. 2000. *Nuestras mejores 30 canciones.* Buenos Aires: Sony 2-493573, CD2.

———. 2007 [1972]. *¡Qué pena!* Montevideo: Orfeo 3764-2.

Olivera, Rubén. 1986. "La canción política." *La del taller* 5/6: 2–9. Montevideo: Talleres Latinoamericanos de Música Popular.

Oporto, Lucy. 2007. *El Diablo en la Música: La muerte del amor en "El gavilán" de Violeta Parra.* Viña del Mar: Altazor.

Orellana, Carlos. 1978. "Discusión sobre la música chilena." *Araucaria de Chile* 2: 109–173. , Accessed February 27, 2012, http://www.patriciocastillo.com/textos.htm.

Orquera, Yolanda Fabiola. 2008. "Marxismo, peronismo, indocriollismo: Atahualpa Yupanqui y el norte argentino." *Studies in Latin American Popular Culture* 27: 185–205.

Orrego Salas, Juan. 1980. "La Nueva Canción Chilena: tradición, espíritu y contenido de su música." *Literatura Chilena en el exilio,* XIV abril, primavera. Los Angeles, California, Ediciones de la frontera: 2–7.

———. 1985. "Espíritu y contenido formal de su música en la Nueva Canción Chilena." *Literatura Chilena en el Exilio* 9 (3–4): 5–13.

Osorio, José (ed.). 1996. *Ricardo García: Una obra trascendente.* Santiago: Pluma y Pincel.

Osorio Fernández, Javier. 2005. "Postcolonialidad y música popular: Violeta Parra y los usos de lo popular en la Nueva Canción Chilena." Paper presented at VI Congreso de la Asociación Internacional para el Estudio de la Música Popular (IASPM-AL). Instituto Carlos Vega, Buenos Aires, Argentina.

Otano, Rafael. 2006. *Nueva crónica de la transición,* 2nd ed. Santiago: LOM

Padilla, Alfonso. 1985. "El grupo Illapu." *Literatura chilena, creación y crítica* 9: 54–55.

Paez Villaró, Carlos. 2000. *Entre colores y tambores: Viaje desde la punta de la cerbatana, hasta la lonja del tamboril.* Austin: University of Texas.

Pallares, Ricardo. 1992. *Tres mundos en la lírica uruguaya actual: Washington Benavides, Jorge Arbeleche, Marosa Di Giorgio.* Montevideo: Ediciones de la Banda Oriental.

Palombo, Bernardo and Damián Sánchez. 2009. "Canción por el fusil y la flor." In *Canción con todos: Mercedes Sosa: En vivo en Casa*, by Mercedes Sosa. Casa de las Américas CMA 005, compact disc. Recorded October 24, 1974.

Parada, Rodolfo. 1988. "La articulación entre tradición y modernidad en la cultura. La Nueva Canción Chilena, 1960–1975." Inedit abstract of Phd Thesis, París III.

———. 1990. "La Nueva Canción Chilena ha muerto: ¡Viva la música Popular Chilena!" Accessed December, 21, 2009, http://www.quilapayun.info.

———. 2008. "La Nueva Canción Chilena 1960–1970: Arte y política, tradición y modernidad." *Patrimonio Cultural* 13 (49): 17–20.

Parra, Ángel. 1977. *Chacabuco* [LP]. Mexico: Discos NCL NCL-LP-0011.

Parra, Isabel. 1985. *El libro mayor de Violeta Parra*. Madrid: Michay.

Parot, Carmen Luz. July 2, 2007. Historia del Inti-Illimani. EncontrArte, 67. Retrieved from http://encontrarte.aporrea.org/67/.

Party, Daniel. 2009. "Beyond 'Protest Song': Popular Music in Pinochet's Chile (1973–1990)." Pp. 671–684 in *Music and Dictatorship in Europe and Latin America*, edited by Roberto Illiano and Massimiliano Salas. Turnhout: Brepols Publishers.

———. 2010. "Beyond 'Protest Song': Popular Music in Pinochet's Chile (1973–1990)." Pp. 671–684 in *Music and Dictatorship in Europe and Latin America*, edited by Roberto Illiano and Massimiliano Salas. Turnhout: Brepols Publishers.

Pellegrino, Guillermo and Jorge Basilago. 2002. *Las cuerdas vivas de América Latina: Chabuca Granda, Víctor Jara, Violeta Parra, Daniel Viglietti, Atahualpa Yupanqui*. Buenos Aires: Sudamericana.

———. 2003. *Cantares del alma: Biografía definitiva de Alfredo Zitarrosa*. Buenos Aires: Planeta.

———. 2009. *Rubén Lena, maestro de la canción*. Montevideo: Banda Oriental.

Perrone, Charles. 1988. *Letras e Letras da Música Popular Brasileira*. Trad. De José Luiz Paulo Machado. Rio de Janeiro: Elo Editora e Distribuidora Ltda.

Perrone, Marcela. 2010. "Música de fronteiras: O estudo de um campo creativo situado entre a música popular e a música erudita de vanguarda." Universidade Federal do Estado de Río de Janeiro, Masters Thesis.

Perez Luna, Elizabeth. July 7, 1975. "Ángel Parra en México." *El Nacional* (Caracas) Suplemento 7 Día, 14.

Petronio Arapí, Tabaré. 2006. *Las voces del silencio: Historia del Canto Popular 1973–1984*. Montevideo: FONAM.

Pincheira Albrecht, Rodrigo (ed.). 2010. *Schwenke & Nilo: Leyenda del Sur*. Hualpén, Chile: Ediciones Nuevos Territorios.

Pino-Robles, Rodolfo. 1999. "Music and Social Change in Argentina and Chile: 1950–1980 and Beyond." Conference Paper, Canadian Association of Latin American and Caribbean Studies. Ottawa, Canada. 1–5.

Ponce, David. 2008. *Prueba de sonido: Primeras historias del rock en Chile (1956–1984)*. Santiago: Ediciones B/ Comisión de Publicaciones de la Sociedad Chilena del Derecho de Autor, SCD.

Portales, Carlos. 1991. "External Factors and the Authoritarian Regime." Pp. 251–275 in *The Struggle for Democracy in Chile, 1982–1990*, edited by P. W. Drake and I. Jaksić. Lincoln: University of Nebraska.

Portorrico, Emilio Pedro. 2004. *Diccionario biográfico de la música argentina de raíz folklórica*, 2nd ed. Buenos Aires: Emilio Pedro Portorrico.

Prada, Teresinha. 2006. "A utopia no horizonte da música nova." Universidad de San Pablo, Faculdade de Filosofia, Letras e Ciências Humanas (FFLCH). Universidad Estadual de Campinas, Instituto de Filosofía y Ciencias Humanas, Masters Thesis.

Prieto, Adolfo. 1988. *El Discurso criollista en la formación de la Argentina moderna*. Buenos Aires: Sudamericana.

Puebla, Carlos. 1970. "Hasta siempre." In *Cuba traditionnel: Cuba révolutionnaire*, Volume 2, compiled by Alain Gheerbrant. Festival FLDX505, 33⅓ rpm.

Quilapayún. 2003. *¡En Chile!* [CD]. Alerce CDA 0472/CDA 0473.

————. 2012a. Por Vietnam. Retrieved from http://www.quilapayun.com/canciones/porvietnam.html.

————. 2012b. Canción final, Cantata Santa María de Iquique. Retrieved from http://www.quilapayun.com/canciones/csmcfinal.html.

————. 2013a. El pueblo unido jamás será vencido. Retrieved from http://www.quilapayun.com/canciones/elpueblounido.html.

————. 2013b. Quilapayún en Mendoza, Noviembre 1983. Retrieved from http://www.youtube.com/watch?v=xc33psKhKGo.

Qureshi, Lubna Z. 2009. *Nixon, Kissinger, and Allende.* Lanham, MD: Lexington.

"Resolución final del Encuentro de la Canción Protesta." November–December 1967. Casa de las Américas, año VIII, No. 45. La Habana, Cuba, pp. 143–144.

Rey Tristán, Eduardo. 2002. "Movilización estudiantil e izquierda revolucionaria en el Uruguay (1968–1973)." *Revista Complutense de Historia de América,* Volume 28, 185–209.

Richards, Keith. 2005. "Nueva canción." Pp. 36–39 in *Pop Culture Latin America: Media, Arts and Lifestyle,* edited by Stephanie Dennison and Lisa Shaw. Santa Barbara, California: ABC-CLIO

Ridenti, Marcelo. 2009. "Artistas de la revolución brasileña en los años sesenta." Trans. Ada Solari. *Prismas* 13: 211–223.

Rios, Fernando. 2008. "La Flute Indienne: The Early History of Andean Folkloric-Popular Music in France and Its Impact on Nueva Canción." *Latin American Music Review* 29 (2): 145–189.

————. 2012. "The Andean *conjunto,* Bolivian *sikureada* and the Folkloric Musical Representation Continuum." *Ethnomusicology Forum* 21 (1): 5–29.

Ríos, Mary. 1995. *Guía de la Música Uruguaya 1950/1990.* Montevideo: Arca.

Rivera, Hernán. 2010. *Santa María de las flores negras.* Santiago: Alfaguara Editores.

Rodríguez, Ileana. 1996. *Women, Guerrillas, and Love: Understanding War in Central America.* Trans. Ileana Rodríguez with Robert Carr. Minneapolis: University of Minnesota Press.

Rodríguez, Javier. 2008. "Hacia un análisis intertextual de la propaganda musical durante la Unidad Popular." *Intersecciones, Revista de Ensayos* 1: 54–63.

————. 2012. "La madre del hombre nuevo se llama revolución: Música popular e imaginario del hombre nuevo durante la Unidad Popular en Chile." Universidad de Chile, Masters Thesis.

Ródriguez, Osvaldo. 1984. *Cantores que reflexionan.* Madrid: Literatura América Reunida (LAR).

Rodríguez Barilari, Elbio. 1977. "Música Popular '77: Una notoria superación." *El País.* Montevideo, 30 de diciembre, p. 29.

————. 1982. "Música, cultura y soberanía." *Propuesta* 1 (4): 42–43.

————. 1983a. "Preparando futuros carnavales." *Propuesta* 1 (8): 44–46.

————. 1983b. "Una ecuación colectiva." *Propuesta* 1 (10): 40–41.

————. 1984a. "Eduardo Darnauchans: El rock revisitado." *Nueva Viola* 1 (1): 8–11.

————. 1984b. "Quién conoce a Schellemberg?" *Nueva Viola* 1 (1): 23.

————. 1985. "Darnauchans: Informe especial." *Nueva Viola* 2 (7): 24–34.

————. 1999. "Canto Popular Uruguayo." Pp. 99–100 in *Diccionario de la Música Española e Hispanoamericana,* Volume 3, edited by Emilio Casares Rodicio. Madrid: Sociedad General de Autores y Editores.

Rodríguez Musso, Osvaldo. 1984. "Antes de la Nueva Canción." In *Cantores que reflexionan.* Madrid: LAR ediciones. Accessed February 28, 2012, http://www.abacq.net/imagineria/disc004.htm.

————. 1989. *La Nueva Canción Chilena: Continuidad y reflejo.* La Habana: Casa de las Américas.

Rojas Sotoconil, Araucaria. 2009. "Las cuecas como representaciones estético-políticas de chilenidad en Santiago entre 1979 y 1989." *Revista Musical Chilena* 63 (212): 51–76.

Rolle, Claudio. 2000. "La 'Nueva Canción Chilena,' el proyecto cultural y la campaña presidencial y gobierno de Salvador Allende." Paper presented at the III IASPM-AL Conference, Bogotá, August 23–27. Accessed December 21, 2008, http://www.iaspmal.net/wp-content/uploads/2011/10/Rolle.pdf.

———. 2005. "Del *Cielito lindo* a *Gana la gente*: Música popular, campañas electorales y uso político de la música popular en Chile." Paper presented at IV Congreso de la Rama Latinoamericana de IASPM. Instituto Carlos Vega, Buenos Aires, Argentina.

Román, Nicolás. 2011. "La guitarra trabajadora: El oficio del cantor popular y su hibridación a la canción de protesta." *Revista Chilena de Literatura* 78, Accessed January 8, 2012.

Rothstein, Edward. 1996. "La música amenaza a los dictadores." *Relaciones* 140–141: 27–28.

Ruiz, Agustín. 2006. "Cubanidad en el discurso musical del canto progresista chileno. I Parte: Lo cubano en la Nueva Canción Chilena 1967–1973." Paper presented at VII Congreso de la Asociación Internacional para el Estudio de la Música Popular (IASPM-AL). Casa de las Américas, La Habana, Cuba.

Sábato, Ernesto and Eduardo Falú. 1965. "El sueño de Celedonio Olmos." In *Romance de la muerte de Juan Lavalle*, 3rd ed. Philips 5085519, 33⅓ rpm.

Said, Edward. 2007. "Daniel Barenboim (Bonding Across Cultural Boundaries)." *Music at the Limits*. New York: Columbia University Press.

Salas, Rosario. 2001. "Problemática de la música popular en Chile." *Revista Musical Chilena* 55 (195): 65–66.

Saldaña-Portillo, María Josefina. 2003. *The Revolutionary Imagination in the Americas and the Age of Development*. Durham: Duke University Press.

Salinas, Horacio. 2010. Presentación de Horacio Salinas para el libro "Conversaciones conmigo mismo" de Eduardo Carrasco. Retrieved from http://quilapayun.wordpress.com/2010/11/08/presentacion-de-horacio-salinas-para-el-libro-conversaciones-conmigo-mismo-de-eduardo-carrasco/.

Salinas, Mónica. 2006. *Poesía y mito: Alfredo Zitarrosa*. Montevideo: Seix Barral.

Sampayo, Aníbal. 1972. "Hasta la Victoria." In *Hasta la Victoria* by Mercedes Sosa. Philips 6347068, 33⅓ rpm.

Santander, Ignacio Q. 1983. *Quilapayún*. Madrid: Ediciones Júcar.

Santos, Laura, Alejandro Petrucelli, and Pablo Morgade. 2008. *Música y dictadura, por qué cantábamos*. Buenos Aires: Capital Intelectual.

Scagliola, Ricardo. 2002. Review. *Hispamérica* 31 (92): 113–115.

Segura, Henry. 1977. "Caminos para una identidad." *Nota sin datos, archivo Bonaldi*.

Sigal, Silvia. 1996. *Le rôle politique des intellectuels en Amérique latine: La dérive des intellectuels en Argentine*. Paris: L'Harmattan.

Sigal, Silvia, and Eliseo Verón. 2004. *Perón o muerte: Los fundamentos discursivos del fenómeno peronista*. Rev. ed. Buenos Aires: Eudeba.

Sigmund, Paul. 1977. *The Overthrow of Allende and the Politics of Chile, 1964–1976*. Pittsburgh: University of Pittsburgh.

Silber, Irwin. October–November 1967. "Canción protesta." *Sing Out* 17 (5).

Sorensen, Diana. 2007. *A Turbulent Decade Remembered: Scenes from the Latin American Sixties*. Stanford: Stanford University Press.

Sosnowski, Saúl. 1987. "Dentro de la otra orilla: La cultura uruguaya: Represión, exilio y democracia." Pp. 11–22 in *Represión, exilio y democracia: La cultura uruguaya*, edited by Saúl Sosnowski. Montevideo: Universidad de Maryland—Ediciones de la Banda Oriental.

Sotelo, Gerardo. 1982. "Cantar abriendo fronteras." *Opción* 1 (16): 41–43.

Štambuk, Patricia and Patricia Bravo. 2011. *Violeta Parra: El canto de todos*. Santiago: Pehuén.

Stern, Steve J. 2006a. *Remembering Pinochet's Chile: On the Eve of London 1998*. Durham, NC: Duke University Press.

———. 2006b. *Battling for Hearts and Minds: Memory Struggles in Pinochet's Chile, 1973–1988*. Durham, NC: Duke University Press.

Stortini, Julio. 2004. "Polémicas y crisis en el revisionismo argentino: El caso del Instituto de Investigaciones Históricas 'Juan Manuel de Rosas' (1955–1971)." Pp. 81–106 in *La historiografía académica y la historiografía militante en Argentina y Uruguay*, edited by Fernando Devoto and Nora Pagano. Buenos Aires: Biblos.

Taffet, Jeffrey F. 1997. "'My Guitar Is Not for the Rich': The New Chilean Song Movement and the Politics of Culture." *Journal of American Culture* 20 (2): 91–103.

Taylor, Diana. 1997. *Disappearing Acts: Spectacles of Gender and Nationalism in Argentina's "Dirty War."* Durham, NC: Duke University Press.

Tejada Gómez, Armando, Tito Francia, Oscar Matus, Mercedes Sosa, Víctor Gabriel Nieto, Martín Ochoa, et al. 2003. "Manifiesto del Nuevo Cancionero." *Página Oficial: Armando Tejada Gómez*, Last modified March 3. http://www.tejadagomez.com.ar/. First published 1963.

Terán, Oscar. 1991. *Nuestros años sesentas: La formación de la nueva izquierda intelectual en la Argentina 1956–1966*. 2nd ed. Buenos Aires: Puntosur Editores.

Torre Nilsson, Leopoldo (director). 2008. *Güemes, la tierra en armas*. DVD. Music by Ariel Ramírez. Buenos Aires: A.V.H. Originally released in 1971.

Torres, Rodrigo. 1980. *Perfil de la creación musical en la Nueva Canción Chilena desde sus orígenes hasta 1973*. Santiago: Ceneca.

———. 1983. "Presencia de Gabriela Mistral y Pablo Neruda en la música chilena." Tesis (Licenciatura en Musicología). Universidad de Chile, Thesis.

———. 2003. "Tiple." Pp. 293–294 in *Continuum Encyclopedia of Popular Music of the World, Volume II, Performance and Production*, edited by John Shepherd and David Horn. New York: Continuum.

———. 2004. "Cantar la diferencia: Violeta Parra y la canción chilena." *Revista Musical Chilena* 58 (201): 53–73.

Trigo, Abril. 1989. "Leo Masliah: Kamikaze de la cultura popular uruguaya." *Revista de Crítica Literaria Latinoamericana*, Año XV, No. 30: 105–116.

———. 1990. "Contracultura del insilio en Uruguay (1973–1985)." *Revista Hispánica Moderna* 43 (2): 228–238.

———. 1991. "Words and Silences in Uruguayan Canto Popular." *Studies in Latin American Popular Culture* 10: 215–237.

———. "*Candombe* and the Reterritorialization of Culture." 1993. *Callaloo* 16 (3): 716–728.

———. 1997. *¿Cultura uruguaya o culturas linyeras? (Para una cartografía de la neomodernidad posuruguaya)*. Montevideo: Vintén Editor.

———. "The Gaucho and the Gauchesca." 2008. Pp. 279–292 in *The Blackwell Companion to Latin American Studies Culture and Literature*, edited by Sara Castro-Klaren. New York: Blackwell Publishing.

Tumas-Serna, Jane. 1992. "The 'Nueva Canción' Movement and Its Mass-Mediated Performance." *Latin American Music Review* 13 (2): 139–157.

Undurraga, Vicente. September 6, 2007. "Eduardo Carrasco, fundador de Quilapayún y filósofo: 'Cada generación reinventa la Cantata Santa María.'" *The Clinic* 216: 20–22.

Unidad Popular. 1969. Programa básico de gobierno de la Unidad Popular. Retrieved from http://www.bicentenariochile.cl/index.php?option=com_content&view=article&id=19: progamabasico.

United States. Department of State. 1975. *Church Report: Covert Action in Chile 1963–1973*. Retrieved from http://foia.state.gov/reports/churchreport.asp.

Valko, Marcelo. 2007. *Los Indios invisibles del Malón de la Paz*. Buenos Aires: Ed. Madres de Plaza de Mayo.

Valladares, M. Carlos and P. Manuel Vilches. 2009. *Rolando Alarcón: La canción en la noche*. Santiago: Quimantú.

Valenzuela, Arturo. 1978. *The Breakdown of Democratic Regimes: Chile*. Baltimore: Johns Hopkins.

Van Der Lee, Pedro. 1997. "Latin American Influences in Swedish Popular Music." *Popular Music and Society* 21 (2): 17–45.

Varas, José Miguel and Juan Pablo González. 2005. *En busca de la música chilena: Crítica y antología de una historia sonora*. Santiago: Publicaciones del Bicentenario.

Vega, Carlos. 1947. *La forma de la cueca chilena*. Santiago: Instituto de investigaciones musicales.

———. 1944. *Panorama de la música popular argentina*. Buenos Aires: Losada.

———. 1979. "Mesomúsica: Un ensayo sobre la música de todos." *Revista del Instituto de Investigación Musicológica Carlos Vega*. Año 3, No. 3: 4–16.

Velasco Castillo, Fernando. 1969. Opening remarks, Primer Festival de la Nueva Canción Chilena. Tape recording.

Velásquez, Marcos. 1996. *Nuestro camino: Antología*. Montevideo: Ayuí/Tacuabé, AE154K.

Verani, Hugo J. 1977. "Muestra de la poesía uruguaya actual." *Hispamérica* 6 (16): 61–65.

Vidart, Daniel. 1968. *Poesía y campo*. Capítulo Oriental 23. Montevideo: Centro Editor de América Latina.

Viglietti, Cédar. 1968. *Folklore musical del Uruguay*. Montevideo: Ediciones del Nuevo Mundo.

Viglietti, Daniel. 1968. *Canciones para mi América*. Le Chant du Monde LDXC74362, 33⅓ rpm.

———. 1971. *Canciones chuecas*. Orfeo ULP 90.558.

———. 1985. "Vigencia de la nueva canción." Pp. 22–24 in *La del taller*, No. 2. Montevideo: Talleres Latinoamericanos de Música Popular.

———. 1999a [1970]. *Canto libre*. Montevideo: Ayuí A/M 34 CD.

———. 1999b [1971]. *Canciones chuecas*. Montevideo: Ayuí A/E 212 CD.

———. 2001. *Canciones para el hombre nuevo*. Montevideo: Ayuí A/M 35 CD.

Vila, Pablo. 1982. "Música popular y auge del folklore en la década del '60." *Crear* 10: 24–27. Buenos Aires.

———. Forthcoming. "Narrative Identities and Popular Music: Linguistic Discourses and Social Practices." In *Music and Youth Culture in Latin America: Identity Construction Processes from New York to Buenos Aires*, edited by Pablo Vila. Oxford and New York: Oxford University Press.

Vilariño, Idea. 1980. "La canción." Pp. 73 in *Segunda antología*. Buenos Aires: Arca.

———. 1993a. *Canciones*. Montevideo: Ediciones de la Banda Oriental.

Vilariño, Idea and Alfredo Zitarrosa. 1993. "La canción y el poema." Pp. 5–7 in *Canciones*. Montevideo: Ediciones de la Banda Oriental.

Vilches, Patricia. 2004. "De Violeta Parra a Víctor Jara y Los Prisioneros: Recuperación de la memoria colectiva e identidad cultural a través de la música comprometida." *Latin American Music Review / Revista de Música Latinoamericana* 25 (2): 195–215.

Villegas, Sergio. 1974. *Chile-el estadio: Los crímenes de la junta militar*. Buenos Aires: Cartago.

Williams, Raymond. 1985. *Marxism and Literature*. Oxford: Oxford University Press.

Wilson, S. R. 1980. "Eduardo Galeano: Exile and a Silenced Montevideo." *Chasqui* 9 (2/3): 30–38.

Wright, Thomas and Rody Oñate Zúñiga. 2007. "Chilean political exile." *Latin American Perspectives* 34 (4): 31-49.

———. 1998. *Flight from Chile: Voices of exile*. Albuquerque: University of New Mexico.

Yépez, Benjamín. 2000–2001. "Nueva canción." Pp. 1076–1083 in *Diccionario de la Música \Española e Hispanoamericana*, Volume 7, edited by Emilio Casares Rodicio. Madrid: Sociedad General de Autores y Editores.

Yupanqui, Atahualpa. 1967 [1947]. *Cerro Bayo*. Buenos Aires: Siglo XX.

———. 2006 [1948]. *Tierra que Anda*. Buenos Aires: Corregidor.

———. 1965a. *El Canto del Viento*. Buenos Aires: Honegger.

———. 2003 [1965]. *El Payador perseguido*. San Luis, Argentina: Nueva editorial universitaria-UNSL.

———. 2008. *Este Largo Camino-Memorias*. Buenos Aires: Cántaro Editores.

Zitarrosa, Alfredo. 1970. *Milonga madre*. Montevideo: Orfeo ULP 90539.

———. 1980. *Textos políticos*. México: Fotón LPF 030.

———. 1991. *Alfredo Zitarrosa*. Montevideo: Orfeo CDO 004-2.

———. "La canción y el poema." *Antología: 1936–1989*. Compact disc. Buenos Aires: Discos Micrófon.

———. 1997 [1967]. *La ley es tela de araña*. Buenos Aires: EMI-Odeón 821304-2.

———. 1999a. *Y yo salí cantor*. Julio C. Corrales and Carlos J. Castillos, comps. Montevideo: n.p., Impr. Atlántica.

———. 1999b. *Por si el recuerdo: Cuentos*. Montevideo: Banda Oriental.

————. 2001a. *El oficio de cantor y canciones: Obras de Alfredo Zitarrosa 1*. Prefacio de Wáshington Benavídes. Montevideo: Ediciones de la Banda Oriental.

————. 2001b. *Crónicas: Entrevistas para Marcha: Obras de Alfredo Zitarrosa 2*. Montevideo: Ediciones de la Banda Oriental.

Zolov, Eric. 2008. "Expanding Our Horizons: The Shift from an Old to a New Left in Latin America." *A Contracorriente* 5 (2): 47–73, http://www.ncsu.edu/acontracorriente/winter_08/documents/Zolov.pdf.

Index

About the Contributors

Illa Carrillo Rodríguez is a postdoctoral fellow at the McGill University site of the Improvisation, Community, and Social Practice (ICASP) project, a major collaborative research initiative funded by the Social Sciences and Humanities Research Council of Canada. She received her PhD from the Doctoral School of Plastic Arts, Aesthetics, and Art Sciences of the University of Paris 1. Her dissertation examined the cultural and political history of Argentine folk and rock music in the second half of the twentieth century, with an emphasis on the performance practices through which artists Mercedes Sosa and León Gieco interrogated and reformulated dominant paradigms of national culture and identity. She has written papers and published articles and chapters on this topic and on the impact of the Falklands/Malvinas War on Argentine rock culture. Her current research focuses on the cultural politics of human rights activism and the role of popular music and other embodied forms of performance in the enactment of generational and political memory narratives in contemporary Argentina.

María Figueredo is associate professor at the Department of Languages, Literatures, and Linguistics at York University. She teaches courses in Latin American literature, and is a fellow at Massey College, University of Toronto. She has published in the area of literature and music, literary theory, and Latin American culture in specialized journals and book collections. Her book *Poesía y canto popular: Su convergencia en el siglo XX. Uruguay, 1960-1985* [*Poetry and Popular Song: Their Convergence in the Twentieth Century. The Case of Uruguay, 1960–1985*] (2005), studied the socio-cultural process of poetry that is set to music at particular times in the history of Latin America. Recent publications of her research include "From Pablo Neruda to Luciana Souza: *Latin America* as Poetic-Musical Space" in *Latin*

American Identities After 1980, edited by Gordana Yovanovich and Amy Huras (2003) and "Trayectoria y proyección del enunciado femenino, o la revolución en poesía musicalizada, del Canto Popular Uruguayo: El caso del dúo Cristina Fernández y Washington Carrasco en 'Canto de madre,'" *Cuadernos de música, artes visuales y artes escénicas* 6: 1 (January-March 2011): 53–64. She has also studied music as a subtext in women's prose, and music in the twentieth century Latin American novel. Current projects include a book titled *Latin American Writers in Song*, and work on the role of music in the novel such as Laura Esquivel's *La ley del amor*.

Laura Jordán González holds a scholarship awarded by the *Observatoire Interdisciplinaire de Création et de Recherche en Musique* (OICRM). She is a PhD candidate in musicology at Laval University, in Quebec. Her doctoral thesis addresses the relationship between singing and social representations associated with vocals in the Chilean cueca. She has published articles in specialized journals such as *Revista Musical Chilena, IASPM@Journal, Volume!* and *Boletín Música*. She currently serves on the Executive Committee of the International Association for the Study of Popular Music (2013-2015).

Camila Juárez has PhDs in history and theory of arts (University of Buenos Aires). She has obtained a scholarship from CONICET and currently teaches at Instituto Universitario Nacional del Arte (IUNA) and the National University of Avellaneda (UNDAV). She participates in several research groups at the University of Buenos Aires, at the Instituto Universitario Nacional del Arte (IUNA) and has been a member of ANR Globamus, at the Ecole des Hautes Etudes en Sciences Sociales, EHESS (Paris). She has published several chapters in books and articles in specialized journals.

Eileen Andrea Karmy Bolton has a degree in sociology from Universidad Alberto Hurtado and a master of arts in musicology from Universidad de Chile. Since 2010, she has researched cumbia in Chile, her work becoming the first national academic approach of this musical genre, spread throughout the website www.tiesosperocumbiancheros.cl. She has also researched about tango and its spaces in Chile, coediting a documental film about Tanguerías in Santiago de Chile (1960–2010) and publishing a book (*Travelling Tango: Typical Orchestras in Valparaíso 1950–1973*). She is currently working on a second book, a coedited volume called *Palimpsestos Sonoros: La Nueva Canción Chilena ayer y hoy*, and developing a study about the working conditions of the musicians in Chile and their relation to public policy supported by a research grant from CLACSO–Asdi.

Carlos Danilo Molinero has a degree in engineering from the University of Buenos Aires, a masters degree in business administration from Universidad

Politécnica de Madrid, a masters degree in direction of building enterprises from the Universidad Católica Argentina and a masters degree in history from the University Torcuato Di Tella. He is the author of two books on folk music in Argentina: *Militancia de la Canción—política en el Canto folklórico de la Argentina* (2012) and *Cantos Con-Juntos* (2013). And he has published several articles on the topic, such as: "Atahualpa: Voz y silencio del indio en la canción," "Raza y Canción: La representación del indígena en la canción folklórica argentina," "Poetas de la tierra," "El Folklore del Vino," "Riquezas Criticadas," "Historia de Pago Chico," and "Literatura Folklorica Comentada." He is also the author of the lyrics of several folk songs, which were recorded by the most important singers of Argentina, such as Hernán Figueroa Reyes, Roberto Rimoldi Fraga, Luis Mansini, Gerardo Macchi Falú, Carlos Pino, Lucrecia Longarini, César Isella, and Los Huanca Huá.

Nancy Morris is professor in the Department of Media Studies and Production, Temple University, Philadelphia, United States. She taught at the University of Stirling, Scotland, from 1993–1998. Her research centers on collective identity and international communication, with a focus on Latin America. She is author of *Puerto Rico: Culture, Politics and Identity* (1995), coeditor of *Media and Globalization: Why the State Matters* (2001), and has published in various communications and culture journals. She has published articles on Chilean New Song in *Latin American Research Review* and *Literatura Chilena*. In 2012 she was a Fulbright Scholar and visiting professor at the University of Chile; in 2002 she held the Unesco Communications Chair at the Autonomous University of Barcelona, Spain.

Abril Trigo is Distinguished Humanities Professor and director of the Center for Latin American Studies at the Ohio State University. He has published extensively on Latin American cultural studies, particularly on the historical formation of national imaginaries and their articulation to the popular. He is the author of *Caudillo, estado, nación: Literatura, historia e ideología en el Uruguay* (1990), *¿Cultura uruguaya o culturas linyeras?* (*Para una cartografía de la neomodernidad posuruguaya*) (1997), *Memorias migrantes: Testimonios y ensayos sobre la diáspora uruguaya* (2003), *The Latin American Cultural Studies Reader*, coauthored with Ana Del Sarto and Alicia Ríos (2004), and *Crisis y transfiguración de los estudios culturales latinoamericanos* (2012). He is currently working on *A Critique of the Political-Libidinal Economy of Culture* and is on the editorial committee of *Alter/Nativas, Journal of Latin American Cultural Studies*.

Pablo Vila is professor of sociology at Temple University. His research focuses on the social construction of identities on the U.S.-Mexico border and in Argentina. He has researched issues of national, regional, racial, ethnic, religious, gender, and class identities on the U.S.-Mexico border and has written *Crossing Borders, Reinforcing Borders: Social Categories, Metaphors, and Narrative Identities on the U.S.-Mexico Frontier* (2000); *Border Identifications: Narratives of Religion, Gender, and Class on the U.S.-Mexico Border* (2005); and *Ethnography at the Border* (2003). In his work on identification processes in Argentina, he has researched the way different social actors use popular music to understand who they are and act accordingly. This part of his research has resulted in several articles and the books *Troubling Gender: Youth and Cumbia in Argentina's Music Scene* (2011); *Youth Identities and Argentine Popular Music: Beyond Tango* (2012); *Cumbia! Scenes of a Migrant Latin American Music Genre* (2013); and *Music and Youth Culture in Latin America: Identity Construction Processes from New York to Buenos Aires* (Forthcoming 2014).